DATE DUE

MAY 9 2001	
JUN - 6 2002	
AUG 1 1 2003	
NOV 2 7 2004	

BRODART   Cat. No. 23-221

INTRODUCTION TO ADDICTIVE BEHAVIORS

Introduction
to
Addictive Behaviors

Second Edition

Dennis L. Thombs

THE GUILFORD PRESS
New York   London

© 1999   The Guilford Press
A Division of Guilford Publications, Inc.
72 Spring Street, New York, NY 10012
http://www.guilford.com

Printed in the United States of America

This book is printed on acid-free paper.

Last digit is print number: 9   8   7   6   5   4   3   2   1

Library of Congress Cataloging-in-Publication Data
available from the Publisher.

ISBN 1-57230-411-1

About the Author

Dennis L. Thombs, PhD, is an associate professor in the Department of Adult, Counseling, Health, and Vocational Education at Kent State University in Kent, Ohio. His research and teaching focus is addictive behavior and his interests include the conceptualization of alcohol and drug abuse problems and the processes individuals, families, schools, and communities use to address these problems as well as to resist change. Much of his work is concerned with the social conditions that influence the adoption of innovation and change. Dr. Thombs is also interested in the application of multivariate statistical procedures to measure theoretical constructs.

Acknowledgments

The following publishers have generously given permission to use extended quotations or paraphrases, and/or to reprint or adapt tables or figures, from published works:

"Alcohol Problems in Adoptees Raised Apart from Alcoholic Biologic Parents" by D. W. Goodwin, F. Schulsinger, L. Hermansen, S. B. Guze, and G. Winokur, 1973, *Archives of General Psychiatry, 28,* 238–243. Copyright 1973 by the American Medical Association.

Beyond Freedom and Dignity by B. F. Skinner, 1975, New York: Bantam. Copyright 1975 by B. F. Skinner. Used by permission of Random House, Inc.

"Theory in the Practice of Psychotherapy" by M. Bowen, 1976, in P. J. Guerin (Ed.), *Family Therapy: Theory and Practice,* New York: Gardner Press. Copyright 1976 by Gardner Press, Inc.

Theories of Personality (3rd ed.) by C. S. Hall and G. Lindzey, 1978, New York: Wiley. Copyright 1978 by John Wiley & Sons, Inc.

"Principles of Alcoholism Psychotherapy" by S. Zimberg, 1978, in S. Zimberg, J. Wallace, and S. Blume (Eds.), *Practical Approaches to Alcoholism Psychotherapy,* New York: Plenum Press. Copyright 1978 by Plenum Publishing Corporation.

"Function of Theory in Counseling" by B. Steffire and H. M. Burks, 1979, in H. M. Burks and B. Steffire (Eds.), *Theories of Counseling,* New York: McGraw-Hill. Copyright 1979 by McGraw-Hill, Inc.

I'll Quit Tomorrow (rev. ed.) by V. E. Johnson, 1980, San Francisco: Harper & Row. Copyright 1980 by V. E. Johnson. Used by permission of HarperCollins Publishers, Inc.

Broken Bottles, Broken Dreams: Understanding and Helping the Children of Alcoholics by C. Deutsch, 1982, New York: Teachers College Press. Copyright 1982 by Teachers College, Columbia University.

Alcoholism and the Family: A Guide to Prevention and Treatment (2nd ed.) by A. Lawson and G. Lawson, 1998, Gaithersburg, MD: Aspen Publishers. Copyright 1998 by Aspen Publishers, Inc.

Drugs and Behavior: An Introduction to Behavioral Pharmacology by W. A. McKim, 1986, Englewood Cliffs, NJ: Prentice-Hall. Copyright 1986 by Prentice-Hall, Inc.

"Alcohol and Tension Reduction: An Update on Research and Theory" by H. Cappell and J. Greeley, 1987, in H. T. Blane and K. F. Leonard (Eds.),

Preface

This book was written for the entry-level substance abuse counselor and the practicing mental health professional with no formal training in the addictions. It is intended for students who want to establish careers as substance abuse counselors, and for those professionals currently in practice who have never had the opportunity to study the transdisciplinary foundations of substance abuse counseling. The book has two primary goals. The first is to challenge and strengthen the reader's understanding of addiction by exploring how others in the field have come to know it; I hope that this will enable the reader to create a clear and logically consistent perspective on addiction. The second goal is to show the reader how theory and research are important to clinical practice. This should provide the reader with an array of treatment strategies that are vital to the principle of individualized treatment planning, and help make him or her an effective practitioner.

There are a number of good books currently available on alcoholism and other drug dependencies. For the most part, however, either these books are written at an advanced level for the sophisticated practitioner or researcher or they focus on a limited set of theoretical orientations. The present text is unique in that it attempts to present a comprehensive and thoughtful review of theory and research with the front-line practitioner in mind. Those in the "trenches" have often operated in isolation, separated from the research community. Exposure to complex and divergent theories of addictive behavior has often been neglected in the preparation and training of mental health and allied health professionals, including substance abuse counselors, social workers, psychologists, nurses, and so forth. Some of these practitioners are familiar with one or more of the disease models, but even here they often have not had the opportunity to examine its propositions critically. This book assumes virtually no preexisting knowledge in the biological or behavioral sciences. In every case, a careful attempt has been made to explain the concepts that construct each theory, as well as the research generated by it.

This book is also distinctive in that it emphasizes behavioral science perspectives on addiction. The chapter on the disease models does highlight important information from behavioral genetics, neuroscience, psychopharmacology, and drug metabolism that addiction practitioners should understand. However, extensive knowledge in these areas would be presented in specialized, advanced courses in a university curriculum, and there are a number of adequate texts that focus on these areas. This text is best suited for use in those university courses designed to introduce the student to the transdisciplinary foundations of substance abuse counseling.

Special thanks are in order to those who helped me complete the second edition. I am grateful to The Guilford Press, and especially to Seymour Weingarten, for his encouragement and assistance in its preparation. A number of reviewers provided feedback that was extremely helpful in steering the direction of the book. Most notable among these were Kenneth Leonard and Howard Blane of the Research Institute on Addictions in Buffalo, New York. Colleen, Ryan, and Ben deserve credit as well for the love and support they have provided me.

DENNIS L. THOMBS
Kent State University

Contents

6 The Family System   184

7 Social and Cultural Foundations   236

CHAPTER ONE

The Multiple Conceptions of Addictive Behavior and Clinical Practice Today

CONCEPTIONS OF ADDICTION IN U.S. HISTORY

For most of U.S. history, habitual drunkenness and drug use have been viewed as both sinful conduct and disease. In recent decades, they also have been considered maladaptive behavior (i.e., debilitative behavior that is "overlearned"). Today, some insist that addiction evolves from all three sources—namely, that it is a *disease* in which people *learn* to act in *immoral* ways. This incongruent vision of addiction has a long history. In the United States, the conception of addiction to alcohol has been evolving since the colonial period. At that time, alcohol consumption in the populace was high (by today's standards) and inebriety was quite common (Goode, 1993); there was little concern about excessive drinking and drunkenness. Americans generally had a high tolerance for social deviance, and thus they were mostly indifferent to the problems caused by heavy drinking. Alcohol was used as a beverage, as medicine, and as a social lubricant. The town tavern was at the center of social and political life. Workers often drank throughout the day and some employers actually supplied them with free liquor.

During the 17th century and for most of the 18th, alcohol was not seen as an addictive substance and habitual drunkenness was not viewed as a disease (Levine, 1978). Moreover, frequent, heavy drinking was not understood to be a compulsion involving "loss of control," nor was it considered a progressive, deteriorative disorder. Though most Americans considered excessive drinking to be of little importance, some prominent figures did warn and chastise about drunkenness. In these instances, it often was defined as immoral behavior. In sermons, Puritan ministers warned that drunkards faced eternal suffering in hell,

1

and though Cotton Mather referred to alcohol as the "good creature of God," he also described drunkenness as "this engine of the Devil" (Mather, 1708). In the 1760s, John Adams proposed restrictions on taverns and Benjamin Franklin described these establishments as "pests to society" (Rorabaugh, 1976). The first American to clearly articulate the modern conception of alcoholism as a disease state was Dr. Benjamin Rush. He was a Philadelphia physician, signer of the Declaration of Independence, and surgeon general of the Continental Army who, in 1784, authored a pamphlet titled *An Inquiry into the Effects of Ardent Spirits on the Human Mind and Body.* In this work, Rush challenged the conventional view that habitual drunkenness was an innocuous activity. He did not condemn alcohol use per se but, rather, excessive consumption and drunkenness. Throughout his writings on alcohol, he made an attempt to alert Americans to dangers of unrestrained drinking. He emphasized that alcohol misuse was contributing to an array of social problems: disease, poverty, crime, insanity, and broken homes.

Rush's writings greatly contributed to a paradigm shift that redefined the problem of "habitual drunkenness." According to Levine (1978), Rush's new construction was based on four propositions which are still relied on today to explain problematic alcohol and drug use:

1. Hard liquor is an addictive substance.
2. There exists a compulsion to drink that arises from a loss of control.
3. Frequent drunkenness is a disease.
4. Total abstinence from alcohol is the only way to cure the drunkard.

Though Rush was not optimistic about reform in the United States, his writings laid the groundwork for the temperance movement. The first temperance society was formed in 1808. Three years later a number of independent groups united, and in 1826 the American Society for the Promotion of Temperance (later renamed the American Temperance Society) was founded. Consistent with the views of Dr. Rush, the initial objective of the Society was to promote moderation—not prohibition. To accomplish this, the Society organized itself into local units that sent lecturers out into the field, distributed information, and served as a clearinghouse for movement information.

By the mid-1830s, over half a million Americans had joined the temperance movement *and* made a pledge to abstain from all alcoholic beverages (Levine, 1978). The emphasis on moderation gave way to a commitment to the necessity of abstinence for all citizens. Thus, the "temperance" movement became a "prohibitionist" movement, and increasingly inebriety was seen as immoral conduct. After the Civil

War, this view was applied to opium and morphine, which also came to be seen as inherently addicting poisons.

Those in the American Temperance Society worked hard to proselytize others, and to an extent they were successful. Employers stopped supplying alcohol to their employees on the job. Politicians were more restrained in their relations with alcohol producers and distributors. In many areas, local legislation was passed to regulate taverns—an outcome of lobbying by the Society. Goode (1993) reports that between 1830 and 1840, annual alcohol use dropped from 7.1 gallons per person (age 15 or older) to 3.1 gallons.

Leaders in the temperance movement held assumptions about the "disease" of alcoholism that are quite similar to those espoused today in Alcoholics Anonymous (AA). Levine's (1978) historical review found that habitual drunkards were described as having the following disease symptoms and features:

1. Loss of control.
2. Intense cravings when not drinking.
3. A physical compulsion to drink because of the power of alcohol.
4. A vulnerability to excessive drinking determined by hereditary characteristics.
5. Complete abstinence as the only cure.

John B. Gough (1881), a prominent temperance lecturer, said that he considered "drunkenness as sin, but I consider it also disease. It is a physical as well as moral evil" (p. 443). Levine (1978) found the following passage from a 1873 annual report of the Society: "The Temperance press has always regarded drunkenness as a sin and a disease—a sin first, then a disease; we rejoice that the Inebriate Association are now substantially on the same platform."

Thus, much of the modern, post-Prohibition thinking about alcoholism can be traced back through the temperance movement, and to Benjamin Rush's early conceptualization in the late 1700s. This construction of substance abuse combines notions of sin and disease without much concern for the inconsistencies and inevitable questions that it generates. For instance, are we free to choose disease—as well as free to avoid it? Such questions were not addressed by temperance leaders.

Yalisove (1998) has noted that AA is largely responsible for the adoption of the disease concept in most treatment settings in the United States. The only significant difference between temperance ideology and the views promoted by AA, beginning in the late 1930s, is the emphasis placed on the *source of alcohol addiction.* Prior to National Prohibition, temperance leaders blamed both the agent (alcohol) and the drinker. Later, AA shifted the focus to characteristics within the drinker, chiefly "loss of control," a problem sometimes responsive to mutual social support, and one certainly not requiring the social activism embedded in temperance ideology. This modification of the conception of alcoholism was in line with the post-Prohibition climate in the nation. After its repeal in 1933, national Prohibition was perceived to have been a failure and public policies shifted to alcohol control. There was little interest in sharply curtailing the alcohol supply—the intervention of choice in an "agent-focused" conceptualization.

It should be noted that the mixed "disease–moral model," cultivated by the temperance movement, still guides alcohol and drug control policies today. For instance, drug courts "sentence" offenders to "treatment," DWI (driving while intoxicated) offenders are required to participate in treatment and/or attend AA meetings, employers make workers' continued employment contingent on seeking treatment, and so on. Peele (1996) describes this as the "disease law enforcement model" and states: "When public figures in the United States discuss drug policy, they generally veer between these two models, as in the debate over whether we should imprison or treat drug addicts. In fact, the contemporary U.S. system has already taken this synthesis of the law enforcement approach to drug abuse and the disease approach almost as far as it can go" (p. 204).

This brief historical review shows that the U.S. conception of addiction, particularly alcoholism, has long been defined by incongruous assumptions involving morality and disease. Neither perspective has entirely supplanted the other. Thus, much disagreement and confusion remains about the nature of addiction. This confusion tends to impede progress toward developing widely shared social norms about acceptable and unacceptable substance use, and it spurs acrimonious debates about public drug control policy.

For the purpose of examining treatment implications, perspectives on addiction can be classified into three groups. These distinct views point to different strategies for controlling the problem of addiction in our society. This chapter examines each in greater detail.

ADDICTION AS IMMORAL CONDUCT

The first position maintains that addiction represents a refusal to abide by some ethical or moral code of conduct. Excessive drinking or drug use is considered freely chosen behavior that is at best irresponsible and at worst evil. By identifying addiction as sin, one does not necessarily ascribe the same level of "evilness" to it as one would to rape, larceny, or murder. Nevertheless, in this view it remains a transgression, a wrong.

Note that this position assumes that alcohol and drug abuse are freely chosen—in other words, that in regard to this sphere of human conduct, people are free agents. Alcoholics and addicts are not considered "out of control"; they choose to use substances in such a way that they create suffering for others (e.g., family members) and for themselves. Thus, they can be justifiably blamed for having the alcohol/drug problem.

Because addiction results from a freely chosen and morally wrong course of action, the logical way to "treat" the problem is to punish the alcoholic or addict. Thus, from this perspective, legal sanctions such as jail sentences, fines, and other punitive actions are seen as most appropriate. The addict is not thought to be deserving of care or help. Rather, punishment is relied on to rectify past misdeeds and to prevent further chemical use. Relapse is considered evidence of lingering evil in the addict; again, then, punishment is believed to be needed to correct "slipping."

In our society today, this perspective on substance abuse is typically advocated by politically conservative groups, law enforcement organizations, zealous religious factions, and groups of individuals who have been personally harmed by alcoholics/addicts (e.g., Mothers Against Drunk Driving). During political campaigns, candidates frequently appeal to this sentiment by proposing tougher legal penalties for possession and distribution of illicit drugs and for drunken driving. U.S. history is marked by repeated (and failed) government efforts to eliminate addiction with such legal sanctions. The crackdown on Chinese opium smokers in the 1800s and the enactment of Prohibition in the early 20th century stand as two noteworthy examples.

The "addiction as sin" position has several advantages, as well as disadvantages. One advantage is that it is straightforward and clear. There is little ambiguity or murkiness associated with this stance. Furthermore, it is absolute; there is no need for theorizing or philosophizing about the nature of addiction. It is simply misbehavior and as such needs to be confronted and hence punished. Scientific investigation of the problem is believed to be unnecessary, because that which must be done to correct it (i.e., application of sanctions) is already well understood. In this view, our society's inability to adequately address the problems of alcoholism and addiction reflects widespread moral decay. Proponents of the "addiction as sin" model typically call for a return to "traditional" or "family" values as the way to ameliorate the problem.

There are at least three disadvantages to the "addiction as sin" model as well. First, science suggests that alcoholism and addiction are anything but simple phenomena. They appear to be multifactorial in origin, stemming from pharmacological, biological, psychological, and social factors. The apparent complexity of addiction is underscored by the variety of diverse theories seeking to explain it (many of which are described in this volume). Moreover, as science has begun to shed light on various aspects of compulsive chemical use, it has become clearer that much still remains to be learned. The genetic vulnerability hypothesis, alcohol expectancy theory, and the purported stabilizing effects of alcoholism on family structure are all cases in point.

Another disadvantage of the moral point of view is that it is not at all clear that chemical dependencies are freely chosen. In fact, the disease models (see later) maintain that exactly the opposite is the case. That is, excessive drinking or drugging represents being out of control, or a loss of control exists; in either case, the individual does not freely choose substance abuse. A further point of departure is offered by the behavioral sciences, where, at least in several theoretical perspectives, a high rate of chemical self-administration is understood to be under the control of social or environmental contingencies. These contingencies are usually external to alcoholics or addicts and are not under their personal control. Thus, both the disease models and the behavioral sciences challenge the notion that addiction is willful misconduct.

A third disadvantage with the addiction-as-sin position is that history suggests that punishment is an ineffective means of reducing the prevalence of addictive problems in the population. Aside from the issue of inhumane sanctions (a real possibility if a political majority adopts the moral view of addiction), a reasonably strong case can be made, based on historical precedents, that striking back at substance abusers via governmental authority simply does not work over an extended period. In fact, law enforcement crackdowns often have the unintended effects of being an impetus for strengthening organized crime networks, creating underground markets, bolstering disrespect for the law, clogging court dockets, and overloading prisons (at substantial cost to the taxpayer).

ADDICTION AS A DISEASE

In the second view, excessive consumption of alcohol or drugs is the result of an underlying disease process. The disease process is thought to cause compulsive use; in other words, the high rate and volume of use are merely the manifest symptoms of an illness. The exact nature of the illness is not fully understood at this point, but many proponents of the disease models believe that it has genetic origins. For these reasons, it is hypothesized that individuals cannot drink or drug themselves into alcoholism or drug addiction. If the disease (possibly arising from a genetic vulnerability) is not present, dependencies cannot develop, no matter how much of the substance is ingested.

The addiction-as-a-disease conception maintains that the alcoholic and addict are victims of an illness. The afflicted individual is not evil or irresponsible, just sick. Thus, the chemical abuse is not freely chosen; rather, the excessive drinking or drugging is seen to be beyond the control of the sufferer. In fact, a common feature of the disease conceptions is the loss of control over substance use. It is hypothesized that once an addict has consumed a small amount of a drug, intense cravings are triggered via unknown physiological mechanisms, and these cravings lead to compulsive overuse. This mechanism is beyond the personal control of the addict.

Because alcoholics and addicts are seen as suffering from an illness, the logical conclusion is that they deserve compassionate care, help, and treatment. Because the condition is considered a disease, medical treatment is appropriate. Competent treatment, then, especially on an inpatient basis, should be supervised by physicians. Traditionally, treatment based on the disease models emphasized the management of medical complications (e.g., liver disease, stomach ulcer, and anemia), as well as patient education about the disease model and about recovery.

Disease models are strongly advocated by at least three groups in our society today. One of these is the profession of medicine. Critics have indicated that physicians have a vested interest in convincing society that addiction is a disease. As long as it is considered such, they can admit patients to hospitals, bill insurance companies, and collect fees. However, in today's health care system, the pressure of "managed care" has greatly reduced physician authority, making such criticism seem less relevant. Another group that has strongly advocated the disease conception is the alcohol industry (i.e., the brewers, distillers, and winemakers), which also has a vested interest in viewing alcoholism, specifically, as a disease. As long as it is a disease suffered by only 10% of all drinkers, our society (i.e., our government) will not take serious steps to restrict the manufacture, distribution, sale, and consumption of alcoholic beverages. In other words, the alcohol industry wants us to believe that the problem lies within the "host" (i.e., the alcoholic) and not with the "agent" (i.e., alcohol). A third group that strongly advocates the disease notion is the "recovery movement," which is made up of individuals and families recovering from chemical dependencies. This group can also be considered to have a vested interest in identifying alcoholism and addiction as diseases. First, calling alcoholism or addiction a disease makes it more respectable than labeling it a moral problem or a mental disorder. Second, maintaining that it is a disease can reduce possible guilt or shame about past misdeeds. This stance may allow recovering individuals to focus on the work that they need to do to maintain a chemical-free life.

There are a number of advantages to the disease models. Most important, addiction is taken out of the moral realm, and its victims are helped rather than scorned and punished. In addition, society is more willing to allocate resources to help persons who have a disease than to help individuals who are merely wicked. It is also clear that the disease models have helped hundreds of thousands of alcoholics and addicts to return to healthful living. Thus, their utility in assisting at least a large subset of addicts is beyond question.

There are also a number of disadvantages to the disease models; only a few are discussed here. (Chapter Two includes a more extensive discussion of these.) Briefly, several of the key concepts of these models have not held up under scientific scrutiny. For example, the loss-of-control hypothesis, the supposedly progressive course of alcoholism, and the belief that a return to controlled drinking is impossible are all propositions that have been seriously challenged by scientific investigations. Within the scientific community, it is acknowledged that these assumptions are not well supported by empirical evidence. Unfortunately, a large segment of the treatment community appears to be unaware of this literature, or perhaps chooses to ignore it.

ADDICTION AS MALADAPTIVE BEHAVIOR

The third position holds that addiction is a behavioral disorder; as such, it is shaped by the same laws that shape all human behavior. Essentially, then, addiction is learned. It is neither sinful (as the moral model purports) nor out of control (as the disease models purport). Instead, it is seen as a problem behavior that is clearly under the control of environmental, family, social, and/or even cognitive contingencies. As in the disease models, the person with an addiction problem is seen as a victim—not a victim of a disease but a victim of destructive learning conditions. For the most part, addictive behavior is not freely chosen, although some behavioral science theories (e.g., social learning theory) do assert that addicts retain some degree of control over their drinking or drugging.

It is important to understand the value placed on objectivity in the behavioral sciences. When alcoholism (or addiction) is described as a "maladaptive behavior," this is different from describing the condition as "misbehavior" (a moral perspective). Behavioral scientists avoid passing judgment on the "rightness" or "wrongness" of substance abuse. By "maladaptive," the behavioral scientist means that the behavior pattern has destructive consequences for addicts and/or their families (and possibly society). It does not imply that the addicts are bad or irresponsible.

In the behavioral science view, the most appropriate treatments are based on learning principles. Specifically, "clients" (this term is preferred over "patients") are taught skills to prevent relapse. The medical aspects of treatment are attended to when necessary, but they are generally deemphasized. The emphasis instead is placed on client training and on experimentation with these procedures. Behavioral scientists are most heavily involved in this treatment approach.

Behaviorally oriented treatment is labor intensive and evaluation focused. In such programs, clinical practice tends to be directed by data and, as a result, is subject to frequent change. Though these characteristics are consistent with today's managed care emphasis on efficiency and accountability, many community-based treatment programs are slow to adopt this approach to clinical practice (Lamb, Greenlick, & McCarty, 1998). This reluctance is part of the problem known as "technology transfer," which is discussed later in this chapter.

At present, the strong advocacy groups for an empirical approach to treatment tend to be found in the field of psychology. Division 50 (the Addictions) of the American Psychological Association is one example. This group, as well as others like it (e.g., the International Coalition for Addictions Studies Education), is relatively small in number and has yet to have a major impact on public policy toward addiction treatment.

THE NEED FOR THEORY

Why a book on theories of addictive behavior? As the discussion up to this point has outlined, three broad perspectives (i.e., sin, disease, and maladaptive behavior) on the nature of addiction exist today. The first, the moral model, is not a theory, at least as the term "theory" is understood in science. The disease models are the theoretical base from which most treatment providers operate in the United States today. The behavioral science perspectives, though sharing an emphasis on faulty learning, are represented by an array of distinctive theoretical positions.

It is my own belief that the addiction-as-sin position is the only perspective that is clearly understood by the majority of professionals working in the alcohol and drug abuse field today. This is not to say that they rely on it; indeed, the moral model is almost universally rejected by competent practitioners (with good reason, as was mentioned earlier). Unfortunately, it appears that critical examination of the disease model and the various behavioral science theories has been largely ignored by many in the alcohol and drug abuse field. All too often, practitioners rigidly cling to their favorite theory, in many cases without fully understanding all its concepts and implications. At the same time, other theories may be callously disregarded. Stefflre and Burks (1979) maintain that because all counselors necessarily operate from a theory (it may be informal or personal, but it nevertheless exists), it is essential that they hold the theory "explicitly"—that is, that they understand it with great clarity. They explain: "Just as the personality defects and emotional problems of the counselor need not preclude the possibility of effective work if they are taken into account and corrected for, so theory may be used better in counseling if we are aware that the theory is held, and if we acknowledge its limitations and some of the sources of its attraction to us" (p. 10).

The nearly dogmatic stance that some practitioners have taken regarding the disease models has slowed the development of the addictions treatment field. Clearly, the disease models have helped a large number of chemically dependent clients. However, as judged by the large number of addicts who refuse treatment, drop out of treatment, and/or relapse, it can be reasonably asserted that these models are not a "good fit" for many (perhaps most) chemically dependent clients. It is imperative that practitioners consider alternative models of recovery for clients who cannot work within the disease model. All too often, such clients are labeled as "being in denial." This tendency to reduce all client resistance to denial can obscure the possibility that the problem may lie in the treatment model, not in the clients. Rather than forcing a model on clients, perhaps we should work to help clients discover their own paths to recovery. If these paths include traditional approaches, that is fine. However, as practitioners, we should possess the flexibility to guide clients in different directions as well. The theories and models outlined in detail in this volume will inform and assist counselors in identifying appropriate options.

WHAT EXACTLY IS A THEORY?

The popular understanding of the term "theory" is usually "a belief that stands in opposition to fact." Many of us have heard someone retort, "Oh, that's just a theory." In other words, theories are commonly thought to be unsubstantiated hypotheses or speculation. Furthermore, there is a tendency to equate theory with things that are impractical or devoid of common sense. However, as Monette, Sullivan, and De Jong (1990) note, all of us necessarily rely on theories to function in our relationships with family members, friends, professional colleagues, and others. In most cases, these theories are crude and not explicit; nonetheless, they exist, if only in our minds. Thus, to dismiss theory as useless is to fail to recognize its universal application, both in science and in everyday life.

In the behavioral sciences, the term "model" is often used in place of "theory." When a paradigm is not well developed or it attempts to only explain a narrow aspect of some behavior, we often refer to it as a model. In this volume, both terms are used and attempts to distinguish between them are not made.

Hall and Lindzey (1978) define the term "theory" as a "set of conventions created by the theorist" (p. 10). This straightforward definition underscores the fact that theories are not predetermined by nature or data or any other orderly process. It rests largely on the theorist's prior knowledge and creativity. In the following passage, Hall and Lindzey (1978) insightfully describe it this way:

> Just as the same experiences or observations may lead a poet or novelist to create any one of a multitude of different art forms, so the data of investigation may be incorporated in any of countless different theoretical schemes. The theorist in choosing one particular option to represent the events in which he or she is interested is exercising a free creative choice that is different from the artist's only in the kinds of evidence upon which it focuses and the grounds upon which its fruitfulness will be judged. . . . There is no formula for fruitful theory construction any more than there is a formula for making enduring literary contributions. (p. 10)

The basic function of a theory is to organize data or our observations of some phenomenon (Monette et al., 1990). Theories allow us to impose order and meaning on a collection of isolated observations. Thus, they attempt to make sense of dissimilar findings and to explain relationships among variables of interest.

Because a theory is provisional (i.e., it does not explain in absolute or final terms), it is inappropriate to characterize it as "true" or "false." Instead, it is best described as "useful" or "not useful" (Hall & Lindzey, 1978). A theory's utility, then, can be assessed by its ability to predict events, or by how closely the data generated in research support hypothesized relationships.

FORMAL ATTRIBUTES OF A GOOD THEORY

Stefflre and Burks (1979) have identified five formal attributes of a good theory. They are described in the following paragraphs:

1. *Clarity.* A good theory must exhibit clarity in a number of ways. First, there should be agreement among its general assumptions (i.e., its philosophical foundation), as well as agreement between its consequences and generated data or observations (i.e., its scientific foundation). Second, the propositions of a good theory should be clearly described and easily communicated. Third, a good theory should serve as "an easily read map" (Stefflre & Burks, 1979, p. 9).

2. *Comprehensiveness.* A good theory can be applied to many individuals in many different situations. Its ability to explain events should extend across a variety of time periods, geographic areas, sociocultural contexts, and sociodemographic variables (gender, race, religion, etc.).

3. *Explicitness.* Precision is a chief characteristic of a good theory. Important theoretical concepts must be capable of being defined operationally. That is, concepts must be measurable with a high degree of reliability. Theories that rely on vague, ill-defined, or difficult-to-measure concepts cannot be checked against clear referents in the real world (Stefflre & Burks, 1979).

4. *Parsimony.* A good theory explains phenomena in a relatively simple and straightforward manner. A theory that can explain behavioral events in innumerable ways is suspect. A theory that "overexplains" something may be creative, but it may also be fiction. That is, it may not accurately reflect reality.

5. *Generation of useful research findings.* A good theory has a history of generating research findings (i.e., data) that support its concepts. Theories that have little or no empirical support are less useful than those that have considerable data driving further investigation of its propositions. Stefflre and Burks (1979) summarize these formal attributes by stating the following: "A theory is always a map that is in the process of being filled in with greater detail. We do not so much ask whether it is true, but whether it is helpful" (p. 9).

SUBSTANTIVE ATTRIBUTES OF THEORIES ON ADDICTIVE BEHAVIOR

In the previous section, the formal attributes of a good theory are identified as value-based standards against which a theory can be compared. In other words, the adequacy or inadequacy of a theory can be gauged by the formal attributes presented earlier. The substantive attributes, discussed here, possess no such evaluative quality; they are neutral relative to a theory's adequacy or inadequacy (Hall & Lindzey, 1978). These substantive attributes are the particular assumptions that undergird various theories on addictive behavior.

1. *Purposive versus mechanistic nature of the behavior.* This is a very old issue in philosophy and psychology. As it relates to addiction, the question is this: Should the abuse of alcohol or drugs be seen as purposeful and goal directed? Or, rather, should it be seen as one element in a larger dynamic system of behavior? Typically, those holding to the former position maintain that chemical use has an immediate benefit of some kind for the addict. In the other camp are those who maintain that addiction (e.g., drug-seeking behavior) is instead a symptom of a larger destructive process. The view that drug use is purposive does not necessarily suggest that it is sinful or freely chosen. For example, conditioning theory maintains that compulsive use is goal directed, but it relies on the concept of reinforcement as an explanation. Examples of mechanistic theories include the disease models and family systems theory.

2. *Conscious versus unconscious determinants.* This is another very old debate. At issue is whether addictive behavior is determined by conscious or by unconscious factors. Some theories on addictive behavior question the very existence of the unconscious. Others assert that it cannot be measured and therefore is not within the realm of scientific inquiry. Still other theories (e.g., psychoanalysis) give it a central role in the development of alcohol/drug problems. Interestingly, some treatment providers today unwittingly assign little importance to unconscious factors, yet in counseling practice they focus on clients' defense mechanisms. Such an apparent inconsistency suggests an incomplete analysis of the problem.

3. *Degree of emphasis on reward.* Theories of addictive behavior vary as to the role of reinforcement in driving compulsive use. This is a central concept in conditioning theory, and in social learning theory as well. However, other theories assign little significance to the rewards derived from chemical use and instead only emphasize the negative consequences (e.g., the disease model). Other theories stress reward only as it relates to family or social relationships (e.g., family systems theory and sociocultural perspectives).

4. *Learning process versus stable structures.* An important distinction between theories on addictive behavior has to do with those that outline a specific process of behavior change, in contrast to those that deal primarily with stable structures of the personality, the family, or the society. Those theories that emphasize a learning process usually seek to explain how an individual moves from drug experimentation to drug abuse to drug dependence. Theories emphasizing stable structures do not usually detail such a progression.

5. *Genetic versus environmental factors.* This issue is the center of much contemporary controversy. The disease models have traditionally em-

phasized genetic determinants of alcoholism, and in recent years other drug addictions as well. Most behavioral science theories, by contrast, have paid less attention to hereditary influences. Chapter Two discusses the role of genetics in addictive behavior in detail.

6. *Degree of emphasis on the operation of homeostatic mechanisms.* Some theories of addictive behavior emphasize the need of the individual or the family to maintain "homeostasis" or "balance" (e.g., psychoanalytic theory and family systems theory). This process is seen as a vital, automatic tendency to preserve the unity and integrity of the psyche or the social unit. The homeostatic mechanisms are seen as operating in much the same manner as biological mechanisms. Conditioning theories and other learning theories generally place little emphasis on homeostatic mechanisms. Such theories do not assume that addiction is related to being in or out of balance.

7. *Degree of emphasis on sociocultural determinants.* Most theories of addictive behavior focus on factors (genetic, physiological, psychological) within the individual. To date, relatively little emphasis has been placed on such factors as institutional structure and change, cultural beliefs, government actions and policies, tax law, the deterrent effect of criminal law, ethnic and racial identity, subcultures, or the like. In general, those theories that most strongly emphasize genetic determinants of addiction are those that tend to disregard the sociocultural context completely. Theories based on the learning process are usually more sympathetic toward sociocultural perspectives. This volume presents various sociocultural perspectives; none of them can be considered an elegant theory by itself.

THEORY, RESEARCH, AND CONTEMPORARY CLINICAL PRACTICE

One of the fundamental assumptions of science is that virtually all phenomena have multiple causes (Hardyck & Petrinovich, 1975). The implication is that theories on addiction should integrate biological, psychological, and social factors in an effort to explain compulsive substance use. Unfortunately, this is not yet the case in the addictions field. To date, none of the major contemporary theoretical perspectives has adequately accounted for the enormous amount of data collected on substance abuse and dependence. Some are best described as "single-factor" theories (Fingarette, 1988); that is, a single factor (such as a genetic predisposition, or the reinforcement value of a drug) is relied on to explain all compulsive use. Other theories are limited because they narrow themselves to one level of analysis (e.g., biochemical reactions, personality dynamics, family structure, or social relations) and ignore data that do not fit into their conceptual scheme.

The theories to be discussed in this volume can be accurately described as single-factor and one-level-of-analysis explanations of addiction. Some of them probably fall into both categories. Separately, they represent distinct visions of the problem of substance abuse. In many cases, a theory or model is built on assumptions that place it squarely at odds with the other theories; thus, it is difficult to imagine how the theories presented here could be integrated. This dilemma poses a special challenge to professionals in the field. Although practitioners need a theoretical framework from which to work, they also need to keep in mind that the scientific understanding of addiction is still in its infancy, and that none of the theories and models presented in this volume can justifiably be discarded with ease. This ambiguity must be tolerated for the foreseeable future. Though this may be uncomfortable, it is preferable to developing a ideology that espouses one theory and rejects all others. Above all, I hope that this book will instill cognitive flexibility as well as an appreciation for how each theoretical position contributes to our understanding of addiction.

In most conventional addiction treatment programs in the United States today, there is little integration of theory and research into clinical practice (Caldwell, 1991; Lamb et al., 1998). Knowledge about alcoholism, other addictions, and their treatment grew during the 1970s and 1980s. However, the use of this knowledge base by substance abuse counselors has been minimal. The gap has grown so great that the National Institute on Alcohol Abuse and Alcoholism (NIAAA) sponsored a 1990 conference titled "Linking Alcoholism Treatment Research with Clinical Practice" (Gordis, 1991). It was unique in that it allowed researchers and practitioners to address one another. In commenting on the meeting, Enoch Gordis (1991), the director of the NIAAA, noted:

> In theory, alcohol researchers seek knowledge about alcohol-related health conditions, and practitioners use this knowledge to help their patients recover. In practice, however, we often find that alcohol researchers and alcohol practitioners travel in two largely unrelated circles; they speak different languages, attend different meetings, and generally view problems—and their solutions—from very different perspectives. (p. 173)

The origins of this schism between theory-based research and clinical practice are multiple. Historically, alcoholism treatment programs in the United States have been staffed primarily by counselors who are themselves in recovery from alcoholism. This has also often been true of the nurses and physicians who work in alcoholism treatment programs. For many years, the theory and research base in addictions treatment was minimal. Practitioners were therefore forced to rely on what worked for them (i.e., the disease models). Thus, a tradition of using theory and research to guide clinical counseling practice never evolved. According to Caldwell (1991),

> most people entering treatment were considered to fit Jellinek's description of the gamma alcoholic and were treated as such. (The gamma alcoholic is the physiologically addicted alcoholic.) This is somewhat understandable, because the practitioner was, more often than not, himself or herself a recovering gamma alcoholic who had entered the field in response to years of neglect by the professional community. Such practitioners tended to view other alcoholics as fitting this pattern and delivered treatment accordingly. (p. 175)

The division between researchers and practitioners also stems from the fact that multiple disciplines have been involved in alcoholism research and treatment. The professions have included medicine, psychology, nursing, social work, and many others. Each of these disciplines has different views on the relative importance of research versus clinical practice. For instance, whereas some physicians have been heavily involved in research, most are more concerned with the delivery of services, program administration, and other aspects of clinical practice. The reverse can often be said of psychologists who work in the addictions field. Moreover, the relatively distinct training in each of the disciplines often makes it awkward for professionals from different backgrounds to communicate with one another. Physicians are often confused by behavioral science concepts and helping strategies, and nonmedical professionals may be ignorant of biomedical issues.

BARRIERS TO CHANGE IN THE TREATMENT COMMUNITY

Probably the single greatest barrier to the integration of theory, research, and clinical practice is the treatment community's strong tradition of relying on personal experience, clinical anecdotes, and testimonials. These sources of knowledge are limited because they assume that all addicts or alcoholics are alike. The belief here is this: "It worked for me, so it will work for everyone." It has been clear for some time, however, that alcoholism and addictions to other drugs are not unitary disorders (Cloninger, Christiansen, Reich, & Gottesman, 1978; McLellan, Luborksy, Woody, Druley, & O'Brien, 1983). They require different treatment modalities to maximize client outcomes (McLellan et al., 1997).

It is often asserted that resistance to change is normal and should be expected. Most organizations work to resist innovation, even when science calls for change. Caldwell (1991) notes that this resistance is hardly unique to the addictions treatment community. He cites a statement made by the famous physicist Max Planck more than 50 years ago about the field of physics: "An important scientific innovation rarely makes its way by gradually winning over and converting its opponents. What does happen is that its opponents gradually die out and that growing generation is familiarized with the idea from the beginning" (Planck, 1936, p. 50). This is likely to be the case with the addictions field as well. It is regrettable that change occurs so slowly.

Another barrier to change is the common belief among treatment providers that experimentation with clinical procedures is too risky. The fear, as often expressed, is that some treatment failures will occur with experimentation, so the best course of action is to "stick with what we're doing now." Indeed, it is true that some clients may not respond favorably to a new treatment protocol. However, given the fact that relatively high relapse rates occur in conventional treatment now, this argument seems specious. This position is probably related more simply to a fear of change or of doing something different. Furthermore, experimentation implies that treatment knowledge is incomplete—that there is still more for researchers and treatment providers to learn. This position is uncomfortable for counselors, who are often faced with convincing clients of the effectiveness of their particular program.

Today, substantial numbers of counselors and other practitioners in the addictions treatment field lack adequate preparation in terms of formal education, counselor skills, and in-service training (Lamb et al., 1998). This is another significant barrier to the collaboration of researchers and treatment providers. Many practitioners today do not understand research reports (Huey, 1991). Others have no access to important research literature; unfortunately, still others do not even know that it exists. This should not be surprising given that in many states, the minimum formal educational requirements for the entry-level chemical dependency counselor do not even include the baccalaureate degree.

A final barrier to the synthesis of research and clinical practice deserves mention here. It consists of the often overwhelming caseloads carried by many counselors, and the lack of time and resources necessary for the improvement of skills. The use of theory-based relapse prevention strategies requires not only a highly skilled practitioner but also a great deal of individual attention to each client. Most conventional treatment programs today are forced to rely heavily on group counseling because they lack the resources for more individualized care.

This is a problem not only in publicly funded programs but in private ones as well.

PRACTICAL ISSUES IGNORED BY RESEARCHERS

The research community has also been faulted for the gap between treatment research and clinical practice. Let us examine some of the concerns the treatment community has had about research endeavors. First, it has been pointed out that relapse prevention programs are often designed for mildly to moderately impaired clients. These are clients who are typically young, have no biomedical complications, and have a great deal to gain by maintaining abstinence. Huey (1991) notes, however, that practitioners are most interested in learning how to assist severely impaired clients. In some treatment programs, the majority of the client pool can be described as severely impaired. Thus, relapse prevention programs based on learning principles could be more challenging to implement in some programs.

Another practical problem often ignored by researchers also pertains to client characteristics. It is the problem of the client who demonstrates little or no commitment to recovery. Again, some relapse prevention strategies assume that all clients are motivated to change. A small but significant portion of clients may have no intention to change. They sometimes enter treatment simply to escape or avoid some punitive action by a court, an employer, or some other authority. More research is needed about this important issue.

Archer (1991) has stated that researchers have not paid enough attention to marketing new ideas to practitioners. He has suggested that researchers should devise ways to disseminate their research findings to counselors. Brown (1998) echoes this vision and asks treatment researchers to reconsider their professional priorities:

> For us to succeed in encouraging the adoption of innovation by treatment programs, community agencies, and state and county governments requires a focus that has been virtually absent to date. . . . If we are to meet the lofty—and appropriate—objective of "helping the frontline practitioner to deal more effectively with [our] patient population," we will need to make the adoption of new treatment technologies and access to treatment research findings a significant issue for both the treatment research community and the federal research establishment. (p. 88)

RECENT EFFORTS TO BRIDGE THE GAP: TECHNOLOGY TRANSFER

Across a broad range of human endeavors (business, agriculture, government, education, human services, etc.), specialists in the diffusion of innovation have recognized that people often find it difficult to adopt new practices or products in their occupations. This is particularly the case when the rationale for change is based on information generated from behavioral science research where the new "technology" is abstract or "soft" (Tenkasi & Mohrman, 1995). Many reasons have been given for why employees and organizations resist change and innovation. However, as Diamond (1995) notes, at a deeper level, change is experienced as an emotional and cognitive loss. Typically, change evokes anxiety, insecurity, and fear in the worker.

The issues related to dissemination, adoption, and implementation of research-based information are commonly referred to as problems in "technology transfer" or the "adoption of innovation." In the substance abuse prevention and treatment fields, the diffusion of innovation has not followed the expanding knowledge base (Brown, 1995; Rogers, 1995). Thus, interest in these problems has grown in recent years. Backer, David, and Soucy (1995) have identified the following six strategies to optimize adoption of innovation in substance abuse settings.

1.) *Interpersonal contact.* To get an innovation used in new settings, there needs to be direct, personal contact between those who will be adopting the innovation and its developers or others with knowledge about the innovation.

2.) *Planning and conceptual foresight.* A well-developed strategic plan for how an innovation will be adopted in a new setting . . . is essential to meet the challenges of innovation adoption and sustained change.

3.) *Outside consultation on the change process.* Consultation can provide conceptual and practical assistance in designing the adoption or change effort efficiently and can offer useful objectivity about the likelihood of success, cost, possible side effects, and so forth.

4.) *User-oriented transformation of information.* What is known about an innovation needs to be translated into language that potential users can readily understand. Materials must be abbreviated so that attention spans are not exceeded, and it is important that the focus remain on two key issues: "Does it work?" and "How can it be replicated?" Attempts in recent years to address these questions have lead to the increasing reliance on manual-driven treatment.

5.) *Individual and organizational championship.* An innovation's chances for successful adoption are much greater if influential potential adopters (opinion leaders) and organizational or community leaders express enthusiasm for its adoption.

6.) *Potential user involvement.* Everyone who will have to live with the results of the innovation needs to be involved in planning for innovation adoption, both to get suggestions for how to undertake the adoption effectively and to facilitate ownership of the new program or activity (thus decreasing resistance to change). (pp. 4–5)

The National Institute on Drug Abuse (NIDA) has provided leadership in stimulating technology transfer in the substance abuse prevention and treatment communities. NIDA's Technology Transfer Program was officially formed in 1989. The goals of the program are twofold: (1) reduce demand for drugs by improving prevention and treatment practices, and (2) enhance drug abuse-related HIV/AIDS risk reduction. The program's objective is not simply to disseminate research findings but to assist practitioners with actually implementing new treatment protocols in their programs. The products of the program include conferences, a videotape series, technology transfer packages (treatment protocol materials), and clinical reports.

Professional organizations, such as the International Coalition for Addictions Studies Education (INCASE) and the National Association of Alcoholism and Drug Abuse Counselors (NAADAC), also have been involved in encouraging innovation in treatment and prevention by enhancing the skills of front-line practitioners. For instance, both INCASE and NAADAC sponsor conferences and websites that serve the practitioner as well as the counselor educator.

Despite the efforts noted previously, insufficient resources are being directed to technology transfer for the front-line practitioner (Brown, 1998). To enhance the quality and consistency of service delivery, new innovation adoption initiatives are needed. Unfortunately, significant resources to support such activity probably will not be forthcoming until there is a shift in federal drug control policy *away* from drug interdiction/user criminalization and *toward* prevention and treatment. Drug interdiction, user accountability initiatives, and mandatory minimum prison sentences have been costly practices to carry out, and their effectiveness as public policies is questionable at best (Caulkins, Rydell, Schwabe, & Chiesa, 1997; Hepburn, 1995; Ray & Ksir, 1999). Furthermore, there is a strong need to educate the public that substance abuse prevention and treatment do "work." A number of public policy groups have been pushing for fundamental changes in our drug control policies (e.g., Join Together, 1996). However, to date, their efforts have not been successful.

COMPETENTLY ADMINISTERED PREVENTION AND TREATMENT PROGRAMS ARE EFFECTIVE

Successful advocacy in the drug control policy arena depends on positive program outcomes. It is a bit of a paradox then that the major problem in U.S. drug control policy today is the lack of awareness, among both the general public and political leaders, that competently administered prevention programming and addiction treatment are effective approaches to dealing with the problem of substance abuse. In recent years, numerous empirical studies show that prevention and treatment do "work." Nevertheless, public funding to control drug use continues to be heavily invested in law enforcement first, followed by treatment and then prevention (Haaga & Reuter, 1995).

Why should addictions professionals advocate for drug abuse prevention? Since 1989, there have been five well-controlled preventive interventions that have demonstrated a number of effective approaches to deterring tobacco, alcohol, and illegal drug use among youth (Botvin, Baker, Dusenbury, Botvin, & Diaz, 1995; Ellickson, Bell, & McGuigan, 1993; Hansen & Graham, 1991; Pentz et al., 1989; Perry et al., 1996). Some of these approaches are school based (e.g., Botvin et al., 1995; Ellickson et al., 1993), whereas others have been community based with parent and school components (e.g., Pentz et al., 1989; Perry et al., 1996). Among the lessons learned from these trials was that positive program outcomes decay over time and as a result, ongoing "booster sessions" are essential to maintain gains (Botvin et al., 1995; Ellickson et al., 1993). Of course, this requires resources and at the local level, community/school/parent commitment and cooperation. Another finding of these studies was that "perceived social norms" are an important mediator between program activities and outcomes (Hansen & Graham, 1991; Pentz et al., 1989; Perry et al., 1996). Prevention programming appeared to be effective to the extent that it could instill conservative norms about substance use. In other words, if youth were influenced to perceive that substance use was uncommon (not prevalent) and socially unacceptable among their peers, they were less likely to initiate or continue substance use. Interestingly, normative education may be more effective than peer pressure resistance training in deterring use in children and teens (Hansen & Graham, 1991). This also may be part of the explanation for the failure of Drug Abuse Resistance Education (DARE) to demonstrate much in the way of positive program outcomes (Ennett, Tobler, Ringwalt, & Flewelling, 1994).

Recent research also provide a strong rationale for greater public support of addiction treatment programs (Center for Substance Abuse Treatment, 1997; Mueller & Wyman, 1997; Project MATCH Research Group, 1997). The National Treatment Improvement Evaluation Study (NTIES) assessed 4,411 clients of treatment programs from across the United States. One year after treatment, clients' use of their primary drug of choice was 48.2% lower than in the 12 months before entering treatment (Center for Substance Abuse Treatment, 1997). During the same period, cocaine use dropped by 54.9%, followed by reductions in crack cocaine (50.8%), and heroin (46.6%). NTIES found that addiction treatment reduces crime. Among the sample, shoplifting decreased by 81.6%, with reductions also observed for selling drugs, 78.3%; beating someone up, 77.7%; and arrested for any crime, 64.3%. NTIES also revealed that addiction treatment has a positive impact on job income, homelessness, mental and physical health, and involvement in high-risk sexual behavior (Center for Substance Abuse Treatment, 1997).

Another recent nationwide study, the Drug Abuse Outcomes Study (DATOS) yielded results similar to those of NTIES. The DATOS sample consisted of 10, 010 clients from nearly 100 treatment programs in 11 U.S. cities (Mueller & Wyman, 1997). In a subsample of 3,000 randomly selected clients, investigators compared clients' weekly and daily drug use in the year before entering treatment to that 12 months after treatment ended. The clients came from four types of treatment programs: methadone maintenance, outpatient, short-term inpatient, and long-term residential. Regardless of the type of program in which clients participated, drug use declined substantially after treatment (Mueller & Wyman, 1997). For example, among clients who participated in outpatient treatment, cocaine, alcohol, and marijuana use were each reduced by at least 50% at the 12-month follow-up. In addition, all types of treatment had a positive effect on illegal conduct, employment, and suicide thoughts and attempts.

Project MATCH was a recent major study of alcoholism treatment which assessed the benefits of matching clients to three different forms of therapy (Project MATCH Research Group, 1997). In both aftercare and outpatient settings, 1,726 alcoholic clients were randomly assigned to one of three 12-week, individually delivered treatments: cognitive-behavioral coping skills therapy, motivation enhancement therapy, or Twelve-Step facilitation therapy. Clients were assessed 15 months after completing treatment. Though there was little difference in outcomes by type of treatment, Project MATCH significantly reduced drinking in alcoholic clients (Project MATCH Research Group, 1997). The investigators found that at follow-up, inpatient clients were abstinent on almost 90% of the days, compared to 20% before treatment. Outpatient clients were abstinent on almost 80% of days. Among the inpatient sample, 35% were continuously abstinent during the 15-month follow-up period, compared to 19% of the outpatients. Furthermore, 60% of the inpatients never had 3 consecutive days of drinking during follow-up, compared to 46% of outpatients.

Treatment not only produces positive outcomes but is cost-effective as well. For example, the Rand Corporation (1994) found that for every dollar spent on treatment, $7 is saved on crime-related costs and lost workplace productivity. Another Rand study has found that treatment is more cost-effective than either conventional law enforcement or mandatory minimum drug sentences in reducing both cocaine consumption and related violence (Caulkins et al., 1997). Furthermore, it appears that publicly funded substance abuse treatment can reduce Medicaid medical expenses among the poor by as much as 50% over a 5-year period (Washington State Department of Social and Health Services, 1997).

The outcomes of the major prevention and treatment studies described here indicate that competently administered interventions are effective in deterring youth from beginning to use drugs and in helping those persons with addiction problems. Though much remains to be learned, it appears that the quality of service delivery makes a difference across a variety of approaches. Still, there is a continuing need for research, especially where the products are reports that are accessible to front-line practitioners, the public, and policymakers (Join Together, 1998). A major challenge facing the substance abuse field is developing the educational and training programs needed to prepare highly competent practitioners for the next century.

PURPOSE OF THE BOOK

Recently, INCASE, NAADAC, and several other professional organizations collaborated with the federal government's Center for Substance Abuse Treatment to identify the competencies necessary for effective addiction counseling. The outcome of this effort was a technical assistance document known as the *Addiction Counseling Competencies: The Knowledge, Skills, and Attitudes of Professional Practice* (Center for Substance Abuse Treatment, 1998). The document identifies the "transdisciplinary foundations" that are prerequisite to the development of professional competency. Among these foundations are the following:

1. An understanding of addiction models and theories.
2. An understanding of the social, economic, and cultural context of addiction.
3. Knowledge of the behavioral, psychological, physical health, and social effects of substance abuse.
4. Knowledge of treatment practices.
5. Recognition of the importance of family, social networks, and community systems in the recovery process (Center for Substance Abuse Treatment, 1998).

This book should be of great assistance in developing the transdisciplinary foundation that is unique to the addictions field and essential for clinical practice. Though idealistic, I do hope that at least in a small way, the book helps to bridge the gap that exists between theory and research, on one side, and clinical practice, on the other. I also hope students and in-service professionals will find the review of theory and research to be provocative enough to cause them to reconsider their conceptions of alcohol and drug abuse. The text should serve to strengthen professionals' understanding of diverse theoretical perspectives on addiction and assist them in helping clients find a path to recovery.

REVIEW QUESTIONS

1. What are the three fundamentally different views of addiction? How has the conception of addiction changed during U.S. history?
2. What are the characteristics of these three views that make them distinctive and logically exclusive of one another?
3. What are the advantages and disadvantages of each view?
4. According to the author of this book, which view is best understood? Which is most utilized by the treatment community?
5. According to the author, what theory-related issue threatens the continuing development of the field?
6. What are the basics of theory?
7. What are the formal attributes of a good theory?
8. What are the substantive attributes of theories of addictive behavior?
9. What are single-factor and one-level-of-analysis theories?
10. What fundamental assumption of science suggests that addiction is a biopsychosocial phenomenon?

11. What dilemma faces the practitioner in applying theory to practice?

12. What are some of the reasons for the gap between treatment research and clinical practice? What are the origins of this schism?

13. What are the barriers to the use of research findings in the treatment community?

14. What practical issues do researchers tend to ignore in regard to the use of their findings?

15. How does the problem of "technology transfer" affect the substance abuse field? What is being done to facilitate the adoption of innovation?

16. How do we know that prevention and treatment services are effective in addressing substance abuse problems?

REFERENCES

Archer, L. (1991). Marketing new ideas about treatment. *Alcohol Health and Research World, 15*, 213–214.

Backer, T. E., David, S. L., & Soucy, G. (Eds.). (1995). *Reviewing the behavioral science knowledge base on technology transfer* (NIDA Research Monograph 155; NIH Publication No. 95-4035). Rockville, MD: National Clearinghouse on Alcohol and Drug Information.

Botvin, G. J., Baker, E., Dusenbury, L., Botvin, E. M., & Diaz, T. (1995). Long-term follow-up results of a randomized drug abuse prevention trial in a white middle-class population. *Journal of the American Medical Association, 273*, 1106–1112.

Brown, B. S. (1995). Reducing impediments to technology transfer in drug abuse programming. In T. E. Backer, S. L. David, & G. Soucy (Eds.), *Reviewing the behavioral science knowledge base on technology transfer* (NIDA Research Monograph 155; NIH Publication No. 95-4035). Rockville, MD: National Clearinghouse on Alcohol and Drug Information.

Brown, B. S. (1998). Making a difference: Is journal publication enough? *Journal of Substance Abuse Treatment, 15*, 87–88.

Caldwell, F. (1991). Refining the link between research and practice. *Alcohol Health and Research World, 15*, 175–177.

Caulkins, J. P., Rydell, C. P., Schwabe, W. L., & Chiesa, J. (1997). *Mandatory minimum drug sentences: Throwing away the key or the taxpayers' money?* Santa Monica, CA: Rand Corporation, Drug Policy Research Center.

Center for Substance Abuse Treatment. (1997). *The national treatment improvement evaluation study* (DHHS Publication No. SMA 97-3154). Rockville, MD: Substance Abuse and Mental Health Services Administration.

Center for Substance Abuse Treatment. (1998). *Addiction counseling competencies: The knowledge, skills, and attitudes professional practice* (Technical Assistance Publication Series—21; DHHS Publication No. SMA 98-3171). Rockville, MD: Substance Abuse and Mental Health Services Administration.

Cloninger, C. R., Christiansen, K. O., Reich, T., & Gottesman, I. I. (1978). Implications of sex differences in the prevalence of antisocial personality, alcoholism, and criminality for familial transmission. *Archives of General Psychiatry, 35,* 941–951.

Diamond, M. A. (1995). Organizational change as human process, not technique. In T. E. Backer, S. L. David, & G. Soucy (Eds.), *Reviewing the behavioral science knowledge base on technology transfer* (NIDA Research Monograph 155; NIH Publication No. 95-4035). Rockville, MD: National Clearinghouse on Alcohol and Drug Information.

Ellickson, P. L., Bell, R. M., & McGuigan, K. (1993). Preventing adolescent drug use: Long-term results of a junior high program. *American Journal of Public Health, 83,* 856–861.

Ennett, S. T., Tobler, N. S., Ringwalt, C. L., & Flewelling, R. L. (1994). How effective is drug abuse resistance education?: A meta-analysis of Project DARE outcome evaluations. *American Journal of Public Health, 84,* 1394–1400.

Fingarette, H. (1988). *Heavy drinking: The myth of alcoholism as a disease.* Berkeley: University of California Press.

Goode, E. (1993). *Drugs in American society.* New York: McGraw-Hill.

Gordis, E. (1991). Linking research with practice. *Alcohol Health and Research World, 15,* 173–174.

Gough, J. B. (1881). *Sunlight and shadow.* Hartford, CT: Worthington.

Haaga, J. G., & Reuter, P. H. (1995). Prevention: The (lauded) orphan of drug policy. In R. H. Coombs & D. M. Ziedonis (Eds.), *Handbook on drug abuse prevention: A comprehensive strategy to prevent the abuse of alcohol and other drugs.* Boston: Allyn & Bacon.

Hall, C. S., & Lindzey, G. (1978). *Theories of personality* (3rd ed.). New York: Wiley.

Hansen, W. B., & Graham, J. W. (1991). Preventing alcohol, marijuana, and cigarette use among adolescents: Peer pressure resistance training versus establishing conservative norms. *Preventive Medicine, 20,* 414–430.

Hardyck, C., & Petrinovich, L. F. (1975). *Understanding research in the social sciences.* Philadelphia: Saunders.

Hepburn, J. R. (1995). User accountability. In R. H. Coombs & D. Ziedonis (Eds.), *Handbook on drug abuse prevention: A comprehensive strategy to prevent the abuse of alcohol and other drugs.* Boston: Allyn & Bacon.

Huey, F. (1991). Finer points about new treatment approaches. *Alcohol Health and Research World, 15,* 219–220.

Join Together. (1996). *Fixing a failed system.* Boston: Author.

Join Together. (1998). *Treatment for addiction: Advancing the common good.* Boston: Author.

Lamb, S., Greenlick, M. R., & McCarty, D. (1998). *Bridging the gap between practice and research: Forging partnerships with community-based drug and alcohol treatment.* Washington, DC: National Academy Press.

Levine, H. G. (1978). The discovery of addiction: Changing conceptions of habitual drunkenness in America. *Journal of Studies on Alcohol, 39,* 143–174.

Mather, C. (1708). *Sober considerations on a growing flood of iniquity.* Boston.

McLellan, A. T., Grissom, G. R., Zanis, D., Randall, M., Brill, P., & O'Brien, C. P. (1997). Problem-service "matching" in addiction treatment: A prospective study in 4 programs. *Archives of General Psychiatry, 54,* 730–735.

McLellan, A. T., Luborsky, L., Woody, G. E., Druley, K. A., & O'Brien, C. P. (1983). Predicting response to alcohol and drug abuse treatments: Role of psychiatric severity. *Archives of General Psychiatry, 40,* 620–635.

Monette, D. R., Sullivan, T. J., & DeJong, C. R. (1990). *Applied social research: Tool for the human services.* Fort Worth, TX: Holt, Rinehart & Winston.

Mueller, M. D., & Wyman, J. R. (1997). Study sheds light on the state of drug abuse treatment nationwide (NIH Publication No. 97-3478). *NIDA Notes, 12,* 1, 4–8.

Peele, S. (1996). Assumptions about drugs and the marketing of drug policies. In W. K. Bickel & R. J. DeGrandpre (Eds.), *Drug policy and human nature: Psychological perspectives on the prevention, management, and treatment of illicit drug abuse.* New York: Plenum Press.

Pentz, M. A., Dwyer, J. H., MacKinnon, D. P., Flay, B. R., Hansen, W. B., Wang, E. Y. I., & Anderson-Johnson, C. (1989). Multicommunity trial for primary prevention of adolescent drug abuse. *Journal of the American Medical Association, 261,* 3259–3266.

Perry, C. L., Williams, C. L., Veblen-Mortenson, S., Toomey, T. L., Komro, K. A., Anstine, P. S., McGovern, P. G., Finnegan, J. R., Forster, J. L., Wagenaar, A. C., & Wolfson, M. (1996). Project Northland: Outcomes of a community-wide alcohol use prevention program during early adolescence. *American Journal of Public Health, 86,* 956–965.

Planck, M. (1936). *The philosophy of physics.* New York: Norton.

Project MATCH Research Group. (1997). Matching alcoholism treatments to client heterogeneity: Project MATCH posttreatment drinking outcomes. *Journal of Studies on Alcohol, 58,* 7–29.

Rand Corporation. (1994). *Controlling cocaine: Supply versus demand programs.* Santa Monica, CA: Author.

Ray, O., & Ksir, C. (1999). *Drugs, society, and human behavior* (8th ed.). Boston: MCB/McGraw-Hill.

Rogers, E. M. (1995). Diffusion of drug abuse prevention programs: Spontaneous diffusion, agenda setting, and reinvention. In T. E. Backer, S. L. David, & G. Soucy (Eds.), *Reviewing the behavioral science knowledge base on technology transfer* (NIDA Research Monograph 155; NIH Publication No. 95-4035). Rockville, MD: National Clearinghouse on Alcohol and Drug Information.

Rorabaugh, W. J. (1976). *The alcoholic republic; America, 1790–1840.* PhD dissertation, University of California, Berkeley.

Stefflre, B., & Burks, H. M. (1979). Function of theory in counseling. In H. M. Burks & B. Stefflre (Eds.), *Theories of counseling.* New York: McGraw-Hill.

Tenkasi, R. V., & Mohrman, S. A. (1995). Technology transfer as collaborative learning. In T. E. Backer, S. L. David, & G. Soucy (Eds.), *Reviewing the behavioral science knowledge base on technology transfer* (NIDA Research Monograph 155; NIH Publication No. 95-4035). Rockville, MD: National Clearinghouse on Alcohol and Drug Information.

Washington State Department of Social and Health Services. (1997). *Cost savings in Medicaid medical expenses: An outcome study of publicly funded chemical dependency treatment in Washington State* (Briefing paper No. 4.30 [June]). Olympia, WA: DSHS Division of Research and Data Analysis.

Yalisove, D. (1998). The origins and evolution of the disease concept of treatment. *Journal of Studies on Alcohol, 59,* 469–476.

CHAPTER TWO

The Disease Models

In the United States today, the predominant model for understanding alcoholism and other addictions is the view that these disorders are diseases (Yalisove, 1998). This view is particularly strong within the treatment community and within self-help fellowships such as Alcoholics Anonymous (AA) or Narcotics Anonymous (NA). The vast majority of treatment programs rely on the disease (or medical) model for a conceptual base; it shapes selection of treatment options and focuses the content of patient and family education. Thus, most treatment programs in this country employ a supervising physician, require AA or NA attendance, advocate abstinence, teach that the disorder is a chronic condition, and so forth. To the credit of the treatment community, these efforts have lessened the stigma associated with chemical dependency. Compared to 50 years ago, alcoholics and addicts today are less likely to be scorned and more likely to be offered help.

However, enormous controversy continues to surround the disease concept of addiction. Some legal experts and criminologists insist that the use and abuse of chemical substances are intentional acts that deserve punishment (Wilbanks, 1989). In such a view, substance abuse results from a lack of self-restraint and self-discipline. Herbert Fingarette (1988), a philosopher, maintains that the disease model is a myth that endures because it fulfills economic or personal needs of some groups (i.e., the medical community and recovery groups, respectively). Fingarette (1988) strongly supports helping alcoholics or addicts, but he believes that the "disease myth" limits treatment options for many needy individuals. Behavioral science researchers have questioned the validity of the model (Peele, 1985). Some have argued that it is patently unscientific (Alexander, 1988).

Such disparate views are not likely to be resolved in the near future. To evaluate these arguments and counterarguments knowledgeably, it is essential that counselors and other human service professionals understand exactly what is meant by addiction as a disease. Only then can the advantages and disadvantages of this model (i.e., its utility) be intelligently weighed.

DIFFERENT DISEASE CONCEPTIONS

Before we review the core concepts of the disease model, readers should note that there is not just one disease model. A number of proponents of the model, though not necessarily in disagreement, have emphasized different elements. The differences can be striking. For instance, Johnson's (1980) description of the dynamics of alcoholism progression is different from the description of Milam and Ketcham (1983), and Vaillant (1990) provides yet another perspective. The models differ with respect to the importance of physical, psychological, and spiritual factors in the etiology of alcoholism. These different emphases are probably related to the authors' personal experience with alcoholism (whether or not they are recovering alcoholics) and their professional training (i.e., whether they are physicians, psychiatrists, psychologists, etc.).

Peele (1996) provides a useful distinction for thinking about the different disease models. He suggests there are relatively distinct *susceptibility* and *exposure* constructions. The susceptibility variant emphasizes that genetic factors play an important role in the development of substance dependence. These factors influence the individual's vulnerability to the disorders. In contrast, the exposure position holds that chemicals and their actions on the brain are the primary causes of addiction. Here, risk for these disorders is determined by the extent to which the individual is exposed to drugs of abuse. These two disease models are not in conflict with one another. They simply represent different emphases. Each is discussed in detail in this chapter.

The disease model of AA differs somewhat from that espoused by the medical community. The disease model as emphasized by AA stresses the importance of spirituality in the etiology of, and recovery from, alcoholism. In fact, many AA members report that they are recovering from a "spiritual disease." Though many outsiders to AA consider this an oxymoron (i.e., a figure of speech that is a contradiction in terms), many recovering persons feel that it accurately describes their drinking problems. AA encourages its members to find a "Higher Power" and to turn their wills and lives over to a supernatural being. These spiritual conversions are considered crucial to recovery.

In contrast, the medical community tends to point to the significance of biological factors in alcoholism. Physicians often emphasize the role of genetic susceptibilities, increasing tolerance, withdrawal symptoms, liver disease, brain abnormalities, and so forth. Of course, this biomedical approach is consistent with their training. It is not that they ignore spiritual elements; rather, they tend to give such factors less weight than, for example, laboratory test results.

There is another difference between the disease model of AA and that of the medical community. It is a subtle difference, and it is closely related to the dichotomy of spirituality versus science. In AA, members often use the disease concept in a metaphoric sense; that is, they describe their alcohol problems as being "like" a disease. In many cases, recovering individuals do not intend (or perhaps even care) to convey that they literally have a disease. They are simply trying to express that the experience of compulsive chemical use feels like having a disease. It is characterized by feelings of loss of control and hopelessness, conditions familiar to the victims of other diseases (cancer, heart disease, emphysema, etc.).

Most often, physicians do not use the term "disease" as a metaphor. They tend to use the term in a literal sense—that is, "Alcoholism *is* disease." Consider the following statement by a physician who directs a chemical dependency rehabilitation program:

> Whether you become an alcoholic or not depends on genetic predisposition. We know the reason the compulsivity exists is because of a change in the endorphin and cephalin systems in a primitive portion of the brain. The reason for this disturbance in the biochemistry of the primitive brain is a predisposition. Nobody talks any longer about becoming an alcoholic. You don't become an alcoholic—you are born an alcoholic. (Talbott, 1989, p. 57)

As this discussion illustrates, the disease model is not a unitary framework for understanding addiction. However, despite the nuances and ambiguities, certain concepts exist that have traditionally represented the disease model of addiction. Let us examine these concepts in light of the current scientific literature.

TOLERANCE AND WITHDRAWAL

The two clinical features of substance dependence or addiction that are commonly viewed as disease symptoms are tolerance and withdrawal. Drug tolerance is the need to use increasingly greater amounts of a substance to obtain the desired effect. With regular use, tolerance develops to most of the commonly abused psychoactive drugs, including alcohol, cocaine, heroin, and LSD. Though some substance users may initially take pride in their ability to consume large amounts of a drug, increasing tolerance is regarded as an early symptom of dependence (Milam & Ketcham, 1983).

Acute drug withdrawal results when blood or body tissue concentrations of a substance decline following a period of prolonged heavy use (American Psychiatric Association, 1994). The duration, symptoms, and severity of withdrawal vary across drugs and according to the amount of the substance being consumed prior to cessation. Alcohol withdrawal, in particular, varies significantly in both its symptoms and its severity (Saitz, 1998). Clinical manifestations in alcohol withdrawal can range from insomnia to severe conditions such as delirium tremens (DTs) and possibly even death.

Prolonged use of most psychoactive drugs can produce a withdrawal syndrome. These drugs include opiates, heroin, barbiturates, cocaine, and a variety of other substances. The exceptions are several of the commonly abused hallucinogens (LSD, psilocybin, mescaline). The unpleasant symptoms of withdrawal provide motivation for the person to self-administer more of the drug to relieve or even to avoid discomfort.

It is important to note that the contemporary view of drug dependence does not require the presence of either tolerance or withdrawal. According to the diagnostic criteria that appear in the current *Diagnostic and Statistical Manual of Mental Disorders* (DSM-IV), there are seven major symptoms of "substance dependence" (American Psychiatric Association, 1994). As illustrated in Table 2.1, the presence of any three symptoms justifies the dependence diagnosis.

ADDICTION AS A PRIMARY DISEASE

Addiction, especially alcoholism, is often described as a "primary disease"; that is, it is not the result of another condition. This is usually taken to mean that the disease is not caused by heavy drinking or drug use, stress, or psychiatric disorders; rather, it is thought to be the cause of these very conditions. In other words, heavy drinking/drug use, stress, psychiatric disorders, and so forth are secondary symptoms or manifestations of an underlying disease process known as addiction. If the drinking or drug use is stopped, it is believed that the symptoms will, for the most part, disappear (Milam & Ketcham, 1983; Talbott, 1989).

This view is contrary to popular conceptions of addiction, especially alcoholism. To take alcoholism as an example, many laypeople (even those who view alcoholism as a disease) feel that alcoholism results from abusive drinking, which in turn stems from irresponsibility, stress, or emotional problems. The disease model, properly understood, disputes these ideas (Milam & Ketcham, 1983). The model proposes that alcoholics are not responsible for contracting their disease; the disease itself causes or drives the heavy drinking. Furthermore, it is maintained that those drinkers who lack genetic susceptibility to the

TABLE 2.1. DSM-IV Criteria for Substance Dependence

A maladaptive pattern of substance use, leading to clinically significant impairment or distress, as manifested by three (or more) of the following, occurring at any time in the same 12-month period:

(1) tolerance, as defined by either of the following:
    (a) a need for markedly increased amounts of the substance to achieve intoxication or desired effect
    (b) markedly diminished effect with continued use of the same amount of the substance
(2) withdrawal, as manifested by either of the following:
    (a) the characteristic withdrawal syndrome for the substance
    (b) the same (or closely related) substance is taken to relieve or avoid withdrawal symptoms
(3) the substance is often taken in larger amounts or over a longer period than was intended
(4) there is a persistent desire or unsuccessful efforts to cut down or control substance use
(5) a great deal of time is spent in activities necessary to obtain the substance (e.g., visiting multiple doctors or driving long distances), use the substance (e.g., chain-smoking), or recover from its effects
(6) important social, occupational, or recreational activities are given up or reduced because of substance use
(7) the substance use is continued despite knowledge of having a persistent or recurrent physical or psychological problem that is likely to have been caused or exacerbated by the substance (e.g., current cocaine use despite recognition of cocaine-induced depression, or continued drinking despite recognition that an ulcer was made worse by alcohol consumption)

Specify if:
    With Physiological Dependence: evidence of tolerance or withdrawal (i.e., either Item 1 or 2 is present)
    Without Physiological Dependence: no evidence or tolerance or withdrawal (i.e., neither Item 1 nor 2 is present)

Note. From American Psychiatric Association (1994). Copyright 1994 by the American Psychiatric Association. Reprinted by permission.

disease cannot drink themselves into alcoholism (Milam & Ketcham, 1983).

In recent years, however, various lines of research have developed data that contradict the primary-disease concept for all alcoholics. For example, researchers note that there may be multiple types of alcoholisms (National Institute on Alcohol Abuse and Alcoholism, 1990). Some forms may be more sensitive to genetic factors, whereas others are influenced by environmental conditions (Cloninger, 1987). Environmental factors (stress, marital and family problems, depression, anxiety, etc.) may cause some forms of alcoholism. Schuckit (1989) has reported that a proportion of alcoholics "fulfill criteria for a clearly preexisting antisocial personality disorder (ASPD)" (p. 2). This suggests that severe antisocial life problems may cause alcoholism in some.

Cox (1985) has noted that certain psychological traits predispose individuals to substance abuse in general:

> Specifically, future substance abusers are characterized by disregard for social mores, independence, impulsivity, and affinity for adventure. These are enduring personality characteristics that appear to be biologically mediated (Eysenck, 1981; Zuckerman, 1983). Persons exhibiting these personality characteristics are able to satisfy their psychological needs through substance use, and they appear to be especially susceptible to environmental influences promoting substance use. (p. 233)

This passage cogently describes how genetics and environment interact to promote alcohol and drug abuse. It also suggests that a "sensation-seeking" alcoholic personality will not disappear upon cessation of alcohol use. Successful recovery may often depend on the alcoholic's finding alternative (i.e., nonchemical) ways to fulfill psychological needs for excitement and risk taking.

Findings such as these suggest that the causes of alcoholism (and probably other addictions as well) are multiple and mediated by both genetic and environmental factors. Each alcoholic probably has a relatively unique combination of forces that led to the development of his/her drinking problem. Some cases may be strongly influenced by genetic factors; others may be mediated solely by environmental ones. In the future, the concept of "primary" alcoholism is likely to be further and further restricted as various types of the disorder continue to be identified.

GENETIC ORIGINS OF ADDICTION: THE SUSCEPTIBILITY MODEL

There is compelling evidence of the familial transmission of substance use disorders (e.g., Bierut et al., 1998; Merikangas et al., 1998). This familial transmission is thought to occur via both genetic and psychosocial pathways. The genetic factors may involve individual differences in drug metabolism, tolerance, sensitivity, and/or side effects (Merikangas et al., 1998). The accompanying psychosocial (or environmental) pathways are numerous and may include inadequate parental monitoring and supervision, child–parent modeling processes, marital discord, family stress, child abuse, and so on (Patterson, 1996). Thus, the clustering of substance use in families is thought to be determined by the confluence of genetic and environmental variables.

As noted in Chapter One, the idea that alcoholism, in particular, has genetic origins that can be traced back to the 19th century (Levine,

1978). More recently, scientists also have examined the role of genetic influence on other drugs of abuse. Interest in the general field of behavioral genetics has grown for three reasons (Mann, 1994). First, a large body of research shows hereditary influence on animal behavior. Second, the methodologically sound twin studies conducted since the 1980s have consistently found that genes contribute to the development of complex disorders, such as alcoholism. Third, and perhaps of greatest importance, there is an increasing awareness that genes and the environment *jointly* determine human behavior—particularly addictive behavior.

Genotype and Phenotype

The study of genetics deals with characteristics that are transmitted from parents to their offspring via biological mechanisms. These characteristics are not acquired as a result of learning, modeling, socialization, or other postnatal experiences; they are hereditary or inborn. Such human characteristics as eye color and blood type are determined by genetic factors.

"Genes" are the basic structural units of heredity. Each person shares 50% of the genes of each parent in a unique arrangement that is different from that of both parents. This assemblage of genes is the person's "genotype." During both pre- and postnatal development, the individual is exposed to a variety of environmental influences. This interaction between genotype and environment generates an enormous number of individual traits and characteristics, which are referred to as the person's "phenotype." The phenotype, then, is the outcome of the interaction between genes and environment. It should be noted that fetal exposure to alcohol or other drugs is an environmental influence on the phenotype; fetal alcohol syndrome and related conditions among newborns are not genetic disorders.

During the last 10 years, the advances made in the field of behavioral genetics have generated evidence to support claims that heredity plays a role in a wide range of human behavior. Frequently, these claims have been distorted by the popular press with superficial reports describing an "intelligence gene" and a "violence gene" (Mann, 1994). Too often, the magnitude of the genetic influence is exaggerated or relevant environmental factors are unduly minimized, often as a result of ignorance about the interactive nature of each. This lack of understanding also has fueled the mistaken belief in "genetic determinism." Clearly, for complex human traits, genes are not destiny but parameters of risk as well as protection. According to Kenneth Kendler, a behavioral genetics researcher, "genes and environment loop out into each other and feed back on each other in a complex way that we have just begun to understand" (Mann, 1994). The important point is that genes operate in a probabilistic manner in addictive behavior (Goldman & Bergen, 1998). They are not deterministic factors.

Researchers acknowledge that genetic factors play a role in the development of the substance use disorders. However, there is considerable disagreement about the relative contribution of "nature" and "nuture." Lester (1988), Searles (1988), and others have been highly critical of heritability measures that genetic researchers use to claim, for instance, that a trait is "60% inherited." According to Lester (1988), "For concepts like intelligence, or schizophrenia, or alcoholism, there is no evidence that simple relationships exist; indeed, there is every reason to believe that the highest levels of organismic function are involved, embracing the most complex developing and evolving relationships of humans as social beings" (p. 2). Yet, heritability measures are typically based on the assumption that the relationship between inherited characteristics and environmental variables is additive—when it is not. These two sets of influence are most likely reciprocal or interactive in influencing addiction. In a related point, Searles (1988) notes that a serious flaw in the genetic research on the addictions is the inadequate measurement of environmental variables. He states: "What is termed 'environment' in most studies is usually not the complex, multifaceted construct that the word implies. It often is simply what is left after genetic factors are removed, or it reflects overly broad influences of crudely measured variables" (p. 164). Given the inadequacy of current research methods to accurately assess "nature versus nuture," we should not dismiss, but should rather view as tentative, those findings that assign values to the respective contributions of genetic factors and the environment. The following discussion reviews some of what is known about the roles of genetics and the environment in shaping alcohol and drug dependence.

Early Work: Goodwin's Adoption Study

Donald Goodwin, a psychiatrist and widely respected alcoholism researcher, was among the first to establish a link between genetics and alcoholism. His well-known adoption study is usually cited as the basis for the claim often made that children of alcoholics are four times more likely to develop alcoholism than are children of nonalcoholics (Goodwin, Schulsinger, Hermansen, Guze, & Winokur, 1973). The study is particularly important because it rekindled interest in the genetic origins of alcoholism (Searles, 1988). Today, it is still cited by treatment professionals as evidence that alcoholism is a "true disease." Unfortunately, few have closely evaluated the methods used in the study.

The Goodwin study relied on a pool of Danish children ($n = 5,483$) who were given up for adoption shortly after birth during the period from 1924 to 1947. The pool of adoptees was originally created for a study on schizophrenia. The study was conducted in Denmark because that country maintains national adoption registries, which are available for scientific investigations.

The design of an adoption study is relatively simple. It is based on the principle that children born to alcoholic parents but adopted and raised by others (probably by nonalcoholic adoptive parents) may have a greater likelihood of developing alcohol problems than adopted children born to nonalcoholic parents (and most likely raised by nonalcoholic adoptive parents). Any differences in the rates of problem drinking or alcoholism between the two groups of adoptees can then be attributed to heredity rather than to family rearing practices. Furthermore, because both groups of children are adoptees, any relationships between being adopted and later alcoholism should be the same for both groups.

Goodwin et al. (1973) identified a group of 67 male adoptees who had an alcoholic parent (85% of these were fathers), who were adopted by nonrelatives before the seventh week of life, and who had no known contact with biological relatives. These subjects were referred to as "probands." In addition, two control groups (adoptees born to nonalcoholic parents) were identified. One of these consisted of 70 adoptees who were matched to the probands on age, sex, and time of adoption. The biological parents of these control group adoptees had no hospital record of problem drinking, alcoholism, or psychiatric disorder. The second group of controls consisted of 37 adoptees who were born to nonalcoholic parents but "had a biological parent hospitalized for a psychiatric condition other than alcoholism" (Goodwin et al., 1973, p. 238). Of the sample of 174 adoptees (who by the time of the study were adults), 41 could not be found or refused to be interviewed for the study. In a structured interview, information was obtained on demographic variables, parents, drinking practices, and other relevant factors. Later, it was found that the two control groups did not differ substantially from each other, so they were combined (Goodwin et al., 1973).

Table 2.2 shows the drinking problems and patterns in the two adoptee groups. As can be seen, the two groups differed significantly on five variables. One was "Hallucinations"; according to Goodwin (1988), "hallucinations" referred to "auditory or visual perceptual distortions associated with withdrawal from alcohol" (pp. 102–103). The second variable on which there was a significant difference, "Lost control," referred to the experience of wanting not to use alcohol on an occasion but being unable to do so. The variable "Morning drinking"

TABLE 2.2. Drinking Problems and Patterns in Two Adoptive Groups

	Probands ($n = 55$)	Controls ($n = 78$)
Problems		
Hallucinations*	6%	0%
Lost control*	35%	17%
Amnesia	53%	41%
Tremor	24%	22%
Morning drinking*	29%	11%
Delirium tremens	6%	1%
Rum fits (seizures after withdrawal)	2%	0%
Social disapproval	6%	8%
Marital trouble	18%	9%
Job trouble	7%	3%
Drunken-driving arrests	7%	4%
Police trouble, ever	15%	8%
Treated for drinking, ever *	9%	1%
Hospitalized for drinking	11%	0%
Patterns		
Moderate drinker	51%	45%
Heavy drinker, ever	22%	36%
Problem drinker, ever	9%	14%
Alcoholic, ever*	18%	5%

Note. From Goodwin, Schulsinger, Hermansen, Guze, and Winokur (1973).
Copyright 1973 by the American Medical Association. Reprinted by permission.
* Indicates statistically significant differences between groups.

assessed repeated drinking in the morning, rather than just one or two drinks on an occasion. The other two variables on which there were significant differences—"Alcoholic, ever" and "Treated for drinking, ever"—are self-explanatory. On each of these five variables, the probands were overrepresented, compared to controls. Notice that on most of the remaining drinking problems (i.e., those not followed by an asterisk), the probands also reported greater levels of alcohol problems than did controls. However, these differences did not reach statistical significance (as determined by chi-square analyses and student's t-tests). Thus, they could have occurred by chance.

For a full understanding of the findings in Table 2.2, it is important to consider the classification criteria for the four drinking patterns. These appear in Table 2.3. As one can see (in Table 2.2), 18% of the probands were alcoholic, compared to 5% of the controls. In other words, the rate of alcoholism among adopted sons with an alcoholic biological parent was 3.6 times greater than that among adopted sons whose biological parents were not alcoholic. This finding has been widely used to support the claim that alcoholism is genetically determined (e.g., Goodwin, 1988; Milam & Ketcham, 1983).

Unfortunately, as evidence for a genetic basis of alcoholism, the importance of these particular findings have been exaggerated (Fingarette, 1988; Lester, 1988; Murray, Clifford, & Gurling, 1983; Peele, 1985). Consider, for example, the fact that relatively small proportions of both groups (i.e., proband and control) actually became alcoholic later in life. As Fingarette (1988) notes:

> In Goodwin's study, about 18 percent of the sons who had an alcoholic parent became alcoholics, compared to 5 percent of the sons of nonalcoholic parents. The hypothesis is that the difference between these groups is attributable to heredity. But to see the full picture, let's turn the numbers around: 82 percent of the sons who had an alcoholic parent—more than four out of five—did not become alcoholics. So if we generalize from Goodwin's results, we must say that

TABLE 2.3. Criteria for Drinking Categories

Moderate drinker	Neither a teetotaler nor heavy drinker
Heavy drinker	For at least 1 year drank daily and had six or more drinks at least two or three times a month, or drank six or more drinks at least once a week for more than a year but reported no problems.
Problem drinker	(A) Meets criteria for heavy drinker (B) Had problems from drinking but insufficient in number to meet alcoholism criteria
Alcoholic	(A) Meets criteria for heavy drinker (B) Must have had alcohol problems in at least three of the following four groups:
	Group 1: Social disapproval of drinking by friends or parents Marital problems from drinking
	Group 2: Job trouble from drinking Traffic arrests from drinking Other police trouble from drinking
	Group 3: Frequent blackouts Tremor Withdrawal hallucinations Withdrawal convulsions Delirium tremens
	Group 4: Loss of control Morning drinking

Note. From Goodwin, Schulsinger, Hermansen, Guze, and Winokur (1973). Copyright 1973 by the American Medical Association. Reprinted by permission.

about 80 percent of persons with an alcoholic parent will not become alcoholics. Either the relevant genes are usually not transmitted or the genes are transmitted but are usually out-weighed by
other factors. (pp. 52–53)

Moreover, if alcoholism is always determined by genetic factors,
how is it that 5% of the control group (i.e., sons of nonalcoholic parents) developed alcoholism in later life? The reluctance to acknowledge the potent influence of environmental factors is highlighted by
Goodwin's (1988) admission that the genetic hypothesis "certainly may
not apply to all alcoholics. Even the possibility of environmental influence cannot be entirely ruled out" (p. 107).

The other serious data-analytic problem in the Goodwin et al.
(1973) study rests with the distinction made between problem drinkers and alcoholics. Goodwin (1988) admits that the criteria employed
were "arbitrary" (p. 105). This being the case, it is important to consider the results of combining the problem drinkers and the alcoholics
into one group. Lester (1988) and Murray et al. (1983), using Goodwin
et al.'s (1973) data, did just this. The result was that there was no
statistically significant difference between the proband and control
groups in regard to number of problem drinkers/alcoholics. Murray et
al. (1983) have noted: "If the cut-off point for abnormality is widened
to include not just alcoholism but also problem drinking, then evidence for any genetic predisposition vanishes. . . . Could it be that
Goodwin's findings are simply an artifact produced by the threshold
for alcoholism accidentally dividing heavy drinkers in the index and
control groups unevenly?" (p. 42).

Twin Studies

Before findings from twin studies are examined, let us examine the
logic, design, and limitations of a twin study. There are two types of
twins: "monozygotic" (MZ) and "dizygotic" (DZ). MZ twins develop
from a single ovum and sperm, whereas DZ twins develop from separate ova and sperm. MZ twins share identical genotypes; however, DZ
twins share only half of their genes. MZ twins are usually referred to
as "identical" twins, whereas DZ twins are often known as "fraternal"
twins. Of course, MZ twins are always of the same gender. DZ twins
may be of different genders and are no more alike (in terms of genetic
makeup) than any two siblings.

In twin studies, concordance rates are determined for a specific
characteristic or trait. A "concordance rate" is the degree of similarity
between the twins in each pair in a series on any given characteristic.

The greater the concordance between MZ twins, as compared to DZ twins, is taken as evidence of the degree of genetic determination for a characteristic. Stated in another way, the concordance rate of the DZ twins serves as a baseline representing environmental input on a characteristic. The greater the degree to which the MZ twins' concordance rate exceeds that of the DZ twins, the greater the role heredity plays in determining that characteristic.

Lester (1988) points out that twin studies are based on a set of assumptions. Though these problems do not discredit well-designed twin studies, we should be aware that the following problems may exist:

1. Twin studies assume that mating of the parents is random or "nonassortative." More specifically, it is assumed that the selection of a mate is not influenced by drinking or drug use habits.
2. [It is assumed that] no dominance or other genetic effects are involved in the particular disorder (alcohol or other drug use).
3. The within-pair environmental variance is the same in DZ twins as in MZ twins. That is, the post-natal experience of the identical twin pairs is roughly equivalent to that of fraternal twins. It is assumed that fraternal twins have the same degree of social contact with each other as do identical twins. (p. 6)

The first assumption involving random mating is particularly problematic and could lead to inflated estimates of the genetic contribution to alcoholism or other drug dependencies. In regard to the third assumption, recent twin studies have used statistical controls to adjust for MZ/DZ differences in social environment.

Findings from Alcohol-Specific Twin Studies

Twin studies conducted since the late 1980s have established that both environmental and genetic factors play a role in the development of alcoholism. Kaprio et al. (1987) conducted a twin study involving 2,800 male pairs from Finland. The subjects responded to a questionnaire that assessed quantity and frequency of drinking, density of drinking (i.e., regularity of drinking at particular times, such as weekends), frequency of passing out from drinking, and frequency of social contact between twins (including cohabitation). Kaprio et al. (1987) found that (1) identical twins had more social contact with each other (as adults) than fraternal twins, (2) frequent social contact between twins was significantly correlated with concordance rates in drinking patterns, (3) the concordance rate among the identical twins was somewhat higher than that for the fraternal twins, and (4) the higher concordance rate among the identical twins was explained by both social contact (an environmental factor) and genetic variables.

Kaprio et al. (1987) estimated that for measures of quantity, frequency, and density of drinking, "environment" accounted for 60 to 64% of the variance in these three variables. Frequency of drinking to unconsciousness was completely explained by environmental factors.

Insight into how genetic and environmental factors interact has emerged from a twin study conducted by Heath, Jardine, and Martin (1989). This is one of the few studies that has relied on female twins. The sample was obtained through the Australian National Twin Register; it consisted of 1,200 identical twin pairs and 750 fraternal twin pairs (all twins were female). The most important finding of this study was that marital status was a major modifier of genetically influenced drinking patterns. Among both younger and older adult women, being married (or living with a man but not actually being married) suppressed the emergence of genetically influenced drinking patterns. Women who were not married (or not in a similar relationship) tended to drink more heavily (Heath et al., 1989). This supports the notion that both environment and genetics are important, and that they interact in a variety of complex ways to spur the development of alcoholism. In other words, genetics set the stage for vulnerability to later environmental influences.

Further support for the interactive influence of both genetics and environment comes from a recent twin study (McGue, Pickens, & Svikis, 1992). The investigation located co-twins of probands (i.e., patients) from alcohol and drug abuse treatment programs in Minnesota. About 57% of the same-sex twin pairs had their zygosity (MZ vs. DZ status) determined by blood test, whereas the remainder were determined by self-report questionnaire administered to both the probands and their co-twins. Approximately 8% of the pairs were eliminated from the data analyses because the questionnaire method could not confirm their zygosity. The sample of twin pairs was then broken down by gender and age of first symptom of alcoholism. Within each gender, "early-onset" twin pairs were identified as those where the probands reported a symptom of alcoholism prior to the age of 20. Otherwise, the pairs were classified as "late-onset" (McGue et al., 1992).

As shown in Table 2.4, .725 (or 73%) of the variance in alcoholism among the male early-onset twin pairs could be accounted for by genetic factors. This compared to about 30% of the variance in the male late-onset pairs and to about 54% of the variance among the total number of male twin pairs. In contrast, the data provided no evidence of genetic influence in female alcoholism for either age group (McGue et al., 1992). These data suggest that genetic factors play a strong role in male alcoholism that appears prior to the age of 20. Genetic variables seem to have only a moderate influence on male alco-

TABLE 2.4. Sex and Age Effects on the Inheritance of Alcohol Problems: A Twin Study

Group	Monozygotic		Dizygotic		Proportion of variance		
	Number of pairs	Concordance rate	Number of pairs	Concordance rate	Genetic	Shared environmental	Unshared environmental
			Males				
Early onset	52	.865	44	.568	.725	.232	.043
Late onset	33	.606	52	.509	.295	.372	.333
Total	85	.765	96	.536	.543	.331	.126
			Females				
Early onset	20	.500	22	.500	.000	.732	.268
Late onset	24	.292	21	.333	.000	.525	.475
Total	44	.386	43	.419	.000	.635	.367

Note. Adapted from McGue, Pickens, and Svikis (1992). Copyright 1992 by the American Psychological Association. Adapted by permission.

holism that begins later in life, and inheritance may play no role in the development of female alcoholism (McGue et al., 1992).

Areas of scientific inquiry that are in formative stages, such as the role of genetics in alcoholism, often include investigations that yield inconsistent or contradictory results. Another twin study from the same year is a case in point. Directly contradicting the work of McGue et al. (1992), an investigation by Kendler, Heath, Neale, Kessler, and Eaves (1992) found evidence supporting a genetic basis for female alcoholism. In this study, data analyses used 1,030 female–female twin pairs of known zygosity from the Virginia Twin Registry. The data were collected from structured psychiatric interviews. The interviewer was "blinded" as to the psychopathological status of each co-twin.

The feature of this study that distinguishes it from the McGue et al. (1992) study is that it did not use a co-twin's admission to an alcoholism treatment facility as the basis for selecting the twin pair for the study. The Kendler et al. (1992) study was a population-based study in which twin pairs were identified through a registry. The proportion of the twins who had received treatment for a drinking problem was not reported.

Kendler et al. (1992) used four different definitions of alcoholism. They found that genetics account for 50 to 60% of the variance in female alcoholism. However, these estimates assumed that the environmental experiences of the MZ and DZ twins were equal. When this factor was controlled for, the heritability of liability to alcoholism in women was in the range of 40 to 50% (Kendler et al., 1992).

Why are the findings of McGue et al. (1992) and Kendler et al. (1992) so contradictory with respect to the role of genetics in female alcoholism? The authors of the second study state it best: "One plausible hypothesis is that the genetic loading for alcoholism in the modest proportion of women who seek treatment may not be typical of that found in the entire population of women with alcoholism. It is possible, for example, that patients seen in treatment settings may have been particularly influenced by social or environmental factors" (Kendler et al., 1992, p. 1881).

Following this line of reasoning, it would also then be plausible to conclude that males who seek treatment for alcoholism tend to have a stronger genetic loading than do their female counterparts. The reasons for this difference are not clear. Age may play a role: Women entering treatment facilities for the first time may tend to be older than the men who do so. Perhaps women are more likely to have a form of alcoholism caused primarily by social/environmental factors. Further research is needed before firm conclusions can be reached about the role of genetics in alcoholism and about any possible differences in its etiology in women and men.

Twin Studies of Other Drug Use

Initial twin study research reported that there were modest genetic influences on cigarette smoking (Carmelli, Swan, Robinette, & Fabsitz, 1992) and illicit drug use in general (Jang, Livesley, & Vernon, 1995). These findings were replicated recently in a rigorous investigation conducted by Tsuang et al. (1998). The investigators studied 3,373 male twin pairs from the Vietnam Era Twin Registry. The population-based sample represented 65% of the pairs in the registry. In addition to finding that the use of different drugs tends to co-occur in individuals, Tsuang et al. (1998) developed statistical models indicating the presence of a latent or underlying *vulnerability* to substance abuse. This vulnerability was influenced jointly by: (1) genetic factors, (2) family environmental factors, and (3) nonfamily environmental factors. The respective contributions of each of these three factors varied by drug of abuse. These additive influences can be seen in Table 2.5.

The data from the Tsuang et al. (1998) study suggest that genetic factors play the greatest role in heroin abuse. Marijuana abuse appears to be influenced substantially by all three sources of influence. In contrast, nonfamily environmental variables appear to be the predominant influences on stimulants, sedatives, and psychedelics. The reader should note that these estimates of additive influence were based on data collected from males only and that for particular individuals the contribution of genotype and environment varies (Goldman & Bergen, 1998). Nevertheless, the data are evidence that a genetic susceptibility to drug abuse exists.

TABLE 2.5. Additive Influences of Genetic, Family Environmental, and Nonfamily Environmental Factors on Substance Abuse

Drug	Genetic influence	Family environmental	Nonfamily environmental
Heroin	54%	13%	33%
Marijuana	33%	29%	38%
Stimulants	33%	19%	48%
Sedatives	27%	17%	56%
Psychedelics	26%	21%	53%

Note. Data from Tsuang et al. (1998).

The Discredited Dopamine D_2 Receptor Gene Theory

In 1990, with much fanfare, Kenneth Blum, Ernest Noble, and colleagues published a paper in the *Journal of the American Medical Association* in which they reported that they had discovered the gene that causes alcoholism (Blum et al., 1990). The researchers focused on a single gene for the dopamine D_2 receptor subtype. There are different subtypes of receptors that respond to dopamine in the mesolimbic pathway. The investigators' rationale for examining the D_2 receptor subtype was its location in the nucleus accumbens, a pleasure center of the brain, as well as in other sites that are implicated in the mediation of reward. DNA samples from 35 deceased alcoholics and 35 deceased nonalcoholics revealed that one structural mutation of the gene for the D_2 receptor, the A1 allele, was observed in 77% of the alcoholics but in only 28% of the nonalcoholics (Blum et al., 1990). In a subsequent study of the dopamine D_2 receptor gene, Noble, Blum, Ritchie, Montgomery, and Sheridan (1991) were more circumspect and concluded that ". . . the present study has not established unequivocally a genetic link between the functioning of the dopaminergic system and severe alcoholism" (p. 653).

Soon after the Blum et al. (1990) article was published in the *Journal of the American Medical Association,* other studies appeared that did not support the association between alcoholism susceptibility and the suspect A1 allele (e.g., Bolos et al., 1990; Gejman et al., 1994; Parsian et al., 1991). Criticisms of the work of Blum and Noble included reliance on small samples, inadequate methods, and conclusions that went far beyond their data. To their credit, Blum and Noble participated in some of the work that disputed the findings of their 1990 study (e.g., Gejman et al., 1994). However, in the journal *Science,* one researcher was quoted as saying that Blum and Noble had built a "castle in the air" (Holden, 1994, p. 1696). One unfortunate aspect of this episode is the confusion it generates among the general public, who often do not understand the tentative nature of findings from scientific studies.

Collaborative Study on the Genetics of Alcoholism

Recent work on identifying alcoholism susceptibility genes has employed a different strategy from that used by Blum, Noble, and others. A $60 million project known as the Collaborative Study on the Genetics of Alcoholism (COGA) is mapping the sequence of human DNA, rather than using the "hit or miss" approach of the past (Begleiter et al., 1995). Funded by the National Institute on Alcohol Abuse and Alcoholism (NIAAA), this project is a component of the larger Human Genome Project (HGP). The HGP is a massive research program designed to map the entire human genome (Collins & Fink, 1995). COGA seeks to identify the specific genes that increase alcoholism susceptibility through one or more channels including neuron communication and alcohol metabolism.

Preliminary COGA findings indicate that alcoholism susceptibility is probably linked to several genes (Reich et al., 1998). In other words, the disorder is likely "polygenic" and not the result of a mutation in a single gene. This may point toward alcoholism subtypes, which may vary with respect to gene–environment contributions. Interestingly, initial COGA work has not found evidence to link the dopamine D_2 receptor gene to alcoholism susceptibility (Reich et al., 1998). Furthermore, it appears that there may be "protective genes" against alcoholism (Reich et al., 1998). Thus, genetic characteristics may decrease, as well as increase an individual's risk for alcoholism.

The Social Impact of Genetic Research

The information and technology gained as a result of the HGP (and COGA) are expected to have a profound social impact. Stigmatization and discrimination based on hereditary characteristics and other misuses and misinterpretations of genetic information are significant social and public policy concerns (Khoury & Genetics Work Group, 1996). Predictive genetic screening of complex traits, such as alcoholism susceptibility, raises conceptual and philosophical questions about personal responsibility for one's conduct, future reproductive decisions, genetic determinism and one's health, and the definition of "normal" and "abnormal" drinking practices. Furthermore, multiple, and often contradictory, values and belief systems influence public and personal views about the morality of genetic technologies. Therefore, the psychosocial aspects of genetic technology in disease prevention and treatment require evaluation before genetic testing should be introduced into medical practice (Khoury & Genetics Work Group, 1996).

The translation of genetic technologies into patient care brings with it special concerns about how these tools will be applied, and because of this, the HGP has committed research money to study the ethical, legal, and social implications of the emerging genetic testing technology (Collins & Fink, 1995). Results of genetic studies can be interpreted in such a way that the causes of disease, disability, and behavioral characteristics (traits) are reduced to the expression of particular genes, thereby excluding the contribution of psychosocial and environmental factors (Croyle & Lerman, 1995). An important and challenging role for addictions practitioners will be to educate clients and their families about genetic test technology so that they make informed decisions about testing.

Utilization of Genetic Testing for Various Diseases

Past studies on attitudes toward genetic testing have found that both general (Croyle & Lerman, 1995) and at-risk (Kessler, Field, Worth, & Mosbarger, 1987) groups tend to express favorable attitudes toward, and interest in, being tested. However, research on the actual utilization of genetic testing shows that use tends to be much lower (Croyle & Lerman, 1995). Furthermore, studies on attitudes toward genetic testing for Huntington's Disease and cystic fibrosis have shown that "hypothetical testing" (Kessler et al., 1987; Williamson et al., 1989) described as available sometime in the future, draws substantially more interest than "currently available testing" (Craufurd, Dodge, Kerzin-Storrar, & Harris, 1989; Tambor et al., 1994).

In general, relatively little is known about whether at-risk individuals will want to know their risk status. The process involved in arriving at a decision for or against testing is complex and not well understood at this time. Compared to other diseases, utilization of screening for alcoholism susceptibility may have unique features in that persons at high risk may be those least likely to use the test (Thombs, Mahoney, & Olds, 1998).

Application of a Bogus Testing Procedure to Determine
College Students' Interest in Genetic Screening

In 1997, Drs. Colleen Mahoney, R. Scott Olds, and I conducted a quasi-experimental study to assess college student interest in using genetic screening for alcoholism susceptibility (Thombs et al., 1998). Of course, the test did not exist at the time. We deceived 181 students at Kent State University by concocting a bogus story that they were part of large, multicampus study to determine interest in "a newly available" genetic test for alcoholism susceptibility. They were debriefed about the true nature of the study during the following week. The purpose of this study was to assess the extent to which we could predict genetic screening intentions and utilization in a college student sample.

A questionnaire was administered before and after the students viewed a presentation that accurately explained genetic susceptibility to alcoholism. We lied to the students because findings from past studies suggested that a test described as a "procedure available sometime in the future" would provoke unrealistically positive testing intentions. Test utilization was assessed by providing students with a mechanism to actually schedule a test during the week following the data collection.

A large majority of the students were opposed to being tested for alcoholism susceptibility (Thombs et al., 1998). Only 7% indicated a strong intention to schedule a test. With the exception of frequent drunkenness before age 16, alcohol indicators had little relationship to test-seeking intention. Moreover, in the week following the data collection, only seven participants (4%) requested to schedule a test. These findings are consistent with previous investigations on use of genetic screening for other disorders (Craufurd et al., 1989; Kessler et al., 1987; Tambor et al., 1994; Williamson, et al., 1989).

If the sample used in the investigation was representative of young adults in general, this raises the concern that if or when such a test becomes available in the future, a large segment of at-risk young adults will simply avoid using it (Thombs et al., 1998). The lack of interest in the (bogus) test may have resulted from the participants' relatively high level of alcohol involvement and their need to reduce the cognitive dissonance that they were experiencing during and immediately after the presentation. Across all levels of alcohol use, rejection of the test may have been the easiest way to reduce the dissonance between their drinking behavior and the opportunity to be screened for alcoholism. For many students, this option would allow for denial of the risks associated with alcohol use and it would protect their current drinking practices, whether they were problematic or not. When genetic screening for alcoholism susceptibility is introduced into the health marketplace in the future, initial use may find more acceptance among high-risk families and as part of patient assessment in alcoholism treatment.

Genetic Risk Summary

There are six essential points that the addiction practitioner should understand about the genetics of addictive behavior.

1. *Genes and the environment jointly determine alcohol and drug addictions.* Mann (1994) quotes research scientist Robert Plomin as saying, "Research into heritability is the best demonstration I know of the importance of the environment" (p. 1689).

2. *The inherited characteristic is not a disease but a predisposition or susceptibility.* In other words, addiction is not an inherited disease caused by a variant in a single gene, such as in the cases of cystic fibrosis or Huntington's Disease. Rather, addiction is a complex disorder caused by a variety of genetic and environmental variables. Genetic risk factors either increase or decrease risk for developing the disorder. It may be found that some gene mutations actually provide protection against alcoholism and some drug addictions.

3. *Among persons with addiction problems, there is heterogeneity to the contribution of genes and environment that influence individual patterns of substance use.* In the future, it may be discovered that there are subtypes of alcoholism, for example, ranging from those that are largely genetic in origin, at one extreme, to those determined entirely by the environment, on the other end of the spectrum. Alcoholism subtypes also may be based on the presence or absence of antisocial personality traits and age of onset (Anthenelli & Tabakoff, 1995).

4. *Recognizing the role of genetic risk factors does not require that alcoholism and other drug dependencies be defined as disease states.* A wide range of human traits are influenced by genes, including physical endurance (Montgomery et al., 1998) and perceived social support (Kendler, 1997), that by social convention are not considered diseases.

5. *Research on the genetics of addiction is important because it may lead to more effective ways to prevent and treat the problem of addiction.* According to research scientist Xandra Breakefield, "The purpose of behavioral genetics is not to push people into trouble but to pull them out" (Mann, 1994). For example, a genetic test for alcoholism could identify children who are at risk for developing the disorder in the future. Such a test also could be used in the assessment and diagnosis of alcoholic clients and as motivation enhancement for ambivalent clients.

6. *In the future, clients in treatment and their families will need assistance with the genetic testing decision and how to interpret test results.* Individuals may respond differently to positive test results depending on one's perceived capability to change their drinking behavior. A posi-

tive test result could exacerbate a person's alcohol problems by inducing a sense of futility and hopelessness. On the other hand, some might interpret a negative test result to mean that they can continue to drink with impunity. A range of other client responses probably exist as well. At this point we can only speculate on how the results of a genetic test for alcoholism susceptibility will be used by clients.

Alcohol Metabolism: Liver Enzymes
and the Possibility of Genetic Regulation

A variety of processes are involved in the metabolism of drugs. These processes break down or inactivate drugs so that they can be eliminated from the body. For some time researchers have been interested in alcohol metabolism because of speculation that alcoholics may suffer from an inherited "error in metabolism" and because there is ethnic variation in the liver enzymes that break down alcohol (NIAAA, 1994). This section provides an overview of work in this area.

Alcohol is absorbed from the stomach and the small intestine into the circulatory system and transported to the liver for metabolism. The first step in alcohol metabolism involves the conversion of alcohol to acetaldehyde by a liver enzyme known as alcohol dehydrogenase or "ADH" (see Figure 2.1). Acetaldehyde, in turn, is converted to acetic acid by another liver enzyme—aldehyde dehydrogenase (ALDH). Acetic acid is metabolized further into carbon dioxide and water, which is eliminated from the body (NIAAA, 1994).

During the 1970s, several medical researchers published studies purporting to show that alcoholics and relatives of alcoholics tend to metabolize (i.e., to break down) alcohol in abnormal ways. In most of these studies, the alcohol metabolite of concern was acetaldehyde. Acetaldehyde is a rather toxic breakdown product; it was postulated to be responsible for the increasing tolerance and physical dependency that are sometimes part of alcoholism. Some studies that measured blood levels of acetaldehyde found higher levels in alcoholics and relatives of alcoholics than in individuals with no positive family history of alcoholism (Schuckit, 1984). However, as the NIAAA has observed, the hypothesis that acetaldehyde is a genetic marker for alcoholism predisposition is not well supported by evidence. In 1987, the NIAAA concluded:

> On balance, these studies suggest a probable increase in acetaldehyde in alcoholics, but the measurement of acetaldehyde in biological fluids is fraught with technical difficulties and is subject to significant errors. In any case, the positive studies provide no informa-

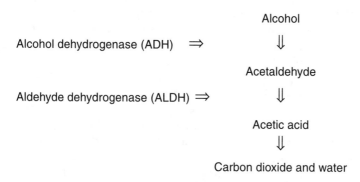

FIGURE 2.1. Metabolism of alcohol via the ADH pathway. From National Institute on Alcohol Abuse and Alcoholism (1994).

     tion as to whether this tendency is antecedent to the development of alcoholism or is a consequence of it. (p. 36)

This highlights two serious problems with this line of research—that is, measurement of acetaldehyde in body fluids and uncertainty about whether acetaldehyde is a cause or a consequence of years of heavy drinking. For a technical review of the problems with these studies, readers should see Lester (1988).

    Another set of studies has examined alcohol elimination in certain ethnic groups (e.g., Japanese and Native Americans) (Okada & Mizoi, 1982; Tsukamoto, Sudo, Karasawa, Kajiwara, & Endo, 1982). The hypothesis here is that rates of alcoholism among an ethnic group are determined by an inborn reaction to ethanol, called a "flushing response." Members of some groups tend to flush (reddening of the face, warm sensations, dizziness) when they drink because they are relatively deficient in ALDH. As a result of this deficiency, acetaldehyde is metabolized more slowly, allowing the toxic substance to accumulate in body fluids (and cause flushing).

    Here, the hypothesis becomes contradictory, or at the very least it branches into two inconsistent ones. One hypothesis is that ethnic groups that eliminate alcohol slowly and tend to flush (e.g., East Asians) will have lower rates of alcoholism because the flushing is an aversive consequence that discourages heavy drinking. As a result, members of these groups will not abuse alcohol because of this uncomfortable reaction when ethanol is consumed. However, others put forth the hypothesis that those groups that eliminate alcohol slowly and tend to flush (e.g., Native Americans) will be very susceptible to alcoholism because the high levels of acetaldehyde cause tolerance to alcohol to increase. Clearly, alcohol elimination cannot be used to explain alcoholism etiology in opposite directions. Schwitters, Johnson, McClearn, and Wilson (1982) comment on these studies: "Once persons drink at all, whether flushing occurs following the use of alcohol has only a trivial effect on drinking behavior" (p. 1262).

Findings from a cross-cultural study of Asian and North American populations support this view. Though East Asian populations have been identified as having an ALDH deficiency, which presumably would protect them from alcoholism, Helzer et al. (1990) found that a Korean sample had the highest rate of alcohol abuse and alcohol dependence among five studied groups. The samples were from: St. Louis, Missouri; Taiwan; Puerto Rico; and Canada. About 43% of the Koreans met criteria for alcohol abuse or alcohol dependence. Again, this suggests that social influences that promote abusive drinking can override alcohol metabolism deficits.

It is important to note that these studies ignore important differences among ethnic subgroups. This is particularly true of such ethnic groups as "Asians" (who include Chinese, Japanese, Koreans, Vietnamese, etc.) and "Native Americans" (who come from dozens of different clans) (NIAAA, 1990). For example, Christian, Dufour, and Bertolucci (1989) found that among 11 Native American tribal groups in Oklahoma, the alcohol-related death rate ranged from less than 1% to 24%. Such a finding suggests that abuse of alcohol among Native Americans is much more closely related to the norms and customs of specific tribal groups than it is to any supposed metabolic abnormalities of genetic origin.

Genetic Regulation of Nicotine Metabolism

Recent genotype studies have begun to identify variables that may influence smoking initiation, nicotine dependence, and smoking cessation. Pianezza, Selles, and Tyndale (1998) report that individuals who lack a genetically variable enzyme known as CYP2A6 have impaired nicotine metabolism. Persons with the CYP2A6 deficiency smoked significantly fewer cigarettes than did those with normal metabolism. As a result, these individuals appear to be somewhat "protected" from developing tobacco dependence (Pianezza et al., 1998).

Other studies have examined the relationship between smoking and dopamine regulation. In a case control study of 289 smokers and 233 nonsmoking controls, Lerman et al. (1999) found that individuals with a specific genotype known as SLC6A3-9 were significantly less likely to be smokers. Sabol et al. (1999) extended the findings of Lerman et al. (1999) by discovering that the effect of SLC6A3-9 was on smoking cessation rather than on smoking initiation. Sabol et al. (1999) also found that the SLC6A3-9 genotype was correlated with low scores on the personality trait known as novelty seeking. The correlation suggests that individuals carrying the SLC6A3-9 sequence have altered dopamine transmission, and thereby less need for reward from external stimuli, including that provided by cigarettes. Although these findings await replication, the relationship between SLC6A3-9, novelty seeking, and tobacco use may represent a possible mechanism by which genotype exerts influence on smoking behavior.

Event-Related Potentials: The P3 Brain Wave Studies

Event-related potentials (ERPs) are brain electrical signals that are generated in response to a specific stimulus, such as a light or a sound (National Institutes of Health, 1998). These electrical signals of the brain provide a sensitive measure of cognitive activity. ERPs are measured at the scalp of the head with standard electroencephalography (EEG) technology and displayed as wave-like lines. They are assessed according to their height (or amplitude) and elapsed time following a stimulus. The P3 (or P300) component of ERP peaks between 300 and 500 milliseconds after a stimulus. P3 amplitude is higher for significant stimuli than for insignificant stimuli.

The brain wave is thought to be associated with information processing, decision making, and memory (Donchin & Coles, 1988). Individuals with low P3 amplitude are thought to have difficulty distinguishing between significant and insignificant stimuli. Research has established that low P3 voltage is found in persons suffering from alcoholism (Cohen, Wang, Porjesz, & Begleiter, 1995), schizophrenia (Ford, White, Lim, & Pfefferbaum, 1994), and attention-deficit disorder (Klorman, Salzman, Pass, Borgstedt, & Dainer, 1979).

Interest in the P3 deficit in alcoholism began in the mid-1980s. In a seminal study, Begleiter, Porjesz, Bihari, and Kissin (1984) reported that in a sample of preadolescent sons of alcoholics who had never themselves consumed alcohol or illicit drugs, the P3 wave amplitude was greatly reduced compared to a control group of similar-age sons of nonalcoholic fathers. This was a remarkable finding because previously it had been assumed that the P3 deficit was a consequence of the deleterious effects of alcohol on the brain (Porjesz & Begleiter, 1985). Instead, it appeared that the P3 deficit may precede the development of alcoholism; that is, it may be a biological marker for susceptibility to the disorder.

During the next few years, several laboratories replicated the findings of Begleiter et al. (1984). One rigorous study found that the amplitude of the P3 wave in abstinent alcoholics was not associated with avoiding alcohol but was significantly related to the number of problem drinkers in their family (Pfefferbaum, Ford, White, & Mathalon, 1991). However, some studies failed to observe the expected differences in P3 wave amplitude between high-risk and low-risk subjects (e.g., Polich & Bloom, 1988). These inconsistencies were addressed in a meta-analysis of the P3 literature, where it was concluded that the expected differences can be observed with the application of difficult visual tasks (Polich, Pollock, & Bloom, 1994). Today, among neurophysiology researchers, there is consensus that reduced P3 wave amplitude is associated with alcoholism susceptibility (NIAAA, 1997).

Recently, Begleiter et al. (1998) reported preliminary findings on the "hunt" for the genes associated with P3 wave abnormalities in alcoholism. Genetic analysis of 103 "dense alcoholic" and random control families has revealed a number of candidate genetic loci. The strongest linkages were found on chromosomes 2 and 6, with suggestive evidence on chromosomes 5 and 13 (Begleiter et al., 1998). Each chromosomal region contains several hundred genes that will require high-resolution mapping to determine whether they are actually associated with P3 wave abnormalities.

EFFECTS OF DRUGS ON BRAIN STRUCTURE AND FUNCTION: THE EXPOSURE MODEL

Cell Activity of the Brain

Cells of the brain are known as "neurons." The structural features of a presynaptic and postsynaptic neuron appear in Figure 2.2. It should be noted that this figure depicts only two neurons and thus is quite simplistic. In the brain, each neuron forms synapses with many other neurons and, in turn, receives synaptic connections from an equally large number of neurons.

The brain's signaling functions are primarily conducted by the neurons of the brain. There are approximately one trillion neurons in the brain (NIAAA, 1997). They provide the capacity for sensation, movement, language, thought, and emotion. Though neurons in different parts of the brain vary in size, shape, and electrical properties, most share the common features that appear in Figure 2.2. The cell body containing the nucleus holds the cell's genetic information. Dendrites are the tree-like projections which integrate information from other neurons. Many neurons have a single axon which conducts electrical signals away from the cell body. At the end of each axon, branches terminate at a microscopic gap known as the synapse. Thus, neurons

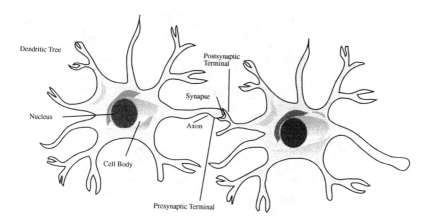

FIGURE 2.2. Structural features of a presynaptic and postsynaptic neuron. This schematic drawing depicts the major components of neuronal structure, including the cell body, nucleus, dendritic trees, and synaptic connections. From National Institute on Alcohol Abuse and Alcoholism (1997).

do not physically connect with one another but are separated by a very small fluid-filled gap (see Figure 2.3).

The presynaptic axon terminals release brain chemicals, known as neurotransmitters, into the synapse in response to electrical stimuli. There are homeostatic mechanisms in operation that attempt to maintain the appropriate concentration or balance of neurotransmitter in the synapse. One mechanism involves the action of enzymes that break down available neurotransmitters. (Enzymes are specialized proteins that serve as a catalyst for a specific chemical reaction.) When the concentration of a neurotransmitter becomes too great, enzymatic activity in the synapse increases to reduce it. A second mechanism is known as "reuptake." Here, presynaptic "pumps" draw neurotransmitter molecules back into the presynaptic terminal. This reabsorption process intensifies when the concentration of neurotransmitter in the synapse becomes too great. In tandem, the processes of enzymatic activity and reuptake work to maintain optimal neurotransmitter concentration. (Some of the ways that drugs of abuse alter normal brain chemistry are described later.)

Postsynaptic dendritic terminals (see Figure 2.3) receive and respond to the particular neurotransmitter for which it is designed to operate. At the postsynaptic terminals, there are target areas for the neurotransmitter molecule. These target areas are known as "receptor sites," or just "receptors." Typically, each neurotransmitter has an affinity for a specific type of receptor, and, in fact, their relationship has

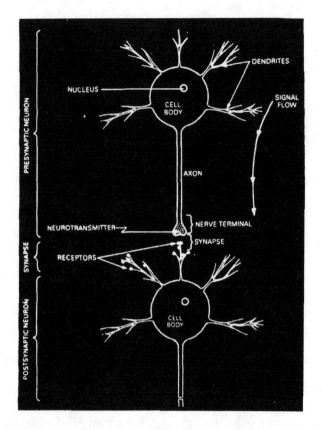

FIGURE 2.3. Typical nerve cell. Provided by Dr. Boris Tabakoff. From National Institute on Alcohol Abuse and Alcoholism (1997).

often been described as akin to that of a key (the neurotransmitter) to its lock (the receptor). In some cases, a receptor may recognize more than one chemical. Nevertheless, the design of the receptor is such that it usually responds only to the specific molecular structure of its neurotransmitter. The postsynaptic terminals respond to the presence of a neurotransmitter by sending an electrical signal toward its cell body. In this way, the neurons relay information to one another in a rapid manner.

Mesolimbic Dopamine Pathway: The Brain's Reward Center

One characteristic that all commonly abused drugs share is their ability to stimulate reward centers in the brain. Many drugs stimulate a chemical circuit in the brain known as the mesolimbic dopamine pathway (Gardner, 1992). This pathway is a system of neurons that operates primarily on dopamine and extends through several regions of the brain. Other chemical pathways, using serotonin and glutamate, also are implicated in the reinforcing effects of particular drugs, but these are not reviewed here in an extensive manner.

As shown in Figure 2.4, the mesolimbic system is composed of the medial forebrain bundle, the ventral tegmental area, and the nucleus accumbens, with projections to the limbic system and the frontal cortex (Julien, 1998). The medial forebrain bundle, sometimes known as the brain's seat of pleasure, links the ventral tegmental area with the nucleus accumbens. When activated by drugs, the medial forebrain bundle scatters impulses to a number of reward centers throughout the mesolimbic system (Palfai & Jankiewicz, 1997). Of particular importance is the nucleus accumbens; when stimulated, it provides pleasure and thus serves as a strong reinforcer. Humans and animals will repeat any behavior that evokes stimulation from this part of the brain, even if it requires a great deal of effort.

Drugs stimulate the reward centers of the mesolimbic system by rapidly intensifying the actions of the neurotransmitter dopamine

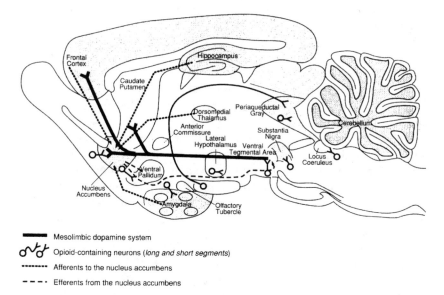

FIGURE 2.4. Section of the rat brain illustrating several neurochemical systems prominently implicated in the rewarding and dependence-inducing effects of alcohol and other drugs of abuse. Adapted from Koob (1992) by National Institute on Alcohol Abuse and Alcoholism (1997). Copyright 1992 by Elsevier Science Ltd. Adapted by permission.

(Koob, 1992). High levels of dopamine make the mesolimbic reward pathway more sensitive, whereas low levels decrease its sensitivity. These changes in the mesolimbic system may be the neurobiological basis for "wanting," but not necessarily "liking," the effects of a drug (White, 1998).

Drugs of abuse alter the cellular activity of neurons that use dopamine and other neurotransmitters. For instance, cocaine blocks the "reuptake" or reabsorption of dopamine by the neurons (brain cells) that release it (Leshner, 1996). This reduction in neuronal reuptake of dopamine increases the neurotransmitter's concentration in the extracellular spaces known as synapses. When dopamine levels are elevated, activation of the reward pathway occurs, thereby reinforcing the behavior associated with it (e.g., smoking crack cocaine). It is interesting to note that even nondrug behaviors, such as playing video games, stimulate dopaminergic neurotransmission (Koepp et al., 1998). Though it is not clear that this is the basis for "nondrug addictions," such as gambling, advances in neuroscience will continue to encourage such speculation.

Recent rat research suggests that serotonin, another neurotransmitter, also may be implicated in cocaine's activation of the mesolimbic system. The absence of a particular type of serotonin receptor—1B—appears to potentiate the rewarding effects of cocaine (Rocha et al., 1998). Rats without serotonin-1B receptors were found to be much more willing than control rats to "work" for cocaine. The lack of modulation from this serotonin receptor subtype may increase stimulation of the mesolimbic dopamine system. Thus, serotonin may play a role in susceptibility to cocaine addiction. This discovery may eventually lead to a clearer understanding of the individual variation in cocaine abuse and dependence.

Other stimulants, such as amphetamine, cause an excessive release or "leaking" of dopamine into the synapse. The increased concentration sensitizes the mesolimbic system. The presence of nicotine in the brain prompts a series of chemical changes that somewhat elevate dopamine levels by slowing the breakdown of its molecules in the synapse. However, it is known from animal research that nicotine is less effective as a positive reinforcer than other commonly abused drugs (Risner & Goldberg, 1983). It appears that nicotine dependence is motivated more by negative reinforcement (relief from withdrawal) than by stimulation of reward pathways. Recently, Epping-Jordan, Watkins, Koob, and Markou (1998) found that the decrease in brain reward function during nicotine withdrawal is "comparable in magnitude and duration to that of other major drugs of abuse" (p. 76).

Other commonly abused drugs initiate their action on the mesolimbic system through a "second stage" of dopamine neurons found in the ventral tegmental area (Julien, 1998). Opiates, such as heroin and morphine, act on an endogenous opioid circuitry that loops into the mesolimbic pathway. Recently, alcohol was demonstrated to activate this reward pathway as well (Ingvar et al., 1998). Alcohol also stimulates release of glutamate, an excitatory neurotransmitter, and some opiate receptors. Furthermore, alcohol, barbiturates, and the benzodiazepine tranquilizers increase the release of gamma-aminobutyric acid (GABA), an inhibitory neurotransmitter found in many areas of the brain. The GABA$_A$ subtype of receptors is thought to contribute to the depressant effects of alcohol (NIAAA, 1997).

The biological purpose of the mesolimbic system probably is to mediate reward and pleasure and to create motivation to engage in life-sustaining tasks (e.g., eating and reproduction). However, motivation has both cognitive and emotional dimensions. Cognitive expectations in the form of anticipated reinforcement arise from previous life experiences and influence motivation. It is likely not an accident that our expectations of future events are formed in the prefrontal cortex, which is linked to the nucleus accumbens. Previous drug "highs" may be preserved as memories and may motivate the user to engage in repeated self-administration of a euphoric substance. Furthermore, as this region of the brain becomes increasingly exposed to excess dopamine during a period of substance abuse, its natural production may decline, resulting in fewer and less sensitive receptors for the neurotransmitter. This is one mechanism for the development of drug tolerance.

As a result of these changes to the brain, the addicted person gradually relies more and more on the drug as the source of gratification and pleasure. In this process, addicts tend to develop the perception that they have an inability to regulate their desire for the drug (i.e., perceived loss of control). As interest in nondrug activities diminishes, involvement in drug-related behaviors increases. Drug seeking, intoxication, and recovering from the deleterious effects (e.g., hangover) typically become the central activities in the addict's life.

Is Addiction a Brain Disease?

Since 1997, the National Institute on Drug Abuse (NIDA) has been actively promoting the notion that addiction is a "brain disease." The director of NIDA published an article in the prestigious journal *Science* (and later reprinted in the *National Institute on Justice Journal*) in which he laid out a rationale for the brain disease conception based largely on knowledge of the mesolimbic reward pathway (Leshner, 1997, 1998). An NIDA website on the neurobiology of addiction promotes this view (http://www.nida.nih.gov), and at professional conferences it is echoed by NIDA officials (e.g., Vereen, 1998).

NIDA's position is based on two observations. First, the brain of the addict is different from the brain of the nonaddict. Second, all addictive substances activate the brain's reward circuit thereby increasing the likelihood of repeated self-administration. According to Leshner (1997):

> The addicted brain is distinctly different from the nonaddicted brain, as manifested by changes in brain metabolic activity, receptor availability, gene expression, and responsiveness to environmental cues. Some of these long-lasting changes are idiosyncratic to specific drugs, whereas others are common to many different drugs. The common brain effects of addicting substances suggest common brain mechanisms underlying all addictions.
>
> That addiction is tied to changes in brain structure and function is what makes it, fundamentally, a brain disease. A metaphorical switch in the brain seems to be thrown as a result of prolonged drug use. Initially, drug use is a voluntary behavior, but when that switch is thrown, the individual moves into the state of addiction, characterized by compulsive drug seeking and use. (p. 46)

Leshner (1997) goes on to say that "addiction is not just a brain disease" (p. 46). He calls the "brain disease" conception too simple, citing the critical importance of behavioral and social-context features of addiction. In the *Science* article, Leshner (1997) concludes that this understanding of addiction is "a totally new concept for much of the general public, for policymakers, and, sadly, for many health care professionals" (p. 46).

Some psychologists have been quite critical of the brain disease concept. Leccese (1996) asserts that the extent of brain damage resulting from acute and chronic exposure to cocaine, marijuana, and heroin has been grossly exaggerated. He suggests that exposure to alcohol may present the greatest risks to brain structure and function. Falk (1996) challenges the brain disease conception by referring to it as "pharmacological determinism." His thesis is that behavioral and social variables are given much too little emphasis in the explanation of drug and alcohol abuse. In the biomedical view, they are seen as merely tempering drug–brain interactions but not as important independent predictors of drug use in their own right. According to Falk (1996):

> It is facile, and most acceptable politically, to say that drug abuse is ultimately a function of how drugs affect the central nervous system and that any structural and behavioral toxicities are simply consequences of that basic interactional surface. This view, that drug

abuse is a kind of "brain disease," is quite conservative in that it relegates social and economic circumstances as permissive factors rather than as the basic determinants of drug abuse. In another sense, it is a socially liberal view, for if drug abuse is a brain disease requiring medical attention, then treatment costs legitimately require coverage by medical insurance. In this scheme, a host of "soft" determinants can be generously admitted as "modulators" of the brain locus where the basic mechanisms of action reside. Soft determinants include a person's subcultural values, peer pressure, drug availability, legal and other social constraints, family structure, educational status, social responsibilities, and alternative opportunities. The data languages and theoretical constructs of these putative modulator disciplines are usually quite different from those that describe molecular and central nervous events, and they lack the scientific prestige of biochemical and brain parlance. (p. 7)

That NIDA chose to employ a "brain disease" conception rather than a "brain injury" conception also raises some questions. Certainly, psychoactive drugs alter brain function and structure. Yet, there is no clear scientific basis for distinguishing between diseases and injuries (Baker, Teret, & Daub, 1987). It can be argued that the brain of the addict is not so much "diseased" as "injured" by exposure to self-administered toxins. With abstinence, much of the damage done to the brain often heals by itself eventually (Vereen, 1998). In other words, healing can occur without active medical intervention, such as medication or surgery. This is the case with many common injuries. Furthermore, the injury model can fit because just as addiction involves relapse, many injuries have a persistent, recurring nature as well.

From a public-policy perspective, it certainly is easy to see that the disease conception would be more useful than the injury model in cultivating societal support for more treatment resources. The former may be more likely to reduce the blame directed at the individual user and quiet the calls for punishment of addicts. In contrast, the conception of injury has long been associated with self-infliction, "bad" or reckless behavior, and blaming the victim (Baker et al., 1987). This issue is raised not to inflame a debate nor even to argue for a "brain injury" position but simply to point out that neuroscience findings do not necessarily compel us to adopt the disease conception.

LOSS OF CONTROL

Loss of control is a central premise of the traditional disease model of alcoholism. Indeed, Step One of AA's "Twelve Steps" is an admission that alcoholics are "powerless over alcohol" (AA, 1981). It is asserted that the alcoholic's loss of control stems from some unknown defect or abnormality. This abnormality is described as a compulsion or an intense craving (Milkman & Sunderwirth, 1987). More rigorous examinations of drug urges and cravings have been conducted in cognitive psychology (e.g., Tiffany, 1990) and these appear in Chapter Five.

In the traditional disease model, the exact nature of the abnormal craving for alcohol is not claimed to be well understood, but the "Big Book" of AA teaches as follows: "We are equally positive that once he takes any alcohol whatever into his system, something happens, both in the bodily and mental sense, which makes it virtually impossible for him to stop. The experience of any alcoholic will abundantly confirm this" (AA, 1976, pp. 22–23). As this passage indicates, the notion of loss of control is consistent with the subjective experience of many alcoholics. Why, then, do so many of the leading alcoholism researchers reject the concept?

Logical Inconsistency

Fingarette (1988), a philosopher, has pointed out that the classical loss-of-control concept is illogical. It maintains that after a minimal amount of alcohol enters the body, all ability to control drinking disappears. If this were actually the case, an alcoholic would have no desire, cravings, or compulsion to drink when sober. Abstention from drinking and recovery from alcoholism would actually by quite easy. Fingarette (1988) observes:

> If the loss of control is triggered by the first drink, then the only hope for an alcoholic is to refrain from that first drink, that is, total abstention. But if loss of control is triggered only after the first drink, and not before, why should the alcoholic have any special difficulty mustering the self-control to simply avoid that first drink? Why should abstinence pose any special problem? (p. 34)

Long ago, practitioners recognized that many alcoholics would terminate use of disulfiram (Antabuse) in order to resume drinking several days later (Merry, 1966). Behavior of this type suggests that the loss-of-control construct is invalid because at least among some alcoholics, the intention to drink is formed prior to any consumption. In such situations, binge drinking may not be impulsive at all but actually is planned for a future point in time.

Why is it maintained that control is lost after consumption has begun? One can only speculate, but it may be related to the alcoholic's need to blame the drug (alcohol) or some unknown biological mechanism. If the hypothesis did not first require alcohol to be introduced into the body, then the only possible explanations would be psychological or behavioral in nature. Proponents of the traditional disease model typically prefer to avoid nonbiological explanations.

Laboratory Experiments

Conclusive evidence exist that chronic alcoholics (including those who have previously experienced alcohol withdrawal sickness) can drink in a controlled manner in laboratory settings (Pattison, Sobell, & Sobell, 1977). A 1977 review of the alcoholism research literature found that in almost 60 laboratory studies, some involving experiments lasting as long as 2 months, alcoholics demonstrated no loss of control (Pattison et al., 1977). Fingarette (1988) points out that the amount of alcohol consumed by alcoholics is a function of the "costs and benefits perceived by the drinker—an observation that radically contradicts the idea of some overpowering inner drive that completely overwhelms all reason or choice" (p. 36). The contingencies (i.e., rewards and punishers) attached to drinking (as perceived by the drinker) appear to control the amount consumed. The arrangement of contingencies in three different studies involving alcoholics (Cohen, Liebson, Fallace, & Speers, 1971; Bigelow & Liebson, 1972; Cohen, Liebson, Fallace, & Allen, 1971) are concisely described by Fingarette (1988):

> One research team was able, by offering small payments, to get alcoholics to voluntarily abstain from drink even though drink was available, or to moderate their drinking voluntarily even after an initial "priming dose" of liquor had been consumed. (The larger the "priming dose," the less moderate the subsequent drinking, until a modest increase in the amount of payment offered prompted a resumption of moderation.) In another experiment, drinkers were willing to do a limited amount of boring work (pushing a lever) in order to earn a drink, but when the "cost" of a drink rose (that is, more lever pushing was asked of them) they were unwilling to "pay" the higher price. Still another experiment allowed alcoholic patients access to up to a fifth of liquor, but subjects were told that if they drank more than five ounces they would be removed from the pleasant social environment they were in. Result: Most of the time subjects limited themselves to moderate drinking. (p. 36)

A common counterargument to these findings is that the drinking occurred in artificial or unnatural drinking environments (i.e., hospital units or laboratories), and that because of this fact, the data have little relevance for understanding typical alcoholic drinking. In other words, drinking in a clinic under the observation of investigators radically affects alcoholics' self-control and drinking behavior. This counterargument is faulty and does not adequately address deficiencies in the loss-of-control hypothesis. If it is argued that the social setting and/or observation by others affects alcoholic drinking, it cannot be argued that loss of control stems from the effects of alcohol or some biological abnormality. Thus, even though the experimental settings may have been anomalous, the findings indicate that frequency and quantity of drinking among alcoholics are not determined solely, or even in a significant way, by ethanol or endogenous mechanisms.

ADDICTION AS A PROGRESSIVE DISEASE

In the classic disease model, addiction is believed to follow a "progressive" course (Talbott, 1989). That is, if alcoholics or addicts continue to abuse chemicals, their condition will deteriorate further and further. Marital, family, work, and medical problems only worsen over time; they do not get better with continued use. Life becomes increasingly unmanageable.

Johnson (1980) has described the progression of alcoholism in terms of the alcoholic's emotional relationship to the drug. His scheme has four phases. The first two phases represent "normal" drinking; the third and fourth are typical of alcoholic drinking. Johnson identifies these four phases as (1) learning the mood swing, (2) seeking the mood swing, (3) harmful dependence, and (4) drinking to feel normal.

In phase 1, learning the mood swing, the drinker is initiated into the use of alcohol. In our culture, it usually occurs at a relatively young age. The drinking is associated with pleasant feelings. There are no emotional "costs" as a result of the consumption. In phase 2, seeking the mood swing, the drinker purposely drinks to obtain euphoria. The amount of alcohol increases as intoxication becomes desired; however, in this phase, there are still no significant emotional costs or adverse consequences. In phase 3, harmful dependence, an "invisible line" is crossed (Johnson, 1980, p. 15). In this first stage of alcoholic drinking, the individual still finds euphoria in excessive consumption, but there is a price to pay. Following each drinking episode are consequences (e.g., hangovers, damaged relationships, and arrests for driving while intoxicated). Despite such problems, the alcoholic continues to drink excessively. In the last phase, the alcoholic's condition has deteriorated to the point that he/she must drink just to feel "normal." When the alcoholic is sober, he/she is overwhelmed by feelings of remorse, guilt, shame, and anxiety (Johnson, 1980); the natural tendency is to drink to block out these feelings. Johnson (1980) describes the alcoholic in this last phase as at risk for premature death.

Milam and Ketcham (1983) describe the progression of alcoholism in somewhat different terms. Their scheme focuses more on physiological deterioration than on the emotional relationship with the chemical. It consists of three stages: (1) the adaptive stage, (2) the dependent stage, and (3) deterioration.

In the adaptive stage, the chief characteristic is increasing tolerance to the drug. Alcoholics believe they are blessed by having such a capacity for alcohol because they experience no negative symptoms. They typically do not appear to others to be grossly intoxicated; thus, there is no apparent behavioral impairment. However, physiological changes associated with increasing tolerance are occurring. The drinker is not aware of these changes (Milam & Ketcham, 1983).

The chief characteristic of the dependent stage is physical withdrawal. These symptoms build gradually during this stage. Initially, they are not recognized as withdrawal symptoms but are confused with symptoms of a hangover. To manage these symptoms "effectively," many alcoholics fall into a "maintenance drinking" pattern in which they drink relatively small amounts at frequent intervals to avoid withdrawal sickness. They usually avoid gross intoxication out of a fear of having their problem exposed to others (Milam & Ketcham, 1983).

The last stage, deterioration, is characterized by major medical problems. Various organs are damaged as a result of long-term heavy drinking. In addition to the liver, the brain, the gastrointestinal tract, the pancreas, and even the heart may be affected. These pathological organ changes will cause death if an alcoholic does not receive treatment (Milam & Ketcham, 1983).

Johnson (1980) and Milam and Ketcham's (1983) cogent descriptions of the progression of alcoholism (and possibly other addictions) are not consistent with epidemiological findings, however. Studies that examine large populations, rather than just those alcoholics who present themselves for treatment, indicate that alcoholism and other addictions do not follow a predictable sequence of stages in which the user inevitably deteriorates (NIAAA, 1990). On the contrary, so-called natural remission (disappearance of an alcohol problem without treatment) is not uncommon among men as they move into older age categories (Fillmore, 1987a). Furthermore, it appears that among males there is a relationship between dependence problems and alcohol-related social problems on the one hand and age on the other. Generally, by the time men reach their 40s, alcohol problems have declined; in many cases, such men still drink, but more moderately (Fillmore & Midanik, 1984). In women, alcohol problems appear to peak in the 30s (compared to the 20s for men). Also, women are more likely than men to display considerably higher rates of remission across all decades of life (Fillmore, 1987b).

Even among clinical populations (treated alcoholics and problem drinkers), there is evidence to dispute the conception of alcoholism as a progressive disorder. For example, in Norway, Skog and Duckert (1993) tracked the drinking behavior of 182 alcoholics (men and women) over a 4½-year period following inpatient treatment and 135 problem drinkers (men and women) over a 2¼-year period following outpatient treatment. All clients were assessed by a standardized alcoholism assessment instrument and by a personal interview which focused on patterns of drinking during the previous year. In the outpatient group, blood samples were collected and analyzed for a liver enzyme (GT) which is responsive to the presence of alcohol. This was done to determine whether self-reported light drinking was actually the result of consistent underreporting (i.e., minimizing alcohol intake). The data analyses included calculating one-step transition matrices that estimated the likelihood that a participant would move from one level of drinking to another between two successive follow-up assessments.

Skog and Duckert (1993) found that 1 year after treatment, only 11% of the inpatients and 5% of the outpatients were abstinent. However, treatment appeared to have a substantial positive impact on the drinking practices of both client groups. At each follow-up, self-reported alcohol intake was considerably lower than at admission to treatment. This was true for both groups of clients. Among the outpatient group, liver enzyme levels were consistent with self-report intake— making it unlikely that the results (at least for this group) were biased by underreporting.

Though there was a good deal of change in the drinking patterns of individuals from one assessment interval to the next, the investigators could find no strong or clear trends for the groups as a whole (Skog & Duckert, 1993). Some participants were increasing their drinking, while a nearly equal number were consuming less. When change did occur, it most likely was to a neighbor consumption category (e.g., abstinence to moderation). According to the investigators, "Very large and dramatic jumps are, in effect, unlikely. Hence, the data suggest that processes of change are reasonably smooth" (Skog & Duckert, 1993, p. 183). Furthermore, there was no evidence of loss of control or heavy consumption following periods of abstinence or light drinking, and heavy drinkers tended to gradually decrease their intake rather than quit abruptly. None of these findings fit with the conception of a "progressive disease." Skog and Duckert (1993) conclude that among treated clients, "the observed pattern of change more resembles an indeterministic (or stochastic) process than a systematic natural history of a disease" (p. 178).

Peele (1985) has advanced a concept called "maturing out" to explain how many alcoholics and addicts give up substance abuse without the benefit of treatment or self-help programs. The term was coined earlier by Winick (1962), who sought to explain the process by which many heroin addicts cease using the drug as they grow older. Today, the concept has been applied more broadly to include alcohol and other drugs.

This natural remission is thought to be related to developmental issues. Peele (1985) suggests that addiction is a maladaptive method of coping with the challenges and problems of young adulthood. Such challenges may include establishing intimate relationships, learning to manage one's emotions, finding rewarding work, and separating from one's family of origin. Abuse of alcohol or drugs is a way to evade or postpone dealing with these challenges. Peele (1985) contends that as addicts tire of the "night life" and the "fast lane" and become more confident in their ability to take on life challenges (i.e., responsibilities), they will gradually (in most cases) give up substance abuse.

In a series of empirical studies, the process of maturing out was examined among a group of heroin addicts who had been admitted to the California Civil Addict Program during the years 1962 to 1964 (see Anglin, Brecht, Woodward, & Bonett, 1986). In 1974–1975, the investigators conducted a follow-up assessment of the original sample using a longitudinal retrospective procedure. The studies revealed that maturing out was prevalent in this population, but it was conditional on a number of factors. For example, 75% of "older addicts" and 50% of "younger addicts" had ceased heroin use if they lacked antisocial characteristics and were not involved in crime/drug dealing (Anglin et al., 1986). However, among those still involved in crime/drug dealing to some degree, there was no relationship between maturing out and age. Furthermore, younger addicts assessed as high in "personal resources," an aggregate measure combining educational status, post–high school vocational training, employment history, and parents' socioeconomic status, were found to cease heroin use at a somewhat earlier point in their addiction careers (Brecht, Anglin, Woodward, & Bonett, 1987). Finally, participation in methadone maintenance facilitated maturing out in older addicts more than in younger addicts, but legal supervision had no differential effect across age categories (Brecht & Anglin, 1990).

Evidence also shows that the alcohol consumption of young adults tends to follow the process of maturing out. Similar to heroin, the process seems to be conditional on a number of individual characteristics and social variables. Gotham, Sher, and Wood (1997) assessed 284 college students, most of whom were seniors. Three years later, after all had earned bachelor's degrees, they were assessed a second time. At this follow-up, the cohort's frequency of weekly intoxication had dropped substantially. Three variables were associated with decreased college drinking: a full-time job, being male, and being less "open to experience." Individuals who scored relatively high on a measure of extraversion were most likely to have continued a pattern of frequent intoxication during the 3-year period. In another study, Miller-Tutzauer, Leonard, and Windle (1991) conducted a 3-year longitudinal study of 10,594 persons, ages 18 to 28. The purpose of their investigation was to examine the impact of marriage on alcohol use. They found that individuals tended to moderate their alcohol use prior to actually becoming married and that drinking continued to decline into the first year of marriage. This decline in alcohol use appeared to stabilize by the end of the first year. Miller-Tutzauer et al. (1991) concluded that the transition to marriage is often associated with a maturation in drinking behavior.

How is it that the disease model has emphasized that the course of addiction is invariably progressive (a notion supported by many in recovery), and yet empirical data indicate that natural remission increases with age? This discrepancy can probably be traced to the fact that the disease model emerged from recovering alcoholics' first-person accounts and from clinical anecdotes. All of these were given by alcoholics who recovered through AA or presented themselves for treatment. Such individuals probably represent just a subgroup of all those persons with addiction problems. So, although the concept of addiction as a progressive disease may fit some alcoholics and addicts, it does not apply to most with these problems.

ADDICTION AS A CHRONIC DISEASE

Questions about the "chronicity" of addiction constitute one of the most controversial issues in the field, and have become a source of great tension between the treatment and research communities (Marion & Coleman, 1990; Peele, 1985). The disease model maintains that addiction is a chronic disorder, meaning that it never disappears (e.g., "Once an alcoholic, always an alcoholic"). The disease can be readily treated with sustained abstinence and growth within AA or NA, but it is never "cured." For this reason, most individuals in AA or NA refer to themselves as "recovering" rather than "recovered." In this way, chemical dependence is likened to other chronic diseases, such as cancer, diabetes, or heart disease.

Abstinence from all mood-altering substances, then, is the goal of virtually all treatment programs in the United States (it should be noted, however, that caffeine and nicotine are not prohibited). Marion and Coleman (1990) admit that the basis for this treatment goal is not based on science but rather on folklore. They write: "Abstinence in recovery is supported by the knowledge gained by the experience of drug addicts and alcoholics in their attempts to recover. Through A.A./N.A. 'leads' and testimonials, alcoholics and drug abusers daily report their inability to recover while using any mood- and mind-altering chemicals" (p. 103).

In contrast, the research community has produced a relatively large body of data indicating that controlled drinking is a viable treatment strategy for many alcoholics, particularly those of younger ages (Heather & Robertson, 1981; Miller, 1982). In addition, it appears that it may produce better posttreatment outcomes than abstinence-oriented treatment (Sobell & Sobell, 1976). However, more comparative research is needed. Unfortunately, in the United States today few grant providers are willing to fund such investigations.

DENIAL

Denial is another central feature of the traditional disease model. According to Massella (1990), it is the "primary symptom of chemical dependence" (p. 79). Denial is best characterized as an inability to perceive an unacceptable reality; the unacceptable reality is being an "alcoholic" or an "addict." Denial is not lying. It is actually a perceptual incapacity—the most primitive of the psychological defenses. Denial protects the ego from the threat of inadequacy. George (1990) recognizes that it also "protects the option to continue to use, which for the addicted individual is the essence of life" (p. 36). Further discussion of denial and other defense mechanisms is reviewed in Chapter Three.

Stories of alcoholic denial are legendary. I have personally consulted with so-called end-stage alcoholics, who were gravely ill (pancreatitis, gastrointestinal bleeding, liver cirrhosis) and hospitalized and have heard them deny that alcohol had any role in causing their medical crises. Certainly, denial is a common aspect of alcoholism and other addictions. However, instead of narrowly defining it as a symptom of a disease, it is useful to take a broader view and to consider how other forces, in combination, foster its use. For instance, the general social stigma attached to addiction is responsible in part for the frequent emergence of the defense. There are few labels today worse than that of "alcoholic" or "addict." With this moral condemnation, it is no wonder that individuals unconsciously react the way they do when initially offered help. Another contributing factor is the coercive methods that are sometimes used to force clients into treatment. The use of confrontative procedures (e.g., family interventions, employee assistance program efforts, and group confrontation) to break down the denial may in many situations have the unintended effect of actually strengthening it.

This is not to say that chemical abuse should be ignored or "enabled." However, it should be kept in mind that at least in some cases, denial is a product of well-intentioned coercion by "concerned others" or treatment personnel. To describe it as a disease symptom is to ignore its social origins and the universality of its use by almost all humans, addicted as well as nonaddicted.

STRENGTHS OF THE DISEASE MODELS

The enduring value of the disease models is that it removes alcohol and other drug addictions from the moral realm. It proposes that addiction sufferers should be treated and helped rather than scorned and ridiculed. Though the moral model of addiction has by no means disappeared in the United States, today more resources are directed toward rehabilitation rather than just toward punishment. The emergence of the disease model is largely responsible for this shift in resources. Increasingly, it is being recognized that harsh penal sentences do little to curb substance abuse in our society.

The contributions of molecular biology and neuroscience in recent years have begun to elucidate the genetic parameters of addiction. These developments will likely solidify the treatment community's conception of addiction as a disease state. If technological advances lead to implementation of genetic screening as a diagnostic tool, the credibility of the disease view may increase among the general public. From a public-policy perspective, the more addiction can be attributed to genetic factors (as opposed to willful misconduct), the greater the likelihood of public support for increased resources being directed to treatment.

Putting science aside, another strength of the *classical* disease model is its simplicity. Recall from Chapter One that a good theory is one that is parsimonious. This applies to the traditional disease model: It can be taught to clients in a relatively simple and straightforward manner. Clients, in turn, are often comfortable with the disease conception because it is familiar. Most clients have known someone with a disease (heart disease, diabetes, etc.), so it is not a foreign notion.

The disease models provide the individual who is new to recovery with a mechanism for coping with any guilt and shame stemming from past misdeeds. This framework teaches that problem behaviors are symptoms of the disease process. The alcoholic or addict is not to blame; the fault rests with the disease process. As one alcoholic with many years in recovery shared with me, "Calling it [alcoholism] a disease allows us to put the guilt aside so that we can do the work that we need to do."

The unwavering commitment to abstinence as the goal of treatment and sobriety as a way of life are principles promoted by the disease models and a source of their strength as well. Clearly, the large majority of clients who appear for treatment would benefit most by complete abstinence from psychoactive drugs (other than prescribed medications). Hundreds of thousands, if not millions, of recovering persons have rebuilt their lives as the result of achieving and maintaining a sober life. In this regard, disease models are distinguished from other theories on addiction. On the issue of abstinence, the disease models are clear and direct. Other models dodge the issue a bit, do not address it directly, or contend that "it depends" on the individual client.

WEAKNESSES OF THE DISEASE MODELS

The weaknesses of the disease models have been identified throughout this chapter; they are not repeated here in detail. Simply put, some of the propositions of the disease models are not well supported by science. The notions that have been particularly discredited are that addiction is a "progressive disease" and that it involves a literal "loss of control." Clearly, the best-supported proposition is that alcoholism and other substance use disorders have varying degrees of genetic etiology. However, as argued earlier, the fact that a human trait, behavior, condition, syndrome, disorder, and so on, is to some degree rooted in genes does not necessarily require us to think of it as disease. Furthermore, it is clear that environmental factors contribute greatly to all forms of substance use, abuse, and dependence.

The major limitation of the disease conception in general is that it gives too little emphasis to the impact of psychosocial variables and particularly the role of learning as etiological bases. Furthermore, the classical disease model has contributed little to skill-based prevention strategies that rely on learning principles to enhance coping. Subsequent chapters in this volume explore some alternatives to the disease model. None of them is without significant limitations either, as we will see.

REVIEW QUESTIONS

1. Why is the disease model of alcoholism/addiction controversial in many quarters?

2. How does Peele distinguish between types of disease models?

3. Along which dimensions and among which groups do different conceptualizations of the disease model emerge?

4. What is meant by addiction as a "primary disease"?

5. In what ways do research data restrict the applicability of the primary-disease concept?

6. According to Kendler, what is the relationship between genes and the environment in influencing complex human traits?

7. What is meant by the terms "genes," "genotype," and "phenotype"?

8. Why should we be cautious about the assignment of numerical values to the contributions of "nature" and "nurture"?

9. How is an adoption study designed?

10. Why is Donald Goodwin a significant figure in the work on the hereditabiity of alcoholism? What commonly cited statistic stems from his work?

11. What are the weaknesses of Goodwin et al.'s (1973) study?

12. How are MZ and DZ twin pairs different?

13. How is a twin study designed?

14. What are three assumptions on which twin studies rest?

15. According to the twin study research, what are the respective roles of genetics and environment in the etiology of alcoholism and other drug dependencies?

16. What was the D_2 receptor gene episode?

17. What is COGA?

18. What questions are raised by the prospect of genetic screening for alcoholism? In the future, will such a test be widely used?

19. What should the addiction practitioner know about the genetics of addiction?

20. What is the ADH pathway? What are the major limitations of the alcohol metabolism studies?

21. Is there evidence that ALDH deficiencies influence alcohol abuse/alcoholism?

22. Do genetic characteristics influence nicotine metabolism?

23. Why might the P3 wave findings be evidence of a true biological marker for alcoholism?

24. What is the structure and function of the neuron?

25. What is the significance of the mesolimbic dopamine pathway? How do various drugs interact with this system?

26. What is the "brain disease" conception? Why is it controversial?

27. What is meant by "loss of control" in the disease model? Why does Fingarette maintain that it is illogical?

28. Does laboratory research support the loss-of-control concept?

29. How do Johnson's and Milam and Ketcham's descriptions of the progression of alcoholism differ?

30. In what ways do research findings dispute the concept of alcoholism as a "progressive disease"?

31. What is "maturing out"? Is there evidence for this construct?

32. What is meant by addiction as a "chronic disease"?

33. Do research data support the use of controlled drinking as a treatment for alcoholism?

34. How is denial different from lying? What are the problems with calling denial a "symptom" of a disease?

35. What are the strengths of the disease model?

36. What are the weaknesses of the disease model?

REFERENCES

Alcoholics Anonymous. (1981). *Twelve steps and twelve traditions.* New York: AA World Services.

Alcoholics Anonymous. (1976). *The story of how many thousands of men and women have recovered from alcoholism* [the "Big Book"]. New York: AA World Services.

Alexander, B. K. (1988). The disease and adaptive models of addiction: A framework evaluation. In S. Peele (Ed.), *Visions of addiction: Major contemporary perspectives on addiction and alcoholism.* Lexington, MA: Heath.

American Psychiatric Association (1994). *Diagnostic and statistical manual of mental disorders* (4th ed.). Washington, DC: Author.

Anglin, M. D., Brecht, M. L., Woodward, J. A., & Bonett, D. G. (1986). An empirical study of maturing out: Conditional factors. *International Journal of the Addictions, 21,* 233–246.

Anthenelli, R. M., & Tabakoff, B. (1995). Hypothesized subtypes of alcoholism. *Alcohol Health and Research World, 19,* 178.

Baker, S. P., Teret, S. P., & Daub, E. M. (1987). Injuries. In S. Levine & A. M.

Lilienfeld (Eds.), *Epidemiology and health policy.* New York: Tavistock.

Begleiter, H., Porjesz, B., Bihari, B., & Kissin, B. (1984). Event-related potentials in boys at risk for alcoholism. *Science, 225,* 1493–1496.

Begleiter, H., Porjesz, B., Reich, T., Edenberg, H. J., Goate, A., Blangero, J., Almasy, L., Foroud, T., et al. (1998). Quantitative trait loci analysis of human event-related brain potentials: P3 voltage. *Electroencephalography and Clinical Neurophysiology, 108,* 244–250.

Begleiter, H., Reich, T., Hesselbrock, V., Porjesz, B., Li, T., Schuckit, M. A., Edenberg, H. J., & Rice, J. P. (1995). The collaborative study on the genetics of alcoholism. *Alcohol Health and Research World, 19,* 228–236.

Bierut, L. J., Dinwiddie, S. H., Begleiter, H., Crowe, R. R., Hesselbrock, V., Nurnberger, J. I., Porjesz, B., Schuckit, M. A., & Reich, T. (1998). Familial transmission of substance dependence: Alcohol, marijuana, cocaine, and habitual smoking. A report from the Collaborative Study on the Genetics of Alcoholism. *Archives of General Psychiatry, 55,* 982–988.

Bigelow, W., & Liebson, J. (1972). Cost factors controlling alcoholic drinking. *Psychological Record, 22,* 305–314.

Blum, K., Noble, E. P., Sheridan, P. J., Montgomery, A., Ritchie, T., Jagadeeswaran, P., Nogami, H., Briggs, A. H., & Cohn, J. B. (1990). Allelic association of human dopamine D_2 receptor gene in alcoholism. *Journal of the American Medical Association, 263,* 2055–2060.

Bolos, A. M., Dean, M., Lucas-Derse, S., Ramsburg, M., Brown, G. L., & Goldman, D. (1990). Population and pedigree studies reveal a lack of association between the dopamine D_2 receptor gene and alcoholism. *Journal of the American Medical Association, 264,* 3156–3160.

Brecht, M. L., & Anglin, M. D. (1990). Conditional factors of maturing out: Legal supervision and treatment. *International Journal of the Addictions, 25,* 393–407.

Brecht, M. L., Anglin, M. D., Woodward, J. A., & Bonett, D. G. (1987). Conditional factors of maturing out: Personal resources and preaddiction sociopathy. *International Journal of the Addictions, 22,* 55–69.

Carmelli, D., Swan, G. E., Robinette, D., & Fabsitz, R. (1992). Genetic influence on smoking: A study of male twins. *New England Journal of Medicine, 327,* 829–833.

Christian, C. M., Dufour, M., & Bertolucci, D. (1989). Differential alcohol-related mortality among American Indian tribes in Oklahoma. *Social Science and Medicine, 28,* 275–284.

Cloninger, C. R. (1987). Neurogenetic adaptive mechanisms in alcoholism. *Science, 236,* 410–416.

Cohen, H. L., Wang, W., Porjesz, B., & Begleiter, H. (1995). Auditory P300 in young alcoholics: Regional response characteristics. *Alcoholism: Clinical and Experimental Research, 19,* 469–475.

Cohen, M., Liebson, J., Fallace, L., & Allen, R. (1971). Moderate drinking by chronic alcoholics: A schedule-dependent phenomenon. *Journal of Nervous and Mental Disease, 153,* 434–444.

Cohen, M., Liebson, J., Fallace, L., & Speers, W. (1971). Alcoholism: Controlled drinking and incentives for abstinence. *Psychological Reports, 28,* 575–580.

Collins, F. S., & Fink, L. (1995). Tools of genetic research: The human genome project. *Alcohol Health and Research World, 19,* 190–195.

Cox, W. M. (1985). Personality correlates of substance abuse. In M. Galizio & S. A. Maisto (Eds.), *Determinants of substance abuse.* New York: Plenum Press.

Craufurd D., Dodge A., Kerzin-Storrar L., & Harris, R. (1989). Uptake of presymptomatic predictive testing for Huntington's disease. *Lancet, 2,* 603–605.

Croyle, R. T., & Lerman C. (1995). Psychological impact of genetic testing. In R. T. Croyle (Ed.), *Psychosocial effects of screening for disease prevention and detection.* New York: Oxford University Press.

Donchin, E., & Coles, M. G. (1988). Is the P300 component a manifestation of context updating? *Behavioral and Brain Sciences, 11,* 357–427.

Epping-Jordan, M. P., Watkins, S. S., Koob, G. F., & Markou, A. (1998). Dramatic decreases in brain reward function during nicotine withdrawal. *Nature, 393,* 76–79.

Eysenck, H. J. (1981). *A model for personality.* Berlin: Springer-Verlag.

Falk, J. L. (1996). Environmental factors in the instigation and maintenance of drug abuse. In W. K. Bickel & R. J. DeGrandpre (Eds.), *Drug policy and human nature: Psychological perspectives on the prevention, management, and treatment of illicit drug abuse.* New York: Plenum Press.

Fillmore, K. M. (1987a). Prevalence, incidence and chronicity of drinking patterns and problems among men as a function of age: A longitudinal and cohort analysis. *British Journal of Addiction, 82,* 77–83.

Fillmore, K. M. (1987b). Women's drinking across the adult life course as compared to men's. *British Journal of Addiction, 82,* 801–811.

Fillmore, K. M., & Midanik, L. (1984). Chronicity of drinking problems among men: A longitudinal study. *Journal of Studies on Alcohol, 45,* 228–236.

Fingarette, H. (1988). *Heavy drinking: The myth of alcoholism as a disease.* Berkeley: University of California Press.

Ford, J. M., White, P., Lim, K. O., & Pfefferbaum, A. (1994). Schizophrenics have fewer and smaller P300's: A single trial analysis. *Biological Psychiatry, 35,* 96–103.

Gardner, E. L. (1992). Brain reward mechanisms. In J. H. Lowinson, P. Ruiz, R. B. Millman, & J. G. Langrod (Eds.), *Substance abuse: A comprehensive textbook* (2nd ed.). Baltimore: Williams & Wilkins.

Gejman, P. V., Ram, A., Gelernter, J., Friedman, E., Cao, Q., Pickar, D., Blum, K., Noble, E. P., Kranzler, H. R., & O'Malley, S. (1994). No structural mutation in the dopamine D_2 receptor gene in alcoholism or schizophrenia. Analysis using denaturing gradient gel electrophoresis. *Journal of the American Medical Association, 271,* 204–208.

George, R. L. (1990). *Counseling the chemically dependent: Theory and practice.* Englewood Cliffs, NJ: Prentice-Hall.

Goldman, D., & Bergen, A. (1998). General and specific inheritance of substance abuse and alcoholism. *Archives of General Psychiatry, 55,* 964–965.

Goodwin, D. W. (1988). *Is alcoholism hereditary?* New York: Ballantine.

Goodwin, D. W., Schulsinger, F., Hermansen, L., Guze, S. B., & Winokur, G. (1973). Alcohol problems in adoptees raised apart from alcoholic biological parents. *Archives of General Psychiatry, 28,* 238–243.

Gotham, H. J., Sher, K. J., & Wood, P. K. (1997). Predicting stability and change in frequency of intoxication from the college years to beyond: Individual-difference and role transition variables. *Journal of Abnormal Psychology, 106,* 619–629.

Heath, A. C., Jardine, R., & Martin, N. G. (1989). Interactive effects of genotype and social environment of alcohol consumption in female twins. *Journal of Studies on Alcohol, 50,* 38–48.

Heather, N., & Robertson, I. (1981). *Controlled drinking.* London: Methuen.

Helzer, J. E., Canino, G. J., Yeh, E. K., Bland, R. C., Lee, C. K., Hwu, H. G., & Newman, S. (1990). Alcoholism: North America and Asia. *Archives of General Psychiatry, 47,* 313–319.

Holden, C. (1994). A cautionary tale: The sobering story of D$_2$. *Science, 264,* 1696–1697.

Ingvar, M., Ghatan, P. H., Wirsén-Meurling, Risberg, J., Von Heijne, G., Stone-Elander, S., & Ingvar, D. H. (1998). Alcohol activates the cerebral reward system in man. *Journal of Studies on Alcohol, 59,* 258–269.

Jang, K. J., Livesley, W. J., & Vernon, P. A. (1995). Alcohol and drug problems: A multivariate behavioural genetic analysis of co-morbidity. *Addiction, 90,* 1213–1221.

Johnson, V. E. (1980). *I'll quit tomorrow* (rev. ed.). San Francisco: Harper & Row.

Julien, R. M. (1998). *A primer of drug action* (8th ed.). New York: Freeman.

Kaprio, J., Koskenvuo, M., Langinvainio, H., Romanov, K., Sarna, S., & Rose, R. J. (1987). Genetic influences on use and abuse of alcohol: A study of 5638 adult Finnish twin brothers. *Alcoholism: Clinical and Experimental Research, 11,* 349–356.

Kendler, K. (1997). Social support: A genetic–epidemiologic analysis. *American Journal of Psychiatry, 154,* 1398–1404.

Kendler, K. S., Heath, A. C., Neale, M. C., Kessler, R. C., & Eaves, L. J. (1992). A population-based twin study of alcoholism in women. *Journal of the American Medical Association, 268,* 1877–1882.

Kessler, S., Field, T., Worth, L., & Mosbarger, H. (1987). Attitudes of persons at risk for Huntington's disease toward predictive testing. *American Journal of Human Genetics, 26,* 259–270.

Khoury, M. J., & Genetics Work Group. (1996). From genes to public health: The applications of genetic technology in disease prevention. *American Journal of Public Health, 86,* 1717–1722.

Klorman, R., Salzman, L., Pass, H., Borgstedt, A. D., & Dainer, K. B. (1979). Effects of methylphenidate on hyperactive children's evoked responses during passive and active attention. *Psychophysiology, 16,* 23–29.

Koepp, M. J., Gunn, R. N., Lawrence, A. D., Cunningham, V. J., Dagher, A., Jones, T., Brooks, D. J., Bench, C. J., & Grasby, P. M. (1998). Evidence of striatal dopamine release during a video game. *Nature, 393,* 266–268.

Koob, G. F. (1992). Drugs of abuse: Anatomy, pharmacology, and function of reward pathways. *Trends in Pharmacological Sciences, 13,* 177–182.

Leccese, A. P. (1996). The pharmacological understanding of psychoactive drugs: Basic science in the context of differential prohibition. In W. K. Bickel & R. J. DeGrandpre (Eds.), *Drug policy and human nature: Psychological per-*

spectives on the prevention, management, and treatment of illicit drug abuse. New York: Plenum Press.

Lerman, C., Caporaso, N. E., Audrain, J., Main, D., Bowman, E. D., Lockshin, B., Boyd, N. R., & Shields, P. G. (1999). Evidence suggesting the role of specific genetic factors in cigarette smoking. *Health Psychology, 18,* 14–20.

Leshner, A. I. (1996). Molecular mechanisms of cocaine addiction. *New England Journal of Medicine, 335,* 128–129.

Leshner, A. I. (1997). Addiction is a brain disease, and it matters. *Science, 278,* 45–47.

Leshner, A. I. (1998, October). Addiction is a brain disease—and it matters. *National Institute of Justice Journal,* 2–6.

Lester, D. (1988). Genetic theory: An assessment of the heritability of alcoholism. In C. D. Chaudron & D. A. Wilkinson (Eds.), *Theories on alcoholism.* Toronto: Addiction Research Foundation.

Levine, H. G. (1978). The discovery of addiction: Changing conceptions of habitual drunkenness in America. *Journal of Studies on Alcohol, 39,* 143–174.

Mann, C. C. (1994). Behavioral genetics in transition. *Science, 264,* 1686–1689.

Marion, T. R., & Coleman, K. (1990). Recovery issues and treatment resources. In D. C. Daley & M. S. Raskin (Eds.), *Treating the chemically dependent and their families.* Newbury Park, CA: Sage.

Massella, J. D. (1990). Intervention: Breaking the addiction cycle. In D. C. Daley & M. S. Raskin (Eds.), *Treating the chemically dependent and their families.* Newbury Park, CA: Sage.

McGue, M., Pickens, R. W., & Svikis, D. S. (1992). Sex and age effects on the inheritance of alcohol problems: A twin study. *Journal of Abnormal Psychology, 101,* 3–17.

Merikangas, K. R., Stolar, M., Stevens, D. E., Goulet, J., Preisig, M. A., Fenton, B., Zhang, H., O'Malley, S. S., & Rounsaville, B. J. (1998). Familial transmission of substance use disorders. *Archives of General Psychiatry, 55,* 973–979.

Merry, J. (1966). The "loss of control" myth. *Lancet, I,* 1257–1258.

Milam, J. R., & Ketcham, K. (1983). *Under the influence.* New York: Bantam.

Milkman, H. B., & Sunderwirth, S. G. (1987). *Craving for ecstasy: The consciousness and chemistry of escape.* Lexington, MA: Heath.

Miller, W. R. (1982). Treating problem drinkers: What works. *The Behavior Therapist, 5,* 15–19.

Miller-Tutzauer, C., Leonard, K. E., & Windle, M. (1991). Marriage and alcohol use: A longitudinal study of "maturing out." *Journal of Studies on Alcohol, 52,* 434–440.

Montgomery, H. E., Marshall, R., Hemingway, H., Myerson, S., Clarkson, P., Dollery, C., Hayward, M., Holliman, D. E., Jubb, M., World, M., Thomas, E. L., Brynes, A. E., Saeed, N., Barnard, M., Bell, J. D., Prasad, K., Rayson, M., Talmud, P. J., & Humphries, S. E. (1998). Human gene for physical performance. *Nature, 393,* 221.

Murray, R. M., Clifford, C. M., & Gurling, H. M. D. (1983). Twin and adoption studies: How good is the evidence for a genetic role? In M. Galanter (Ed.), *Recent developments in alcoholism* (Vol. 1). New York: Plenum Press.

National Institute on Alcohol Abuse and Alcoholism. (1987). *Alcohol and health: Sixth special report to the U.S. Congress* (DHHS Publication No. ADM 87-1519). Washington, DC: U. S. Government Printing Office.

National Institute on Alcohol Abuse and Alcoholism. (1990). *Alcohol and health: Seventh special report to the U.S. Congress* (DHHS Publication No. ADM 90-1656). Washington, DC: U.S. Government Printing Office.

National Institute on Alcohol Abuse and Alcoholism. (1994). *Alcohol and health: Eighth special report to the U.S. Congress* (NIH Publication No. 94-3699). Bethesda, MD: National Institutes of Health.

National Institute on Alcohol Abuse and Alcoholism. (1997). *Alcohol and health: Ninth special report to the U.S. Congress* (NIH Publication No. 97-4017). Bethesda, MD: National Institutes of Health.

National Institutes of Health. (1998, May 20). COGA suggests genetic loci for P3 brain wave activity. *NIH News Release*. Bethesda, MD: Author.

Noble, E. P., Blum, K., Ritchie, T., Montgomery, A., & Sheridan, P. J. (1991). Allelic association of the D_2 dopamine receptor gene with receptor-binding characteristics in alcoholism. *Archives of General Psychiatry, 48,* 648–654.

Okada, T., & Mizoi, Y. (1982). Studies on the problem of blood acetaldehyde determination in man and level after alcohol intake. *Japanese Journal of Alcohol and Drug Dependence, 17,* 141–159.

Palfai, T., & Jankiewicz, H. (1997). *Drugs and human behavior* (2nd ed.). Madison, WI: Brown & Benchmark.

Parsian, A., Todd, R. D., Devor, E. J., O'Malley, K. L., Suarez, B. K., Reich, T., & Cloninger, C. R. (1991). Alcoholism and alleles of the human D_2 dopamine receptor locus: Studies of association and linkage. *Archives of General Psychiatry, 48,* 655–663.

Patterson, G. R. (1996). Some characteristics of a developmental theory for early onset delinquency. In M. F. Lenzenweger & J. J. Haugaard (Eds.), *Frontiers of psychopathology.* New York: Oxford University Press.

Pattison, E. M., Sobell, M. B., & Sobell, L. C. (1977). *Emerging concepts of alcohol dependence.* New York: Springer.

Peele, S. (1985). *The meaning of addiction: Compulsive experience and its interpretation.* Lexington, MA: Heath.

Peele, S. (1996). Assumptions about drugs and the marketing of drug policies. In W. K. Bickel & R. J. DeGrandpre (Eds.), *Drug policy and human nature: Psychological perspectives on the prevention, management, and treatment of illicit drug abuse.* New York: Plenum Press.

Pfefferbaum, A., Ford, J. M., White, P. M., & Mathalon, D. (1991). Event-related potentials in alcoholic men: P3 amplitude reflects family history but not alcohol consumption. *Alcoholism: Clinical and Experimental Research, 15,* 839–850.

Pianezza, M. L., Sellers, E. M., & Tyndale, R. F. (1998). Nicotine metabolism defect reduces smoking. *Nature, 393,* 750.

Polich, J., & Bloom, F. E. (1988). Event-related brain potentials in individuals at high and low risk for developing alcoholism: Failure to replicate. *Alcoholism: Clinical and Experimental Research, 12,* 368–373.

Polich, J., Pollock, V. E., & Bloom, F. E. (1994). Meta-analysis of P300 amplitude from males at risk for alcoholism. *Psychological Bulletin, 115,* 55–73.

Porjesz, B., & Begleiter, H. (1985). Human brain electrophysiology and alcoholism. In R. E. Tartar & D. H. van Thiel (Eds.), *Alcohol and the brain.* New York: Plenum Press.

Reich, T., Edenberg, H. J., Goate, A., Williams, J. T., Rice, J. P., Van Eerdewegh, P., Foroud, T., Hesselbrock, V., Schuckit, M. A., Bucholz, K., Porjesz, B., Li, T. K., Conneally, P. M., Nurnberger, J. I., Tischfield, J. A., Crowe, R. R., Cloninger, C. R., Wu, W., Shears, S., Carr, K., Crose, C., Willig, C., & Begleiter, H. (1998). Genome-wide search for genes affecting the risk for alcohol dependence. *American Journal of Medical Genetics, 81,* 207–215.

Risner, M. E., & Goldberg, S. R. (1983). A comparison of nicotine and cocaine self-administration in the dog: Fixed-ratio and progressive-ratio schedules of intravenous drug infusion. *Journal of Pharmacology and Experimental Therapeutics, 224,* 319–326.

Rocha, B. A., Scearce-Levie, K., Lucas, J. J., Hiroi, N., Castanon, N., Crabbe, J. C., Nestler, E. J., & Hen, R. (1998). Increased vulnerability to cocaine in mice lacking the serotonin-1B receptor. *Nature, 393,* 175–178.

Sabol, S. Z., Nelson, M. L., Fisher, C., Marcus, S. E., Gunzerath, L., Brody, C. L., Hu, S., Sirota, L. A., Greenberg, B. D., Lucas, F. R., Hamer, D. H., Benjamin, J., & Murphy, D. L. (1999). A genetic association for cigarette smoking behavior. *Health Psychology, 18,* 7–13.

Saitz, R. (1998). Introduction to alcohol withdrawal. *Alcohol Health and Research World, 22,* 5–12.

Schuckit, M. A. (1984). Biochemical markers of a predisposition to alcoholism. In S. B. Rosalki (Ed.), *Clinical biochemistry of alcoholism.* Edinburgh: Churchill Livingston.

Schuckit, M. A. (1989). Familial alcoholism. *Drug Abuse and Alcoholism Newsletter, 18,* 1–3.

Schwitters, S. Y., Johnson, R. C., McClearn, G. E., & Wilson, J. R. (1982). Alcohol use and the flushing response in different racial–ethnic groups. *Journal of Studies on Alcohol, 43,* 1259–1262.

Searles, J. S. (1988). The role of genetics in the pathogenesis of alcoholism. *Journal of Abnormal Psychology, 97,* 153–167.

Skog, O. J., & Duckert, F. (1993). The development of alcoholics' and heavy drinkers' consumption: A longitudinal study. *Journal of Studies on Alcohol, 54,* 178–188.

Sobell, M. B., & Sobell, L. C. (1976). Second-year treatment outcome of alcoholics treated by individualized behavior therapy: Results. *Behaviour Research and Therapy, 14,* 195–215.

Talbott, G. D. (1989). Alcoholism should be treated as a disease. In B. Leone (Ed.), *Chemical dependency: Opposing viewpoints.* San Diego: Greenhaven.

Tambor, E. S., Bernhardt, B. A., Chase, G. A., Fadden, R. R., Geller, G., Hofman, K. J., & Holtzman, N. A. (1994). Offering cystic fibrosis carrier screening to an HMO population: Factors associated with utilization. *American Journal of Human Genetics, 55,* 626–637.

Thombs, D. L., Mahoney, C. A., & Olds, R. S. (1998). Application of a bogus testing procedure to determine college students' utilization of genetic screening for alcoholism. *Journal of American College Health, 47,* 103–112.

Tiffany, S. T. (1990). A cognitive model of drug urges and drug-use behavior: Role of automatic and nonautomatic processes. *Psychological Review, 97,* 147–168.

Tsuang, M. T., Lyons, M. J., Meyer, J. M., Doyle, T., Eisen, S. A., Goldberg, J., True, W., Lin, N., Toomey, R., & Eaves, L. (1998). Co-occurrence of abuse of different drugs in men: The role of drug-specific and shared vulnerabilities. *Archives of General Psychiatry, 55,* 967–972.

Tsukamoto, S., Sudo, T., Karasawa, S., Kajiwara, M., & Endo, T. (1982). Quantitative recovery of acetaldehyde in biological samples. *Nihon University Journal of Medicine, 24,* 313–331.

Vaillant, G. E. (1990). We should retain the disease concept of alcoholism. *Harvard Medical School Mental Health Letter, 6,* 4–6.

Vereen, D. (1998, May 29). News from NIDA: A research update. *Annual Conference of the International Coalition for Addictions Studies Education (INCASE),* Minneapolis.

White, F. J. (1998). Cocaine and the serotonin saga. *Nature, 393,* 118–119.

Wilbanks, W. L. (1989). Drug addiction should be treated as a lack of self-discipline. In B. Leone (Ed.), *Chemical dependency: Opposing viewpoints.* San Diego: Greenhaven.

Williamson, R., Allison, M. E. D., Bentley, T. J., Lim, S. M. C., Watson, E., Chapple, J., & Adam, S. (1989). Community attitudes to cystic fibrosis carrier testing in England: A pilot study. *Prenatal Diagnosis, 9,* 727–734.

Yalisove, D. (1998). The origins and evolution of the disease concept of treatment. *Journal of Studies on Alcohol, 59,* 469–476.

Zuckerman, M. (1983). *Biological bases of sensation seeking, impulsivity, and anxiety.* Hillsdale, NJ: Erlbaum.

CHAPTER THREE

Psychoanalytic Formulations

Sigmund Freud (1885–1939) made the first systematic attempt to explain the origins of mental disorders . His theory is known as "psychoanalysis." Freud derived psychoanalytic concepts from his clinical practice. His patients were predominantly white female residents of Vienna, Austria, from the 1890s to the 1930s. Psychoanalytic concepts continue to influence clinical practitioners in the mental health field today, particularly in some psychiatric circles (Gabbard, 1999). These concepts also have historical significance and provide perspective on the evolution of addictions treatment.

FREUD

As Peter Gay's (1988) biography of Freud attests, the Viennese physician was indeed a remarkable man. His ideas have had a lasting impact on our culture in ways that are sometimes no longer traced to Freud. For example, he originated the notion of defense mechanisms (denial, rationalization, etc.). He brought attention to the significance of anxiety in the human experience. He was the first to give an extensive description of the unconscious mind. He pointed to the importance of early childhood experience, and he was the first to insist that human sexual behavior is an appropriate subject for scientific scrutiny. These achievements show that Freud's theory of psychoanalysis has had a major impact on the contemporary understanding of human behavior.

PSYCHOANALYSIS: A TYPE OF PSYCHOTHERAPY

The terms "psychoanalysis" and "psychotherapy" are not synonymous, though they are sometimes mistakenly thought to be. "Psychotherapy" is a more general term describing professional services aimed at helping individuals or groups overcome emotional, behavioral, or relationship problems. There are more than 240 methods of counseling and psychotherapy (George & Cristiani, 1995). Psychoanalysis is one of these approaches.

Traditional psychoanalysis involves an "analyst" and an "analysand" (i.e., the client). Typically, the analysand lies comfortably on a couch while the analyst sits behind him/her, out of view. Often, the analyst takes notes while the analysand describes whatever comes into his/her mind. Interestingly, Freud discouraged analysts from taking notes; he cautioned that doing so would distract their attention (Gay, 1988).

Interpretation

Psychoanalysis relies heavily on the analyst's interpretation of the analysand's concerns. To this end, the analyst encourages the analysand to say absolutely everything that comes to mind. By contrast, the analyst remains as silent as possible, hoping that this will stimulate uninhibited verbal activity on the part of the analysand. Gay (1988) describes the process in this way:

> In the strange enterprise that is psychoanalysis, half the battle and half alliance, the analysand will cooperate as much as his neurosis lets him. The analyst for his part is, one hopes, not hampered by his own neurosis; in any event, he is required to deploy a highly specialized sort of tact, some of it acquired in his training analysis, the rest drawn from his experience with analytic patients. It calls for restraint, for silence at most of the analysand's productions and comments on a few. Much of the time patients will experience their analyst's interpretations as precious gifts that he doles out with far too stingy a hand. (p. 298)

Free Association

According to Freud, the fundamental principle of psychoanalysis is that "free association" should be encouraged. The analysand should be free to reveal the most sensitive things that come to mind, so that the analyst can interpret them. For this reason, the analyst positions himself/herself behind the analysand. The analyst's reactions to shocking disclosures could cause the analysand to be distracted and inhibit the free flow of associations.

Dream Interpretation

Another feature of psychoanalysis is dream interpretation. Its purpose is to uncover unconscious material, which the analysand typically represses. The task of the analyst is to study the symbols presented in the dreams and to interpret their disguised meanings. Psychoanalysts believe that dreams have two types of content: "manifest" and "latent." The manifest content is the dream as it appears to the dreamer; latent content is what is disguised to the dreamer. The latent content is composed of the analysand's actual motives that are seeking expression but are very painful or personally unacceptable (Coleman, Butcher, & Carson, 1980).

Resistance

In *The Interpretation of Dreams*, Freud (1900/1953) defined resistance as simply "whatever interrupts the progress of analytic work" (p. 555). According to Gay (1988), Freud warned: "Resistance accompanies the treatment at every step; every single association, every act of the patient's must reckon with this resistance, represents a compromise between the forces aiming at cure and those opposing it" (p. 299).

For the psychoanalyst, resistance arises because the analysand becomes threatened by the uncovering of unconscious material. At such times, the analysand may attempt to change the subject, dismiss its importance, become silent, forget dreams, hold back essential information, be consistently late for appointments, become hostile, or employ other defensive mechanisms. Gay (1988) describes resistance as a "peculiarly irrational" but universal human tendency. The contradictory nature of resistance is underscored by the pointlessness of voluntarily seeking help (and paying for it) and then fighting against it.

Resistance can be viewed as a significant problem in counseling individuals with alcohol and drug problems. Taleff (1997) argues that addiction practitioners who value the concept will see it in their clients and adopt helping strategies in accordance with it. However, practitioners who reject psychoanalytic formulations typically will not rely on the resistance "construction," and as a result will not "see it" or use it to guide practice.

Taleff (1997) has elaborated on the sources of resistance. Although traditional psychoanalytic thinking maintains that resistance arises solely from personality dynamics, Taleff (1997) recognizes that counselor practices, family and group dynamics, and the structure of treatment are other sources as well. In a synergistic way, these sources of resistance can interact with one another to delay treatment seeking or to undermine recovery. A major challenge in helping people with substance abuse problems is to properly assess and attend these complex issues.

Transference

In the process of psychoanalysis, the relationship between analyst and analysand becomes emotionally charged. In this situation, the analysand frequently applies to the analyst particular feelings, thoughts, attributes, and motives that he/she had in a past relationship with a parent or other significant person (a teacher, coach, clergyman, etc.). As a result, the analysand may respond to the analyst as he/she did to that particular person in the past. If the past relationship was characterized by hostility or indifference, the analysand may feel the same way about the analyst. The tasks of the analyst, then, are to help the analysand (1) "work through" these feelings, (2) recognize that the analyst is not the parent or significant other figure, and (3) stop living within the confines of past relationships.

PERSONALITY STRUCTURE

In the psychoanalytic perspective, human behavior is thought to result from the interaction of three major subsystems within the personality: the "id," the "ego," and the "superego." Although each of these structures possesses unique functions and operating principles, they interact so closely with one another that it is often impossible to separate their distinct effects on behavior. In most cases, behavior is the result of the dynamic interaction among the id, ego, and superego. Each subsystem does not typically function in the absence of the other two (Hall & Lindzey, 1978).

The id is the original source of the personality and consists largely of instinctual drives. Psychoanalytic theorists have a specific understanding of the term "instinct." It is defined as an "inborn psychological representation of an inner somatic source of excitation" (Hall & Lindzey, 1978, p. 39). The psychological representation is more commonly referred to as a "wish," "internal urge," or "craving." The bodily excitations that give rise to wishes or urges are called "needs." Thus, the sensation of hunger represents the physiological need of the body for nutrients. Psychologically, this need is expressed as a wish or craving for food. In addiction, drugs become sources of bodily excitation, which in turn give rise to cravings for that chemical. The chemical craving motivates the addict to seek out the drug of choice. Psychoanalysts note that addicts' instinctual drives make them hypersensitive to environmental stimuli (offers from friends to "get high," the smell of a burning match, advertisements for alcohol, etc.). These stimuli elicit cravings and make addicts vulnerable to "slips" and relapses.

The id is present from birth. It is the basic life force from which the ego and the superego begin to differentiate themselves. It supplies the psychic energy necessary for the operation of the ego and superego. "Psychic energy" is defined as mental activity, such as thinking and remembering. Freud believed that the id is a bridge that connects the energy of the body to that of the personality. Interestingly, Freud noted that this psychic energy is not bound by logic and reality. It allows us to do such impossible things as be in two places at once or move backward in time.

Some of the instinctual drives of the id are constructive (e.g., sex). However, others are destructive (e.g., aggression, destruction, and death). Because the id cannot tolerate increases in psychic energy (they are experienced as uncomfortable states of tension), it is identified as the component of personality that is completely selfish. The id is only concerned with immediate gratification (i.e., discharge of tension). It has no consideration for reality demands or moral concerns.

The id is said to operate via the "pleasure principle." That is, high tension levels (e.g., sexual urges or drug cravings) prompt the id to act to reduce the tension immediately and return the individual to a comfortably constant level of low energy. Thus, the id's aim is to avoid pain (e.g., the discomfort of abstinence) and to increase pleasure (e.g., drug-induced euphoria). (Table 3.1 outlines the effects of intoxication on the id and the other personality subsystems of both nonalcoholics and alcoholics.) The operation of the pleasure principle makes frustration and deprivation difficult to tolerate. Clearly, both frustration and deprivation are common in early recovery, and they make the addict susceptible to relapse.

The ego emerges from the id to satisfy the needs of the individual that require transactions with the external world (i.e., reality). Survival requires the individual to seek food, water, shelter, sex, and other basic needs. The ego assists in this effort by distinguishing between subjective needs of the mind (an id function) and the resources available in the external world.

Ultimately, the ego must answer to the demands of the id. How-

TABLE 3.1 The Effects of Intoxication on the Personality Subsystems of Nonalcoholic and Alcoholic Drinkers

Subsystem	Nonalcoholics		Alcoholics	
	Sober	Intoxicated	Sober	Intoxicated
Id	Striving	Disinhibited	Craving	Triumphant
Ego	Controlling	Exhilarated	Anxious	Overwhelmed
Superego	Restraining	Weakened	Punishing	Disrupted

Note. Adapted from Berry (1988). Copyright 1988 by the Addiction Research Foundation. Adapted by permission.

ever, it does so in such a way as to ensure the survival and health of the individual. This response requires the use of reason, planning, delay of immediate gratification, and other rational resources in dealing with the external world. In "normal" individuals, the ego is able, to some degree, to control the primitive impulses of the id. As a result, the ego is said to operate via the "reality principle." The aim of the ego is to suspend the pleasure principle temporarily, until a time that an appropriate place and object can be found for the release of tension. In this way, the ego is the component of personality that mediates between the demands of the id and the realities of the external world.

The third subsystem of the personality is the superego, which is the moral component of the personality. It emerges from the learning of moral values and social taboos. The superego is essentially that which is referred to as the "conscience"; it is concerned with "right" and "wrong." The superego develops during childhood and adolescence as a result of reward and punishment. It has three main functions. One is to suppress impulses of the id, particularly sexual and aggressive urges. The second function is to press the ego to abandon realistic goals in exchange for moralistic ones. The third is to impel the individual to strive for perfection.

Hall and Lindzey (1978) aptly describe the nature of the superego in the following passage: "That is, the superego is inclined to oppose both the id and the ego, and to make the world over into its own image. However, it is like the id in being nonrational and like the ego in attempting to exercise control over the instincts. Unlike the ego, the superego does not merely postpone instinctual gratification; it tries to block it permanently" (p. 39).

Though the three subsystems of personality operate as a whole, each represents distinct influences on human behavior (see Figure 3.1). The id is the biological force that influences human behavior. The ego represents the psychological origins of behavior, whereas the superego reflects the impact of social and moral forces. Both the id and superego can be thought of as the irrational components of personality; the id strives for pleasure at all costs whereas the superego always works to prevent it.

ANXIETY, DEFENSE MECHANISMS, AND THE UNCONSCIOUS

Anxiety plays a prominent role in psychoanalytic theory. The purpose of anxiety is to warn the individual that there is impending danger (i.e., pain). It is also a signal to the ego to take some preventive measure to reduce the threat. According to Hall and Lindzey (1978), "Anxiety is a state of tension; it is a drive like hunger or sex but instead of

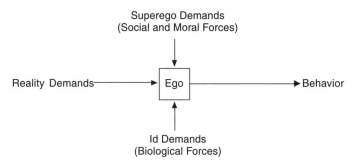

Superego Demands
(Social and Moral Forces)

Reality Demands ──────► Ego ──────► Behavior

Id Demands
(Biological Forces)

FIGURE 3.1. Influence of the id, ego, and superego and of reality demands on human behavior.

arising from internal tissue conditions it is produced originally by external causes. When anxiety is aroused it motivates the person to do something. He or she may flee from the threatening region, inhibit the dangerous impulse, or obey the voice of conscience" (p. 48). Often the ego can cope with anxiety by rational measures. For example, a nervous student with an upcoming exam can spend extra time studying. A "stressed-out" employee can exercise, meditate, or turn to other constructive diversions. A parent can begin to save money now for a child's college education in 15 years. A recovering alcoholic who has cravings can call his/her Alcoholics Anonymous (AA) sponsor. Such actions require reason, the ability to plan, and the delay of immediate gratification for long-term gain.

Frequently, the ego is overcome by anxiety it cannot control. In such situations, rational measures fail and the ego resorts to irrational protective mechanisms, which are often referred to as "defense mechanisms." The defense mechanisms, such as denial and rationalization, alleviate the anxiety. However, they do so by distorting reality instead of dealing directly with the problem. This distortion creates a discrepancy or gap between actual reality and the individual's perception of it. As a consequence, the ego's ability to cope with reality demands becomes increasingly diminished. Such is the case with alcoholics, who, on being confronted with their problematic drinking, rely on denial and rationalization. These defenses, in turn, allow the abusive drinking to continue and become increasingly dysfunctional.

Typical ego defense mechanisms among the chemically dependent include the following:

1. *Compensation*: making up for the deprivation of abstinence by overindulging in another pleasure. (Example: A recovering drug addict becomes compulsive about gambling, work, eating, etc.)

2. *Denial*: inability to perceive an unacceptable reality. (Example: An employee denies he is suffering from alcoholism when confronted about the bottle he keeps hidden in his desk.)

3. *Displacement*: directing pent-up feelings of hostility toward objects less dangerous than those that initially aroused the anger. (Example: An addict in treatment comes home from a group counseling session and screams at his wife. In group, he received feedback from the facilitator indicating that he was not actively participating.)

4. *Fantasy:* gaining gratification from the loss of intoxicants by imagining the euphoria and fun of one's past drug abuse. (Example: While in rehabilitation, a group of addicts experience cravings as they reminisce about the "good ol' times.")

5. *Isolation*: withdrawing into a passive state in order to avoid further hurt. (Example: A depressed alcoholic in early recovery refuses to share her problems in group.)

6. *Projection*: assuming that others think badly of one even though they have never communicated this in any way. (Example: An addict unexpectedly blurts out to a counselor, "I know you think I'm a worthless piece of ___.")

7. *Rationalization*: attempting to justify one's mistakes or misdeeds by presenting rationales and explanations for the misconduct. (Example: An addict reports that he missed a Narcotics Anonymous meeting because he had to make a very important telephone call to his attorney.)

8. *Regression:* retreating to an earlier developmental level involving less mature responses. (Example: In a therapeutic community, an adult resident "blows up" and makes a huge scene when she learns that iced tea is not available for lunch that day.)

9. *Undoing*: atoning for or making up for an unacceptable act. (Example: An alcoholic goes to a bar after work and gets "smashed." He doesn't get home until 4:00 A.M. His wife is furious. The next day he brings her flowers and cooks dinner.)

The defense mechanisms and other processes operate on an unconscious level. The unconscious, according to Freud, represents the largest part of the human mind. The individual is generally unaware of the content and process of this part of mind. The conscious mind, by contrast, is a function of the ego that has often been likened to the "tip of an iceberg" (see Figure 3.2).

The unconscious mind holds forbidden desires, painful memories, and unacceptable experiences that have been "repressed," or pushed out of consciousness. Although individuals are unaware of unconscious material, it possesses energy and seeks expression. Thus, at times, unconscious material successfully penetrates the conscious mind. Typical examples include so-called Freudian slips (e.g., using the word "sex"

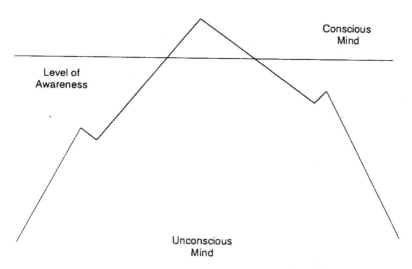

FIGURE 3.2. The "iceberg" view of the conscious versus the unconscious mind.

when the word "stress" would have been appropriate). Unconscious material also surfaces during fantasies, dreams, and hypnosis. In each case, ego controls are lowered, allowing the unconscious to appear. Psychoanalysts believe that as long as unconscious material is repressed and not integrated into the ego (presumably through psychoanalysis), maladaptive behavior (e.g., addictions) will be maintained.

PSYCHOSEXUAL DEVELOPMENT

Freud believed that the early childhood years are critical to the development of a person's personality—in fact, that one's state of mental health as an adult is largely determined by the degree to which one resolves conflicts at each childhood stage.

According to Freud, children pass through three stages in the first 5 years of life. Together, these are referred to as the "pregenital stages." Then, at about the age of 5, children enter the "latent stage," a relatively quiet and uneventful period of about 5 to 6 years. As adolescence nears, the dynamics again become less stabilized; impulses, particularly sexual ones, reappear at this time. This is called the "genital stage."

Freud made sharp distinctions between the dynamics of each of the stages. However, he did not believe that there are abrupt transitions as a person moves from one stage to the next; rather, passage from stage to stage is gradual and often incomplete. According to Hall and Lindzey (1978), "The final organization of personality represents contributions from all four stages" (p. 58).

Freud described each stage of psychosexual development in terms of libidinal drives that are associated with specific zones of the body (Arlow, 1979). The stages are summarized in the following paragraphs.

Oral Stage

The oral stage covers the period from birth to about 18 months. During this phase, the infant's main source of libidinal gratification is derived from sucking, which, of course, involves the mouth, lips, and tongue. As the infant's needs for oral gratification are fulfilled, he/she is freed from a state of tension and frustration. This satisfied state induces calm in the infant and allows the infant to sleep. The theory of psychoanalysis asserts that these dynamics form one's basic orientation to frustration. Persons who never had their oral needs met during infancy tend to anticipate disappointment at every turn and adopt a pessimistic outlook on life.

In the psychoanalytic framework, alcoholism is thought to be the result of these very dynamics. It is considered an ineffective and destructive attempt at resolving conflicts from the oral period (Blume, 1966). Thus, it has been described as an "oral fixation" (Kinney & Leaton, 1987). That is, alcoholics are persons with unmet oral needs who are easily frustrated and thus turn to the bottle for relief. The act of drinking, especially from a bottle, is thought to be symbolic of a desire to return to the security and comfort of suckling from the mother's breast. The reader should note that today, "oral fixation" is seen as an outdated concept by many within and outside psychoanalytic circles.

According to Blume (1966), the infantile behavior exhibited by alcoholics (narcissism, demandingness, passivity, etc.) results from their being "stuck" in the oral stage. The fixation stems from parental deprivation during this period of childhood. Anxiety and compensatory needs for control, power, and achievement manifest themselves during adulthood. Alcohol abuse is thought of as an attempt to find relief from anxiety, as well as an effort to boost one's feelings of strength and invulnerability. This is referred to as "false courage" (Blume, 1966).

Anal Stage

The anal stage covers the period from about 18 months to 3 years of age. The child obtains libidinal gratification chiefly through activities associated with the retention and elimination of feces. During this phase, the child believes that feces are an extruded portion of the self; he/she considers the feces to be a valuable and highly prized possession. Typically, the child's caretakers attempt to shame the child for such attitudes, which often leads to feelings of low self-worth. A child with such attitudes is described as having an "anal retentive" personality. According to Arlow (1979), it is characterized by "stubborn assertiveness, contrary rebelliousness, and by the determination to be in control of whatever happens to him" (p. 13).

Phallic Phase

From the ages of 3 to 5, self-manipulation of the genitals is assumed to be the primary source of libidinal gratification. The dynamics of the phallic phase are thought to be extremely complicated, though subtle. Among boys, the "Oedipus complex" is played out; among girls, essentially the same dynamics occur, but they are referred to as the "Electra complex." Each represents a myth of ancient Greek origin. Boys and girls, during this phase, are thought to symbolically relive these Greek dramas. In each case, the child desires to overthrow the same-sex parent and to possess the opposite-sex parent. For children of both genders, resolution of this conflict is considered essential for the later development of satisfactory heterosexual relationships. Homosexual tendencies are thought to stem from an unsatisfactory resolution of this conflict during the phallic phase.

Under propitious conditions, the child puts aside the hostility of the Oedipus or Electra complex and establishes an identification with the parent of the same gender. Part of this identification process includes the adoption of the parent's moral standards and prohibitions. This results in the emergence of the superego.

Latency Stage

The latency stage extends from the age of 5 or 6 to about the age of 12. It ends with the onset of adolescence. Presumably, during this period, the child's sexual urges recede as the child develops talents and directs energies toward the outside world. Thus, it is thought of as a relatively quiet period during which the child is socialized.

Genital Stage

The genital stage appears after puberty. The young teen supposedly experiences a "sexual reawakening." From this point on, individuals derive the greatest pleasure from the genitals. Freud described this period as one of great turbulence. The adolescent makes second attempts to master the conflicts arising from desires of the oral, anal, and phallic phases. Successful resolution of these conflicts results in a con-solidation of one's identity in terms of sexual orientation, moral stan-dards, and choice of work or profession. However, in most persons, the resolution of at least some of these conflicts remains incomplete. Many individuals are thought to pass into adulthood with a variety of neu-rotic tendencies. Thus, it becomes the ego's obligation to mediate be-tween the urges of the id and the demands of the superego.

INSIGHTS INTO COMPULSIVE SUBSTANCE USE

Early psychoanalytic formulations insisted that chemical dependency stems from unconscious death wishes and self-destructive tendencies of the id. It was believed that among alcoholics and drug addicts, the id is oriented toward death instincts rather than constructive (e.g., sexual) instincts. Thus, many early psychoanalysts viewed compulsive sub-stance abuse as a form of "slow suicide" (Khantzian, 1980). The focus in treatment was on the tendencies of the id. This traditional school of thought, known as "drive reduction," holds that substance abuse is merely a manifest symptom of a repressed idea (or memory) that comes to consciousness. The repressed idea is unrecognizable, that is, appears as substance abuse, because it is distorted by psychological defenses (Leeds & Morgenstern, 1996). In essence, substance abuse can be thought of as a compromise resulting from the conflict between a re-pressed idea and the defense against it (Leeds & Morgenstern, 1996).

A second school of thought, within the psychoanalytic tradition, is sometimes referred to as "ego psychology." Contemporary psycho-analytic treatment of chemical dependence seems to draw heavily on this conceptualization of addiction (Murphy & Khantzian, 1995). Here, substance abuse is seen as a symptom of a deficient ego. According to Murphy and Khantzian (1995), "it is the vulnerable and disregulated self which is the central problem in addiction" (p. 162). Individuals with addiction problems are seen as lacking the capacity to adequately care for themselves; they expose themselves unnecessarily to a variety of risks: health, safety, financial, legal, and so on. The consequences of risky or dangerous behavior can be ignored because a sense of well-being, security, and pleasure is provided by the drug intoxication (Murphy & Khantzian, 1995). In this psychoanalytic approach, the goal of treatment is to build ego strength by helping the person de-velop the capabilities to cope with the demands of the external world.

Despite the differences just described, psychoanalytic formulations of addiction share a set of assumptions. According to Leeds and Morgenstern (1996), these are as follows:

1) the act of drug use is a symptom of some type of underlying psychological disorder,
2) the psychological problems of the addict precede and cause the substance abuse—there is little recognition that psychological problems are the consequence of substance abuse,
3) addiction is seen as a uniform disorder—there is relatively little consideration given to disorder subtypes, different drugs of abuse, to the course or severity of the addiction problem, etc., and
4) the presence of addiction indicates severe psychopathology. (p. 76)

Contemporary psychoanalysts tend to view chemical dependency as a symptom of a deficient ego. Essentially, they believe that substance abuse is only the obvious and outward manifestation of deeper personality problems. The goal of treatment in such cases is to build ego strength so that the demands of the id can be better managed.

Two Necessary Conditions

According to Wurmser (1974), two general factors are always present in the development of compulsive substance use. The first is described as the "addictive search." This internal urge is a psychological hunger or craving for an entire group of activities; the urge precedes the onset of chemical dependency but accompanies it and follows it, even after abstinence has been established. The activities may include compulsive gambling, overeating, indiscriminate sexual activity, irresistible violence, compulsive shoplifting, endless television viewing, and/or running away. All these activities can be used to provide external relief from overpowering internal drives.

The second necessary factor is referred to as the "adventitious entrance" of chemicals (Wurmser, 1974). This is the random introduction (in terms of accessibility and seductiveness) of alcohol or drugs into a person's life. They are typically introduced by peers, or perhaps by drug dealers in the case of illicit drugs. Without access to and experimentation with these substances, addiction is obviously not possible.

Together, these two predisposing factors (i.e., the addictive search and the adventitious entrance) set the stage for the development of chemical dependency. Both must be present for the disorder to appear. According to Wurmser (1974), some people are driven by an addictive search, but they have not been exposed to the world of drug or alcohol abuse. In such cases, "there is no compulsive drug use without this trigger factor; but there is still an overriding emotional compulsiveness directed toward other activities and objects" (Wurmser, 1974, p. 829).

This may also be the case for many chemically dependent persons in recovery. That is, they have removed themselves from the drinking/drugging scene and are abstinent, but they may continue old compulsions or develop new ones. They may be said to be continuing an addictive search even though they are abstinent.

These two predisposing factors may also explain why some people who gain access to the world of drug or alcohol abuse never become dependent upon them. Despite the availability of various drugs, they may not possess the psychological hunger that is necessary to initiate or maintain compulsive drug or alcohol abuse. In other words, they may not need external relief from internal cravings or urges. Of course, an alternative "disease" explanation is simply that such individuals lack the *genetic* vulnerability to alcoholism and other drug addictions.

Abuse as Affect Defense

Contemporary psychoanalytic thinking maintains that substance abuse itself is a defense mechanism (Khantzian, 1980; Wurmser, 1980). Addicts abuse alcohol or drugs to protect themselves from overwhelming anxiety, depression, boredom, guilt, shame, and other negative emotions. Wurmser (1974) has stated that compulsive drug use is "an attempt at self-treatment" (p. 829). That is, it represents an attempt at self-medication, a way to relieve psychic pain.

For the most part, contemporary psychoanalysts do not view negative affective states (e.g., anxiety, depression) as consequences of substance abuse but, rather, as its causes. According to Khantzian (1980):

> I have become convinced, as has Wurmser, that becoming and remaining addicted to drugs is in most instances associated with severe and significant psychopathology. Necessarily, some of the deserved pathology evident in addicts is the result of drug use and its attendant interpersonal involvements. However, it is my opinion that drug-dependent individuals are predisposed to use and become dependent upon their substances mainly as a result of severe ego impairments and disturbances in the sense of self. . . . (p. 29)

Wurmser's (1978) analysis of this problem goes further. He believes that the greater the legal penalties and social stigma against a drug, the more likely its user is to have severe psychopathology. The lack of internal controls to resist engaging in conduct which society condemns is seen as pathology. Thus, Wurmser (1979) concludes that "a compulsive alcohol or nicotine abuser shows far less preexisting psychopathology than a compulsive (or even casual) user of heroin, LSD, or cocaine" (p. 9).

Wurmser (1978) refers to the link between severe psychopathology and addiction as the "hidden problem." He contends that drug control bureaucrats, law enforcement officials, many physicians (including psychiatrists), and drug users themselves are in denial about this relationship. According to Wurmser (1978), this collective unwillingness to acknowledge the emotional conflict underlying addiction has led to the development of misguided drug control policy and ineffective approaches to prevention and treatment. He believes legal controls do little to address the demand for drugs and that much treatment is superficial because it focuses on the use/nonuse of substances rather than on underlying personality and emotional issues.

Does Research Support the "Self-Medication" Hypothesis?

The psychoanalytic belief that individuals are predisposed to addiction by negative affective states is not supported by research findings. According to Cox's (1985) review of the personality correlates of substance abuse, there is little evidence that psychological distress (e.g., anxiety, depression, and low self-esteem) leads to addiction. Rather, studies of young people indicate that future substance abusers tend to show three character traits: independence, nonconformity, and impulsivity (Cox, 1985). It appears that negative affective states are usually the consequences of years of substance abuse, not the precursors, as claimed by psychoanalysts.

Psychopathology and substance use disorders do commonly coexist within individuals. Findings from the Epidemiologic Catchment Area Study show that substance use disorders co-occur with other psychiatric disorders at a rate that far exceeds that predicted by chance (Regier et al., 1990). Among 20,000 persons surveyed in the community as well as in institutional settings, 20% had at least one psychiatric disorder. However, among those with an alcohol (nondrug) disorder, the rate of psychiatric disorders increased to 37%, and among those with a drug (nonalcohol) disorder, the rate reached 50%. For patients in treatment for an addiction problem, the rate of psychiatric problems appears to range from 67% to 95%, depending on whether the diagnosis involves alcohol, other drugs, or both (Ross, Glaser, & Germanson, 1988). The most prevalent psychiatric disorders in addiction treatment patients are antisocial personality disorder, phobia, psychosexual disorder, and major depression, in that order.

Though the empirical research supports the assertion that a variety of psychiatric disorders tend to coexist in persons who have addiction problems, the co-occurrence appears to be more complex than Wurmser contends, and sometimes the connection may not be causal

(National Institute on Alcohol Abuse and Alcoholism, 1994). A substance use disorder may result from a psychiatric disorder, but in other cases, it may cause a psychiatric problem. It also is possible that a "common factor" could cause both types of disorders. Finally, in some cases, a reciprocal relationship may exist in which the substance use disorder and other psychiatric problem influence one another in a synergistic manner.

Although order of symptom onset cannot conclusively determine the causal sequence for comorbid disorders, it is useful to consider the temporal pattern to them. In a treatment sample, Ross et al. (1988) found that the development of antisocial personality disorder nearly always preceded the onset of alcohol abuse. However, the percentage in which other psychiatric disorders appeared prior to alcohol abuse was lower: schizophrenia, 60%; phobia, 60%; and panic disorder, 58%. Conversely, alcohol abuse seemed to be somewhat more likely to precede the onset of major depression (57%) and obsessive–compulsive disorder (54%).

These data suggest that the "self-medication" hypothesis is too simplistic. Clearly, persons with substance use problems are at risk for having other psychiatric conditions. However, it cannot be concluded that compulsive substance use is always an attempt to manage negative emotions. Frequently, the co-occurring condition is a character disorder (which presumably does not cause distress) rather than an affective disorder.

Where affective disorders, such as major depression, do coexist with alcohol or drug abuse, often the substance use preceded it in time. This time order does not rule out the possibility that depression which is secondary to substance use is "self-treated" with alcohol and/or drugs, but it suggests there is a need for explanatory models that are much more complex than those provided by psychoanalytic theory. Substance use and psychopathology may well have a complex relationship that varies across individuals according to the specific drugs involved, age of onset, and whether it is a mechanism for initiation, maintenance, or cessation of drug use.

Specific Drugs to Correct Different Affects

Psychoanalysts generally dispute the notion that an addict's drug of choice is determined by economic, environmental, or sociocultural factors. Instead, they maintain that addicts become dependent on the drug that will correct or counteract the specific negative emotional state from which they want relief. For example, Wurmser (1980) puts it this way: "The choice of drugs shows some fairly typical correlations with otherwise unmanageable affects (moods): narcotics and hypnotics are deployed against rage, shame, and jealously, and particularly the anxiety related to these feelings; stimulants against depression and weakness; psychedelics against boredom and disillusionment; alcohol against guilt, loneliness, and related anxiety" (p. 72).

Khantzian, Halliday, and McAuliffe (1990) have recently outlined the differing types of emotional pain that they believe lead to dependence on opiates, sedative–hypnotics, or cocaine. They propose that opiate or narcotic addicts are typically the victims of traumatic abuse and violence. As a result, they eventually become perpetrators of violence themselves. This history causes them to suffer with acute and chronic feelings of hostility and anger. According to Khantzian et al. (1990), "Narcotic addicts make the powerful discovery that both the distress they suffer, and the threat they pose with their intense aggression are significantly reduced or contained when they first use opiates. Thus addicts have repeatedly described the anti-rage, anti-aggression action of opiates as 'calming-feeling mellow-safe-or, normal for the first time' " (p. 35).

In contrast, these authors propose that sedative–hypnotics, including alcohol, are abused by individuals who are anxious and inhibited. This class of drugs is used to overcome deep-seated defenses and fears about interpersonal intimacy. Sedative–hypnotic addicts (alcoholics, tranquilizer addicts, etc.) select these drugs in order to dissolve their defenses, thereby allowing brief and safe expressions of love or anger to emerge. Essentially, these addicts feel separate, lonely, or cut off from others when not intoxicated (Khantzian et al., 1990).

Cocaine addicts are thought to select cocaine for its energizing qualities. These addicts are seeking relief from depression, boredom, or emptiness. In addition, cocaine is found to be appealing because it bolsters feelings of self-esteem and assertiveness. Its use may also be thought of as a means of augmenting an already "hyperactive, restless lifestyle" (Khantzian et al., 1990).

As noted previously, empirical data often appear to refute psychoanalytic concepts. This seems to be the case for "specific drugs to correct different affects." For example, alcoholism appears to co-occur frequently with antisocial personality disorder and depression (Holdcraft, Iacono, & McGue, 1998) ,which is somewhat inconsistent with the psychoanalytic profile of the alcoholic as guilt-ridden, lonely, and anxious. In teenagers, epidemiological data indicates that marijuana abuse is correlated with delinquency and depression (Greenblatt, 1998). These associations do not neatly fit in the psychoanalytic model either. This illustrates the lack of precision to many of the psychoanalytic formulations of substance abuse.

Ego Deficiency

According to the psychoanalytic view, addicts are thought to have weak or impaired egos (Khantzian, 1980; Wurmser, 1980). They have failed to develop adequate internal controls for coping with the internal drives of the id. This makes addicts dependent on their external environment (i.e., alcohol and drugs) for the satiation of their psychic needs. Over time, addicts become more and more dependent on these external controls (i.e., alcohol and drugs), and their egos become increasingly dysfunctional.

In addition, a weakened ego does not recognize the ever-increasing dangers of continued alcohol and drug abuse. The perception of risk becomes distorted. This distortion is commonly seen among chemically dependent people when they demonstrate an indifference to others' concerns for their physical and mental health or personal safety. It may also explain why factual and rational messages (i.e., education) about the risks of substance abuse often fail to impress alcoholics and addicts.

Wurmser (1974) believes that deficiencies in both the ego and superego result from faulty parenting:

> Parents who did not provide a minimum of consistency, of reliability, of trustworthiness, of responsiveness to the child, especially during his developmental crises, are not usable as inner beacons; instead they become targets of rebellious rage and disdain. Parents who vacillate between temper tantrums and indulgence, who allow themselves to live out their most primitive demands, parents who are more interested in their careers and their clubs and travels than in their children's needs to have them available, or parents who are absent for economic reasons and cannot impart the important combination of love and firmness—all these parents, unless replaced in their crucial functions by capable substitutes, make it very difficult for their children to accept them as secure models. (p. 147)

Concretization

Substance abuse counselors have noted that many chemically dependent clients do not articulate or label feelings. It is as if they have no language for their emotions or inner life. This condition has been referred to as "concretization." Among children and young adolescents, concretization is a normal developmental state. However, many chemically dependent adults exhibit it, as do people with other forms of psychopathology. It can be considered a developmental lag.

Wurmser (1974) believes that the condition of concretization predisposes persons to compulsive drug use. He argues that such persons are unable to find pleasure in everyday life. Because they lack the inner resources to create pleasure, they find the world empty, boring, meaningless, and unstimulating. A vague sense of discomfort and low-level tension fills this emotionless void. To find relief, they turn to alcohol and drugs.

CONTEMPORARY TREATMENT OF ADDICTION

Contemporary psychoanalytically oriented practitioners have outlined a practical approach to the treatment of alcoholism and other addictions (Zimberg, Wallace, & Blume, 1978). First, it is believed that alcohol and drug use must stop completely for treatment to be effective (Zimberg, 1978); if abstinence is not initiated, a power struggle will ensue between client and therapist. Second, the development of transference and countertransference must be understood and properly dealt with in the therapeutic process. Transference appears when the alcoholic or addict applies unresolved past conflicts to the therapist. Typically, the chemically dependent client "tests" the therapist in manipulative ways and displays paradoxical feelings of hostility and dependency. Countertransference, a primitive "parental" reaction by the therapist, is to be avoided (Zimberg, 1978). It is important that therapists understand these tendencies and not allow themselves to be drawn into dysfunctional relationships with addicted clients. The therapists must remain objective, not take the hostility personally, and avoid becoming discouraged or disgusted with such clients. Therapists must also keep in mind that they cannot stop determined alcoholics from drinking or addicts from using drugs. Progress in treatment is largely the alcoholics' or addicts' responsibility (Zimberg, 1978).

The Preferred Defense Structure of Alcoholics

Wallace (1978) has identified a "preferred defense structure" (PDS) among alcoholics. (It may apply to those addicted to other drugs as well.) The concept evolved from his own professional experience in treating alcoholics. He states that this "PDS need not be cast in negative terms" (p. 20). It consists of a set of tactics and strategies that alcoholics use to protect the ego. Furthermore, Wallace (1978) asserts that therapy should not attempt to remove an alcoholic's PDS, but should utilize it to help the client maintain abstinence. In the early stages of treatment, confrontation should be avoided. He recommends that the emphasis should be on sobriety rather than on insight. According to Wallace (1978), "therapeutic efforts that confront the alcoholic PDS prematurely and too heavily will increase rather than reduce the probability of further drinking" (p. 20). According to this perspective, eventually the PDS must be given up for long-term sobriety to be achieved. However, Wallace (1978) suggests that the PDS may be useful in maintaining sobriety for 2 to 5 years. Beyond this period, presence of the PDS signifies a lack of personal growth in recovery and may leave the alcoholic vulnerable to relapse.

Denial is one of the major defenses in the PDS profile (Wallace, 1978). It is believed that denial can actually be used to benefit the alcoholic in early stages of treatment. Alcoholics have a need to "save face" and preserve some self-worth. Rather than making clients face their irresponsible past behavior, therapists should "allow" denial to help them cope with overwhelming anxiety. Wallace (1978) acknowledges that alcoholics must believe in the early stages of treatment that they can no longer drink. However, he does not believe that it is desirable, or even possible, to root out all other vestiges of denial in their personality and behavior.

Another defense in the PDS profile is "all-or-nothing thinking" (Wallace, 1978). Alcoholics tend to exhibit a need for certainty; their personal judgments about people, situations, and events are many times extreme. Wallace (1978) notes: "Decision-making does not often seem to take into account the realistically possible. Decision rules are often inflexible, narrow in scope, and simplistic. Perceived alternatives are few, consisting largely of yes–no, go–no go, black–white dichotomized categories" (p. 23). This tendency leads a recovering alcoholic to prefer predictability and structure. AA meetings certainly provide this condition, and most treatment programs apply these principles as well.

"Conflict minimization and avoidance" constitute another component of Wallace's (1978) PDS profile. He indicates that recovering alcoholics do not like interpersonal conflict and seek to avoid it if at all possible. For this reason, confrontation, especially hostile confrontation, is seen as antitherapeutic. Wallace (1978) recommends that counselors use extreme caution when considering whether to use confrontation in the therapeutic process.

A fourth defense of the PDS is described as "self-centered selective attention." Wallace (1978) claims that alcoholics are usually obsessed with self, and they tend to evaluate events unfolding before them in terms of how the events will affect them personally. Furthermore, they tend to screen out information that is inconsistent with how they view themselves. This "screening out" is linked to low self-worth, guilt, shame, and fear. This is why feedback is often difficult for alcoholics to accept and use in future action. For this reason, it is not imperative that clients in recovery learn the "truth" about themselves immediately. Wallace (1978) maintains that some "myths" may need to be invented to help clients stay sober. In essence, some personal myths may be useful in early recovery.

Still another defense of the PDS is described as "preference for nonanalytical modes of thinking and perceiving" (Wallace, 1978). Alcoholics tend to be persuaded by warm emotional or inspirational appeals rather than by cool logic. In other words, a charismatic, spiritual mode is preferred over reason. Wallace (1978) notes that "the alcoholic is more drawn to the warmth of magic rather than the cold objectivity of science" (p. 25). This has obvious implications for counselor–client relationships. Alcoholics may not want experts for counselors as much as they may want advocates and supporters.

The last defense to be mentioned here is described as "obsessional focusing" (Wallace, 1978). Alcoholics are considered to be intense people by nature; they tend to obsess. Obsessing occurs while they are actively drinking as well as when they are sober. Wallace (1978) notes that many recovering alcoholics become even more compulsive about work, cigarette smoking, and coffee drinking once they stop drinking alcohol. Furthermore, he states that the goal of therapy should not be to reduce this high intensity level but, rather, to redirect it into productive pursuits. A good example would be ritualistic attendance of AA meetings. Though some frown on what they see as a substitute addiction (i.e., AA meetings), Wallace (1978) asserts that this is a good use of obsessional energy because it keeps an alcoholic sober.

Three Stages to Recovery

According to the psychoanalytic perspective, there are three stages to complete recovery, as shown in Table 3.2 (Zimberg, 1978). Stage I is characterized by the self-statement "I can't drink or drug." In this stage, external control (e.g., detoxification and Antabuse) is important. In essence, the clients need protection from their own impulses. The second stage is characterized by the self-statement "I won't drink or drug." Here, the control becomes internalized. Many AA/NA members remain at this level indefinitely. The third stage is represented by "I don't have to drink or drug." Many recovering persons never complete this stage, nor do they necessarily relapse. According to the psychoanalytic perspective, insight-oriented therapy is appropriate at this stage (Zimberg, 1978). However, because a recovering client's perception of the need for change is usually diminished at this point (life is relatively "normal" or "manageable"), few recovering persons pursue insight-oriented therapy.

TABLE 3.2. A Contemporary Psychoanalytic View of Treatment Stages

Stages	Client status	Treatment
Stage I	"I can't drink or drug" (need for external controls)	Detoxification, directive psychotherapy, Antabuse, drug testing, AA/NA, family therapy
Stage II	"I won't drink or drug" (control becomes internalized)	Directive psychotherapy, supportive psychotherapy, AA/NA; Antabuse and drug testing may be discontinued
Stage III	"I don't have to drink or drug" (conflict over abstinence is resolved)	Psychoanalytic psychotherapy

Note. Adapted from Zimberg (1978). Copyright 1978 by Plenum Publishing Corporation. Adapted by permission.

THE IMPORTANCE OF PSYCHOANALYTIC CONCEPTS IN SUBSTANCE ABUSE COUNSELING

Psychoanalytic concepts are widely employed in the practice of substance abuse counseling. However, many counselors are not aware that the concepts are derived from psychoanalytic theory. For example, many counselors make attempts to identify clients' defense mechanisms in an effort to help the clients recognize their perceptual distortions. Denial, rationalization, and fantasy are typical protection mechanisms employed by chemically dependent clients. Closely intertwined with them is the unconscious, an indisputable influence on at least some classes of human behavior.

Psychoanalytic thinking should sensitize substance abuse counselors to the importance of early childhood development and parental influences as possible origins of addictive behavior. Though counselors need not necessarily believe that alcoholics or addicts are "orally fixated" or have unresolved Oedipal conflicts, they should recognize that dysfunctional dynamics in an individual's family of origin often play a role in the development of chemical dependency. Furthermore, the slow progress or frequent relapses that characterize some clients may reflect deep-seated disturbances of personality that originated in childhood.

Psychoanalysts like Khantzian and Wurmser should be credited with making penetrating insights into the personality dynamics of addicts. Wurmser's (1974) notion of an individual's proneness (i.e., the "addictive search") coupled with drug or alcohol availability (i.e., the "adventitious entrance") provides an intriguing explanation for predicting vulnerability to addiction. Likewise, the conceptualization of drug taking as "affect defense" (i.e., a form of self-treatment) is also revealing, particularly when consideration is given to the possibility that an addict's drug of choice is selected in order to provide relief from specific dysphoric moods. The addict's distorted perception of risk, as a function of a weakened ego, sheds light on the weakness of educational approaches (i.e., dissemination of facts) in ameliorating abuse and addiction. Finally, the developmental lag described as "concretization" helps substance abuse counselors to understand the dynamics that underlie the blunted emotional repertoire of many chemically dependent clients.

Many psychoanalysts recognize that traditional analytic treatment methods are largely ineffective with substance dependent clients (e.g., Brickman, 1988). This is not to say that psychoanalytic concepts have no place in addiction assessment and counseling. As Leeds and Morgenstern (1996) have noted ,there has often been confusion between the psychoanalytic *understanding* of addiction and the psychoanalytic *treatment* of the disorder. It should not be assumed that one necessarily leads to the other. In fact, the theory itself, seems to predict that traditional psychoanalytic methods would not work well with the chemically dependent population. Regardless, the concepts can be helpful for analyzing such problems as client resistance.

GENERAL CRITICISMS OF PSYCHOANALYSIS

The theory of psychoanalysis has come under strong attack from many directions. The theory has been criticized for overemphasizing sexual factors. While acknowledging that sexual issues are frequent sources of conflict for many people, critics contend that Freud and his colleagues gave them too central a role in the development of emotional and behavioral disorders (Coleman et al., 1980; Horney, 1967). It has been suggested that a variety of disorders do not stem from unresolved sexual conflicts (depression, anxiety, cocaine addiction, etc.).

Another general criticism of the theory is that it is unduly pessimistic about human nature. That is, psychoanalysis fails to consider positive human motivations for growth and development. Freud perceived humans as being in a constant state of conflict. This is best illustrated by the conflicting tendencies attributed to the id, ego, and superego. Critics maintain that altruism, love, serenity, and personal growth, among other human qualities, are not readily explained by the theory.

A third important criticism involves the unconscious. Freud asserted that the conscious mind comprises a relatively small part of the mind, and that unconscious processes are, for the most part, the determinants of personality and behavior. Critics of psychoanalysis contend that the opposite is true, that most human functioning is under the control of rational, conscious processes. Moreover, many have contended that what Freud considered inaccessibly buried in the unconscious is nothing of the sort; they believe that so-called unconscious thoughts can be brought to awareness with relative ease (i.e., with self-reflection or self-examination).

A fourth criticism is that the theory neglects cultural differences. Freud conceived of psychoanalysis while working with middle- and upper-class white residents of Vienna, Austria, during the last decade of the 19th century and the first three decades of the 20th. In addition, the majority of his clients were female and neurotic. Thus, it is questionable whether the theory can adequately account for the experience of diverse peoples. For example, it is difficult to believe that the Oedipus complex is relevant to the development of all humans, including those of non-Western nations.

There is also little or no empirical evidence to support many of the assumptions of psychoanalysis. The very structure of the personality (id, ego, and superego) may simply be an illusory, though creative, product of Freud's mind. After all, no one has ever seen an ego, measured the unconscious, or found a defense mechanism in the brain. Yet it is interesting that we ascribe much power to these constructs and refer to them as if they have concrete reality.

Finally, it has been pointed out that the penetrating insights offered by psychoanalysts may be of little help to clients suffering from affective or behavioral disorders. Mental health professionals have long recognized that learning why one acts a certain way often does not lead to changes in one's behavior. Some have even gone so far as to say that a cognitive understanding of the past origins of one's problems is irrelevant to the process of change in the present. This may be particularly the case with substance abuse problems.

CRITICISM OF THE PSYCHOANALYTIC VIEW OF ADDICTION

Contemporary psychoanalysts have pointed out that the chemically dependent suffer from poor ego controls. This makes them poor candidates for psychoanalysis, a process that requires significant ego strength. Wurmser (1974), himself a leading psychoanalyst, states that most compulsive drug users are relatively inaccessible by psychoanalysis. There are various reasons for this poor match. Many chemically dependent persons enter treatment with little initial motivation for personal change. Many others require assistance with the ordinary, mundane challenges of staying sober and "straight" a day at a time (e.g., remembering to take Antabuse and finding a ride to an AA meeting). Still others need strong guidance and structure to avoid relapse. These pressing reality-based concerns are not readily addressed in traditional psychoanalysis, with its emphasis on the intellect, the origins of problems, and protracted self-analysis.

In recent years, several psychoanalytically oriented clinicians have recommended that traditional psychoanalytic practice be modified for the treatment of chemical dependency (Yalisove, 1989). The following modifications have been recommended:

1. The initial stage of treatment should be supportive and didactic in nature.
2. Management issues must be emphasized in early phases of treatment (i.e., hospitalization, dangerous behavior, withdrawal symptoms).
3. Sessions should be held once or twice a week.
4. The "couch" should not be used.
5. Interpretation should be minimized.
6. Abstinence should be encouraged.
7. AA attendance should be emphasized.

A consideration of these "modifications" gives rise to this question: Is it still psychoanalysis? The extent of the modifications eliminates most (possibly all) of the distinctive features of traditional psychoanalysis. That which is left appears to be conventional psychotherapy.

REVIEW QUESTIONS

1. What are the origins of psychoanalysis?
2. How are psychotherapy and psychoanalysis distinguished from each other?
3. What are major features of the process of psychoanalytic therapy?
4. According to Taleff, what are the sources of resistance seen in clients?
5. What are the chief characteristics of the id, ego, and superego? How do they interact?
6. What is a defense mechanism? How are defense mechanisms related to anxiety and the unconscious?
7. What are the chief characteristics of the oral, anal, phallic, latency,

and genital stages of psychosexual development? Which stages have significance for substance abuse?

8. How do "drive-reduction" and "ego psychology" hypotheses differ in explaining addiction?

9. What are the "addictive search" and the "adventitious entrance"?

10. What is meant by "abuse as affect defense"?

11. Is the self-medication hypothesis of psychoanalysis supported by empirical research?

12. What specific affects are different drugs thought to correct?

13. Why do addicts not recognize the risks associated with their compulsive use?

14. What is "concretization"?

15. What defenses comprise Wallace's preferred defense structure?

16. What are the three stages of contemporary psychoanalytic treatment?

17. What are the general criticisms of psychoanalysis?

18. What are the criticisms of psychoanalysis as a treatment of addiction?

19. Today, do psychoanalysts recommend traditional methods to treat substancer abusers?

20. What are the features of contemporary psychoanalytically oriented treatment?

REFERENCES

Arlow, J. A. (1979). Psychoanalysis. In R. J. Corsini (Ed.), *Current psychotherapies*. Itasca, IL: Peacock.

Berry, H., III. (1988). Psychoanalytic theory of alcoholism. In C. D. Chaudron & D. A. Wilkinson (Eds.), *Theories on alcoholism*. Toronto: Addiction Research Foundation.

Blume, E. M. (1966). Psychoanalytic views of alcoholism: A review. *Quarterly Journal of Studies on Alcohol, 27,* 259–299.

Brickman, B. (1988). Psychoanalysis and substance abuse: Toward a more effective approach. *Journal of the American Academy of Psychoanalysis, 16,* 359–379.

Coleman, J. C., Butcher, J. N., & Carson, R. C. (1980). *Abnormal psychology and modern life* (6th ed.). Glenview, IL: Scott, Foresman.

Cox, W. M. (1985). Personality correlates of substance abuse. In M. Galizio & S. A. Maisto (Eds.), *Determinants of substance abuse*. New York: Plenum Press.

Freud, S. (1953). The interpretation of dreams. In J. Strachey (Ed. and Trans.),

The standard edition of the complete psychological works of Sigmund Freud (Vols. 4 & 5). London: Hogarth Press. (Original work published 1900)

Gabbard, G. O. (1999). Psychodynamic therapy in an age of neuroscience. *Harvard Mental Health Letter, 15,* 4–5.

Gay, P. (1988). *Freud: A life for our time.* New York: Norton.

George, R. L., & Cristiani, T. S. (1995). *Counseling: Theory and practice.* Needham Heights, MA: Allyn & Bacon.

Greenblatt, J. C. (1998). Practitioners should be aware of co-occurring marijuana use and delinquent/depressive behaviors among youth. (Data from the Substance Abuse and Mental Health Services Administration, Office of Applied Studies). University of Maryland—Center for Substance Abuse Research. *CESAR FAX, 7,* 1.

Hall, C. S., & Lindzey, G. (1978). *Theories of personality* (3rd ed.). New York: Wiley.

Holdcraft, L. C., Iacono, W. G., & McGue, M. K. (1998). Antisocial personality disorder and depression in relation to alcoholism: A community-based sample. *Journal of Studies on Alcohol, 59,* 222–226.

Horney, K. (1967). *Feminine psychology.* New York: Norton.

Khantzian, E. J. (1980). An ego/self theory of substance dependence: A contemporary psychoanalytic perspective. In D. J. Lettieri, M. Sayers, & H. W. Pearson (Eds.), *Theories on drug abuse: Selected contemporary perspectives* (DHHS Publication No. ADM84-967). Washington, DC: U.S. Government Printing Office.

Khantzian, E. J., Halliday, K. S., & McAuliffe, W. E. (1990). *Addiction and the vulnerable self: Modified dynamic group therapy for substance abusers.* New York: Guilford Press.

Kinney, J., & Leaton, G. (1987). *Loosening the grip: A handbook of alcohol information* (3rd ed.). St. Louis: Times Mirror/Mosby.

Leeds, J., & Morgenstern, J. (1996). Psychoanalytic theories of substance abuse. In F. Rotgers, D. S. Keller, & J. Morgenstern (Eds.), *Treating substance abuse: Theory and technique.* New York: Guilford Press.

Murphy, S. L., & Khantzian, E. J. (1995). Addiction as a "self-medication" disorder: Application of ego psychology to the treatment of substance abuse. In A. M. Washton (Ed.), *Psychotherapy and substance abuse: A practitioner's handbook.* New York: Guilford Press.

National Institute on Alcohol Abuse and Alcoholism. (1994). *Alcohol and health: Eighth special report to the U.S. Congress* (NIH Publication No. 94-3699). Bethesda, MD: National Institutes of Health.

Regier, D. A., Farmer, M. E., Rae, D. S., Locke, B. Z., Keith, S. J., Judd, L. L., & Goodwin, F. K. (1990). Comorbidity of mental disorders with alcohol and other drug use. Results from the Epidemiologic Catchment Area (ECA) Study. *Journal of the American Medical Association, 264,* 2511–2518.

Ross, H. E., Glaser, F. B., & Germanson, T. (1988). The prevalence of psychiatric disorders in patients with alcohol and drug problems. *Archives of General Psychiatry, 45,* 1023–1031.

Taleff, M. J. (1997). *A handbook to assess and treat resistance in chemical dependency.* Dubuque, Iowa: Kendall/Hunt.

Wallace, J. (1978). Working with the preferred defense structure of the recovering alcoholic. In A. Zimberg, J. Wallace, & S. Blume (Eds.), *Practical approaches to alcoholism psychotherapy*. New York: Plenum Press.

Wurmser, L. (1974). Psychoanalytic considerations of the etiology of compulsive drug use. *Journal of the American Psychoanalytic Association, 22*, 820–843.

Wurmser, L. (1978). *The hidden dimension: Psychodynamics in compulsive drug use*. New York: Aronson.

Wurmser, L. (1980). Drug use as a protective system. In D. J. Lettieri, M. Sayers, & H. W. Pearson, (Eds.), *Theories on drug abuse: Selected contemporary perspectives* (DHHS Publication No. ADM 84-967). Washington, DC: U.S. Government Printing Office.

Yalisove, D. L. (1989). Psychoanalytic approaches to alcoholism and addiction: Treatment and research. *Psychology of Addictive Behaviors, 3*, 107–113.

Zimberg, S. (1978). Principles of alcoholism psychotherapy. In S. Zimberg, J. Wallace, & S. B. Blume (Eds.), *Practical approaches to alcoholism psychotherapy*. New York: Plenum Press.

Zimberg, S., Wallace, J., & Blume, S. B. (Eds.). (1978). *Practical approaches to alcoholism psychotherapy*. New York: Plenum Press.

Conditioning Models
and Approaches
to Contingency Management

The principal aims of "behaviorism" are to elucidate the conditions of human learning and to develop a technology for behavior change. Behaviorists believe that most or all human behavior is learned, including not only adaptive but also maladaptive behavior (e.g., addiction). One of the major premises, then, is that certain fundamental laws (known and unknown) govern the initiation, maintenance, and cessation of human behavior. Alcohol or drug use is considered a behavior that is subject to the same principles of learning as driving a car, typing a letter, or building a house.

Behavioral psychology, for the most part, restricts itself to the study of overt behavior—that is, behavior that is observable and measurable. There is a heavy emphasis on empirical evidence, as behaviorists are interested in building a true science of human behavior. For this reason, they are usually not interested in internal "mentalistic" constructs, such as mental illness, self-esteem, affective states, thoughts, values, personality structure (e.g., the ego), defense mechanisms, or the unconscious. These concepts cannot be directly observed or measured, and there is no way to prove or disprove their existence. It is thus believed that they are not appropriate subjects for scientific inquiry.

The most prominent behaviorist of the 20th century, B. F. Skinner, commented on how use of mentalistic constructs has distorted (in his view) our society's understanding of addiction and other problem behaviors. He did not believe that it is useful to describe persons as immoral, irresponsible, or diseased. According to Skinner (1975):

> When the control exercised by others is thus evaded or destroyed
> (by the individual), only the personal reinforcers are left. The indi-

vidual turns to immediate gratification, possibly through sex or drugs. If he does not need to do much to find food, shelter, and safety, little behavior will be generated. His condition is then described by saying that he is suffering from a lack of values. As Maslow pointed out, valuelessness is variously described as anomie, amorality, anhedonia, rootlessness, emptiness, hopelessness, the lack of something to believe in and be devoted to. These terms all seem to refer to feelings or states of mind, but what are missing are effective reinforcers. Anomie and amorality refer to a lack of the continued reinforcers which induce people to observe rules. Anhedonia, rootlessness, emptiness, and hopelessness point to the absence of reinforcers of all kinds. . . . If people do not work, it is not because they are lazy or shiftless but because they are not paid enough or because either welfare or affluence has made economic reinforcers less effective. . . . If citizens are not law abiding, it is not because they are scofflaws or criminals but because law enforcement has grown lax. . . . If students do not study, it is not because they are not interested but because the standards have been lowered or because subjects taught are no longer relevant to a satisfactory life. (pp. 112–113)

Skinner (1975) noted that individuals do not choose to become addicted to chemicals. Rather, he believed that they are conditioned to engage in frequent drug-taking behavior by a society that is afraid to implement a scientific technology of behavior. In his view, individuals abuse drugs (or alcohol) because they have not been reinforced for engaging in other kinds of constructive behavior.

CONDITIONED BEHAVIOR

Learned behavior is usually classified according to whether it is the result of "respondent conditioning" or "operant conditioning." This distinction is an important one. However, the two types of conditioning do not represent different kinds of learning but, instead, different types of behavior (McKim, 1986). Respondent behavior is under the control of a well-defined stimulus, whereas operant behavior appears voluntary and is not directly elicited by a stimulus situation. Most human behavior falls into the latter category.

Respondent Conditioning

Respondent conditioning is also known as "classical conditioning" or "Pavlovian conditioning." It was the first type of learning to be studied systematically and was first investigated by the great, Russian physiologist Ivan Pavlov. Respondent behavior is reflexive in the sense that it is under the control of well-defined environmental stimuli. Examples of respondent behavior include the following:

1. Blinking in response to a bright light.
2. Pulling one's hand away from a hot stove.
3. Salivating at the sight or smell of food.
4. Perspiring as the result of walking into a hot room.
5. Jerking one's leg forward when struck on the knee with a physician's hammer.

When a dog salivates at the sight of food, the salivation is considered respondent behavior, under the control of the stimulus of food. Pavlov found that if he paired the sight of food with a neutral stimulus, such as a ringing bell, the bell alone would eventually elicit the salivation. Thus, the bell became a conditioned stimulus able to elicit salivation—a strange situation indeed. Figure 4.1 diagrams respondent or Pavlovian conditioning model.

Operant Conditioning

Operant behavior is different from respondent behavior in that operant behavior appears to be voluntary. In most cases it does not seem to be directly elicited, or caused by, a specific stimulus in the environment. Furthermore, operant behavior is conditioned if it is followed by a reinforcer. In other words, operant behaviors are those that are main-

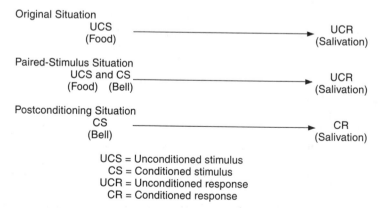

FIGURE 4.1. Model of respondent or Pavlovian conditioning.

tained by events occurring after the behavior, not before it. If a behavior is followed by a reinforcer, the behavior will probably appear again. The subsequent change in rate of behavior is considered "learning."

A "reinforcer" is best defined as any event that increases the probability or rate of a behavior (Miller, 1980). Reinforcers can be any number of things. Some examples include alcohol, drugs, food, sex, verbal praise, money, a good grade, public recognition, and job promotion. Each person finds different things reinforcing. For example, actively drinking alcoholics find alcohol to be a potent reinforcer, whereas recovering alcoholics purposely avoid it as a result of past negative experiences. Furthermore, the potency of a reinforcer is determined by an individual's state of deprivation. For instance, in all probability, a soldier who returns from 6 months of combat duty in a place where no alcohol was available is going to generate much more behavior to obtain a beer than is a civilian who has ready access to alcohol.

The varying effectiveness of alcohol as a reinforcer is further illustrated by the ability of researchers to breed strains of alcohol-craving mice (McKim, 1986). Some strains show a strong fondness for alcohol; others demonstrate a dislike for the beverage. Alcohol-craving mice prefer alcohol to sugar water and will occasionally drink to drunkenness. For these mice, alcohol is a potent reinforcer. They learn new behaviors and engage in high rates of a behavior to continue to get alcohol; in other words, they work for it. Among the mice that do not care for alcohol, the drink cannot be used as a contingency to train them. For this group, alcohol has little reinforcement value.

An important distinction in operant conditioning involves the difference between "positive reinforcement" and "negative reinforcement." In both situations, the rate or probability of a behavior increases. Furthermore, negative reinforcement is not punishment. A negative reinforcement procedure begins with an aversive stimulus; the behavior generated to remove the stimulus results in relief from the noxious stimulus. Thus, in a negative reinforcement procedure, *relief* is the reinforcer. The use of an alarm clock is a good example of negative reinforcement. The alarm sounds until someone awakens to shut it off. The reinforcer in this case is silence (i.e., relief from noise), and the behavior change is reaching to turn off the alarm.

With addictive behavior, the classic example of negative reinforcement is withdrawal sickness. In alcoholic withdrawal, the symptoms include tremors, irritability, restlessness, anxiety, insomnia, and cravings. Alcoholics expect these symptoms to disappear almost immediately upon their taking a drink. Thus, drinking (in the case of chronic alcoholism with the presence of an abstinence syndrome) is reinforced by relief from the withdrawal symptoms. Notice that the reinforcer is not alcohol or withdrawal itself but, rather, *relief from with-*

drawal. In cases of alcohol dependence in which there is no withdrawal sickness (among teens, young adults, binge drinkers, etc.), drinking behavior is contingent upon positive reinforcers, such as euphoria and enhanced sociability.

Punishment can be defined as any event that decreases the probability or rate of a behavior (Miller, 1980). Again, punishment and negative reinforcement have opposite effects: The former decreases behavior; the latter increases it. Punishers can also be any number of things or events. They can include a "dirty" look, ignoring a comment, or even physical abuse. Clearly, people employ punishers quite often in their family, work, and social settings.

In regard to substance use and punishment, it is known that some people have particularly negative physical or psychological reactions to small amounts of alcohol or a drug. The examples of the person who becomes flushed, dizzy, and nauseated after one drink and the person who becomes extremely paranoid and panicky after a couple of puffs on a joint of marijuana illustrate this point. Such persons are essentially punished for substance use. The punisher (i.e., sickness or a paranoid panic attack) decreases the probability of future substance use. In cases such as these, there is little likelihood that substance dependencies will develop.

Generalization and Discrimination

Generalization and discrimination are two types of learning that are influenced by environmental stimuli as well as by reinforcement. Generalization can be defined as the "tendency to perform a response in a new setting because of the setting's similarity to the one in which the response was learned, with the likelihood of the response's occurring being proportional to the degree of similarity between settings" (Mehr, 1988, p. 153). For example, let us imagine that a cocaine addict, 4 years into recovery, goes on a business trip to a distant city. After arriving at the airport, he heads to the subway to catch a train for a downtown meeting. While riding on the subway train, he experiences intense cravings for cocaine. The last time he can remember having such an intense desire for cocaine was when he used to snort the drug with his buddies while riding the trains in his hometown. He essentially generalized cocaine cravings (and use) to all subway trains.

By contrast, discrimination can be defined as the "learning of different responses to two or more similar but distinct stimuli because of the different consequences associated with each one" (Mehr, 1988, p. 153). The failure to discriminate contributes to many relapses during early recovery. For example, let us suppose that an addict is discharged from an inpatient treatment facility. He has many new friends that he has met through Narcotics Anonymous (NA), and many old friends with whom he used to get high. He insists that he can be with his old friends and not "pick up" or "slip." Unfortunately, he soon relapses but gradually learns that his old friends represent a stimulus condition that he must avoid. This gradual recognition is the process of "discriminative learning." This learning process is also important for understanding the dynamics of controlled drinking—an issue discussed later in the chapter.

Extinction

Another conditioning principle is "extinction," which is the absence or removal of a reinforcer. With regard to substance abuse, abstinence and treatment represent extinction procedures. Relapse can be considered evidence of an incomplete extinction procedure. The sheer availability of alcohol and drugs, and their ever-present potential for producing euphoria, make complete extinction of drug-seeking behavior difficult. Thus, from a behavioral perspective, a return to drug use (i.e., relapse) is always a possibility.

INITIATION OF ALCOHOL AND DRUG USE

From a behavioristic perspective, the initiation of substance use is related to three factors: (1) availability, (2) lack of reinforcement for alternative behavior, and (3) lack of punishment for experimenting with alcohol or another drug. Clearly, use cannot begin if a substance is not available; this simple fact is the basis for the federal government's drug interdiction efforts. The second factor, lack of reinforcement, becomes operative when socially approved behavior (e.g., studying, working, attending church, and family recreational activities) that could take the place of drug-using behaviors is not sufficiently rewarded. In such cases, individuals are likely to engage in drug-taking behavior, which is accompanied by more potent or alluring reinforcers. Third, and perhaps most important, many people who experiment with a substance do not receive immediate punishment. As a result of first use, few people get arrested, suffer an adverse physical reaction, lose a job, fail an exam, or receive harsh criticism from peers. The negative consequences of drug use are almost always delayed, sometimes for years or even decades (particularly with alcoholism and nicotine addiction). Not only are people unpunished immediately; they are usually quickly reinforced by euphoria and peer acceptance. Initiation, then, is the result of the combination of availability, reinforcers, and punishers in the social environment.

ADDICTION

McAuliffe and Gordon (1980) have offered the following behavioral definition of "addiction": an operantly conditioned response whose tendency becomes stronger as a function of the quality, number, and size of reinforcements that follows each drug ingestion. Each addict experiences his/her own set of multiple reinforcers. According to McAuliffe and Gordon (1980), there are three classes of reinforcers: (1) euphoria, (2) social variables, and (3) elimination of withdrawal sickness. The combination of these effects vary for each individual and each type of drug. For example, elimination of withdrawal sickness may be a more potent reinforcer for the heroin addict than for the PCP addict. In addition, relief from withdrawal may be a stronger reinforcer for the physically dependent heroin addict than for one who is not physically dependent.

Euphoria is also important. For example, the euphoric consequence of cocaine ingestion may be more important to the maintenance of cocaine addiction than the euphoria that results from drinking alcohol. Furthermore, "peer acceptance," a social variable, may be a more potent reinforcer for the adolescent marijuana smoker than for the 40-year-old marijuana user. Thus, the specific combination of reinforcing effects is what "drives" each addiction.

For behaviorists, the inability to refrain from using a drug (i.e., loss of control) merely indicates that a sufficient history of reinforcement has probably been acquired to impel a high rate of use (McAuliffe & Gordon, 1980). Behaviorists do not believe that there is a single point at which an individual suddenly becomes "addicted." Rather, the word "addiction" is simply a term used to describe an operantly conditioned behavior that occurs at a relatively high rate. The individual's addiction develops gradually and varies continually in response to drug-related contingencies. An "addict" is merely a person who engages in a high rate of drug use, and who has a sufficient history of reinforced drug taking to outweigh the more socially acceptable rewards of life (career accomplishments, family interests, marital sex, material possessions, etc.).

RELATIONSHIP BETWEEN ADDICTION AND PHYSICAL DEPENDENCE

For behaviorists, physical dependence on a drug is neither a necessary nor a sufficient condition for the development of an addiction (McAuliffe & Gordon, 1980). This is consistent with criteria of the fourth edition of the *Diagnostic and Statistical Manual of Mental Disorders* (DSM-IV; American Psychiatric Association, 1994). Physical dependence is simply a side effect of using certain classes of drugs at a high rate over a sufficient amount of time. It merely sets the stage for experiencing withdrawal sickness and its relief. The relief is but one possible reinforcing effect that maintains addictive behavior. Euphoria and peer acceptance are equally potent, and in some cases, more potent, reinforcers. Again, this is especially true of drugs that do not produce physical dependence or do so only minimally (hallucinogens, inhalants, marijuana, etc.)

It may be readily apparent that some addictions are not driven by the reinforcing effects of relief from withdrawal sickness (e.g., marijuana dependence). However, it should also be pointed out that physical dependence can exist in the absence of addiction. The most common example of physical dependence in the absence of addiction involves hospitalized patients recovering from surgery. Such patients are sometimes administered large doses of narcotic analgesics after surgery, over an extended period. When the patients are gradually weaned off the drug, they may experience some symptoms of withdrawal (irritability, diarrhea, headache, muscle ache, depression, etc.). However, because they are not "addicted," they typically do not engage in drug-seeking behavior or verbalize cravings for the drug. In fact, in many cases they do not even recognize the symptoms as those of withdrawal but simply as those of recovery from surgery.

Even in heroin addiction, relief from withdrawal is sometimes not an important reinforcing effect. Three situations involving heroin addicts illustrate the distinction between addiction and physical dependence:

1. Some heroin addicts have been described as having "ice cream habits" because when administered a narcotic antagonist, they are discovered to have no physical dependence on the drug (Ray & Ksir, 1999). They claim they cannot stop using heroin, even though they want to, and are adamant about continuing their use despite the known risks.

2. Many compulsive, long-term heroin addicts go for months, sometimes even years, without ever interrupting their use long enough to experience withdrawal. This pattern indicates that physical dependence (i.e., relief from withdrawal) is not the reinforcer driving their addictive behavior.

3. Many detoxified heroin addicts continue to report that they still feel addicted to the drug many months after last using it. They often continue to express strong desires for heroin.

CESSATION AND RELAPSE

From a behavioristic perspective, cessation of alcohol and drug abuse occurs when the punishers that follow ingestion become less temporally remote (McAuliffe & Gordon, 1980). The immediate severity of punishment effects gradually builds over months or years of abusing a drug. Typically, alcoholics and addicts experience repeated brushes with the law, including perhaps longer and longer jail sentences; sources of money becoming scarce, jobs becoming harder to find and keep, family members and friends becoming increasingly hostile, medical problems worsening, and so on. As these contingencies become more closely linked in time to the chemical use, its rate gradually, or in some cases abruptly, ceases.

Behaviorists expect relapses to occur at relatively high rates among persons in early recovery because drugs are widely available in our society, and because they always retain their ability to cause euphoria. Combined with these factors is the reality that many of the rewards (i.e., reinforcement) that come with abstinence and recovery are delayed. In fact, some abstinence-related reinforcers come only after months or years of sobriety. For example, to regain the trust and respect of family members and coworkers, addicts may have to maintain a year or more of abstinence. Some cocaine addicts have not been able to stabilize their financial affairs for years as a result of the debt they have incurred while using the drug. Drug dealers may not be able to make progress toward life or career goals because of jail time, or simply as a result of their convictions. Whenever reinforcers such as these are delayed to some distant point in the future, their effectiveness in maintaining behavior consistent with recovery is diminished. For these reasons, relapses are always a possibility, especially during early stages of recovery.

BLOOD ALCOHOL DISCRIMINATION

Many alcohol abuse prevention and early intervention programs promote the notion of "sensible" drinking. Controlled-drinking treatment programs for alcoholics essentially teach the same thing. That is, they attempt to arrange contingencies in such a way as to support moderate, nonproblematic consumption. Both types of programs have come under attack from government officials and some proponents of the disease model, who claim that approaches advocating "sensible" or "responsible" drinking are ineffective and dangerous (Harding, 1989). This would particularly be the case if humans were unable to discriminate between particular blood alcohol levels (BALs). In other words, if individuals (nonalcoholic or alcoholic) cannot reasonably estimate their BALs, then efforts aimed at teaching moderate drinking cannot rely on strategies using *perceived intoxication* as a cue to stop or slow one's drinking. A number of studies have examined this issue.

Silverstein, Nathan, and Taylor (1974) attempted to determine whether alcoholics could learn to identify cues linked with intoxication. Using four male alcoholic inpatients who had a strong desire to learn how to control their drinking, the researchers asked the subjects to estimate their BALs on the basis of internal cues. Essentially, they were instructed to link different feelings and sensations with differing BALs. The subjects were initially given no external (accurate) feedback about their performance. As the study progressed, the alcoholic subjects' ability to discriminate between BALs improved as they received more external feedback from the researchers. However, during subsequent training in which the external cues (feedback) were removed, the accuracy of their BAL estimations declined.

The results of Silverstein et al.'s (1974) study indicated that alcoholics could not use internal cues to discriminate between BALs. Subsequent research was conducted with nonalcoholic subjects to determine whether they could rely on internal cues to estimate their BALs and, if so, whether their estimation accuracy could be maintained by internal cues, external cues, or both, subsequent to training. The findings revealed that nonalcoholics were able to use both internal and external cues to estimate BALs. Thus, it appeared that nonalcoholics differed in an important way from alcoholics (Huber, Karlin, & Nathan, 1976).

Several subsequent studies that compared the relative ability of nonalcoholics and alcoholics to estimate their BALs obtained findings consistent with those of the early studies (Brick, 1990). These findings suggest that the differing levels of tolerance among the two groups account for the differences in ability to estimate BALs. Apparently, as a result of chronic, heavy alcohol use and the resultant increase in tolerance to the drug, alcoholics lose the ability to monitor their BALs via internal cues (i.e., feelings and sensations). It seems that chronic alcoholics receive weak, poorly defined, or perhaps nonexistent internal cues as a result of drinking low to moderate amounts of alcohol.

This inability to recognize BALs has important implications for alcoholics in controlled-drinking treatment programs. It suggests that alcoholics must rely exclusively on external cues, such as body weight and number of drinks, to determine their level of intoxication. Those who insist that they can tell when they have had "too much" are likely to be in error (and drunk), which also helps explain why problem drinkers (with high tolerance) insist that they have not had too much to drink and are all right. To the outside observer, they demonstrate noticeable impairment (lack of coordination, slurring of speech, etc.), but internally they lack the cues that can provide this feedback. These findings also suggest that prevention efforts advocating "responsible" drinking, such as those on college campuses, must rely on explicit messages to define an appropriate number of drinks to be consumed at a social event.

BEHAVIORAL TOLERANCE

In regard to alcohol and drug abuse, the term "tolerance" has been defined "either as the decreased effectiveness of a drug which results from the continued presence of the drug in the body, or, the necessity of increasing the dose of a drug in order to maintain its effectiveness after repeated administration" (McKim, 1986, p. 53). Alcoholics and addicts are typically described as having high tolerance for their substance of choice. Those unfamiliar with alcoholism are often surprised to learn that many alcoholics report drinking a quart or more of liquor a day.

Traditionally, tolerance has been thought to be the result of bodily adaption to the drug at the cellular level. That is, the cells of the body, after chronic exposure, adapt to or compensate for the presence of the drug. This compensation explains how alcoholics can drink a six-pack of beer and walk without an impaired gait or without slurring their speech.

Behavioral researchers have determined that learning also plays an important role in the development of tolerance (Brick, 1990). It appears that both biological factors (i.e., cellular adaptation) and nonbiological factors create tolerance. Furthermore, it appears that behavioral tolerance is learned both by respondent (Pavlovian) conditioning and operant conditioning procedures. Shepard Siegel pioneered the Pavlovian model of tolerance (see Figure 4.2). Siegel (1982) hypothesized that drug tolerance is partially conditioned to the environment in which the drug is normally used. If a drug is administered in the presence of usual cues (i.e., the normal environment), the drug effect will be somewhat diminished. In behavioristic jargon, "the drug effect is reduced by these anticipatory conditioned compensatory responses" (Brick, 1990, p. 178). Over time, as a drug is used repeatedly in the same environment, the diminishing effects increase in magnitude. This is the process of building tolerance.

As Figure 4.2 illustrates, after the unconditioned stimulus (pharmacological action of the drug) has been paired with the conditioned stimulus (the normal drug-using environment), placebo and novel stimulus conditions evoke distinctly different responses. Notice that in the placebo condition the usual environmental cues alone will elicit (at least for a while) the drug "high." Also notice that if a drug is used in a novel setting, much of the conditioned tolerance will be lost. In such cases, gross intoxication (alcohol), panic reactions (marijuana, PCP, LSD), and even overdose (heroin) may occur. McKim's (1986) description in Box 4.1 of an experiment by Siegel and his colleagues illustrates this point.

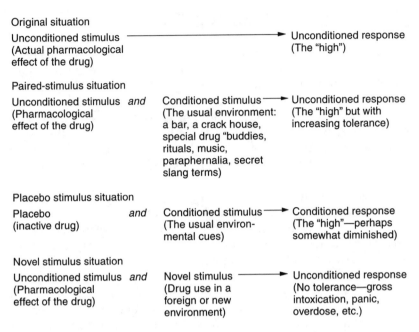

Original situation

Unconditioned stimulus ────────────────────▶ Unconditioned response
(Actual pharmacological   (The "high")
effect of the drug)

Paired-stimulus situation

Unconditioned stimulus *and*   Conditioned stimulus ─▶ Unconditioned response
(Pharmacological   (The usual environment: (The "high" but with
effect of the drug)   a bar, a crack house,   increasing tolerance)
                                special drug "buddies,
                                rituals, music,
                                paraphernalia, secret
                                slang terms)

Placebo stimulus situation

Placebo   *and*   Conditioned stimulus ─▶ Conditioned response
(inactive drug)   (The usual environ-   (The "high"—perhaps
                                mental cues)   somewhat diminished)

Novel stimulus situation

Unconditioned stimulus *and*   Novel stimulus ────────▶ Unconditioned response
(Pharmacological   (Drug use in a   (No tolerance—gross
effect of the drug)   foreign or new   intoxication, panic,
                                environment)   overdose, etc.)

FIGURE 4.2. Pavlovian model of conditioned tolerance.

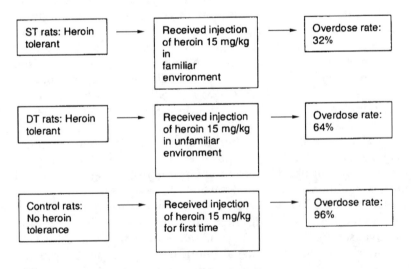

| ST rats: Heroin tolerant | ─▶ | Received injection of heroin 15 mg/kg in familiar environment | ─▶ | Overdose rate: 32% |

| DT rats: Heroin tolerant | ─▶ | Received injection of heroin 15 mg/kg in unfamiliar environment | ─▶ | Overdose rate: 64% |

| Control rats: No heroin tolerance | ─▶ | Received injection of heroin 15 mg/kg for first time | ─▶ | Overdose rate: 96% |

To some degree, drug tolerance is associated with the environment. Tolerance can disappear (to various degrees) if a drug is used in an unfamiliar environment.

FIGURE 4.3. A diagram of Siegel's rat experiment.

BOX 4.1. The Heroin Overdose Puzzle

One of the greatest risks of being a heroin addict is death from heroin overdose. Each year about one percent of all heroin addicts in the United States die from an overdose of heroin despite having developed a fantastic tolerance to the effects of the drug. In a non-tolerant person the estimated lethal dose of heroin may range from 200 to 500 mg, but addicts have tolerated doses as high as 1800 mg without even being sick (Brecher, 1972). No doubt, some overdoses are a result of mixing heroin with other drugs, but many appear to result from a sudden loss of tolerance. Addicts have been killed one day by a dose which was readily tolerated the day before. An explanation for this sudden loss of tolerance has been suggested by Shepard Siegel of McMaster University, and his associates, Riley Hinson, Marvin Krank, and Jane McCully.

Siegel reasoned that the tolerance to heroin was partially conditioned to the environment where the drug was normally administered. If the drug is consumed in a new setting, much of the conditioned tolerance will disappear and the addict will be more likely to overdose. To test this theory Siegel and associates ran the following experiment [see Figure 4.3].

Rats were given daily intravenous injections for 30 days. The injections were either a dextrose placebo or heroin and they were given in either the animal colony room or a different room where there was a constant white noise. The drug and the placebo were given on alternate days and the drug condition always corresponded with a particular environment so that for some rats, the heroin was always administered in the white noise room and the placebo was always given in the colony. For other rats the heroin was always given in the colony and the placebo was always given in the white noise room. Another group of rats served as a control: these were injected in different rooms on alternate dates, but were only injected with the dextrose and had no experience with heroin at all.

All rats were then injected with a large dose of heroin: 15.0 mg/kg. The rats in one group were given the heroin in the same room where they had previously been given heroin. (This was labeled the ST group.) The other rats, the DT group, were given the heroin in the room where they had previously been given the placebo.

Siegel found that 96 percent of the control group died, show-
continued

continued from page 121
ing the lethal effect of the heroin in non-tolerant animals. Rats in the DT group who received heroin were partially tolerant, and only 64 percent died. Only 32 percent of the ST rats died, showing that the tolerance was even greater when the overdose test was done in the same environment where the drug previously had been administered [see Figure 4.3].

Siegel suggested that one reason addicts suddenly lose their tolerance could be because they take the drug in a different or unusual environment like the rats in the DT group. Surveys of heroin addicts admitted to hospitals suffering from heroin overdose tend to support this conclusion. Many addicts report that they had taken the near-fatal dose in an unusual circumstance or that their normal pattern was different on that day (Siegel, 1982).

Note. From McKim (1986). Copyright 1986 by Prentice-Hall, Inc. Reprinted by permission.

The operant type of behavioral tolerance occurs in situations in which individuals learn, while intoxicated, to compensate for the deleterious effect of the drug. Animal research provides evidence of this learned tolerance. Campbell and Seiden (1973) trained rats to obtain food on a schedule that provided reinforcement for responding at a low rate (see Figure 4.4).

The rats were injected with amphetamine, which stimulated responding. Because of the schedule of reinforcement that the rats were on, this increased responding meant that they lost reinforcements. For 28 sessions, the researchers gave amphetamine to one group of rats and then immediately placed them in a "Skinner box," where they were continued on the "slow" reinforcement schedule. A second group of rats received the same 28 sessions; however, they received amphetamine injections *after* each training session.

During the course of the experiment, the rats that received amphetamine prior to their training sessions (i.e., Group One rats) were able to gradually obtain more and more reinforcements by learning to respond more slowly (see Figure 4.4). Essentially, they developed tolerance to the effects of amphetamine. The rats in the second group (i.e., those that had received amphetamine after their training sessions) were then pretreated with amphetamine and tested on the same schedule as before. These rats received very little reinforcement. They essentially had no tolerance in relation to the task of obtaining food, even though they had received the same amount of amphetamine during the course of the experiment. The only difference between the groups was the timing of the amphetamine injection (before or after training). This indicates that cellular adaptation had little to do with the development of tolerance in this case, since both groups received identical doses of amphetamine (Campbell & Seiden, 1973).

Among humans, these findings suggest that cellular adaptation does not, by itself, entirely account for tolerance. This may partially explain why intoxicated teens are much more likely to get into automobile accidents than are equally intoxicated adults: The adult drinkers may have had many more years of "practice" at drunk driving than

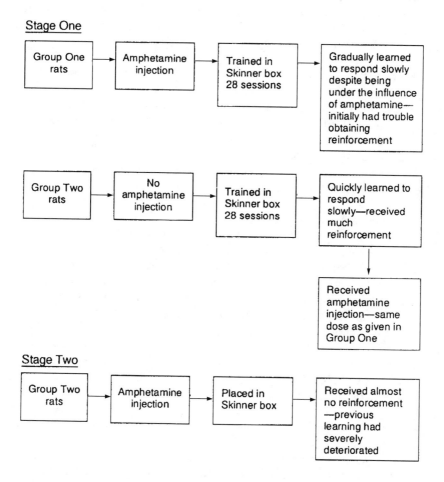

FIGURE 4.4. Tolerance via operant conditioning. This type of tolerance occurs in situations where subjects, while intoxicated, learn to compensate for the deleterious effect of a drug.

the young people. In other words, teens may not have learned how to compensate for the effects of alcohol on driving.

PRINCIPLES OF CONTINGENCY MANAGEMENT

The application of learning principles to the helping process is called "behavioral counseling," "behavior therapy," "behavioral contracting," "contingency management," or simply "contingency contracting." Based on the premise that alcohol and drug use (and addiction) are learned, the counselor's role is to assist clients in learning more effective ways of behaving so that clients reach *their* goals. According to Ullman and Krasner (1965), contingency contracting begins with a functional analysis of behavior that asks the following questions:

1. What behavior is maladaptive? Specifically, what behaviors should be increased or decreased?
2. What environmental contingencies currently maintain or support the behavior? As applied to addiction, what are the rewards that maintain the drug use? Are there punishers associated with avoiding use?
3. What environmental changes can be manipulated to alter the behavior?

In behavioral counseling, the development and maintenance of addiction are the same as the development and maintenance of any other behavior. This view has two important implications. First, drug use is not inherently maladaptive; rather, it becomes inappropriate as the result of labels that significant others assign to it. For instance, an alcoholic is simply a person whose drinking behavior has adversely affected a family member, friend, or coworker. The second implication is that drinking or drug use is maintained because other, more adaptive behaviors are not reinforced or not possible. A typical example would include an alcoholic man in early recovery and his nonsupportive wife. As a result of several months of abstinence, the recovering father begins to demonstrate appropriate parenting behavior (e.g., he takes his son fishing and compliments his daughter's cooking), which his wife criticizes. The lack of reinforcement for these new behaviors soon leads him back to drinking.

According to Dustin and George (1973, p. 12), behavioral counseling is based on four assumptions about human nature and the change process. As applied to substance abusers, these assumptions are often questioned by laypeople and mental health professionals who feel that chemical dependence is driven by unique dynamics. The four assumptions of behavioral counseling are as follows:

1. Humans are viewed as being neither good nor bad intrinsically, but as an experiencing organism that has potential for all kinds of behavior.
2. Humans are able to conceptualize and control their own behavior.
3. Humans are able to acquire new behaviors.
4. Humans are able to influence others' behavior as well as to be influenced by others in their own behavior.

Dustin and George (1973) identified three phases of contingency contracting. The first phase can be described as *problem specification.* With empathetic understanding, the counselor assists clients in identifying their problems in behavioral terms. For example, addicts who say that they are lonely and depressed may lack the kind of social skills necessary for meeting someone new. In teaching such skills, the counselor would help identify the necessary stimulus and reinforcing conditions for meeting someone new. The second phase consists of helping clients to *make a commitment to change.* There are many barriers to achieving this, particularly with chemically dependent clients. The use of incentives to generate and maintain motivation for change is critical. Ignoring this phase or giving it little attention is a major reason that clients drop out of counseling or treatment. The third phase is *specifying goals.* Here it is important that the counselor work toward the clients' goals; the counselor should not impose goals on clients.

APPLICATIONS OF CONTINGENCY CONTRACTING

The following discussion shows how contingency contracting has been applied to a number of treatment issues. These include efforts to (1) establish and maintain controlled drinking; (2) initiate and maintain abstinence, and encourage the adoption of recovery behaviors (taking an Antabuse [disulfiram] tablet, attending Alcoholics Anonymous [AA] each day, etc.); (3) promote positive change in a client's vocational, recreational, social, and familial functioning; (4) motivate the reluctant alcoholic to seek treatment; (5) engage a couple in marital therapy; (6) reduce cocaine and other illicit drug use; (7) enhance compliance with methadone maintenance; and (8) manage residential treatment environments.

Controlled Drinking

With a subset of problem drinkers, perhaps 15 to 25%, controlled drinking, managed by contingency contracting, is a viable alternative to abstinence (Miller, 1982). It should be emphasized that controlled drinking is not an effort to encourage recovering alcoholics to "try drinking again." With selected candidates, it is one of many options at the *onset of treatment.*

A large body of empirical evidence suggests that there should be an expansion of the use of controlled drinking in the United States (see Sobell, Wilkinson, & Sobell, 1990). Controlled drinking appears to be a frequent outcome of both moderation-focused and abstinence-focused treatments; Sanchez-Craig and Lei (1986) found that the overwhelming majority of clients with positive outcomes adopted moderation in both goal conditions. Many successful clients benefit from abstinence-oriented treatment but apparently reject its basic goal and practice controlled use instead.

As a treatment strategy, controlled drinking is usually denounced in the United States (Goode, 1993). Yet, in Canada, Britain, and Scandinavian countries it has much greater acceptance (see review in Rosenberg, Melville, Levell, & Hodge, 1994). For instance, a survey of treatment agencies in England, Scotland, and Wales found that about 75% of service providers reported controlled drinking to be an acceptable treatment goal (Rosenberg et al., 1994). About one-half of these providers thought it to be acceptable for 1 to 25% of their clients. The providers most frequently reported that their position on controlled drinking was based on their own professional experience rather than on research or agency policy.

Heather and Robertson (1983) identified six possible advantages of a controlled-drinking strategy:

1. In our society, abstinence from alcohol is deviant behavior. This is unfortunate. However, the stigma and the label of "alcoholic" pose significant adjustment problems for some people.
2. Among some alcoholics, abstinence may lead to overwhelming states of anxiety or depression that are unlikely to be managed in other ways.
3. Sometimes, overall improvement in life functioning does not result from abstinence.
4. In some alcoholics, abstinence is associated with severe psychosocial problems that lead to frequent relapse.
5. Abstinence during treatment rules out the possibility for changes in drinking behavior.

6. The demand placed on alcoholics to abstain deters many from seeking help until their problem is quite severe.

Miller and Hester (1980) designed a model for controlled drinking based on behavioral principles: *behavioral self-control training* (BSCT). With selected candidates, Miller and Hester (1980) demonstrated an effectiveness rate for BSCT of 60 to 80%. In another study, Harris and Miller (1990) reported that 78% of problem drinkers in a self-directed BSCT group and 63% of those in a therapist-directed BSCT group were rated as maintaining improvement 15 months after initiating treatment. The improved group consisted of abstainers (confirmed by collateral reports) and controlled drinkers. The criteria for being classified as "improved" included (1) on average, no more than 20 standard drinks weekly; (2) not exceeding BALs of .08 to .10 on any occasion (verified by collateral reports); and for those who failed to meet the criteria for controlled drinking, (3) succeeding in reducing their weekly alcohol intake by 30% or more (confirmed by collateral reports).

BSCT comprises the following components (Miller & Hester, 1980):

1. A functional analysis of the drinking behavior is conducted. Together, the client and the counselor determine specific and appropriate limits for alcohol consumption; these depend on body weight and safety concerns. Typically, limits for consumption range from two drinks to perhaps four on one occasion.
2. The client monitors and records consumption.
3. Clients are trained to control the rate of their drinking.
4. Self-reinforcement procedures are created to maintain gains.
5. Emphasis is placed on stimulus control training.
6. In place of alcohol, clients are taught a variety of coping skills for obtaining those outcomes they no longer derive from excessive alcohol use.

Numerous studies have demonstrated the effectiveness of BSCT in helping abusive drinkers to control their drinking. Unfortunately, it is probably not possible to apply BSCT to the broad spectrum of alcoholic clients who appear for treatment. In addition to not being appropriate for clients with certain medical conditions (discussed later), it may be ineffective for the large number of coerced clients (those who are more or less "forced" into treatment by employers, family members, the courts, etc.). Such clients often seek treatment to escape even more aversive sanctions and frequently have little interest in learning to modify their drinking behavior. The limited appeal of BSCT among many abusive drinkers is highlighted by the fact that many controlled-drinking studies have found it difficult to recruit clients (Cameron & Spence, 1976; Robertson, Heather, Dzialdowski, Crawford, & Winton, 1986). Harris and Miller (1990) solicited clients in the Albuquerque, New Mexico, metropolitan area for 6 months via the local news media. Despite the fact that the program was advertised as free of charge, they were able to recruit only 34 clients for their BSCT study.

It should be noted that even the proponents of controlled drinking do not believe that it is a viable strategy for most alcoholics (Miller, 1982). Good candidates are generally young, motivated clients who have no biomedical impairment from alcohol abuse. Lewis, Dana, and Blevins (1988) developed criteria for ruling out controlled-drinking candidates. Those who should not attempt it include the following:

1) clients with liver dysfunction, stomach problems, an ulcer, any other disease of the gastrointestinal tract
2) clients who have cardiac problems that would be adversely affected by alcohol
3) clients who have any physical illness or condition that would be negatively affected by alcohol
4) clients who have a diagnosis of alcohol idiosyncratic disorder intoxication (American Psychiatric Association, 1980, p. 132)
5) clients who are committed to abstinence
6) clients who have strong external demands for abstinence
7) female clients who are pregnant or considering pregnancy
8) clients who lose control of their behavior while drinking
9) clients who have been physically addicted to alcohol
10) clients using any medication or drug that is dangerous when combined with alcohol
11) clients who are abstaining from alcohol
12) those people with the following history: over 40, divorced and not in a supportive relationship, out of work, or with a family history of alcoholism
13) clients who have tried a competently administered moderation-oriented treatment and have failed (p. 153)

Contracting for the Initiation and Maintenance of Abstinence

When abstinence has been chosen and initiated, certain behaviors are conducive to the maintenance of what is commonly called "recovery." They include the following:

1. Attending AA/NA meetings.
2. Calling one's sponsor.
3. Reading self-help literature.
4. Getting to work on time.

5. Avoiding "slipping places."
6. Taking Antabuse as prescribed.
7. Socializing with fellow recovering addicts.
8. Practicing relaxation exercises or other coping skills.
9. Attending to one's family responsibilities.

Contingency contracting can be used to help clients initiate and maintain these behaviors and any others found to be conducive to recovery. Reinforcers and punishers are linked to the occurrence and absence of specified behaviors, as outlined in a written contract. Of course, the contract is not legally binding; however, both client and counselor should sign it, and the client should receive a photocopy. Again, it is not something that is forced on a client but something that counselor and client develop together.

Typically, contracts outline the rewards that clients give themselves if they engage in the specified behaviors. For example, if a client attends five AA meetings a week, he/she can go out for dinner on the weekend. If the client fails to make it to five meetings in a particular week, he/she must forgo the restaurant outing. Likewise, a client may decide to "punish" himself for neglecting to take Antabuse on a particular day. Such oversights can be self-penalized by arranging for donations (perhaps $5.00 or $10.00) to be given to a disliked political or religious organization.

A number of important principles are involved in effective contingency contracting. Two of these are the temporal proximity of the reinforcer or punisher to the specified behavior and the potency of the contingency (Miller, 1980). First, in brief, reinforcers and punishers are most effective when they occur immediately after the specified behavior; those that are delayed are generally less effective. Second, individuals differ considerably in regard to rewards and punishers. For instance, ice cream could be a potent reinforcer for some recovering clients but completely ineffective for others. Thus, effective contracts rely on contingencies that have special significance for the particular client.

Stitzer and Bigelow (1978) examined the desirability of reinforcers among a group of methadone maintenance patients ($n = 53$). Using a questionnaire, they found that the methadone "take-home" privilege was the most effective incentive available to methadone maintenance clinics. The second most effective reinforcer among this group was $30.00 per week, followed in descending order of desirability by $20.00 per week, opportunity to self-select methadone dose, fewer urinalyses, availability of a client representative/advocate, elimination of mandatory counseling, a monthly party, and finally the opportunity to play pool.

The Community Reinforcement Approach

Behavioral therapists have recognized that the application of contingency management procedures to isolated aspects of substance abuse is a narrow approach. To enhance the effectiveness of behavioral treatment, Hunt and Azrin (1973) and Azrin (1976) developed a multicomponent treatment strategy that makes reinforcement in the patient's community contingent upon abstinence from alcohol and/or drugs. A system of contingencies is created for four areas of a client's life: vocational, recreational, social, and familial. As long as the client maintains abstinence, the recovering client receives reinforcers in these areas. Typically, the client's significant others are involved in these contingency contracts, and his/her behavior may be shaped as well.

Hunt and Azrin (1973) compared a community reinforcement program to a standard hospital treatment program and found that the former approach produced significantly better patient outcomes over a 6-month period. Compared to patients in the standard hospital program, those in the community reinforcement program spent less time drinking alcohol, were less likely to be unemployed, and were less likely to be readmitted for treatment. In a second study, Azrin (1976) was able to replicate these findings using a 2-year follow-up assessment.

Motivating the Alcoholic to Seek Treatment

Community reinforcement training (CRT) has been applied to the problem of motivating the violent, alcoholic husband to seek treatment (Sisson & Azrin, 1993). The focus of the training is the wife of the alcoholic. There were four objectives to the CRT program: (1) reduce physical abuse to the wife, (2) encourage sobriety in the husband, (3) increase the likelihood that he would seek treatment, and (4) teach her to assist in the treatment process. The basic premise of the program was that family members learn, by negative reinforcement, to personally avoid the negative consequences of the drinker's behavior. In the alcoholic family, the aversive stimuli are anticipated negative events such as the alcoholic losing his job, obvious drunkenness at a public event, or even physical brutality. From a behavioral perspective, spouses (typically wives) engage in a variety of behaviors to escape from these consequences. These actions are thought not to be an effort so much to protect the alcoholic but to protect self.

The CRT program emphasizes the didactic training of specific skills (Sisson & Azrin, 1993). Wives are taught to be nice to their husbands when they avoid alcohol. They are coached to talk about those topics their husbands enjoy. This is often difficult for wives to carry out because of built-up resentment over past events. A wife is taught how to tell her husband that she likes him sober. The instruction guides her to not be pleasant when her husband is drinking, and not to allow him to escape the consequences of drunkenness, if possible. She also learns to recognize the series of events that lead up to a violent episode, as well as ways to prevent it. Finally, she is taught to take advantage of her husband's saying he would like to cut down or stop drinking. When this happens, she is prepared to act immediately. In the CRT program, the couple would be seen by a counselor the next day.

Before the husband actually begins treatment, the wife is "prepped" to participate in an "Antabuse contract" with her husband (Sisson & Azrin, 1993). The following is explained to the wife:

> "When he comes into counseling we are going to want him to take a pill called Antabuse. Antabuse is a small white pill that, if taken daily, prevents an individual from drinking even small amounts of alcohol. If a person drinks on Antabuse, they become violently ill. An important characteristic of Antabuse that can really help you is that once your husband is taking Antabuse regularly, even if he decides to stop taking it and go back to drinking, he can't for approximately 5 to 14 days because it stays in his system. We'll set up a procedure where you dissolve the pill in a small amount of water and watch him take it. You will know far ahead of time if he's going to drink so you won't have to worry daily if he is going to drink and become violent again. In addition, we have marriage counseling to help you learn to communicate better, and we have a job program to help your husband find a better job." (Sisson & Azrin, 1993, p. 41)

Once in counseling, the couple rehearses a procedure for administering the Antabuse on a daily basis. In addition, the couple practices "Antabuse refusal" procedures in preparation for the possibility that the husband will balk at taking the medication sometime in the future.

In an evaluation of CRT, Sisson and Azrin (1986) found that the program was superior to traditional counseling that relied on Al-Anon. Training of the nonalcoholic family members resulted in a 50% reduction in drinking before the alcoholic entered treatment. The CRT program was much more likely to result in the alcoholic initiating treatment than the traditional approach. Furthermore, abstinence from alcohol was significantly greater for the husbands whose wives received reinforcement training.

Behavioral Marital Therapy for Alcoholism

Recent research suggests that behavioral marital therapy is an effective way to treat married alcoholics (Noel & McCrady, 1993). Investigation into the role of spouse involvement in alcoholism found that the optimal treatment approach has three components: (1) behavioral treatment for the alcoholic, (2) interventions for the spouse to alter behavior that trigger or reinforce drinking, and (3) behavioral marital therapy.

Behavioral treatment for the alcoholic begins with a functional assessment of the alcoholic's drinking behavior and identification of the alcohol use goal. Noel and McCrady (1993) believe that although abstinence is the most realistic goal for most couples, it should not be imposed on them. However, they do request that couples establish an initial period of abstinence—usually 6 months. If reduced drinking is the long-term goal, the couple is asked to specify the parameters of controlled alcohol use. The aims of the behavioral treatment are to teach both the alcoholic and the spouse to (1) control the stimuli that provoke drinking urges and consumption, (2) rearrange the contingencies that prompt drinking, (3) restructure unproductive thoughts, and (4) develop alternatives to drinking.

The spouse intervention also uses stimulus control, contingency management, cognitive restructuring, and alternatives to drinking. Only here they are used to modify those behaviors that trigger or reinforce the spouse's drinking. Noel and McCrady (1993) indicate that cognitive restructuring is especially helpful for teaching the nonalcoholic spouse how to reinforce behavior that supports abstinence and when to ignore drinking behavior or be less alarmed by its consequences for self.

Behavioral marital therapy seeks to improve the couple's ability to communicate and to enhance the relationship. Cognitive restructuring is used here. In addition, the therapy helps couples plan for fun, communicate their needs better, negotiate conflict, and solve problems.

Compared to other forms of alcoholism treatment involving spouses, behavioral marital therapy has better outcomes (Noel & McCrady, 1993). The approach produces increased marital stability and satisfaction and reduced drinking behavior. There was even evidence that after the 1-year follow-up, couples continued to improve even though active treatment had ended.

Behavioral Treatment for Cocaine Dependence

A good illustration of behavioral treatment comes from a study that combined contingency management procedures with the community reinforcement approach. It involved the treatment of cocaine addicts in an outpatient setting (Higgins et al., 1991). The investigation compared the efficacy of behavioral treatment to that of a traditional Twelve-Step drug counseling program. A total of 28 patients participated in the study. The first 13 cocaine-dependent patients were offered the behavioral treatment program; all 13 accepted it. The following 15 patients were offered the Twelve-Step drug counseling program. The authors note that 3 of the 15 patients refused this program option.

The two treatment regimens were quite different, and the investigators describe each in detail. In the behavioral program, patients and therapists jointly selected material reinforcers (Higgins et al., 1991). The goal of the behavioral program was specifically to achieve abstinence from cocaine. The program's contingencies pertained only to cocaine use. Urine specimens were collected four times a week, and patients were breathalyzed at these times as well; however, patients were not penalized for positive test results for drugs other than cocaine. The patients were informed of their urine test results immediately after providing their specimens.

The urine specimens testing negative for cocaine metabolites were rewarded with points that were recorded on vouchers and given to the patient (Higgins et al., 1991). Each point was worth 15 cents. Money was never given directly to patients; rather, staff members actually made the purchases and gave the items to the patients. The first negative urine specimen earned 10 points (i.e., $1.50). The second specimen was worth 15 points ($2.25). The third one earned 20 points ($3.00). The value of each subsequent negative urine specimen increased by 5 points. Furthermore, to bolster the probability of continuous abstinence from cocaine, patients were rewarded with a $10.00 bonus each time they provided four consecutive negative urine specimens. Patients who remained continuously abstinent throughout the entire 12-week treatment program earned points worth $1,038.00, or $12.35 per day.

When the patient tested positive for cocaine or failed to provide a specimen, the value of the vouchers dropped back to 10 points (i.e., $1.50). Items that had previously been purchased did not have to be returned. Higgins et al. (1991) report that the items purchased were "quite diverse and included ski-lift passes, fishing licenses, camera equipment, bicycle equipment, and continuing education materials" (p. 1220). In the program, counselors retained the right to veto purchases. Purchases were approved only if their use was consistent with treatment goals.

The community reinforcement procedures focused on four broad issues: (1) reciprocal relationship counseling, (2) identification of the antecedents and consequences of cocaine use, (3) employment counseling, and (4) development of recreational activities. These issues were addressed in twice-weekly 1-hour counseling sessions throughout the 12-week program. The emphasis appeared to be placed on the first issue, relationship counseling. Eight of the 13 patients in the behavioral program participated in reciprocal relationship counseling. This counseling consisted of procedures "for instructing people how to negotiate for positive changes in their relationship" (p. 1220). The authors describe this process as follows:

> To integrate the community reinforcement approach and contingency management procedures, the patient's significant other was telephoned immediately following each urinalysis test and informed of the results. If the specimen was negative for cocaine, the spouse, friends, or relative engaged in positive activities with the patients that had been agreed upon beforehand. If the result was positive for cocaine use, he or she refrained from the agreed upon positive activities but offered the patient assistance in dealing with difficulties in achieving abstinence. (Higgins et al., 1991, p. 1220)

The Twelve-Step drug treatment consisted of either twice-weekly 2-hour group therapy sessions or once-weekly group sessions combined with 1-hour individual therapy sessions (Higgins et al., 1991). In both formats, the Twelve Steps of NA were emphasized. The patients were informed that cocaine addiction was a treatable but incurable disease. They were required to attend at least one self-help meeting a week and to have a sponsor by the final week of treatment. The counseling sessions provided both supportive and confrontive therapy as well as didactic lectures and videos on vital recovery topics. In the ninth week of treatment, attempts were made to involve family members in the treatment process. Finally, aftercare plans based on Twelve-Step principles were created in the latter weeks of treatment.

After 12 weeks, the two groups (i.e., behavioral treatment vs. Twelve-Step drug counseling) were compared on a variety of outcomes. Across all these measures, the patients in the behavioral treatment showed better outcomes than those in the Twelve-Step group (Higgins et al., 1991). For example, 11 of the 13 patients in the behavioral treatment completed the 12-week program, compared to just 5 of 12 in the Twelve-Step treatment. In the behavioral treatment group, one patient dropped out at week 9 and returned to cocaine use, and the other one had to be admitted to an inpatient unit because of "bingeing." The seven unsuccessful patients in the Twelve-Step treatment terminated for the following reasons: (1) terminated for lack of regular attendance; (2) refused group counseling; (3) refused to abstain from marijuana; (4) did not return after being denied a prescription for antianxiety medication; (5) following a relapse; entered inpatient rehabilitation; (6) decided no longer needed treatment; and (7) murdered.

Patients in behavioral treatment were also more likely than those in the Twelve-Step treatment to have longer periods of continuous abstinence from cocaine (Higgins et al., 1991). Of 13 behavior therapy patients, 10 achieved 4-week periods of continuous abstinence; of the Twelve-Step patients, only 3 of 12 did the same. Furthermore, 6 of the behavioral therapy patients achieved 8-week periods of continuous abstinence, whereas none of the Twelve-Step patients accomplished the same. In the behavioral treatment group, 92% of all collected urine specimens were cocaine free, whereas 78% were "clean" in the Twelve-Step group. This occurred even though many more urine specimens were collected from the behavioral treatment group ($n = 552$) than the Twelve-Step group ($n = 312$).

Interpretation of the Higgins et al. (1991) study has to be qualified by several limitations of the investigation. First, the sample of patients was small ($n = 25$), and all were Caucasian. Second, it is not clear how such a contrived system of contingencies would work over an extended period (6 months or longer). Third, the behavioral treatment focused narrowly on cocaine abstinence and did not address other drug and alcohol use. Fourth, it is difficult to imagine widespread public and/or government support for behavioral treatment programs that pay patients for not using illegal drugs.

With these limitations in mind, the Higgins et al. study (and other behavioral investigations like it) should cause us to reconsider some popularly held notions about the nature of substance dependence and how to treat it. First, the findings indicate that reinforcers can be found to compete with cocaine's intoxicating effects. The popular perception is that cocaine is so reinforcing that food, sex, and all other sources of reinforcement are given up by the addict; the Higgins et al. study shows that money can be an effective alternative reward. Second, the findings suggest that polydrug abusers need not be required to stop use of all drugs at the same time. Contrary to traditional drug treatment philosophy, perhaps it is possible, even preferable, to work on eliminating use of one drug at a time. Finally, the Higgins et al. study demonstrates how important incentives and anticipated benefits are in motivating clients to adopt and maintain abstinence. It appears that many clients drop out of traditional Twelve-Step programs in the early stages (i.e., the first 3 months) because they either do not receive or do not anticipate receiving significant rewards for staying in treatment. There is a vital need to provide incentives to those beginning treatment.

Enhancing Compliance with Methadone Maintenance

Methadone is a relatively long-lasting synthetic opiate that prevents opiate withdrawal symptoms for 24 to 36 hours (National Institute on Drug Abuse, 1987). In proper doses, methadone does not produce sedation or euphoria and therefore has been used for several decades as a treatment for heroin addiction. Though there are positive outcomes to methadone maintenance (Mueller & Wyman, 1997), one common problem is that many clients continue to use a variety of illicit drugs while receiving methadone from a clinic (National Institute on Drug Abuse, 1987).

Contingency contracting has been found to be an effective approach to this problem. A variety of contingencies have been used to increase the rate at which methadone clients produce drug-free urine samples. Money and program privileges have been used as positive reinforcers (e.g., Stitzer, Bigelow, & Liebson, 1980). Aversive consequences, such as contracting for the termination of methadone treatment, also have been found to be effective in reducing positive urine samples (Dolan, Black, Penk, Robinowitz, & DeFord, 1985). Another effective approach has been to make access to methadone maintenance contingent upon cocaine-free urines during the initial phase of treatment (Kidorf & Stitzer, 1993).

The combination of a "take-home" incentive (a positive reinforcer) and a "split-dosing" contingency (an aversive consequence) appears to boost the rate of drug-free urine samples among chronic polysubstance abusers who do not comply with conventional methadone treatment (Kidorf & Stitzer, 1996). A take-home incentive allows a client to leave the clinic with a dose of methadone. This is a convenience for the client because it reduces the frequency with which they must travel to the clinic. A split-dosing contingency requires clients to make two daily visits to the clinic to receive their full dose of methadone. Kidorf and Stitzer (1996) implemented split dosing following a positive urine. They found that the combined use of positive reinforcers and aversive consequences had a marked effect on 28% of a previously noncompliant sample.

Token Economies

To structure an environment that promotes the acquisition of new behaviors, conditioning principles have been applied to entire residential treatment settings. Some therapeutic communities, for example, have employed token economies to shape their clients' behavior. According to Mehr (1988), "the token economy is a system for redesigning total environments to make them supportive of positive or socially desirable behaviors, and capable of extinguishing negative, maladaptive, or socially undesirable behaviors" (p. 163). As applied to chemically dependent populations, token economies encourage the adoption of behaviors that are associated with recovery.

The development of a token economy begins with the identification of "recovery behaviors" (as mentioned previously). Sometimes, the behaviors are prioritized corresponding to differing levels of treatment progress. As clients master certain treatment goals (over weeks and months), they advance to the next level. The reward system is arranged such that clients receive immediate reinforcers (plastic tokens or paper chits) for daily behaviors (attending an AA meeting, cleaning up after lunch, etc.), and special privileges for advancement to a higher treatment level (visits home, their own room, etc.). The tokens are redeemable for material goods such as magazines, cigarettes, food, clothing, or a variety of other things. Advancement in treatment level is thought to signify important treatment gains. In addition, a system of fines is organized in which clients may lose tokens or even be returned to a lower treatment level if they engage in certain behaviors that are inconsistent with recovery.

In Box 4.2, Pickens and Thompson (1984) describe a typical token (or point) economy which they established in a hospital-based drug treatment program.

BOX 4.2. A Point Economy in a Hospital-Based Treatment Program

In the ward-wide program, points are used as the medium for behavioral change. Throughout the 24-hr day, points are given to patients contingent on desired behavior and taken away contingent on maladaptive behavior. Point transactions are administered by all staff who normally work on the ward, including psychiatric nurses, occupational therapists, alcoholism and drug abuse counselors, and psychologists. All point transactions are recorded in a small booklet that each patient is issued daily.

Points are given to patients contingent on three classes of desired behavior: participating in activities considered to be therapeutically helpful to patients, participating in social activities, and grooming and personal care. Participating in therapeutic activities includes attending various classes that are offered on the ward several times each week. The classes are designed to help the patients in rational thinking about themselves, assertiveness, and problem solving, and to improve interpersonal skills and communication. Not only are points earned for attending such activities, but extra points may be earned for being on time and for the quality of participation in the activity. The points are given to patients individually at the end of each activity. At this time a staff person marks the points earned in the patients' point booklet and briefly describes how the quality of participation earned
continued

continued from page 137
them extra points, or how they might improve their participation in the class to earn extra points in the future.

Other therapeutic activities that may earn points on the ward include work on the patient's individualized treatment plan. This plan is devised during the patient's first week of hospitalization. It includes a detailed description of problem behaviors to be changed, the desired behavior, the approach to be taken in changing the behavior, and how the behavioral change is to be "consequated," that is, what the prescribed consequences of the behavior will be. The plan is developed with the patient's cooperation, and is signed by both the patient and the primary staff person. It is considered a document of agreement between the patient and the staff, indicating goals and methods for behavioral change during the patient's stay on the ward.

Points are also given to patients for attendance and for degree of participation in other ward activities, such as planned outings to shopping centers, movies, or parks, as well as various work chores that must be performed on the ward (e.g., watering plants, preparing meals). Personal care activities that earn points include cleaning room, washing clothes, appropriate dress, and regular showers.

The availability of activities for earning points and the number of points to be earned by each activity are clearly defined in the patient's point booklet. However, points can also be given spontaneously by staff to a patient contingent on especially important therapeutic behavior, such as acting responsibly or being particularly helpful. On such occasions, the staff approaches the patient, tells the patient what they observed and liked about his or her behavior, and awards the special points.

As points are given to patients for healthy behavior, points are also taken away from patients for maladaptive behavior. Maladaptive behavior is defined as any behavior that is not in the patient's long-term best interest, regardless of whether it relates directly to drug use or not. Examples of maladaptive behavior would include verbal abuse, assault, theft, or not working on treatment plan. If a particular behavior has been a major problem for the patient in the past, that behavior is typically included in the patient's treatment plan. Otherwise, it is consequated as it occurs on the ward. The same procedure is used in point loss as in point gain. The staff person approaches the patient, tells the patient what was observed and what was inappropriate about the behavior, and then removes points for the behavior in the patient's point booklet.

Points earned by patients are exchangeable on the ward for a variety of goods and services. Points earned during a day are exchangeable for snack food and soft drinks, supplies, cigarettes, or personal care articles. Points not spent on a given day are placed in a savings account, from which the patient may purchase access to visitors, overnight passes, or weekend passes. The major use of points, however, goes towards purchase of the patient's daily privilege or responsibility level on the ward. With a low level of net point earnings, a patient may be able to purchase only the lowest privilege level on the ward—confined to ward. However, with higher levels of net point earnings, the patient may be able to purchase higher and higher privilege levels. At the highest privilege level, patients are able to purchase unlimited and unescorted privileges on the ward. The maximum privilege level obtainable by a patient is set by the staff and typically increases as a patient progresses through treatment.

Thus, the ward's point-economy program can be viewed primarily as a means for getting patients in contact with the therapeutic activities on the ward. Our patients typically attend most classes and participate actively in other ward activities. Though many of our patients are initially very disturbed, there is a low level of maladaptive behavior. While we tend to stress behavioral and cognitive-behavioral approaches in the therapeutic activities available to patients on the unit, the ward program could equally well be used with other treatment approaches.

The program appears to be well liked by both staff and patients. In a study of nursing staff attitudes toward behavior therapy, after working on the ward for one year, the nursing staff said that the behavior therapy approach was less superficial and less mechanistic than did nursing staff working on a more conventional psychiatry unit which emphasized interpretative individual and group psychotherapy (Thompson, Labeck, & Zimmerman, 1980). While some patients may complain initially about the "mickey mouse" nature of the point program, most eventually report liking the program, especially as it provides immediate feedback of progress through treatment. The program seemingly works well with all types of patients. While many of our drug-dependent patients are alcoholics or polydrug abusers from lower socioeconomic levels, patients have also included physicians, psychologists, engineers, and other professionals.

Note. From Pickens and Thompson (1984).

EFFECTIVENESS OF CONTINGENCY MANAGEMENT APPROACHES

An examination of the findings from behaviorally oriented treatment indicates that contingency contracting is an effective strategy for helping those with alcohol and drug problems. The strength of interventions based on operant principles is that they are grounded in *science*. Indeed, this is a principal concern of behaviorally oriented practitioners. Another strength is that these procedures rely on *incentives* to motivate clients. Many treatment programs have failed to incorporate incentives into their intervention strategies as a means of enhancing client motivation. This is a serious oversight.

Interest in behaviorally based interventions is likely to remain strong as long as public officials demand to know "what works." This emphasis on accountability, evidence, and outcomes is inherent to the behavior technology approach.

REVIEW QUESTIONS

1. What are some of the basic characteristics of behaviorism?
2. According to Skinner, who can be faulted for addiction and other problem behaviors?
3. How do respondent and operant conditioning differ?
4. What is the difference between positive reinforcement and negative reinforcement?
5. What is the difference between negative reinforcement and punishment?
6. What relevance do generalization and discrimination have for explaining relapse?
7. From a behavioristic perspective, what three factors predict initiation of substance use?
8. What are the three general classes of reinforcers in addiction? How do they vary across type of drug and characteristics of the user?
9. Why is physical dependence neither a necessary nor a sufficient condition for the development of an addiction?
10. When does cessation from substance abuse usually occur?
11. Why should relapse be expected among those in early recovery (in behavioral terms)?
12. How is tolerance related to one's ability to discriminate blood alcohol levels (BALs)?

13. What is meant by "behavioral tolerance"? How is it learned via respondent and operant principles?

14. What are the assumptions of behavioral counseling? What are the three phases of it as described by Dustin and George?

15. What is behavioral self-control training (BSCT)? Who are good candidates?

16. How can contingency contracting be used to structure and support abstinence?

17. What is community reinforcement training (CRT)?

18. How has CRT been used to help wives of violent alcoholics?

19. What are the features of behavioral marital therapy for alcoholism?

20. How did Higgins et al. treat cocaine dependence?

21. What contingency management procedures have been used to increase compliance with methadone maintenance?

22. How can contingency management be used to structure token economies?

23. What are the strengths of contingency management as a strategy for helping substance abuse clients?

REFERENCES

American Psychiatric Association. (1980). *Diagnostic and statistical manual of mental disorders* (3rd ed.). Washington, DC: Author.

American Psychiatric Association. (1994). *Diagnostic and statistical manual of mental disorders* (4th ed.). Washington, DC: Author.

Azrin, N. H. (1976). Improvements in the community-reinforcement approach to alcoholism. *Behaviour Research and Therapy, 14,* 339–348.

Brecher, E. M., & The Editors of *Consumer Reports.* (1972). *Licit and illicit drugs.* Mount Vernon, NY: Consumers Union.

Brick, J. (1990). Learning and motivational factors in alcohol consumption. In W. M. Cox (Ed.), *Why people drink: Parameters of alcohol as a reinforcer.* New York: Gardner Press.

Cameron, D., & Spence, M. (1976). Recruitment of problem drinkers. *British Journal of Psychiatry, 11,* 544–546.

Campbell, J. C., & Seiden, L. S. (1973). Performance influence on the development of tolerance to amphetamine. *Pharmacology, Biochemistry and Behavior, 1,* 703–708.

Dolan, M. P., Black, J. L., Penk, W. E., Robinowitz, R., & DeFord, H. A. (1985). Contracting for treatment termination to reduce illicit drug use among methadone maintenance treatment failures. *Journal of Consulting and Clinical Psychology, 53,* 549–551.

Dustin, R., & George, R. (1973). *Action counseling for behavior change*. New York: Intext Press.

Goode, E. (1993). *Drugs in American society* (4th ed.). New York: McGraw-Hill.

Harding, F. M. (1989). *Alcohol problems prevention/intervention programs*. Albany: New York State Division of Alcoholism and Alcohol Abuse.

Harris, K. B., & Miller, W. R. (1990). Behavioral self-control training for problem drinkers: Components of efficacy. *Psychology of Addictive Behaviors, 4,* 82–90.

Heather, N., & Robertson, I. (1983). *Controlled drinking*. London: Methuen.

Higgins, S. T., Delaney, D. D., Budney, A. J., Bickel, W. K., Hughes, J. R., Foerg, F., & Fenwick, J. W. (1991). A behavioral approach to achieving initial cocaine abstinence. *American Journal of Psychiatry, 148,* 1218–1224.

Huber, H., Karlin, R., & Nathan, P. E. (1976). Blood alcohol level discrimination by non-alcoholics: The role of internal and external cues. *Journal of Studies on Alcohol, 37,* 27–39.

Hunt, G. H., & Azrin, N. H. (1973). The community-reinforcement approach to alcoholism. *Behaviour Research and Therapy, 11,* 91–104.

Kidorf, M., & Stitzer, M. L. (1993). Contingent access to methadone maintenance treatment: Effects on cocaine use of mixed opiate-cocaine abusers. *Experimental and Clinical Psychopharmacology, 1,* 200–206.

Kidorf, M., & Stitzer, M. L. (1996). Contingent use of take-homes and split-dosing to reduce illicit drug use of methadone patients. *Behavior Therapy, 27,* 41–51.

Lewis, J. A., Dana, R. Q., & Blevins, G. A. (1988). *Substance abuse counseling: An individualized approach*. Pacific Grove, CA: Brooks/Cole.

McAuliffe, W. E., & Gordon, R. A. (1980). Reinforcement and the combination of effects: Summary of a theory of opiate addiction. In D. J. Lettieri, M. Sayers, & H. Wallenstein-Pearson (Eds.), *Theories on drug abuse: Selected contemporary perspectives* (DHHS Publication No. ADM 84-967). Washington, DC: U.S. Government Printing Office.

McKim, W. A. (1986). *Drugs and behavior: An introduction to behavioral pharmacology*. Englewood Cliffs, NJ: Prentice-Hall.

Mehr, J. (1988). *Human services: Concepts and intervention strategies*. Boston: Allyn & Bacon.

Miller, L. K. (1980). *Principles of everyday behavior analysis*. Monterey, CA: Brooks/Cole.

Miller, W. R. (1982). Treating problem drinkers: What works. *The Behavior Therapist, 5,* 15–19.

Miller, W. R., & Hester, R. K. (1980). Treating the problem drinker. In W. R. Miller (Ed.), *The addictive behaviors: Treatment of alcoholism, drug abuse, smoking, and obesity*. Elmsford, NY: Pergamon Press.

Mueller, M. D., & Wyman, J. R. (1997). Study sheds light on the state of drug abuse treatment nationwide (NIH Publication No. 97-3478). *NIDA Notes, 12,* 1, 4–8.

National Institute on Drug Abuse. (1987). *Drug abuse and drug abuse research: The second triennial report to Congress* (DHHS Publication No. ADM 87-1486). Rockville, MD: Author.

Noel, N. E., & McCrady, B. S. (1993). Alcohol-focused spouse involvement with behavioral marital therapy. In T. J. O'Farrell (Ed.), *Treating alcohol problems: Marital and family interventions.* New York: Guilford Press.

Pickens, R. W., & Thompson, T. (1984). Behavioral treatment of drug dependence. In J. Grabowski, M. L. Stitzer, & J. E. Henningfield (Eds.), *Behavioral intervention techniques in drug abuse treatment* (NIDA Research Monograph 46; DHHS Publication No. ADM 86-1281). Washington, DC: U.S. Government Printing Office.

Ray, O., & Ksir, C. (1999). *Drugs, society, and human behavior* (8th ed.). Boston: WCB McGraw-Hill.

Robertson, I., Heather, N., Dzialdowski, A., Crawford, J., & Winton, M. (1986). A comparison of minimal versus intensive controlled drinking treatment interventions for problem drinkers. *British Journal of Clinical Psychology, 25,* 185–194.

Rosenberg, H., Melville, J., Levell, D., & Hodge, J. E. (1994). A 10-year follow-up survey of acceptability of controlled drinking in Britain. *Journal of Studies on Alcohol, 53,* 441–446.

Sanchez-Craig, M., & Lei, H. (1986). Disadvantages of imposing the goal of abstinence on problem drinkers: An empirical study. *British Journal of Addiction, 81,* 505–512.

Siegel, S. (1982). Drug dissociation in the nineteenth century. In F. C. Colpaert & J. L. Slangen (Eds.), *Drug discrimination: Applications in CNS pharmacology.* Amsterdam: Elsevier.

Silverstein, S. J., Nathan, P. E., & Taylor, H. A. (1974). Blood alcohol level estimation and controlled drinking by chronic alcoholics. *Behavior Therapy, 5,* 1–15.

Sisson, R. W., & Azrin, N. A. (1986). Family-member involvement to initiate and promote treatment of problem drinkers. *Journal of Behavior Therapy and Experimental Psychiatry, 17,* 15–21.

Sisson, R. W., & Azrin, N. A. (1993). Community reinforcement training for families: A method to get alcoholics into treatment. In T. J. O'Farrell (Ed.), *Treating alcohol problems: Marital and family interventions.* New York: Guilford Press.

Skinner, B. F. (1975). *Beyond freedom and dignity.* New York: Bantam.

Sobell, M. B., Wilkinson, D. A., & Sobell, L. C. (1990). Alcohol and drug problems. In A. S. Bellack, M. Hersen, & A. E. Kazdin (Eds.), *International handbook of behavior modification* (2nd ed.). New York: Plenum Press.

Stitzer, M., & Bigelow, G. (1978). Contingency management in a methadone maintenance program: Availability of reinforcers. *International Journal of the Addictions, 13,* 737–746.

Stitzer, M. L., Bigelow, G. E., & Liebson, I. (1980). Reducing drug use among methadone maintenance clients: Contingent reinforcement for morphine-free urines. *Addictive Behaviors, 5,* 333–340.

Thompson, T., Labeck, L., & Zimmerman, R. (1980). Nursing staff adjustment as a function of psychiatric treatment modality. *Journal of Behavior Therapy and Experimental Psychiatry, 11,* 200–214.

Ullman, L. P., & Krasner, L. (1965). *Case studies in behavior modification.* New York: Holt, Rinehart & Winston.

Cognitive Models

Substance use and abuse can be explained within a cognitive-behavioral framework. "Cognitive" in this context refers to covert mental processes that are described by a number of diverse terms, including "thinking," "self-talk," "internal dialogue," "expectancies," "beliefs," "schemas," and so on. These "hidden" variables mediate the influence of external stimuli in the production of observable human behavior. Because they represent "behaviors" that are not readily observable, cognitive models are usually distinguished from those that are strictly behavioral. This chapter draws on constructs from a number of cognitive-behavioral approaches including self-efficacy theory (Bandura, 1997) and alcohol expectancy theory (Goldman, Brown, & Christiansen, 1987). The discussion shows how cognitive constructs have been used to explain the initiation and maintenance of addictive behavior; they have also been used to guide the development of relapse prevention strategies based on enhancement of coping and social skills.

BASIC SOCIAL COGNITIVE CONCEPTS

Albert Bandura is recognized as a leader in cognitive psychology. In his early work, he used the term "social learning theory" (SLT). As the theory became increasingly focused on cognition, he adopted the term "social cognitive theory." As the theory continued to evolve, the construct of self-efficacy became central, sometimes leading to use of the term "self-efficacy theory." These propositions about human behavior grew out of dissatisfaction with the deterministic views of human beings as expressed by both psychoanalysis and behaviorism several decades ago. In the orthodox psychoanalytic perspective, humans are considered to be under the control of the unconscious, whereas in the radical behaviorist camp, behavior is controlled by external contingencies (i.e., rewards). In both of those theoretical systems, self-regulation plays no part. Bandura (1977) rejects this view and insists that humans can create and administer reinforcements (rewards and punishers) for themselves and to themselves. He describes it this way:

> Social learning theory approaches the explanation of human behavior in terms of a continuous reciprocal interaction between cognitive, behavioral, and environmental determinants. Within the process of reciprocal determination lies the opportunity for people to influence their destiny as well as the limits of self-direction. This conception of human functioning then neither casts people into the role of powerless objects controlled by environmental forces nor free agents who can become whatever they choose. Both people and their environments are reciprocal determinants of each other. (p. vii)

Note that Bandura indicates that self-direction is possible within limits. These limits vary by both person and environment. For example, a cocaine addict in early recovery who lives in a suburban neighborhood is probably going to have much more control over drug-taking behavior than a similar addict who lives in an inner-city, cocaine-ridden neighborhood. Bandura's (1977) reasoning is apparent in the following passage:

> If actions were determined solely by external rewards and punishments, people would behave like weathervanes, constantly shifting in different directions to conform to the momentary influences impinging upon them. They would act corruptly with unprincipled individuals and honorably with righteous ones, and liberally with libertarians and dogmatically with authoritarians. (p. 128)

In SLT, the consequences of behavior (i.e., reinforcements and punishments) do not act automatically to shape behavior in a mechanistic manner. Rather, these external, environmental contingencies influence the acquisition and regulation of behavior. Internal cognitive processes are also important; they mediate the influence of environmental contingencies. Wilson (1988) states that cognitive processes are based on prior experience and serve to determine (1) which environmental influences are attended to, (2) how these influences are perceived (e.g., as "good" or "bad"), (3) whether they will be remembered, and (4) how they may affect future behavior.

SLT stresses that individuals are actively involved in appraising environmental events. The acquisition and maintenance of behavior are not passive processes. Furthermore, Bandura (1977) maintains that the conditions for learning are facilitated by making rules and consequences known to potential participants. By observing the consequences of someone else's behavior, an individual can learn appropriate actions for particular situations. Bandura (1977) indicates that people create symbolic representations from these observations and rely on them to anticipate the future outcomes that will result from their own behavior. This cognitive process (i.e., symbolic representation) assists in generating motivation to initiate and sustain behavior.

Self-Regulation

Another central concept in SLT, and one of particular importance to the problem of substance use, is "self-regulation" (Abrams & Niaura, 1987). This concept refers to the capability of humans to regulate their own behavior via internal standards and self-evaluative assessments. The concept helps explain how human behavior can be maintained in the absence of external environmental rewards. In the process of self-regulation, humans make self-rewards (and self-punishments) contingent upon the achievement of some specific internal standard of performance. If a discrepancy develops between one's internal standards and one's behavioral performance, the individual will be motivated to change standards, behavior, or both. The internal standards are thought to be the result of one's history of modeling influences and differential reinforcement (Wilson, 1988).

In SLT, alcoholism and addiction are not thought to be conditions characterized by a lack of self-regulation but, rather, forms of self-regulation that are deemed problematic by society (and possibly the family). In other words, the disease model's concept of "loss of control" is disputed by SLT. The alcoholic's or addict's lifestyle is seen as regulated (i.e., organized) around the consumption of alcohol or drugs. The person's behavior is not random or unpredictable; it is purposeful and goal directed. The high degree of self-regulation is clear when consideration is given to the amount of time and effort needed (often daily) to obtain the drug, use the drug, conceal its use, interact with other users, and recover from its effects. Many chemically dependent persons manage such lifestyles for years, even while holding jobs and having families.

In this context, it should be noted that "self-regulation" does not imply "healthy." That is a value-laden term, which by definition is subjective. Furthermore, SLT maintains that in some cases addiction may be a means of coping (i.e., regulating the self) with internal performance standards that are too extreme or unrealistic. For example, an alcoholic may cope with long work hours by consuming many martinis. In other addicts, their evaluation of self is not "activated" by other persons' opinions of their substance use; that is, criticism from others has little impact on how they perceive themselves. Thus, they easily engage in behavior (alcohol/drug abuse) for which there is <u>little external reward and perhaps much punishment</u> (social/family ostracism, arrests, financial debt, health problems, etc.).

Reciprocal Determinism

In Bandura's (1977) view, person, behavior, and environment are continually engaged in "reciprocal determinism." That is, each of the components is capable of changing the nature of the interaction at any time. Individuals are thought to be capable of reassessing their behavior, its impact on the environment, and the environment's impact on themselves and their behavior. In a given situation, one of the three components may gain momentary dominance. Figure 5.1 diagrams the relationship among these components. Notice that in Figure 5.1 an individual is not driven by internal forces alone, nor does he/she passively respond to external forces. Instead, a set of interlocking forces is involved.

Wilson (1988) describes it this way: "<u>a person is both the agent and the object of environmental influence</u>. <u>Behavior is a function of interdependent factors</u>. Thus, cognitions do not operate independently. In a complete analysis of the cognitive control of behavior, mediating processes must be tied to observable action" (pp. 242–243).

Using the concept of reciprocal determinism, White, Bates, and Johnson (1990) have integrated alcohol as a fourth component in the model. The diagram in Figure 5.2 seeks to explain alcohol consumption from an SLT perspective. In this model, White et al. (1990) include perceived actions or "alcohol expectancies" in the alcohol domain. They note that it may be more appropriate to include these under the "person characteristics"; after all, they are cognitive variables. However, they feel that placing them within the alcohol domain emphasizes that many of the effects of alcohol, traditionally attributed to its

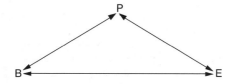

P = Person (cognitive mediating processes)
B = Behavior
E = Environment

FIGURE 5.1. Interactive schema of person, behavior, and environment.

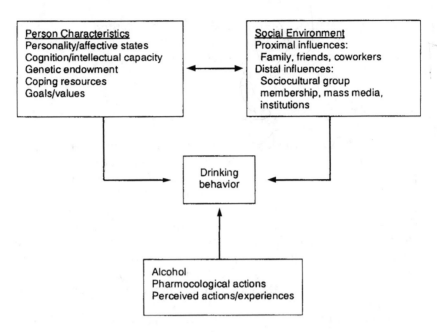

FIGURE 5.2. Interactive schema of person, environment, and drug variables affecting and affected by drinking behaviors. Adapted from White, Bates, and Johnson (1990). Copyright 1990 by Gardner Press, Inc. Adapted by permission.

pharmacological properties, are actually the result of socially mediated beliefs (White et al., 1990). (Alcohol expectancies are discussed in greater detail in a subsequent section of this chapter.)

MODELING AND SUBSTANCE USE

"Modeling," which is vicarious or observational learning, is an important concept in social cognitive paradigms. Wilson (1988) defines it in the following manner:

> In this form of learning people acquire new knowledge and behavior by observing other people and events, without engaging in the behavior themselves and without any direct consequences to themselves. Vicarious learning may occur when people watch what others ("models") do, or when they attend to the physical environment, to events, and to symbols such as words and pictures. (pp. 240–241)

Bandura (1977) has identified three types of effects on behavior that can result from observing a model:

1. *Observational learning effects.* These refer to behaviors acquired through observation of a model that did not previously exist in the individual's behavioral repertoire (e.g., smoking marijuana from a "bong").
2. *Inhibitory–disinhibitory effects.* These refer to increases or decreases in the intensity of a previously learned inhibition. Such behaviors usually result from observing a model's being rewarded or punished for some specific action. Thus a teenage boy may drink a beer—an action he had previously inhibited—when he observes an admired friend (i.e., a model) receive a reward for doing so. In this case, the "reward" may be any number of social consequences (other peers voice their approval, the admired friend becomes more sociable, funny, or easy to talk to, etc.).
3. *Response facilitation effects.* These refer to the appearance of behaviors that are not novel and were not previously inhibited. Examples of such behaviors are as follows: "People applaud when others clap; they look up when they see others gazing skyward; they adopt fads that others display; and in countless other situations their behavior is prompted and channeled by the actions of others" (Bandura, 1971, p. 6).

The pace at which a small group of friends drink beer is another example of a response facilitation effect. In such a group, drinking beer is not a new behavior and it is not inhibited, but the pace of an individual's drinking is influenced by that of the group. If the group is sipping slowly, it is also likely that a particular individual will match that pace. Consider a wine-tasting event in which small amounts are consumed for taste and food is eaten to cleanse the mouth. In such cases, individuals rarely become drunk, as models of such behavior do not normally exist at such events. In contrast, consider a typical college fraternity party, in which models of heavy drinking abound. Again, SLT asserts that the models in both of these drinking situations facilitate the pace of the group's drinking behavior. The models do not cause or require others to increase or decrease their drinking; they simply influence it.

Controlled experiments using a bogus "taste-rating task" have systematically examined the influence of modeling on alcohol consumption. In this procedure, participants are manipulated by the investigator's deception. They are deceived into believing that they are participating in a procedure to evaluate the *taste* of alcoholic beverages. The story is concocted to provide study participants with a rationale for consuming alcoholic beverages in a laboratory setting.

In one such study, Caudill and Marlatt (1975) assigned heavy drinking, male college students ($n = 48$) to one of six groups in a 3×2 design. Without their knowledge, the participants were exposed to different types of "confederate" models who had been trained by the investigators. The participants were exposed to one of three types of drinker models: heavy, light, or nondrinker. In addition, prior to the taste-rating task, they had a brief interaction with a model who was trained to act either "warm" or "cold" toward the participant. The findings showed that participants exposed to heavy drinking models consumed significantly more alcohol than did those exposed to light drinking and no drinking models. The latter two groups did not differ from one another. Though the prior social interaction conditions (warm vs. cold) did not influence consumption, these experimental findings indicate that modeling can be an important social determinant of alcohol consumption (Caudill & Marlatt, 1975).

Collins, Parks, and Marlatt (1985) conducted two similar experiments to study modeling effects. Using male undergraduates who were moderate and heavy drinkers, students were recruited under the pretense of assessing the realism of an on-campus barroom laboratory. They were told that the assessment would involve consumption of alcohol. In one experiment, confederates, under the control of the investigators, acted in a sociable or unsociable fashion while modeling either light or heavy alcohol consumption. Heavy drinking was produced in the participants by exposure to three types of models: sociable heavy drinking, unsociable heavy drinking, and unsociable light drinking. The sociable light-drinking models tended to produce light drinking in confederates. The investigators interpreted these findings in context of the camaraderie and rivalry that exist among young men under differing social conditions. In the second study, the confederates adopted different roles indicating three levels of social status: "transient laborer," "typical college student," and "30-year-old medical resident." Whereas the alcohol consumption of the participants matched that of the confederates, level of status did not influence drinking behavior (Collins et al., 1985).

SELF-EFFICACY AND TREATMENT OUTCOMES

Self-efficacy has become the unifying construct of the social cognitive framework (Bandura, 1997). Previously, it tended to be described as a minitheory within the larger framework of SLT (e.g., Wilson, 1988). Regardless, self-efficacy has been defined as "a perception or judgement of one's capability to execute a particular course of action required to deal effectively with an impending situation" (Abrams & Niaura, 1987, p. 134). Efficacy beliefs have been shown to play an influential role in many classes of human behavior, including coping with stress (Jerusalem & Mittag, 1995), educational attainment (Zimmerman, 1995), career development (Hackett, 1995), health-related behavior (Schwarzer & Fuchs, 1995), and addictive behavior (Marlatt, Baer, & Quigley, 1995).

The two components of self-efficacy are *outcome expectations* and *efficacy expectations*. An outcome expectation is a person's estimate that a particular outcome will occur. In other words, an individual assesses the situation and the various factors involved in his/her own performance and formulates an expectation of the probability that a specific course of action will lead to a particular outcome (Monte, 1980). Of particular relevance here are alcohol and drug expectancies. The next section of this chapter discusses these beliefs more fully.

An efficacy expectation is a person's belief that he/she can carry out the necessary course of action to obtain the anticipated outcome (Bandura, 1997). Thus, an outcome expectation is knowledge of what to do and what will be obtained, whereas an efficacy expectation is the belief (or doubt) that one can do it. Bandura (1995, 1997) contends that people who are healthy, personally effective, and successful tend to have a high sense of perceived self-efficacy. In other words, they believe that they can achieve what they set out to do. Furthermore, people with high self-efficacy are likely to interpret life problems as challenges rather than as threats or unmanageable situations.

Research has demonstrated that psychological treatments alter behavior to the extent that they affect efficacy expectations (Wilson, 1988). Treatment and counseling services that enhance a person's sense of personal competence are likely to lead to improved functioning. According to Wilson (1988):

> Unless treatment creates strong expectations of efficacy, coping behaviors may be easily extinguished following the termination of therapy. The phenomenon of relapse is a problem for all methods of psychological treatment, including behavior therapy. Self-efficacy theory is a means of conceptualizing the relapse process and suggests procedures for facilitating the long-term maintenance of behavior change, especially in the addictive disorders. (p. 243)

According to Bandura (1977), efficacy expectations are based on (and can be altered by) four sources of information. The most powerful influence is thought to be *performance accomplishments* in previous mastery situations. Past failure experiences undermine efficacy beliefs, whereas success boosts them. The second source of efficacy expectations consists of *vicarious experiences*—that is, observation of others' success and failures. A third source is *verbal persuasion*; here, a person is told that he/she can master a task. This source has a relatively weak influence on efficacy expectations because it provides no personal experience of success or failure. The fourth and last source of efficacy expectations is the *emotional arousal* that stems from attempting a demanding task. The experience of anxiety is a powerful cue to people regarding their possibilities for success (or failure) and the amount of effort they will have to exert to achieve mastery. High levels of anxiety and fear are likely to have a debilitating effect on a person's attempts at mastery.

In relation to substance use/nonuse, Marlatt et al. (1995) identified five specific types of self-efficacy. *Resistance self-efficacy* has to do with judgments about one's ability to avoid the initial use of a substance. This type is important for understanding the onset of substance use, particularly in adolescents. *Harm-reduction self-efficacy* involves perceptions of one's ability to avoid harm following initial use of a substance. *Action self-efficacy* pertains to one's perceived ability to achieve abstinence or controlled use. This type is important for understanding initial behavior change efforts among people who have intensified involvement with substance use. *Coping self-efficacy* is concerned with one's anticipated ability to cope with relapse crises. Finally, *recovery self-efficacy* has to do with judgments about one's ability to return to recovery following lapses and relapses.

Efficacy expectations are particularly important in relapse prevention. Addicts who doubt that they can maintain the tasks necessary for recovery (i.e., coping self-efficacy) are likely to relapse. Furthermore, the sources of efficacy expectations suggest specific relapse prevention strategies. Successful efforts are those designed to ensure success (i.e., performance accomplishments) by first providing simple tasks and gradually building to more difficult ones. Successful efforts also expose an addict to other successfully recovering addicts (i.e., vicarious experiences) and teach ways to cope with negative affective states (emotional arousal). Finally, the sources of efficacy expectations suggest that "verbal persuasion" (e.g., "I know you can do it") is an inadequate intervention by itself.

Outcome studies have linked self-efficacy to drinking/drug use status at follow-up and to participation in treatment. Burling, Reilly, Moltzen, and Ziff (1989) examined the relation between self-efficacy and relapse among 81 inpatient substance abuse clients. In general, self-efficacy increased during treatment and at a 6-month follow-up was higher among abstainers than relapsers. Interestingly, they found that low self-efficacy at intake was related to longer stays in treatment and a more positive status at discharge. Self-efficacy ratings at the end of treatment were not related to alcohol and drug use. The investigators speculate that some substance abusers may minimize the severity of their problems and, as a result, report inflated levels of self-efficacy. In such cases, substance abusers may underestimate the difficulties facing hem in recovery and, hence, may be less willing to learn new coping behaviors (Burling et al., 1989). When pressured into treatment by the criminal justice system, an employer, or one's family, clients may exaggerate reports of self-efficacy.

Rychtarik, Prue, Rapp, and King (1992) tracked changes in self-efficacy among a male alcoholic population in treatment and for the 12 months following discharge. They found that clients who had high self-efficacy and actively participated in aftercare had significantly better outcomes than did other groups of clients. Intake self-efficacy ratings were predictive of relapse status at both 6- and 12-month follow-ups, but discharge self-efficacy was not related to relapse at either of these two time intervals. Rychtarik et al. (1992) also conclude that many clients report greatly inflated levels of self-efficacy at the time of discharge from treatment. They speculate that in some cases this may result from genuinely unrealistic expectations about the challenges of recovery, whereas other clients may be actively involved in "impression management."

ROLE OF OUTCOME EXPECTANCY IN ALCOHOL AND DRUG USE

Cognitive models of substance abuse rely heavily on the "outcome expectancy" and "efficacy expectancy" constructs. The former concept has been used to predict and explain drinking behavior and other drug use, whereas both play a role in relapse (and its prevention). This section provides a detailed discussion of both alcohol and other drug outcome expectancies.

There is no widely accepted definition of the term "expectancy." Usually the term refers to a cognitive variable that intervenes between a stimulus and a response. Goldman et al. (1987) define outcome expectancy as the "anticipation of a systematic relationship between events or objects in some upcoming situation" (p. 183). The construction implies an "if–then" relationship between a behavior and any outcome.

Many models of substance abuse and dependence have focused on biological differences among individuals that make some people more susceptible to excessive use than others (e.g., Goodwin, 1990). Other theories have scrutinized the pharmacological effects of drugs (e.g., Koob, 1992). Although it does not completely ignore the biomedical and pharmacological aspects of substance use and abuse, expectancy theory comes close to doing so (Goldman et al., 1987). The theory asserts that drug self-administration is largely determined by the reinforcements an individual expects to obtain as a consequence of putting the substance into one's body. Hence, expectancy theory focuses on the *anticipated* reinforcement of drug use.

Alcohol and other drug expectancies vary in strength from person to person; they are greatly influenced by one's family, peer group, and culture, and perhaps even by the mass media (e.g., alcohol advertising). Goldman et al. (1987) indicate that a lack of positive alcohol expectancies should lead one to abstain from alcohol, whereas heavy drinking can be predicted by a variety of strongly held expectancies. Thus, those drinkers who consume heavily may strongly expect alcohol to make them more relaxed, more sexy, or possibly more aggressive. Moderate and light drinkers may hold weaker expectancies in these areas or may expect no positive outcomes in some of them. Other drug expectancies operate in much the same manner.

The intriguing aspect of alcohol expectancy theory in particular is that it is not necessary to assume that the outcomes of drinking (tension reduction, enhanced sexuality, aggression, etc.) are related to the pharmacological qualities of ethanol. According to Goldman et al. (1987):

> All this model requires is a belief in a relationship between stimuli and outcomes or between behaviors and outcomes. The model operates even if these beliefs are not based on reality. For example, if a person in a typical drinking environment believed they had consumed alcohol, they might produce covert and overt alcohol-related responses (which appear to observers as pharmacologic effects), not because the drug action of alcohol made them do it, but instead because they believed desired outcomes were available if they behaved in this way in this context. (p. 139)

The essence of alcohol expectancy theory, then, is that alcohol's ability to transform an individual's behavior is not attributable so much to the action of ethanol as it is to the anticipated outcomes of consuming alcohol. Whether the same can be said to be true for drugs such as marijuana and cocaine is less clear; there has been little hypothesis testing of illegal drug expectancies.

Laboratory Research

Empirical support for the alcohol expectancy hypothesis comes from laboratory research utilizing placebo and balanced-placebo designs. In early laboratory research on alcohol use, placebo designs were used to control for the effects of expectancy. This was done for the most part as a control formality, following customary practice in pharmacological research (Goldman et al., 1987). It was not hoped that the placebo condition would produce effects similar to that of the actual condition.

One early placebo study tested the disease model's concept of loss of control (Merry, 1966). According to this concept (which has been discussed in detail in Chapter Two of this volume), alcoholics experience intense, probably biologically induced cravings for alcohol after having consumed just a small amount; this intense need for alcohol (once consumed) leads to a loss of control over drinking behavior. Merry (1996) tested this hypothesis by administering alcohol to nine inpatient alcoholics without their knowledge. During an 18-day period, each patient was given an orange-flavored beverage at breakfast. All patients were told that the beverage contained a mixture of vitamins that would help them remain abstinent from alcohol. The beverage was alternated every 2 days such that the patients received either a totally nonalcoholic drink or one that contained 1 ounce of vodka. As a routine part of their treatment regimen, patients were asked to rate their level of alcohol craving later each morning. There was no relationship between their ratings and the beverage consumed, indicating that the basis for alcohol cravings was not pharmacological. Other studies have yielded consistent findings.

In the 1970s, the placebo effects themselves increasingly became the focus of research. Investigators expanded the placebo design. They developed a balanced design that included four cells:

    I.   Told alcohol, given alcohol.
    II. Told alcohol, given only tonic.
    III. Told no alcohol, given alcohol.
    IV. Told no alcohol, given only tonic.

In this balanced-placebo design, an "antiplacebo" condition (III) is added; this condition assesses alcohol effects in the absence of the usual drinking mindset (Goldman et al., 1987). Figure 5.3 illustrates this design.

Using the balanced-placebo design, Marlatt and his colleagues conducted pioneering research on the relationship between alcohol expectancies and drinking behavior. In one landmark study, Marlatt, Demming, and Reid (1973) investigated the loss-of-control hypothesis by presenting separate groups of male alcoholics and social drinkers with the bogus alcohol taste-rating task (as described in the discussion on modeling in this chapter). Both drinker groups had 32 members. The alcoholics (mean age = 47) were actively drinking with no intention to quit. They met at least one of the following criteria: (1) history of alcoholism treatment, (2) five or more arrests for "drunk and disorderly conduct," (3) previous membership in Alcoholics Anonymous (AA) or a vocational rehabilitation program for alcoholics. Most of the

Subject actually receives

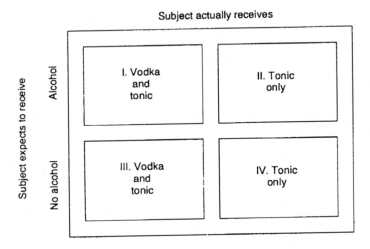

FIGURE 5.3. The balanced-placebo design. From Wilson (1988). Copyright 1988 by the Addiction Research Foundation. Reprinted by permission.

alcoholics (25 of 32) met more than one of these criteria. The social drinkers (mean age = 37) did not meet the criteria stated previously and they were screened out if they described themselves as "heavy" or "problem" drinkers (Marlatt et al., 1973).

The subjects were told that the beverages were either vodka and tonic or tonic only. The actual beverage contents were systematically varied to be either consistent or inconsistent with the instructional set. It was found that both alcoholic and nonalcoholic men drank significantly more when they thought their drinks contained alcohol, regardless of the actual contents. This finding seriously challenges the disease model of alcoholism, which holds that alcoholic drinking is mediated by a physiological mechanism that can be triggered by the introduction of alcohol to the body. Rather, it appears that the subjects' beliefs (expectancies) about beverage content were the crucial factors in determining amount of alcohol consumed.

Survey Research

The results of survey research also provide strong support for the alcohol expectancy theory. Much of this survey work was initiated by Sandra Brown and her colleagues, who developed the Alcohol Expectancy Questionnaire (AEQ). This 90-item self-report questionnaire assesses whether alcohol, when consumed in moderate quantities, produces specific positive effects (Brown, Christiansen, & Goldman, 1987). The AEQ was derived from an initial pool of 216 verbatim statements collected from 125 people who were interviewed individually and in groups. They ranged in age from 15 to 60, and their drinking behavior varied from total abstinence to chronic alcoholism. When the items were factor-analyzed, the following six alcohol expectancy factors emerged:

1. Global positive change.
2. Sexual enhancement.
3. Physical and social pleasure.
4. Increased social assertiveness.
5. Relaxation and tension reduction.
6. Arousal with power.

These factors represent relatively distinct domains of anticipated drinking outcomes. The factors were subsequently used in a large number of survey research studies as variables to predict various drinking practices. In general, the research has consistently linked these expected consumption outcomes to actual use, abuse, and related problem behavior. For example, Brown, Creamer, and Stetson (1987) found that alcohol abusers expected more positive outcomes from drinking than did their nonabusing peers. Similarly, Critchlow (1987) found that heavy drinkers held stronger expectations of positive consequences of alcohol use than did light drinkers, and that they generally evaluated all drinking outcomes more positively. Furthermore, Brown (1985) and this author (Thombs, 1991) reported that alcohol expectancies were better predictors of heavy and problem drinking than was a set of demographic variables.

Among young adolescents, alcohol expectancies have been shown to predict the onset of the initiation of drinking behavior 1 year later (Christiansen, Roehling, Smith, & Goldman, 1989). Among college students, one study found that problem drinkers expected more relaxation/tension reduction than did social drinkers, while the latter group expected more social enhancement (Brown, 1985). Another college student study found that the expectancy profile that distinguished female problem drinkers from female nonproblem drinkers was relatively distinct from the profile that separated these drinker types among males (Thombs, 1993). In this same study, the AEQ factor that had the strongest discriminating value among the women problem drinkers (and thus provided the clearest indication of what they sought through drinking) was arousal with power, whereas for the men it was physical and social pleasure (Thombs, 1993). Finally, one study examined cross-cultural differences in alcohol expectancies (Brown, Christiansen, & Goldman, 1987). A group of Irish (Dublin) adolescents was compared to a group of U.S. (Detroit) adolescents. The groups were matched by age and gender. Results indicated that there were no differences between the two groups on total AEQ scores. However, there were significant differences on subscale scores: The Irish teens expected more arousal and aggression and less sexual enhancement from drinking than did the U.S. teens (Brown, Christiansen, & Goldman, 1987). Irish youth also had significantly lower expectations for enhanced social and cognitive-motor functioning compared to American youth.

Survey research also has identified the outcome expectancies associated with some illegal drugs. In a sample of 704 college students, Schafer and Brown (1991) used factor analysis to identify the anticipated outcomes of marijuana and cocaine use. They identified six marijuana expectancy factors:

1. Cognitive and behavioral impairment.
2. Relaxation and tension reduction.
3. Social and sexual facilitation.
4. Perceptual and cognitive enhancement.
5. Global negative effects.
6. Craving and physical effects.

Though the six sets of items (each factor) had weak to modest internal consistency, multivariate analysis revealed that there were significant correlations between the expectancy measures and patterns of marijuana use and nonuse in college students (Schafer & Brown, 1991). On some of the scales, such as cognitive-behavioral impairment and global negative effects, the nonusers of marijuana had the strongest expectancies, compared to infrequent, recreational, and regular users of the drug. On relaxation and tension reduction measure, the regular users had the greatest score of the four groups. This finding suggests that the perceived negative consequences of marijuana use act as a deterrent to experimentation with the drug, but once use is initiated, strong positive expectations may spur a high level of involvement with marijuana.

Schafer and Brown (1991) identified five cocaine expectancy factors as well:

1. Global positive effects.
2. Global negative effects.
3. General arousal.
4. Anxiety.
5. Relaxation and tension reduction.

The internal consistency for the items comprising global positive effects was good. The other item sets had more modest interitem equivalence. Again, multivariate analysis found significant correlations between the expectancy measures, as a set, and patterns of cocaine use in college students (Schafer & Brown, 1991). Parallel to the marijuana relationships, scores on global positive effects, were highest in the frequent cocaine users, whereas scores for global negative effects were highest among the nonusers of cocaine.

The investigators noted that the identification of relaxation and tension reduction as an anticipated outcome of using cocaine, a stimulant, seems counterintuitive. In all four cocaine user groups, scores on this measure were relatively low. Furthermore, there was little variation across the groups (Schafer & Brown, 1991).

Drug Expectancy: Precursor to or Consequence of Drug Use?

A challenge facing the drug expectancy research has been to demonstrate that the construct is not an epiphenomenal correlate of drug use. The basic question is this: Does expectancy influence drug use or is it merely an artifact of existing drug-taking behavior? This question has important implications for primary prevention and early intervention. A number of studies have examined the question as it pertains to both alcohol and marijuana expectancies.

Miller, Smith, and Goldman (1990) sought to determine whether alcohol expectancies could be detected in a sample of 114 elementary schoolchildren, grades 1–5. The investigators developed an assessment procedure which relied on hand puppets to collect expectancy data from the first- to third-graders. For fourth- and fifth-graders, the adolescent version of the AEQ was administered in addition to the use of handpuppets. Though they were less differentiated than those of adolescents and adults, it was found that alcohol expectancies were present in this age group. As age increased, expectancies about drinking tended to increase as well. Most of the increase occurred during third and fourth grades (children ages 8½ to 10). Because these children presumably had little or no personal drinking experience, it can be assumed that their expectations were the result of exposure to family drinking models, commercial advertising, and other media messages.

In a prospective study, a sample of 422 preteens and teens (mean age at baseline = 12.8) were assessed twice at 12-month intervals (Reese, Chassin, & Molina, 1994). Baseline alcohol expectancies were found to prospectively predict drinking consequences (problems) 12 months later. This relationship was observed even after the effects of the following variables were controlled for: baseline drinking consequences, parental alcoholism, and age. However, expectancies did not predict alcohol use, perhaps because of the relatively high number of abstainers and light drinkers among younger participants.

Another prospective study assessed 461 participants, ages 12 to 14, over a 2-year period (Smith, Goldman, Greenbaum, & Christiansen, 1995). A baseline assessment was followed by two 12-month follow-ups. The purpose of the study was to examine the relationship between expectancy for social facilitation and alcohol use. The investigators found that teenagers' expectations for social facilitation had a reciprocal relationship with their past drinking behavior. In other words, the greater their expectation for social facilitation, the greater their drinking level, followed then by the greater expectations, and so on. Two other directional models were not supported by the data: (1) expectancy influences alcohol use and (2) alcohol use influences expectancy.

In a third prospective study, Stacy, Newcomb, and Bentler (1991) assessed alcohol and marijuana expectancies among 584 participants as they moved from adolescence to young adulthood. Their primary purpose was to determine the nature of the relationship between drug expectancy and drug use. Three possibilities were tested by structural equation models: (1) expectancies predict future drug-taking behavior; (2) expectancies result from drug use, that is, they merely reflect personal experience with a substance; and (3) the relationship between expectancy and drug use is reciprocal.

Stacy et al. (1991) assessed the sample twice at a 9-year interval. At the first assessment interval, the cohort's mean age was about 18. The investigators found that the adolescent measures of expectancy were predictive of adult drug-taking behavior. Furthermore, the data suggested that expectancy is not a consequence or artifact of existing drug use but, rather, is the antecedent of these behaviors. Little evidence was found to support the social learning proposition that expectancy and drug use have a reciprocal relationship (Stacy et al., 1991).

Alcohol Expectancy as a Function of Memory

Theories of human memory have proposed that "expectancy" is a name given to information stored in memory (Bolles, 1972). This information consists of associations between cues and consequences and behaviors and consequences. These two types of associations may combine to influence decision making when cues in the environment match those stored in the predictive relations of memory, which suggests that the structure and function of memory may play a role in drinking behavior.

Recent studies have attempted to link the alcohol expectancy construct more explicitly to cognition and memory (Dunn & Goldman, 1996; Rather & Goldman, 1994; Rather, Goldman, Roehrich, & Brannick, 1992). The conceptualization of Goldman and colleagues is that alcohol expectancies are stored in memory networks. These networks are collections of memories about the predictive relations between drinking and its outcomes. Such information may influence the decision-making process about alcohol use.

Rather et al. (1992) identified a preliminary alcohol expectancy semantic network in college students. They found that though all study participants tended to associate positive/prosocial outcomes with drinking, heavier drinkers tended to expect arousal from alcohol consumption. In contrast, lighter drinkers were more likely to expect sedation. Rather and Goldman (1994) replicated this semantic memory network in a separate sample of college students. They also found that compared to lighter drinkers, the expectancy networks of heavier drinkers were more "tightly configured," meaning more packed with information. By comparison, the networks of lighter drinkers were spatially diffuse, which suggests that when exposed to an alcohol stimulus, heavier drinkers may rapidly associate many positive and arousing effects to alcohol use but be "cognitively insulated" from the sedating and negative outcomes. In lighter drinkers, the network of associations may consolidate more slowly and thereby inhibit alcohol use.

In a sample of 470 second- to fifth-grade children, Dunn and Goldman (1996) found that alcohol expectancy information was organized in memory networks similar to that of adults, even though presumably the subjects had little or no personal drinking experience; they tended to perceive that alcohol generates either arousal or sedation. It also was discovered that older children were more likely to anticipate positive and arousing outcomes from alcohol use. Dunn and Goldman (1996) speculate that as children move through elementary school, they become "cognitively prepared" to drink as a result of being exposed to parental and older peer drinking models and to commercial advertising. These findings suggest that primary prevention strategies should seek to undermine the expectation that alcohol produces positive and arousing effects.

Drug Expectancy as a Comorbidity Mechanism

Alcohol and drug abuse is prevalent among the mentally ill (National Institute on Alcohol Abuse and Alcoholism, 1994). Most mental health professionals agree that alcohol and illegal drug use tend to aggravate the symptoms experienced by the mentally ill and complicates their treatment ("Drug use and the mentally ill," 1994). Yet, many so-called dual-diagnosis clients believe that alcohol, marijuana, and other drugs relieve their symptoms.

The "self-medication hypothesis" has been put forth as an explanation for why, despite the negative consequences, the mentally ill use alcohol and some illegal drugs at rates that exceed that of the general population (National Institute on Alcohol Abuse and Alcoholism, 1994). Kushner, Sher, and Beitman (1990) indicate that some drugs, particularly alcohol, may provide quick, short-term relief for symptoms of anxiety, but repeated drinking bouts usually exacerbate them. Hence, the substance use of dual-diagnosis clients may be influenced by expectations of short-term relief, even though the long-term consequences of such behavior may lead to a worsening of their psychiatric condition.

Research is needed to determine the extent to which mentally ill persons hold expectancies for symptom relief. A competing hypothesis is that mentally ill persons provide reports of self-medication as a post hoc rationalization to divert attention from their actual motivations for substance use (National Institute on Alcohol Abuse & Alcoholism, 1994). In some situations, drinking or drug use simply may be done for convivial reasons.

Expectancy and Treatment Outcomes

Research by Jones and McMahon (1994) indicates that specific types of expectancy predict abstinence rates among alcoholic men in residential treatment. The investigators administered the AEQ and the Negative Alcohol Expectancy Questionnaire to 53 clients at admission and again at 1- and 3-month follow-ups after treatment. The AEQ assessed the immediate, expected, positive outcomes of drinking and the second instrument measured expectations of "same-day," "next-day," and "continued-drinking" negative consequences. Expectancies did not predict 1-month abstinence rates, but at 3 months both Global Positive Change (AEQ subscale) and continued-drinking negative expectancy were predictive of abstinence. The same-day and next-day negative consequences were not as closely related to abstinence. Jones and McMahon (1994) conclude that global positive expectancies combine with long-term negative expectations to influence drinking decisions following treatment.

Caudill and Hoffman (1994) assessed expectancies among a sample of cocaine-dependent clients in treatment. Most of the clients were crack smokers (86%), male (62%), African-American (94%), and self-referred to treatment (92%). The investigators found that clients with strong cocaine expectancies overall tended to remain in treatment longer. However, the expectancy measures were not predictive of long-term treatment outcomes. They speculated that clinical outcomes were related more to coexisting psychiatric disorders than to cocaine expectancies (Caudill & Hoffman, 1994).

ALCOHOL AND STRESS: COGNITION AS A MEDIATING PROCESS

When alcoholics are asked, "Does drinking reduce tension and stress?," the overwhelming majority answer is "yes." Stockwell (1985) found that 93% of a sample of 2,300 alcoholics in treatment reported that they drank to relax. For some time, numerous other studies, using a variety of assessment methodologies, have arrived at similar conclusions for both nonproblem and problem drinkers (Brown, 1985; Masserman, Jacques, & Nicholson, 1945; Wanberg, 1969). Yet the "tension reduction hypothesis" (TRH) has been a long-standing source of controversy in the alcoholism field. There have been two principal reasons for this debate. First, the TRH deviates from some of the tenets of the disease model (e.g., loss of control), and has treatment implications (e.g., the possibility of controlled drinking) that are inconsistent with it (Langenbucher & Nathan, 1990). Second, the findings from studies of the TRH have inconsistently supported its validity (Cappell & Greeley, 1987).

The TRH relies on principles of operant conditioning. As a theory, it is rather simple, straightforward, and readily testable. Furthermore, it is consistent with both folklore and clinical observations. According to Langenbucher and Nathan (1990), "the theory presumes that alcoholic drinking is a product of escape learning; alcoholics drink because they have been negatively reinforced for drinking in the face of life stress" (p. 133). Essentially, the relief from stress (whether it be anxiety, depression, frustration, fear, etc.) maintains high levels of consumption. The relief from these negative emotional states is the reward provided by drinking.

The TRH model actually consists of two subhypotheses, which have been tested in a number of studies: (1) In the presence of stress, alcoholic drinking will increase; and (2) the stress of alcoholics will be relieved by drinking (Cappell & Greeley, 1987; Langenbucher & Nathan, 1990). Before we discuss the evidence for and against these subhypotheses, we will examine some of the early work in this area.

According to a review of the TRH by Cappell and Greeley (1987), E. M. Jellinek, the pioneering alcoholism researcher of the 1940s, was among the first to link alcoholic drinking to tension reduction. Jellinek (1945) proposed that as modern society evolves, it becomes more complex and more difficult for the individual to cope with. As a result, "individuals are more likely to experience increases in frustration, anger, anxiety, and tension. Individual releases are sought. Since there is a substance which can give the desired relief, harassed man will want to take recourse to it" (Jellinek, 1945, p. 19). Jellinek was careful to avoid suggesting that all alcohol use is driven by a desire to find relief from tension; rather, he felt that this desire is one important motivation for drinking, especially for problem drinking. Figure 5.4 illustrates Jellinek's model.

Jellinek did not formally coin the phrase "tension reduction hypothesis," however. About a decade later, Conger (1956), in a seminal study on the relationship between alcohol use and tension, first used the term. Conger was an experimental psychologist who relied on laboratory data from animal studies. In the early 1950s, Conger made use of an approach–avoidance conflict procedure using rats (McKim, 1986). He trained his rats to run down an alley for food (the reward or reinforcer). As they began to eat, he would electrify the grid on which they rested. Clearly, this produced conflict for the hungry rats! They were being reinforced and punished at the same time.

Over time, Conger (1951) adjusted both the food deprivation level (making the food a stronger or weaker reinforcer) and the electric shock level. Eventually, the rats "learned" to run part way down the alley but not to touch the food. Conger found that when one group of rats was injected with alcohol, they would approach and eat the food almost immediately, despite the electric shock. By contrast, a group of rats that received only a placebo injection required many more trials before they would approach and eat the food on an electrified grid. In

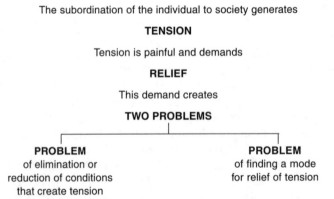

FIGURE 5.4. Jellinek's schematic representation of the origin and consequences of tension. Adapted from Jellinek (1945) by Cappell and Greeley (1987). Copyright 1987 by The Guilford Press. Reprinted by permission.

essence, the alcohol ameliorated the conflict between eating and receiving a shock. Conger (1951) concluded that these findings supported an important element of the TRH—that is, that alcohol mitigates aversive states such as fear or tension.

Since Conger's (1951) early work, numerous TRH studies have been conducted, and several comprehensive reviews of this body of research exist. Each one reaches slightly different conclusions about the validity of the TRH. The most recent review, by Langenbucher and Nathan (1990), indicates that empirical evidence generally supports the validity of the TRH. Specifically, the authors conclude that (1) there is a statistically significant positive correlation between a study's year of publication and its methodological quality, and (2) the greater the methodological adequacy of a study, the more strongly its findings support the TRH (Langenbucher & Nathan, 1990).

A 1987 review of TRH studies is somewhat more cautious in its assessment of the research. Cappell and Greeley (1987) observe that studies relying on *conflict paradigms* (e.g., Conger's work, described previously) in both humans and animals "provide relatively consistent support for the TRH" (p. 44). However, these studies have not specified the exact elements of conflict that alcohol is able to ameliorate.

In contrast, *stress-induction paradigms* produce equivocal results. Under aversive stimuli, such as tension, individuals respond in different ways when given alcohol. It is possible that biological differences among individuals make some much more responsive to the tension-dampening effects of alcohol than others. Furthermore, some studies have suggested that low or moderate amounts of alcohol may dampen responses to stress, whereas high amounts may actually exacerbate it. Finally, studies that have made use of social stressors (those most similar to the "natural" ones most alcoholics would experience) have been least likely to produce findings in support of the TRH. Cappell and Greeley (1987) conclude that the inconsistencies in the "social stressor" class of TRH studies are difficult to explain. However, it is possible that individuals interpret and respond to identical, stressful social situations (e.g., interpersonal conflict) in varied ways, with or without alcohol. Thus, the complexity of the relationship may be especially pronounced. Powers and Kutash (1985) neatly summarized these findings in the following passage:

> Alcohol use does not cause the relief of stress, in that alcohol is neither a necessary nor a sufficient condition for that occurrence. Alcohol is not a necessary condition for stress relief, for very often stress relief occurs without the presence of alcohol. Alcohol is not a sufficient condition, for at times alcohol use results in an increase in stress or no change.

Alcohol is best considered as one of many possible contributors to stress relief. Many interactive factors determine whether alcohol use results in a reduction of stress. The most prominent factors identified thus far include: expectations regarding alcohol's effects, pharmacological effects of alcohol at varying dosages, individual differences in the appraisal of stressors and in coping behaviors, and the entire constellation of stressors and stress responses experienced by the individual. (p. 471)

STRESS RESPONSE DAMPENING

In response to the inconsistent findings of studies testing the TRH, Levenson, Sher, Grossman, Newman, and Newlin (1980) created the stress response dampening (SRD) model. The model builds on the TRH by *specifying the conditions under which alcohol will be used to reduce stress or tension*. The major propositions of the SRD model are summarized as follows:

1. Alcohol is a drug that can dampen the physiological stress response.
2. Drinking behavior tends to be reinforced when alcohol is used in a stressful context.
3. Stress reduction is due to pharmacological mechanisms, not expectancy of alcohol effects.
4. Physiological arousal (i.e., the stress response alone does not predict alcohol use.
5. Instead, alcohol use is likely in stressful situations when there are no negative consequences for drinking and when the individual possesses certain personality traits, particularly antisociality and impulsiveness (Sher, 1987).

Support for the SRD model is demonstrated by findings from an experimental study that compared the alcohol consumption of two groups of social drinkers; half were adult children of biological fathers who abused alcohol (Sayette, Breslin, Wilson, & Rosenblum, 1994). All participants were exposed to a social stressor (anticipation and delivery of a public speech) after consuming either a moderate dose of alcohol or tonic water. The instructional set was varied to be either consistent or inconsistent with the beverage they actually received in the experiment. It was found that alcohol intoxication reduced subjective anxiety and negative self-evaluation in response to the stressor. This was true for both men and women. Parental history and belief about whether they received alcohol or a placebo had no effects on response to the stressor. Furthermore, alcohol expectancies, as assessed by the AEQ, also had no correlation with stress reactivity (Sayette et al., 1994).

The findings support the SRD model by showing that alcohol's ability to reduce stress rests primarily on its pharmacological action. Alcohol expectancies, from the psychological domain, appear to be relatively unimportant moderators of stress reactivity. Expectancy variables may have greater influence on other forms of behavior, particularly those involving social interaction, such as sexual risk taking (Dermen, Cooper, & Agocha, 1998).

Appraisal–Disruption: Alcohol's Ability to Interfere with the Processing of Stressful Information

Further explication of the conditions under which alcohol dampens stress is found in research conducted by Sayette (1993). The following propositions are the major components of his appraisal–disruption model:

1. The pharmacological actions of alcohol interfere with the *initial appraisal of stressful information* by diminishing the power of a stressor to activate associated memories and concepts in long-term memory;
2. Alcohol is most likely to dampen stress when it is consumed *prior to appraisal of the stressor*; and
3. When alcohol is consumed after appraisal of the stressor, *the stress response may be enhanced rather than reduced.*

The thrust of Sayette's appraisal–disruption model is that the *timing of the alcohol consumption,* in relation to the appearance of a stressor, is critical for understanding whether the stress response will be dampened or exacerbated by drinking; it certainly helps explain why negative emotional states are sometimes intensified by drinking (e.g., profound grief reactions among those drinking at an Irish wake).

TIFFANY'S MODEL OF DRUG URGES AND CRAVINGS

The construct of "urge" or "craving" is central to many explanations of addictive behavior. It is used to explain the maintenance of a high rate of use and as well as relapse. The notion that urges or cravings prompt substance use seems to be taken for granted by laypersons, addicts themselves, and many professionals.

Marlatt (1985) proposed a distinction between "urge" and "craving," noting that an urge is an *intention* that motivates use, whereas craving represents the *anticipation* of a positive drug effect (i.e., an outcome expectancy). Regardless of whether this distinction is accepted, Marlatt's conception represents a positive reinforcement model of urge/craving. In contrast, an earlier model by Jellinek (1955) proposed that cravings represented the anticipation of relief from withdrawal, in essence, a negative reinforcement model.

In a review of the empirical research, Tiffany (1990) contends that data do not support either Marlatt's or Jellinek's models. His case is based on an examination of the relationship between drug urge and actual use. Across both self-report and physiological measures, he found that the correlations between urges and drug use were only of modest or moderate magnitude. This suggests that *drug use occurs frequently without being prompted by urges.* Furthermore, Tiffany (1990) observed that *many relapses were not provoked by urges and cravings.* In such cases, he concluded that these episodes could be characterized as "absentminded relapses" (p. 163). To account for these observations, Tiffany created the following cognitive model to explain drug urges and cravings.

Human cognitive processing includes both *automatic* and *nonautomatic* processes (Shiffrin & Schneider, 1977). According to Tiffany (1990), an automatic cognitive process is "a relatively permanent sequence of tightly integrated associative connections in long-term memory that always become active in response to a particular input configuration" (p. 152). Among humans, across many classes of behavior, automatic processes are revealed by the following: (1) speed in task performance; (2) the behavior is executed without intention and is elicited by specific stimuli; (3) under eliciting stimuli, the behavior is difficult to inhibit or curtail; (4) the behavior is easy and nondemanding to carry out; and (5) the behavior can be conducted without much conscious awareness. The common example of automatic cognitive process is driving a motor vehicle to a familiar destination, such as work. Operation of the vehicle occurs automatically and without much conscious awareness.

The same processes guide compulsive drug self-administration, whether it be smoking, alcohol consumption, drug injection, and so on. Tiffany (1990) asserts that with repeated practice, drug acquisition and consumption become behavior produced by automatic processes. He employs the concept of *drug use action plans* to emphasize that over time, the sequence of behaviors involved in using alcohol and/or drugs becomes integrated, efficient, and effortless. In typical situations in which drug use occurs unimpeded, urges do *not* accompany the process. It is on this point that Tiffany's model departs significantly from traditional views of urges/cravings. To explain how urges are generated, Tiffany points to an opposite set of cognitive processes. Nonautomatic cognitive processing is slow, and it depends on careful attention and effort. Other features of nonautomatic processing include (1) identification of strategies, (2) conscious decision making, (3) planning, and (4) monitoring of task performance.

In Tiffany's (1990) model, *both* abstinence–avoidance and abstinence–promotion urges are produced by nonautomatic processes. Abstinence–avoidance urges occur when drug-use action plans are blocked or obstructed by external barriers (e.g., running out of cigarettes late at night), whereas abstinence–promotion urges are produced when the individual is attempting to change drug use or to maintain abstinence (e.g., while in treatment). Tiffany (1990) hypothesizes that stress and other negative emotional states give rise to both types of urges, which generate competing nonautomatic processes that can influence drug use action plans. This competition tends to inhibit the impact of abstinence–promotion urges and thereby increases the likelihood of the individual executing their automatic drug use action plans.

RELAPSE

A "relapse" can be defined as an "uncontrolled return to drug or alcohol use following competent treatment" (Lewis, Dana, & Blevins, 1988, p. 193). It is probably the most significant issue in treating chemically dependent clients. It is often puzzling that individuals who seem to recognize the seriousness of their addiction, who appear committed to recovery, and who have gained some mastery over their drinking or drug-taking behavior often have tremendous difficulty in remaining abstinent.

Historically, views on relapse have tended to be moralistic. Such views still predominate in many segments of our society. Relapsed alcoholics or addicts are scorned: They are thought of as lazy, irresponsible, or possibly weak-willed. Essentially, they are viewed as having a defect of character. Unfortunately, such views, especially when held by legislators, government officials, and other key decision makers, impede progress in treatment approaches by depriving treatment and research centers of much-needed financial support.

Interestingly, the disease model of addiction has traditionally had little to say about relapse prevention. AA folklore, and especially its slogans, provide various messages of caution about "slippery places" and direct members to call their sponsors, but little is provided in the way of skills. Moreover, the disease model has not elaborated on the meaning of relapse. The loss-of-control concept in alcoholism has, in fact, been cited for inadvertently contributing to full-blown relapses (Lewis et al., 1988). The proposal that alcoholics cannot stop drinking once alcohol enters their bodies seems to establish an expectation that 1 drink must lead to 20. Thus, when many alcoholics and other drug addicts do relapse, they often seem to go on extended binges.

Stress as an Impetus for Relapse

Stress is frequently associated with relapse among recovering persons (Hunter & Salmone, 1986; Milkman, Weiner, & Sunderwith, 1984; Marlatt & Gordon, 1979). A review of the research literature indicates that it is the most frequently cited explanation for relapse (Milkman et al., 1984). For instance, of the 20 conditions that Hunter and Salmone (1986) describe as being associated with relapse, 12 are stress-related. One prominent study collected data on 137 relapse episodes reported by groups of alcoholics, cigarette smokers, and heroin addicts (Marlatt & Gordon, 1979). All subjects had completed treatment programs with complete abstinence as the goal. Results revealed that 76% of the relapses studied occurred in three contexts: (1) intrapersonal negative emotional states (37%), (2) social pressure (24%), and (3) interpersonal conflict (15%).

In general, it appears that relapsers evaluate more life situations as threatening than do nonrelapsers. Those who relapse seem to have greater difficulty in coping with unpleasant emotions, frustrating events, and unsatisfactory relations with others. In other words, they demonstrate low frustration tolerance (see next section). The nonrelapsers seem to learn strategies for coping with the problems whereas the relapsers do not. This seems to apply to the gamut of addictions. The cognitive dynamics appear similar in cigarette smoking, overeating, alcoholism, and heroin and cocaine addiction.

Hunter and Salmone (1986) note the role of self-evaluations in relapse in the following passage:

> Stress . . . can become a substantial problem when the feeling of stress underlies a perceived need to make up for lost time, as is frequently the case when a recovering alcoholic becomes a work addict. Impatience represents a lack of preparation for non-chemical coping and includes frustration experienced when one's goals have been set unachievably high. If one is unwilling to admit to mistakes in judgement, or in performance, one is left with two options: (1) being absolutely perfect, or (2) feeling totally worthless. The first of these is unrealistic; the second is a dangerously negative feeling about oneself. Recovering alcoholics cannot afford either of these extremes. (p. 24)

Thinking Patterns and Relapse

Clearly, all those in recovery who have a commitment to abstinence face stressful situations. In fact, stress can be viewed as a natural consequence of taking on the challenge of living drug-free. The key in determining whether recovery stress is facilitative or debilitative is the individual's interpretation of frustrating experiences—that is, how the person thinks about himself/herself, others, and the world. In this view, cognition, thinking, self-statements, internal dialogue, and so forth mediate stress. It is not so much stress itself (which is virtually a universal human experience) as the manner in which people evaluate it that is critical. As the ancient Stoic philosopher Epictetus once said, "Men are disturbed not by things but by the views which they take of them."

The proponents of rational–emotive theory (a cognitive-behavioral psychotherapy) have elaborated on the thinking patterns and emotions of recovering alcoholics and addicts (Ellis, McInerney, DiGiuseppe, & Yeager, 1988). According to Ellis (1985), among the most basic and broadly experienced motivations for continuing with self-defeating behavior patterns are discomfort anxiety and low frustration tolerance; this is particularly true in addictive behaviors (Ellis et al., 1988). "Discomfort anxiety" is the emotion one experiences when anticipating an unpleasant or uncomfortable feeling. Ellis et al. (1988) write, "It is usually brought about by the irrational belief that pain, discomfort, or unpleasantness is unbearable, and that it cannot and must not be tolerated" (p. 25). Accompanying discomfort anxiety is "low frustration tolerance"—that is, the tendency to avoid situations or tasks that may be difficult or painful in some way.

These conditions are thought to be especially prominent in the covert cognitive functioning of the recovering addict. Rational–emotive theorists refer to this as the "abstinence/low-frustration-tolerance pattern" (Ellis et al., 1988). It stems from such dysfunctional beliefs as the following:

1. I cannot stand avoiding a drink.
2. I cannot function without a drink.
3. I am not strong enough to resist alcohol.
4. I cannot stand the deprivation of my desire for a drink.
5. I am a horribly deprived person if I cannot have a drink.
6. Life is too hard so I am entitled to have a drink.
7. To make up for my difficult life, I must have a drink.
8. I must have a drink or I can't go on.
9. I must not abstain when it's so enjoyable to imbibe.
10. I must not abstain when it is so painful to do so. (Ellis et al., 1988, p. 25)

These beliefs (and other similar ones) trigger the pattern as displayed in Figure 5.5.

Ellis et al. (1988) note that the reason addictive behavior is so easy to develop is that no alternative coping strategy (e.g., cognitive or

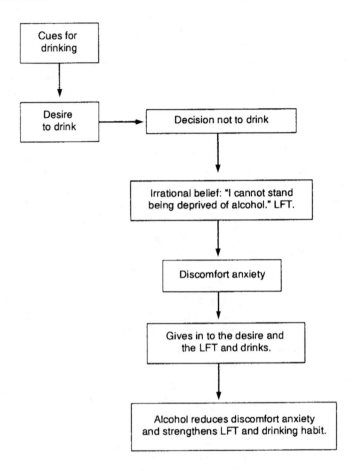

FIGURE 5.5. The abstinence/low-frustration-tolerance (LFT) pattern. Adapted from Ellis, McInerney, DiGiuseppe, and Yeager (1988). Copyright 1988 by Allyn & Bacon. Adapted by permission.

behavioral) can reduce the discomfort anxiety as quickly and effortlessly as alcohol or drugs can. All other strategies require time to work, practice, and individual effort. During such a period, the addict is experiencing discomfort and susceptible to falling back into the habit of relying on chemicals.

Table 5.1 describes five of the most common irrational beliefs associated with low frustration tolerance and relapse. The table also lists rational alternatives that a recovering person can use to dispute these irrational thoughts about the difficulties of recovery.

TABLE 5.1. Self-Defeating Thinking That Might Lead to Relapse, and Some Model Rational Alternatives

Self-defeating thought	Rational alternative
1. "This not drinking is just too hard. I can't stand not having what I want."	"While not drinking is certainly difficult, I have stood it for some time now and one hour or one day at a time I can continue to stand it. I don't need everything I merely want, and while I may want a drink, I don't want all the problems that it will bring."
2. "I need more excitement in my life. I'm so bored without seeing my friends I can't stand it anymore. I'll go visit my friends at the bar, but not take a drink."	"Nobody ever died of boredom. While I certainly would like more excitement in my life right now, the price of associating with my friends might be drinking again. If I want to be less bored, I'd better find some other things to do."
3. "Poor me. I must be so damn worthless to have to give up drinking when so many people can handle it. Nothing is going right for me, so what's the use? How could a drink make my life any worse?"	"Where is the evidence that I am worthless because I can't do 'something that some other people can do'? I can't run a four-minute mile either. Does that prove I'm worthless? While things may not be great right now, it doesn't help to pity myself. It only makes me feel worse. I need to think through that drink I want. Remember the last drink? Did that make life better? Or did it lead to more and more drinks, which made a bad situation so much worse?"
4. "They shouldn't treat me this way. I'll show them who is boss, I'll fix them. I'll go get drunk and then they will be sorry."	"I really hate it when I'm treated this way. I'd better learn to stick up for myself but punishing them may not be the way to do that. Besides, who am I really going to punish if I go out and get drunk?"
5. "I'm so upset and uptight. If I don't have a drink, I'll go crazy. I sure would rather be drunk than out of my mind."	"A drink won't prevent me from going crazy. In fact, it may take me further down the road. Being uptight or upset can be best handled without a drink. People don't go crazy from not getting what they want."

Note. From Ellis, McInerney, DiGiuseppe, and Yeager (1988). Copyright 1988 by Allyn & Bacon. Reprinted by permission.

An Analysis of Relapse and Its Prevention

SLT offers a perspective on relapse that differs from the one put forth by the traditional disease model. According to Lewis et al. (1988), "The social learning perspective . . . looks at a return to substance use as a learning experience that can be successfully used to bolster gains previously made in treatment" (p. 200). In fact, clients are taught to view "slips" in just this way. Relapse is not viewed as something that is "awful" or "terrible," and clients are not taught to fear it. Instead, they are encouraged to understand it as a response to environmental cues that constantly impinge on them. It is not evidence that they are incompetent, stupid, or worthless. The experience of relapse can provide clients with the opportunity to learn about their high-risk situations or "triggers" and to identify strategies that they can use to prevent them.

Much of the work done in relapse prevention has been carried out by Marlatt and Gordon (1985). They view relapse as the result of *high-risk situations* combined with the tendency to engage in *self-defeating thinking*. High-risk situations are those that may trigger a "slip"; they may include visiting a friend at a bar, attending a wedding reception, returning to an old neighborhood, or the like. In AA parlance, they are referred to as "slippery places." Relapse prevention strategies teach clients how to cope better with high-risk situations. Thus, this approach can be viewed as an attempt to enhance coping skills. Client self-efficacy is a critical factor.

Marlatt and Gordon (1985) believe that self-defeating thinking emerges from lifestyle imbalances. These lifestyle imbalances occur when the external demands on an individual's time and energy interfere with their ability to satisfy desires for pleasure and self-fulfillment. In this imbalance, recovering clients feel pressure to "catch up" for lost time and thus feel *deprived* of pleasure, enjoyment, fun, and so on. As a result, they come to feel that they deserve indulgence and gratification. During this state of perceived deprivation, cravings for their preferred substance tend to arise, and they begin to think positively about the immediate effects of the chemical. In other words, they generate positive alcohol or drug expectancies in which substance use is anticipated to make their immediate situation better. At the same time, they deny or selectively forget about all the negative consequences that go along with a reinitiation of use. There is often the tendency to rationalize the return to using (e.g., "I owe myself this drink").

Apparently Irrelevant Decisions

In this process of covert cognitive change, recovering persons may find themselves in more and more high-risk situations prior to the first "slip." As this movement begins, they start making "apparently irrelevant decisions" (AIDs) (Marlatt & Gordon, 1985). According to Lewis et al. (1988):

> These AIDs are thought to be a product of rationalization ("What I'm doing is O.K.") and denial ("This behavior is acceptable and has

no relationship to relapse") that manifest themselves as certain choices that lead inevitably to a relapse. In this respect AIDs are best conceptualized as "minidecisions" that are made over time and that, when combined, lead the client closer and closer to the brink of the triggering high-risk situation. (p. 203)

Figure 5.6 illustrates Lewis et al.'s view of the role of AIDs and other cognitive antecedents of a relapse.

Examples of AIDs abound. Following is a list of typical AIDs as they apply to recovery:

1. A recovering alcoholic begins to purchase his cigarettes at liquor stores. He insists that the liquor stores are more conveniently located than other sales outlets.
2. A recovering alcoholic begins taking a new route home from work. She says she is bored with the old way. The new route is somewhat longer; it also has several liquor stores along the way.

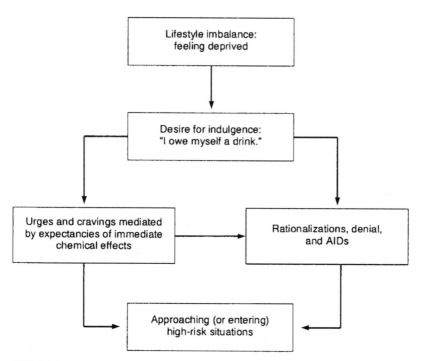

FIGURE 5.6. Covert (cognitive) antecedents of a relapse. Adapted from Lewis, Dana, and Blevins (1988). Copyright 1988 by Brooks/Cole Publishing Company. Adapted by permission.

3. A husband in early recovery begins to offer to run to the store for groceries. His wife is pleased. He regularly goes to the supermarket with a liquor store next door, even though it is further from home. He says that this market has better prices.
4. A recovering substance abuser goes to an old drug buddy's house to borrow a hammer.
5. A recovering alcoholic offers to go alone on out-of-town business trips. Her supervisor says that it is not necessary that she always go, but she says she likes to get away.
6. A recovering alcoholic refuses to get rid of his liquor cabinet. He says he needs it when entertaining friends and relatives.
7. A recovering substance abuser transfers to a new job within the company. It is not a promotion, but it happens to have little direct supervision.

The Abstinence Violation Effect

In the SLT perspective, there is a significant difference between a "lapse" (or a "slip") and a full-blown relapse (Abrams & Niaura, 1987). A lapse is seen as a return to drinking that is brief, involves consuming a small quantity of alcohol, and has no other adverse consequences. By contrast, a relapse involves a return to heavy consumption, perhaps bingeing, and is accompanied by a host of emotional and physical complications. The aim of relapse prevention is to prevent lapses from turning into relapses (Abrams & Niaura, 1987).

The "abstinence violation effect" is the experience of intense shame, guilt, and embarrassment that frequently occurs following a lapse or a slip (Marlatt & Gordon, 1985). It increases the likelihood that a slip will turn into a full-blown relapse. Among those recovering persons who are committed to abstinence, the slip may be interpreted as evidence of personal inadequacy or incompetence. The person can be overwhelmed by intense self-directed negative emotion. One recovering alcoholic told me (DT) that he remembers saying this to himself after he slipped: "I can't believe I did this. I'm so stupid. What I've done is horrible. My wife will have no respect for me. This shows that I really am nothing but a no-good drunk—just a piece of shit. I might just as well keep drinking. It don't matter no more."

Early in treatment, prior to lapses, clients need to be educated about the meaning of slips and relapses. It is important that they not think of relapse as personal failure. This type of cognitive restructuring teaches them that a slip is only a mistake, not global evidence of a character flaw. Furthermore, it is helpful for the clients to attribute the slips to environmental cues rather than to themselves. By doing this, they place the focus properly on dealing effectively with the trigger situations. Such a focus tends to build self-efficacy as the clients learn skills for coping with high-risk situations.

PROJECT MATCH: A TEST OF COGNITIVE THERAPY

In 1989, the National Institute on Alcohol Abuse and Alcoholism initiated a study entitled *Matching Alcoholism Treatments to Client Heterogeneity* (Project MATCH). The project was a national, multisite, randomized clinical trial designed to assess the benefits of matching alcoholic clients to three different psychosocial treatments, while accounting for ten client characteristics (Project MATCH Research Group, 1997). Project MATCH was the largest and most statistically powerful trial of psychotherapy outcomes ever carried out.

Details about the findings of the trial are not fully discussed here. However, in a review of cognitive models it is important to mention that cognitive-behavioral coping skills therapy was one of the tested treatments. The other two were motivational enhancement therapy and Twelve-Step facilitation therapy (Project MATCH Research Group, 1997).

All three therapies, delivered in either aftercare or outpatient settings, had substantial positive effects on measures of "percent days abstinent" and "drinks per drinking day." However, the study yielded little evidence to support the value of matching clients to different treatments. Hence, cognitive-behavioral coping skills therapy was not superior to the other forms of therapy offered in the trial. In fact, evidence suggested that in outpatient settings specifically, Twelve-Step facilitation therapy produced better outcomes than the cognitive therapy in clients with low psychiatric severity. Neither therapy was superior for clients with high psychiatric severity (Project MATCH Research Group, 1997).

SUMMARY

The cognitive-behavioral models provide a sound conceptual base for understanding substance use. The initiation of substance use is influenced by outcome expectancies and by modeling. Young people initiate substance use as a result of observing others. They imitate parents, peers, media figures, and so on, because they anticipate deriving the same rewards they observe others obtain.

Alcohol and drug abuse are self-regulated behaviors. The high degree of self-regulation is demonstrated by the time and effort that are required to maintain a lifestyle centered around drinking and/or drug use. Viewing such behavior as "out of control" is probably inaccurate.

The concept of "self-efficacy" is an extremely important one in assisting chemically dependent persons. Evidence suggests that a crucial determinant in whether treatment will be successful is the client's belief in his/her ability to master the various tasks of recovery. Without this belief, treatment is likely to fail. In addition, research indicates that self-efficacy is most likely to be enhanced by "performance accomplishments." Thus, it is imperative that clients initially be given small tasks at which success is virtually assured before they attempt more difficult ones.

Recent cognitive models have shed light on how drug outcome expectancies influence drug use and related behavior, including treatment outcomes. Some of this work has attempted to tie expectancy formation to human memory and cognitive processing. These important advances in cognitive science have added precision to our understanding of such nebulous topics as alcohol use and stress and drug urges and cravings.

Relapse is often related to an inability to cope with environmental stressors (i.e., high-risk situations). It often appears to result from negative emotional states, social pressure, and interpersonal conflicts, rather than being evidence of a character flaw. Effective relapse prevention strategies anticipate these events by teaching clients specific coping skills tailored to their individual needs.

Finally, cognitive-behavioral relapse prevention considers lapses (and even relapses) to be opportunities for learning. Instead of viewing them as events to be fearful of, and as evidence of treatment failure, treatment providers should assist clients in analyzing their high-risk situations and covert cognitive processes. Helping clients to think differently about the meaning of relapse can result in a reduction of the abstinence violation effect and thus in fewer subsequent full-blown relapses.

REVIEW QUESTIONS

1. As it relates to determinism, how does social learning theory (SLT) differ from both psychoanalysis and conditioning theory?

2. How are expectancies and modeling related to one another?

3. How can alcohol and drug use be influenced by modeling?

4. What is the significance of "self-regulation" and "reciprocal determinism" for understanding substance use?

5. What is "self-efficacy"? How is it influenced?

6. With respect to substance use, what types of self-efficacy exist?

Has research found self-efficacy to be related to treatment outcomes?

7. What are "alcohol and drug expectancies"?

8. How are placebo conditions use to study alcohol expectancies?

9. What is the bogus taste-rating task?

10. How does "sociability" moderate modeling effects on drinking?

11. Has survey research been able to link expectancies to substance use? What are the anticipated outcomes of marijuana and cocaine use?

12. Does the evidence indicate that drug expectancies are the precursors or consequences of substance use?

13. What role does memory play in drinking behavior? How are the memory networks of heavy drinkers different from those of lighter drinkers?

14. What is the role of drug expectancy in psychiatric comorbidity?

15. What types of alcohol expectancies are linked to treatment outcome?

16. What is the tension reduction hypothesis (TRH)? Do existing data support its validity?

17. What are the propositions of the stress response dampening (SRD) model?

18. Under what conditions, does alcohol disrupt the initial appraisal of stressful information?

19. In Tiffany's model, when do drug urges appear in cognitive processing?

20. How has relapse been viewed historically?

21. What is the most frequently cited explanation for relapse in the professional literature?

22. What are "discomfort anxiety" and "low frustration tolerance"? How do they lead to relapse?

23. What are the cognitive patterns that lead to relapse? What is the significance of feeling deprived?

24. In SLT, how are recovering clients taught to view relapse?

25. What are "apparently irrevelant decisions" (AIDs)? How do they lead to relapses?

26. What is the "abstinence violation effect"?

27. What were the outcomes of Project MATCH?

REFERENCES

Abrams, D. B., & Niaura, R. S. (1987). Social learning theory. In H. T. Blane & K. E. Leonard (Eds.), *Psychological theories of drinking and alcoholism.* New York: Guilford Press.

Bandura, A. (1971). Analysis of modelling processes. In A. Bandura (Ed.), *Psychological modelling: Conflicting models.* Chicago: Aldine-Atherton.

Bandura, A. (1977). *Social learning theory.* Englewood Cliffs, NJ: Prentice-Hall.

Bandura, A. (1995). Exercise of personal and collective efficacy in changing societies. In A. Bandura (Ed.), *Self-efficacy in changing societies.* New York: Cambridge University Press.

Bandura, A. (1997). *Self-efficacy: The exercise of control.* New York: Freeman.

Bolles, R. C. (1972). Reinforcement, expectancy, and learning. *Psychological Review, 79,* 394–409.

Brown, S. A. (1985). Expectancies versus background in the prediction of college drinking patterns. *Journal of Consulting and Clinical Psychology, 53,* 123–130.

Brown, S. A., Christiansen, B. A., & Goldman, M. S. (1987). The Alcohol Expectancy Questionnaire: An instrument for the assessment of adolescent and adult alcohol expectancies. *Journal of Studies on Alcohol, 48,* 483–491.

Brown, S. A., Creamer, V. A., & Stetson, B. A. (1987). Adolescent alcohol expectancies as a function of personal and parental drinking patterns. *Journal of Abnormal Psychology, 96,* 117–121.

Burling, T. A., Reilly, P. M., Moltzen, J. O., & Ziff, D. C. (1989). Self-efficacy and relapse among inpatient drug and alcohol abusers: A predictor of outcome. *Journal of Studies on Alcohol, 50,* 354–360.

Cappell, H., & Greeley, J. (1987). Alcohol and tension reduction: An update on research and theory. In H. T. Blane & K. E. Leonard (Eds.), *Psychological theories of drinking and alcoholism.* New York: Guilford Press.

Caudill, B., & Hoffman, J. A. (1994, August). *Cocaine expectancies and treatment outcomes among crack users.* Paper presented at the annual meeting of the American Psychological Association, Los Angeles.

Caudill, B. D., & Marlatt, G. A. (1975). Modeling influences in social drinking: An experimental analogue. *Journal of Consulting and Clinical Psychology, 43,* 405–415.

Christiansen, B. A., Roehling, P. V., Smith, G. T., & Goldman, M. S. (1989). Using alcohol expectancies to predict adolescent drinking behavior after one year. *Journal of Consulting and Clinical Psychology, 57,* 93–99.

Collins, R. L., Parks, G. A., & Marlatt, G. A. (1985). Social determinants of alcohol consumption: The effects of social interaction and model status on the self-administration of alcohol. *Journal of Consulting and Clinical Psychology, 53,* 189–200.

Conger, J. J. (1951). The effects of alcohol on conflict and avoidance behavior. *Quarterly Journal of Studies on Alcohol, 12,* 1–29.

Conger, J. J. (1956). Alcoholism: Theory, problem, and challenge. II. Reinforcement theory and the dynamics of alcoholism. *Quarterly Journal of Studies on Alcohol, 13,* 296–305.

Critchlow, B. (1987). Brief report: A utility analysis of drinking. *Addictive Behaviors, 12,* 269–273.

Dermen, K. H., Cooper, M. L., & Agocha, V. B. (1998). Sex-related alcohol expectancies as moderators of the relationship between alcohol use and risky sex in adolescents. *Journal of Studies on Alcohol, 59,* 71–77.

Drug use and the mentally ill. (1994). *Harvard Mental Health Letter, 11,* 6–7.

Dunn, M. E., & Goldman, M. S. (1996). Empirical modeling of an alcohol expectancy memory network in elementary school children as a function of grade. *Experimental and Clinical Psychopharmacology, 4,* 1–9.

Ellis, A. (1985). *Overcoming resistance.* New York: Springer.

Ellis, A., McInerney, J. J., DiGiuseppe, R., & Yeager, R. J. (1988). *Rational-emotive therapy with alcoholics and substance abusers.* Elmsford, NY: Pergamon Press.

Goldman, M. S., Brown, S. A., & Christiansen, B. A. (1987). Expectancy theory: Thinking about drinking. In H. T. Blane & K. E. Leonard (Eds.), *Psychological theories of drinking and alcoholism.* New York: Guilford Press.

Goodwin, D. W. (1990). Genetic determinants of reinforcements from alcohol. In W. M. Cox (Ed.), *Why people drink: Parameters of alcohol as a reinforcer.* New York: Gardner Press.

Hackett, G. (1995). Self-efficacy in career choice and development. In A. Bandura (Ed.), *Self-efficacy in changing societies.* New York: Cambridge University Press.

Hunter, T. A., & Salmone, P. R. (1986). Dry drunk syndrome and alcoholic relapse. *Journal of Applied Rehabilitation Counseling, 18,* 22–25.

Jellinek, E. M. (1945). The problem of alcohol. In Yale Studies on Alcohol (Ed.), *Alcohol, science, and society.* Westport, CT: Greenwood Press.

Jellinek, E. M. (1955). The "craving" for alcohol. *Quarterly Journal of Studies on Alcohol, 16,* 35–38.

Jerusalem, M., & Mittag, W. (1995). Self-efficacy in stressful life transitions. In A. Bandura (Ed.), *Self-efficacy in changing societies.* New York: Cambridge University Press.

Jones, B. T., & McMahon, J. (1994). Negative and positive alcohol expectancies as predictors of abstinence after discharge from a residential treatment program: A one-month and three-month follow-up study in men. *Journal of Studies on Alcohol, 55,* 543–548.

Koob, G. F. (1992). Drugs of abuse: Anatomy, pharmacology, and function of reward pathways. *Trends in Pharmacologic Sciences, 13,* 177–182.

Kushner, M. G., Sher, K. J., & Beitman, B. D. (1990). The relation between alcohol problems and the anxiety disorders. *American Journal of Psychiatry, 147,* 685–695.

Langenbucher, J. W., & Nathan, P. E. (1990). The tension-reduction hypothesis: A reanalysis of some early crucial data. In W. M. Cox (Ed.), *Why people drink: Parameters of alcohol as a reinforcer.* New York: Gardner Press.

Levenson, R. W., Sher, K. J., Grossman, L. M., Newman, J., & Newlin, D. B. (1980). Alcohol and stress response dampening: Pharmacological effects, expectancy, and tension reduction. *Journal of Abnormal Psychology, 89,* 528–538.

Lewis, J. A., Dana, R. Q., & Blevins, G. A. (1988). *Substance abuse counseling: An individualized approach.* Pacific Grove, CA: Brooks/Cole.

Marlatt, G. A. (1985). Cognitive factors in the relapse process. In G. A. Marlatt & J. R. Gordon (Eds.), *Relapse prevention* (pp. 128–200). New York: Guilford Press.

Marlatt, G. A., Baer, J. S., & Quigley, L. A. (1995). Self-efficacy and addictive behavior. In A. Bandura (Ed.), *Self-efficacy in changing societies.* New York: Cambridge University Press.

Marlatt, G. A., Demming, B., & Reid, J. B. (1973). Loss of control drinking in alcoholics: An experimental analogue. *Journal of Abnormal Psychology, 81,* 233–241.

Marlatt, G. A., & Gordon, J. R. (1979). Determinants of relapse: Implications for the maintenance of behavior change. In P. A. Davidson & S. M. Davidson (Eds.), *Behavioral medicine: Changing health lifestyles.* New York: Brunner/Mazel.

Marlatt, G. A., & Gordon, J. R. (Eds.). (1985). *Relapse prevention.* New York: Guilford Press.

Masserman, J. H., Jacques, M. G., & Nicholson, M. R. (1945). Alcohol as a preventive of experimental neurosis. *Quarterly Journal of Studies on Alcohol, 6,* 281–299.

McKim, W. A. (1986). *Drugs and behavior: An introduction to behavioral pharmacology.* Englewood Cliffs, NJ: Prentice Hall.

Merry, J. (1966). The "loss of control" myth. *Lancet, 1,* 1257–1258.

Milkman, H., Weiner, S. E., & Sunderwirth, S. (1984). Addiction relapse. *Addictive Behaviors, 3,* 119–134.

Miller, P. M., Smith, G. T., & Goldman, M. S. (1990). Emergence of alcohol expectancies in childhood: A possible critical period. *Journal of Studies on Alcohol, 51,* 343–349.

Monte, C. F. (1980). *Beneath the mask: An introduction to theories of personality.* New York: Holt, Rinehart & Winston.

National Institute on Alcohol Abuse and Alcoholism. (1994). *Alcohol and health: Eighth special report to the U.S. Congress* (NIH Publication No. 94-3699). Bethesda, MD: National Institutes of Health.

Powers, R. J., & Kutash, I. L. (1985). Stress and alcohol. *International Journal of the Addictions, 20,* 461–482.

Project MATCH Research Group. (1997). Matching alcoholism treatments to client heterogeneity: Project MATCH posttreatment drinking outcomes. *Journal of Studies on Alcohol, 58,* 7–29.

Rather, B. C., & Goldman, M. S. (1994). Drinking-related differences in the memory organization of alcohol expectancies. *Experimental and Clinical Psychopharmacology, 2,* 167–183.

Rather, B. C., & Goldman, M. S., & Roehrich, L., & Brannick, M. (1992). Empirical modeling of an alcohol expectancy memory network using multidimensional scaling. *Journal of Abnormal Psychology, 101,* 174–183.

Reese, F. L., Chassin, L., & Molina, B. S. G. (1994). Alcohol expectancies in early adolescents: Drinking behavior from alcohol expectancies and parental alcoholism. *Journal of Studies on Alcohol, 55,* 276–284.

Rychtarik, R. G., Prue, D. M., Rapp, S. R., & King, A. C. (1992). Self-efficacy, aftercare and relapse in a treatment program for alcoholics. *Journal of Studies on Alcohol, 53*, 435–440.

Sayette, M. A. (1993). An appraisal–disruption model of alcohol's effects on stress responses in social drinkers. *Psychological Bulletin, 114*, 459–476.

Sayette, M. A., Breslin, F. C., Wilson, G. T., & Rosenblum, G. D. (1994). Parental history of alcohol abuse and the effects of alcohol and expectations of intoxication on social stress. *Journal of Studies on Alcohol, 55*, 214–223.

Schafer, J., & Brown, S. A. (1991). Marijuana and cocaine effect expectancies and drug use patterns. *Journal of Consulting and Clinical Psychology, 59*, 558–565.

Schwarzer, R., & Fuchs, R. (1995). Changing risk behaviors and adopting health behaviors: The role of self-efficacy beliefs. In A. Bandura (Ed.), *Self-efficacy in changing societies*. New York: Cambridge University Press.

Sher, K. J. (1987). Stress response dampening. In H. T. Blane & K. E. Leonard (Eds.), *Psychological theories of drinking and alcoholism*. New York: Guilford Press.

Shiffrin, R. M., & Schneider, W. (1977). Controlled and automatic human information processing: II. Perceptual learning, automatic attending, and a general theory. *Psychological Review, 84*, 127–190.

Smith, G. T., Goldman, M. S., Greenbaum, P. E., & Christiansen, B. A. (1995). Expectancy for social facilitation from drinking: The divergent paths of high-expectancy and low-expectancy adolescents. *Journal of Studies on Alcohol, 104*, 32–40.

Stacy, A. W., Newcomb, M. D., & Bentler, P. M. (1991). Cognitive motivation and drug use: A 9-year longitudinal study. *Journal of Abnormal Psychology, 100*, 502–515.

Stockwell, T. (1985). Stress and alcohol. *Stress Medicine, 1*, 209–215.

Tiffany, S. T. (1990). A cognitive model of drug urges and drug-use behavior: Role of automatic and nonautomatic processes. *Psychological Review, 97*, 147–168.

Thombs, D. L. (1991). Expectancies versus demographics in discriminating between college drinkers: Implications for alcohol abuse prevention. *Health Education Research, 6*, 491–495.

Thombs, D. L. (1993). The differentially discriminating properties of alcohol expectancies for female and male drinkers. *Journal of Counseling and Development, 71*, 321–325.

Wanberg, K. W. (1969). Prevalence of symptoms found among excessive drinkers. *International Journal of the Addictions, 4*, 169–185.

White, H. R., Bates, M. E., & Johnson, V. (1990). Social reinforcement and alcohol consumption. In W. M. Cox (Ed.), *Why people drink: Parameters of alcohol as a reinforcer*. New York: Gardner Press.

Wilson, G. T. (1988). Alcohol use and abuse: A social learning theory analysis. In C. D. Chaudron & D. A. Wilkinson (Eds.), *Theories on alcoholism*. Toronto: Addiction Research Foundation.

Zimmerman, B. J. (1995). Self-efficacy in career choice and development. In A. Bandura (Ed.), *Self-efficacy in changing societies*. New York: Cambridge University Press.

CHAPTER SIX

The Family System

Systems theory and family therapy have been linked with each other for several decades; however, the two are not synonymous. In "systems theory," the unit of analysis is the social system. Relatively little consideration is given to intrapsychic factors. The determinants of behavior are thought to be the "ongoing dynamics and demands of the key interpersonal system(s) within which the individual interacts" (Pearlman, 1988, p. 290). The emphasis is on social roles that are carried out within the context of the organizations to which one belongs. In this culture, the family is usually the dominant influence on behavior, though the workplace, the neighborhood community, and the church can also be considered influential systems.

The literature on addiction and the family has evolved from two sources: (1) the clinical experience of family therapists and (2) empirical research. According to Sher (1997), this has created two bodies of knowledge that are relatively distinct from one another. In this chapter, key concepts from the clinically focused literature are presented first, followed by a review of findings generated from research studies.

CLINICALLY GENERATED CONCEPTS

Social systems, such as families, are complex organizations that are hierarchical in nature. Their dynamics consist of stable, predictable patterns of relationships. Rules (which are often unspoken, but known to members) guide these relationship patterns. Whenever one element in the system is changed (e.g., an alcoholic family member stops drinking), all other elements are affected. The entire system attempts to compensate for the change. Thus, systems theory stresses the wholeness of the social unit and emphasizes the interdependence of all the members of the system. Again, psychological factors are not usually scrutinized. According to Steinglass (1978), the significance assigned to "wholeness" and interdependent relationships is that which distinguishes systems theory from most other perspectives on addiction.

Boundaries

In a family system (as well as other systems), there is organization. Several systems concepts are typically used to describe the nature of the organization. One such concept is referred to as "boundaries." Boundaries exist to

> distinguish those elements contained within the system from other elements within the broader environment. Boundaries are significant within a system framework since they not only define membership within a given system or subsystem but also characterize the quality of the relationship between the system per se and its surrounding milieu. This latter property of a boundary is referred to as its permeability and describes the ease of exchange of information with other systems. (Pearlman, 1988, p. 290)

Boundaries have also been described as "rules of interaction" and "methods of functioning," which fall on a continuum from "very diffuse" to "very rigid"; in the middle of this continuum lie "clear" boundaries (see Figure 6.1). Within most family systems, boundaries lie at some point in the middle, though they may be closer to one extreme or the other. Optimally functioning family relationships are characterized by clear boundaries. That is, they allow for individuality yet maintain intimacy, they are based on mutual respect, the members show

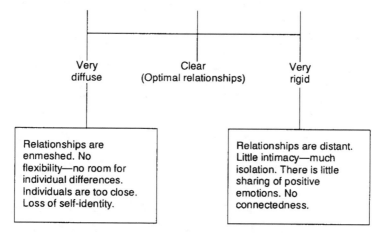

FIGURE 6.1. Family boundaries continuum.

genuine love and concern for one another without attempting to control one another, freedom and flexibility are evident, and communication patterns are clear and direct.

Where very diffuse boundaries exist, relationships are characterized by overinvolvement. There is no room for separateness or individual uniqueness; an overemphasis is placed on sameness and unity (Lawson & Lawson, 1998). Families with diffuse or enmeshed boundaries do not allow adolescents to pull away from the family. They discourage the development of exceptional or unique talents. Some adolescents may rebel against this "smothering" by abusing alcohol or drugs. When marital relationships are characterized by overinvolvement, the individuality of each spouse is "sacrificed" for the "sake of the marriage" (Lawson & Lawson, 1998, p. 58).

In other chemically dependent families, boundaries may be rigid or disengaged. Individual members of the family (particularly the alcoholic or addict) may be isolated, or, at other times, the entire family may be isolated from the community. According to Lawson and Lawson (1998) alcoholic families have three rules:

1. "do not talk about the alcoholism,"
2. "do not confront drinking behavior," and
3. "protect and shelter the alcoholic so that things don't become worse." (p. 58)

Unfortunately, such rules enable an alcoholic or addict to keep drinking or using drugs and inadvertently to contribute to the progression of addictive behavior. A vicious cycle develops in which the isolation imposed by the three rules perpetuates the chemical abuse, and, in turn, the chemical abuse maintains the need for isolation (see Figure 6.2).

When one spouse is an alcoholic or addict, the marital relationship may be disengaged at a fixed distance. That is, the partners may remain married but they lead relatively separate lives. The alcoholic or addict may work and spend much time with drinking or drug-using buddies rather than at home. The nondependent spouse may carry the full parenting load and pursue other interests without the chemically dependent spouse. Children of these disengaged families typically feel rejected and unloved. They may develop emotional problems or "act out." Either way, their maladaptive behavior represents a plea for help.

Subsystems and Hierarchies

"Subsystems" and "hierarchies" also contribute to the organization of the family system. There are several subsystems within the family. The original subsystem is the marital one. Within the marital subsystem, certain privileges, communication patterns, and behaviors are appro-

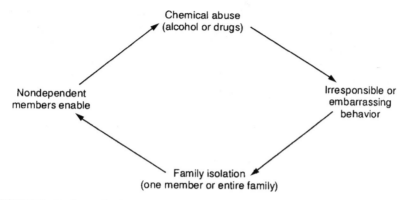

FIGURE 6.2. Reciprocal relationship between family isolation and chemical abuse.

priate (financial decisions, career decisions, sexual relations, etc.). With the birth of the first child, a new subsystem (the parental subsystem) is created. Within this subsystem, the decisions about how to raise the children are made. This power rests with the parents; thus, a hierarchy appears in which parents have more power than the children. In chemically dependent families where the alcoholic or addict is a parent, the nondependent spouse typically assumes most of the parental power. The addicted spouse gives up or turns over power as a parent. This shift in role obligations places a heavy burden on the nondependent spouse and usually creates feelings of resentment. Sometimes a grandparent or older sibling may assume some parental power (as demonstrated by cooking meals, shopping, doing laundry, etc.); in this way, subsystem boundaries may become blurred.

A sibling subsystem also will evolve. Its complexity will depend on the number of children, their age differences, their gender, and their common interests (Lawson & Lawson, 1998). Sibling subsystems may distinguish the sons from the daughters, the oldest from the youngest, or the athletic from the nonathletic. In functional families, these subsystems will remain somewhat fluid and dynamic as time passes and the children mature. In dysfunctional families, the subsystems may remain static as the children are required to assume inappropriate roles, such as that of a parent. Allowing a child into the marital subsystem (e.g., incest) is another example in which subsystems are likely to remain static (Lawson & Lawson, 1998).

Family Rules

Another characteristic of family organization pertains to the rules that govern interactions between and among members. Often these rules are implicit rather than explicit; however, most or all members some-how seem to know them. They define appropriate conduct within the family system. They function to provide order, stability, consistency, and predictability in family affairs. They also restrict behavioral op-tions (e.g., "incest is unacceptable"). Families usually have rules gov-erning the manner in which different emotions are expressed. In some families anger is not allowed, whereas in others shouting is permis-sible. In some families affection is demonstrated with hugs and kisses, while in others physical contact is minimized.

Barnard (1981) noted six areas in which families usually formu-late rules:

1. To what extent, when, and how family members may com-ment on what they see, feel, and think.
2. Who can speak to whom and about what.
3. How a member can be different.
4. How sexuality can be expressed.
5. What it means to be male or female.
6. How a person can acquire self-worth, and how much self-worth is appropriate to possess.

In chemically dependent families, certain family rules are typical. For example, it is usually prohibited to talk openly about the substance abuse; this has been referred to as the "conspiracy of silence" (Deutsch, 1982). A "don't feel, don't trust, don't talk" rule often exists in such families as well. A rule often found in alcoholic families is that anger can only be expressed when the alcoholic is drinking (Lawson & Lawson, 1998). The family's alcoholic sometimes operates according to this rule: "I am comfortable expressing my affection for you only after I have been drinking."

Causality in Family Systems

Systems theory emphasizes reciprocal rather than linear causality. That is, relationships between and among variables or elements in systems include feedback loops. Simple cause-and-effect relationships are viewed as too reductionistic and as incapable of capturing the com-plexity of family interactions. Thus, behaviors that are stimulated by one element themselves become stimuli for other behaviors. Pearlman (1988) notes that most family therapists have firsthand knowledge of the reciprocal patterns in family relationship problems. As an example, Figure 6.3 represents the most common marital pattern in alcoholism.

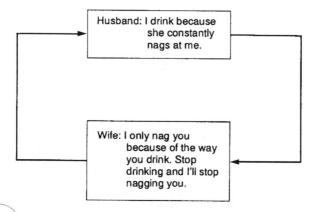

FIGURE 6.3. Reciprocal relationship between husband's abusive drinking and wife's nagging.

Homeostasis

"Homeostasis," a metaphor borrowed from the physiological sciences, has long been an important concept in systems theory (Pearlman, 1988). According to Stanton (1980), homeostasis in a family with an alcoholic or addict is a pathological equilibrium in which the nondependent family members have an emotional investment in the chemically dependent member's maintaining his/her addiction. It explains "the family's tenacity in holding onto existing behavioral repertoires, resisting change, and exerting pressure to minimize or reverse change when it occurs" (Pearlman, 1988, p. 292).

The application of the homeostasis metaphor to alcoholic- or drug-dependent families is at odds with the conventional view that these problems "tear families apart." In the majority of such families, the impact of alcohol and drug use is much more subtle. Alcohol and drug abuse usually do not evoke immediate separation or divorce. According to Steinglass (1981), the more common situation is that "Most families seem to work out a compromise in which the family remains economically and structurally intact despite the presence of a member with chronic alcoholism in its midst" (p. 578).

Rather, the abuse of alcohol and/or drugs may be thought of as an effort to maintain family balance. If the drinking or drug use is stopped (e.g., an attempt at recovery), the family is thrown out of balance. These transition periods typically involve heightened interpersonal interaction, which can be uncomfortable for members (Steinglass, 1981). In order to reestablish greater emotional distance, nondependent family members often (unconsciously) attempt to sabotage the member's recovery effort and thereby return the family to rigid stability. Some treatment programs that work with families are aware of these dynamics and make efforts to help members cope with the anxieties of transitioning from active use to sobriety (Laundergan & Williams, 1993).

The sabotaging behavior of the nondependent members may take many forms. For example, let us suppose that a 40-year-old male alcoholic makes good progress in an aftercare program. After several months of abstinence and frequent Alcoholics Anonymous (AA) attendance, his wife begins to complain bitterly that they never "go out" any more because he is always at "those" meetings. Her nagging eventually prompts him to relapse. She did not intend for him to slip, but her behavior has nevertheless had that result. Another example of sabotaging involves a husband of a female cocaine addict in early recovery. Upon her leaving inpatient rehabilitation, he agrees to care for the kids while she attends aftercare and Narcotics Anonymous (NA) meetings. After a few weeks, he protests that he feels too "tied down" and refuses to continue babysitting. She soon relapses. Other spouses have been known to complain that their recovering spouses are "not the same person"; often, they have ambivalent feelings about the behavioral and personality changes. They may feel that their mates are now too assertive, "kind of boring," or less sociable than when they were drinking or abusing drugs.

The newfound sobriety throws the marital relationship into turmoil; the children are also affected. The following excerpt highlights typical reactions of children to a father in early recovery: "Mother is not needed as the overly responsible martyr when Dad returns to take over running the household. Brother has no reason to stay away from home and must reevaluate his relationship with Dad. The family suddenly notices little sister's hyperactive mannerisms" (Lawson & Lawson, 1998, p. 54).

From a systems point of view, the abusive drinking or drug use has adaptive consequences. That is, it functions to keep the family "in balance"—not a "healthy" balance but a relatively stable one nevertheless. This pathological equilibrium is preferred over continual chaos and crisis. In essence, such families opt for low-level discomfort and "put up" with the substance abuse to avoid grappling with even more painful and sensitive issues.

Alcohol or drug abuse can stabilize a family (i.e., keep it in balance) in a number of ways. It can divert attention from marital problems and allow angry or hurtful feelings to go unexpressed. For example, for married male alcoholics, abusive drinking is often a way to avoid intimacy with their wives. It establishes an emotional distance that can become fixed over time. Frequently, such men feel much ambivalence about their marriages and their children. They may love them but at the same time may believe that their wives and kids are responsible for their lost opportunities. This may be particularly true of men who married and had children relatively young. The family is often seen as a financial and emotional burden, one which many men fear they will not be able to support. In such cases, men feel a loss of freedom, especially when they perceive themselves to be trapped in jobs they dislike. Excessive drinking is one way to cope with these pressures. It serves as an analgesic for the family pain; it also prevents crises that could lead to family breakup if they were faced squarely.

Homeostatic mechanisms, such as drinking, regulate the amount of change to which a family can adapt at any one time. Change can occur in the family, but the need for balance slows it by relying on compensatory measures. In functional families, change is incorporated relatively easily via compensatory efforts that allow all members to get their needs met. If young Johnnie starts Little League baseball, for instance, Dad makes an effort to adjust his work schedule to get him to practice. However, in dysfunctional families, adaptation to the evolving needs of the members is more resistant and less fluid. All members are less likely to get their needs fulfilled.

Pearlman (1988) notes that these family regulatory processes are maintained by feedback loops, which can be points of intervention in family systems therapy. He states:

> Positive feedback loops introduce change into the system. Negative feedback loops, on the other hand, promote a steady state and diminish the impact of change that is introduced into the system. Negative feedback loops are, therefore, closely associated with a system's homeostatic tendencies, and have become an important focal point for the systems therapist in attempting to identify and ultimately overcome a family's seemingly inherent tendency to resist change. (p. 292)

It should be noted that dysfunctional families are not forever locked into maladaptive patterns of interaction. The concept of homeostasis only describes the tendency to regulate change; it does not describe an unalterable pattern of maladaptive interaction.

The Impact of One's Family of Origin

How are dysfunctional marriages and families created? Is the development of such a union predictable, or is it simply the result of choosing the wrong mate? Framo (1976) believes that individuals select mates in an attempt to fill voids they experienced in their own families of origin. This is an unconscious effort for the most part, and it involves bargaining: For example, "I will be your conscience if you act out my impulse" (Framo, 1976, p. 194). In this way, one spouse (typically the woman) seeks to control the other, while the other (typically the man) expresses the rebellion that the first dares not reveal (Lawson & Lawson, 1998). This phenomenon may partly explain why some women are attracted to men who engage in risky behavior (drinking abusively, using drugs, driving fast, fighting, etc.), and why such men often find restrained, traditional women desirable in turn.

Lawson and Lawson (1998) describe in the following passage how alcoholic marriages become increasingly problematic:

> The two personalities become dependent on each other and increasingly intertwined, making it difficult for either to leave regardless of the dysfunction of the relationship. Marital partners enmeshed in these relationships (based on the inability to function as an individual) can manifest dysfunctions leading to superficial relationships, emotional upheaval, and possible drinking behavior (if this drinking model was present in their family of origin). Often these marital partners reach out to each other for identity and fuse into a single entity in the marriage. To achieve some separateness the marital partners must set up emotional distance. One spouse may take the dominant position in the relationship with the remaining spouse adapting to the other and further losing identity. (p. 34)

A marital relationship usually consists of an "emotional pursuer" and an "emotional distancer" (Fogarty, 1976). In U.S. culture (and probably other Western cultures as well), the woman is the pursuer and the man is the distancer. Typically, as the woman strives for intimacy, the man backs away. In healthy marriages, both individuals are at least occasionally pursuers and thus will establish intimacy. In dysfunctional marriages, over time, a fixed emotional distance may occur; that is, neither spouse strives for emotional intimacy. Such is often the case when one spouse abuses alcohol or drugs (or when both do). This underinvolvement often leads the nonabusing spouse to become overinvolved with the children (when there are children). The nonabusing spouse may get some of his/her emotional needs met through the children. In addition, the children may become overly dependent on the nonabusing parent (typically the mother) because of the other parent's distance.

The Teen's Fear of Separation

Dysfunctional marital relationships can have deleterious effects on the teenage children of such unions. Adolescent alcohol or drug abuse is one of the negative consequences of problems between the parents. Stanton (1980) explored the family dynamics that give rise to substance abuse among teens who are themselves children of alcoholics or addicts. He suggests that an overinvolvement with the nonabusing parent creates an intense "fear of separation." At the same time, the teen has normal developmental needs to begin separating from the family of origin. Thus, drug abuse becomes a way in which the teen demonstrates a "pseudoindividuation"—that is, a false independence from the family. The act of abusing drugs or alcohol represents rebellion and autonomy, but, according to Stanton (1980), it is only an "illusory independence." Such a teen establishes a link to the drug subculture (which outwardly suggests adulthood) but also maintains a foothold in the family.

Stanton (1980) cites his own research for evidence of pseudoindividuation among teens and young adults. He found that 66% of heroin addicts, for example, lived with or saw their mothers daily. This may not seem particularly unusual, until consideration is given to the fact that their average age was 28. Considering U.S. cultural norms, this suggests prolonged overdependence on their mothers. Thus, it appears that some young, unmarried addicts vacillate between their families of origin and the drug subculture. They want to appear strong and independent, but they also fear separation from an overinvolved relationship with a parent.

Triads

Bowen (1976), Stanton (1980), and others maintain that dysfunctional families form triadic patterns of interaction, which contribute to the development of addiction in children. "Triads" are family subsystems that consist of three members. Typically, this interactive pattern in a case of chemical dependence involves a young adult (or adolescent) addict and the parents. However, other triads can develop as well, especially in extended families. For example, a triadic subsystem may consist of a young adult male alcoholic, his wife, and his mother (with whom they reside).

In the most common triad, one parent is intensely involved with the addict while the other parent is underinvolved and perhaps punitive. Usually the overinvolved parent is pampering and indulgent of the addicted child. This parent is usually of the opposite sex from the child; thus, the emotionally distant parent is often a father, the overinvolved parent is the mother, and the addict is male.

The triad forms as a means of protecting the marriage and the family. In essence, the triad serves a protective function: It helps maintain the family structure by distracting the parents from their own marital difficulties. The child's drug problem provides a focal point around which they can unify, instead of focusing on their own problems. The drug problem gives them a reason for remaining together. All their emotional energies are directed toward the child rather than toward each other. Thus, the child's drug problem functions to suppress marital conflict.

Stanton (1980) asserts that it is no accident that alcohol or drug abuse typically begins in early or middle adolescence. Parents in a dysfunctional marriage may be threatened by the fact that their child is growing up. They may fear losing the child (to a girlfriend or boyfriend, to military service, to higher education or a career, to a move to a geographically distant area, etc.). This parental anxiety, according to Stanton (1980), stems from the deeper fear that they will have to face their relationship problems. They anticipate that the void in their marriage will no longer be filled by their child. Such parents often feel threatened and incapable of overcoming long-standing marital problems. They only see two options: (1) staying permanently in an unsatisfying relationship or (2) divorce.

The Dance

Stanton (1980) noted that triads become "stuck" in a chronic, repetitive pattern of interaction. He uses the metaphor of the "dance" to describe the process. This is more than simply a description; the "dance" metaphor explains, from a systems viewpoint, how relapse occurs. The dance consists of the various forms of repetitive, consistent, and predictable displays of behavior (Stanton, 1980). One of the steps in the dance is the act of abusing drugs or alcohol. Box 6.1 describes the experience of one 23-year-old polydrug addict who was engaged in a triadic relationship with his parents.

BOX 6.1. Billy and His Parents

For as long as Billy can remember, his parents argued. Sometimes their fights became violent, with many household items being broken. Billy began using drugs in his early teens; by his senior year in high school, he could be described as a drug addict. His drug use came to the attention of his parents because he was "busted" at school. Previously, they had been too involved with their own problems to notice.

Billy's parents reacted in distinctively different ways. His father was enraged and very condemning of Billy; he threatened him with all kinds of consequences. Mom, on the other hand, was very reassuring and protective. She attempted to shield him from his father and to make excuses for him. It appeared that his parents unconsciously welcomed the drug problem because it gave them relief from their own conflict. As a result, they focused much energy on disciplining Billy and helping him with his problem. They arranged for him to be admitted to a drug rehabilitation program.

Upon Billy's discharge, he remained abstinent for several weeks. His parents were on their best behavior during this time. Gradually (and as a result of Billy's abstinence), Mom and Dad began to argue again. Their conflict resurfaced without Billy's "problem" to distract them. In turn, Billy relapsed. It was as if they were in a dance: When Mom and Dad's arguing flared up, so did Billy's drug abuse; when Billy's drug abuse subsided a bit as a result of their efforts and attention, Mom and Dad's arguing again resumed. They were right in step with each other. This pattern continued for 5 years, with four attempts at inpatient rehabilitation. After his fourth discharge, Billy managed to obtain a good-paying job. He remained clean and sober, and he established a relationship with a woman he met through work. Everything was going well until his mother began to harangue him about not visiting and calling. One night she called him while she was drunk and accused him of not really caring for her, and not being appreciative of all of the things she and his father had done for him through the years.

In an aftercare group, Billy reported that he was "shaky" and anxious, and had suddenly begun having drug cravings. He had difficulty linking these symptoms to his conversation with his mother, though he felt her trying to "pull" him back home. Mom was threatened by Billy's increasing independence and maturity.

This story has a happy ending for Billy. He did not relapse, and is doing well in his job and marriage. Mom and Dad are now divorced.

The concept of the dance provides insight into the dynamics behind relapse. Stanton (1980) indicates that these dynamics often go unrecognized and that those who relapse are labeled "unmotivated" or perhaps "emotionally unstable." From a systems perspective, such assessments are superficial; they overlook the addict's enmeshment in the family system. Thus, effective relapse prevention should include intervention with the family rather than just focusing narrowly on intrapsychic factors within the addict.

BOWEN'S FAMILY SYSTEMS THEORY

A relatively large number of family systems theories exist. Each one emphasizes different aspects of the family, though most share common elements as described earlier (Pearlman, 1988). Among the most prominent of these theories is the work of Murray Bowen. The Bowen theory is presented here as the prototypical family systems theory. It should be noted that this is not specifically a theory of addiction but, rather, one of family dysfunction. Addiction is considered an example of dysfunction in the family unit.

Differentiation of Self

Bowen (1976) considers "differentiation of self" to be the central concept of his theory. This concept classifies people on a continuum. On one end of the continuum are people whose lives are extremely dominated by automatic emotional reaction. They are said to be "fused" (Bowen, 1976); that is, no differentiation exists between the emotional and the intellectual self. Emotion, at this extreme, completely dominates the self. According to Bowen (1976), "These are people who are less flexible, less adaptable, and more emotionally dependent on those about them. They are easily stressed into dysfunction, and it is difficult for them to recover from dysfunction. They inherit a high percentage of all human problems" (p. 65).

On the other end of the continuum are those persons who are highly differentiated. That is, they possess a balance between emotional and intellectual responding, and these two processes are more clearly separated. Bowen (1976) maintains that complete differentiation of self is impossible. However, people whose emotional functioning and intellectual functioning are relatively well separated will be more autonomous, more flexible, and better able to cope with stress; they will also demonstrate more independence of emotions. In essence, they possess a high level of emotional maturity. Bowen (1976) states that "their life courses are more orderly and successful, and they are remarkably free of human problems" (pp. 65–66) (see Figure 6.4).

Of those persons on the low end of the continuum (scores = 0–25), Bowen (1976) writes:

> The intellect is so flooded by emotionality that the total life course is determined by the emotional process and by what "feels right," rather

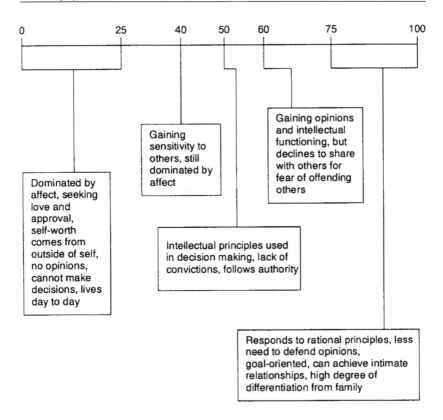

0   25   40   50   60   75   100

Dominated by affect, seeking love and approval, self-worth comes from outside of self, no opinions, cannot make decisions, lives day to day

Gaining sensitivity to others, still dominated by affect

Gaining opinions and intellectual functioning, but declines to share with others for fear of offending others

Intellectual principles used in decision making, lack of convictions, follows authority

Responds to rational principles, less need to defend opinions, goal-oriented, can achieve intimate relationships, high degree of differentiation from family

FIGURE 6.4. Bowen's scale of differentiation.

than by beliefs or opinions. The intellect exists as an appendage of the feeling system. It may function reasonably well in mathematics or physics, or in impersonal areas, but on personal subjects its functioning is controlled by the emotions. (p. 66)

This insight may explain, at least partly, the resistance that many families (and individuals) demonstrate when offered help or therapeutic feedback. The assistance is usually principled; that is, it is formed from reason. It is rational. Thus, it is often rejected because of the overreliance on emotional functioning.

It should be noted here that Bowen does not discount the emotional dimension of human experience. He does not advocate human development that is cold, distant, or uncaring. Rather, he emphasizes that the poorly differentiated individual is "trapped within a feeling world" (Bowen, 1976, p. 67). They have no options in responding; they simply react in an automatic fashion. In contrast, a highly differentiated person can express emotion (both positive and negative) in appropriate, productive ways.

Poorly differentiated persons are "totally relationship oriented" (Bowen, 1976, p. 69). Most of their energy goes into pleasing others and keeping their relationships, especially with family members, in harmony. Conflict is avoided. Typically, these persons say "I feel . . . " when expressing their views. They are unable to form personal beliefs, and thus avoid saying "I think . . . " or "I believe . . . " (Bowen, 1976).

Persons with low levels of differentiation have other difficulties as well. They find it difficult to make plans and carry them out. Long-term goals are almost impossible to form for these individuals. They tend to live from day to day and remain overly dependent on their parents well into adulthood. They are preoccupied with making others happy. Sometimes employers find such characteristics useful, so poorly differentiated individuals may remain in the same low-level positions for many years. Extremely low-functioning individuals in this group may be institutionalized and labeled "psychotic," "schizophrenic," or "mentally ill."

Bowen (1976) describes individuals whose level of differentiation is a bit higher (scores = 25–50) in the following passage:

> Lives are guided by the emotional system, but the life styles are more flexible than the lower levels of differentiation. The flexibility provides a better view of the interplay between emotionality and intellect. When anxiety is low, functioning can resemble good levels of differentiation. When anxiety is high, functioning can resemble that of low levels of differentiation. Lives are relationship oriented, and major life energy goes to loving and being loved, and seeking approval from others. Feelings are more openly expressed than in lower level people. Life energy is directed more to what others think and to winning friends and approval than to goal-directed activity. Self-esteem is dependent on others. It can soar to heights with a compliment or be crushed by criticism. Success in school is oriented more to learning the system and to pleasing the teacher than to the primary goal of learning. . . . They may have enough free-functioning intellect to have mastered academic knowledge about impersonal things; they use this knowledge in the relationship system. However, intellect about personal matters is lacking, and their personal lives are in chaos. (pp. 70–71)

Bowen (1976) indicates that scores of 50 to 75 on his continuum represent moderate levels of self-differentiation. Among this group, the two systems, intellect and emotion, function cooperatively; neither system dominates the other. In particularly stressful situations, the intellectual system may be overwhelmed, but for the most part these individuals lead satisfying lives. The intellectual system learns that discipline is required to obtain long-term gains. Thus, persons in this group are capable to some degree of delaying gratification and planning for the future. They are also somewhat more able to think for themselves. They are aware of differences between thinking and feeling, and at least occasionally are able to state unpopular beliefs or opinions.

The highly differentiated person (scores = 75–100) is "more hypothetical, than real," according to Bowen (1976, p. 73). Few individuals reach such a level of development. Such persons are aware of the relationships around them, but they do not become mired in emotional "stuck-togetherness." They are aware of various response options available to them. They presumably choose how to act instead of automatically reacting to a situation. Again, highly differentiated persons are not emotionally cold or distant; in fact, they welcome and express sincere, authentic emotion. However, they avoid the various insincere expressions of emotion that are often required by unwritten family rules or by social conventions.

Triangles

A triangle (or triad) is thought to consist of a comfortably close twosome and an uncomfortable outsider. To avoid separation, the partners in the twosome work to achieve closeness; often they are overinvolved with each other. The uncomfortable outsider seeks closeness to one of the twosome. These attempts at maneuvering have been described earlier in the chapter as the "dance." Bowen (1976) notes that the constant motion within the triangle results from moderate levels of tension in the twosome, which are felt by only one of them. The other is oblivious to the conflict in the pair. The "uncomfortable other" mediates or diverts some of the tension to himself/herself by engaging the twosome, and thus initiates a new equilibrium within the triangle.

During periods of great stress and tension, the "outsider" position is sought by each member of the triangle. In times of stress, this is the least uncomfortable position. Clearly, all three individuals cannot shift to the outside position. When such shifts are prevented, one of the twosome involves a new outsider, and a new triangle is formed. Bowen (1976) believes that these shifting dynamics often result in all family members being "triangled" at different points in time. Furthermore, when all available family triangles have been exhausted, the family typically seeks to form triangles with people outside itself (members of the clergy, police officers, mental health professionals, social service agencies, school officials, etc.).

Bowen (1976) describes the typical triangle in the following passage:

> The best example of this is the father–mother–child triangle. Patterns vary, but one of the most common is basic tension between the parents, with the father's gaining the outside position—often being called passive, weak, and distant—leaving the conflict between the mother and child. The mother—often called aggressive, dominating, and castrating—wins over the child, who moves another step toward chronic functional impairment. . . . Families replay the same triangular game over and over for years, as though the winner were in doubt, but the final result is always the same. Over the years the child accepts the always-lose outcome more easily, even to volunteering for this position. (pp. 76–77)

The Emotional System in the Nuclear Family

In each generation of a family, certain patterns of emotional functioning appear. These patterns, involving parents and children, are replicated from the mother's and father's separate families of origin. According to Bowen (1976), families transmit these patterns of emotional responding from generation to generation. These patterns are readily observable in most families.

Typically, the nuclear family begins with a marriage. Bowen (1976) maintains that individuals of similar levels of differentiation will be attracted to each other. The lower their level of differentiation, the more intense the emotional fusion in the marriage. In most marriages, one spouse becomes more dominant in decision making for the couple. The other spouse adapts to the arrangement. Bowen (1976) describes the fusion that occurs among most couples in the following passage:

> One [spouse] may assume the dominant role and force the other to be adaptive, or one [spouse] may assume the adaptive role and force the other to be dominant. Both may try for the dominant role, which results in conflict; or both may try for the adaptive role, which results in decision paralysis. The dominant one gains self at the expense of the more adaptive one, who loses self. More differentiated spouses have lesser degrees of fusion, and fewer of the complications. The dominant and adaptive positions are not directly related to the sex of the spouse. They are determined by the position that each had in their families of origin. From my experience, there are as many dominant females as males, and as many adaptive males as females. These characteristics played a major role in their original choice of each other as partners. (p. 79)

When there is a high degree of fusion in the relationship, spouses are preoccupied with the behavior of the other and as a result tension increases to high levels. Spouses with relatively high degrees of differentiation make minor adjustments to cope with the anxiety that results from emotional fusion. Less differentiated spouses develop more problematic symptoms. Bowen (1976) describes four common manifestations of marital fusion:

1. Emotional distancing.
2. Marital conflict.
3. Dysfunction in one spouse.
4. Impairment of one or more children.

The first symptom, emotional distancing, occurs among couples of moderate levels of self-differentiation, as well as among those who are highly fused (and anxious about being so). It is extremely common among most couples, almost universal. Few couples want to maintain the degree of fusion they experienced during their courtship and the early days of their marriage. The loss of self (adaptive role) and the burden of decision making (dominant role) exact too great an emotional cost over prolonged periods of time. Thus, emotional distancing occurs to various degrees in most marital relationships.

Marital conflict results when neither spouse is willing to "give in" to the other—that is, neither spouse is willing to assume the adaptive role. Bowen (1976) indicates that marital conflict does not involve the children. The spouses are intensely involved with each other, with occasional periods of emotional distancing.

Dysfunction in one spouse results when one spouse absorbs a large amount of undifferentiation into himself/herself while assuming the adaptive role (Bowen, 1976). In this situation, the dysfunctional spouse strains to adapt to the other over prolonged periods. There is a loss of self. The adaptive spouse develops such symptoms as physical illness, substance abuse, mental disorders, or irresponsible behavior. These disorders become chronic. Bowen (1976) notes that such marriages tend to be enduring, for this reason: "The underfunctioning one is grateful for the care and attention, and the overfunctioning one does not complain" (p. 81).

When the parents project their undifferentiation onto one or more of the children, they are likely to become emotionally impaired as well. According to Bowen (1976), the intensity of the parents' projection is related to two variables. The first variable has to do with the degree of emotional isolation of the family—that is, the degree to which the family is withdrawn from its extended family, its church, its community, and so on. The second variable pertains to the level of tension in the family: The greater the levels of anxiety (and isolation), the more pronounced the parental projection. Bowen (1976) considers this process of projection to be fundamental to most human problems. As such, he more fully develops the concept by describing it as the "family projection process."

The Family Projection Process

The family projection process involves a father–mother–child triangle. The parents' undifferentiation is projected onto a child. Because the mother gives birth to the child and because she is usually the primary nurturer, Bowen (1976) believes that the process revolves around her emotional energy, which in turn originates in her family of origin. The family projection process can be the principal cause of a child's emotional impairment, or it can superimpose itself on a child's preexisting illness (e.g., leukemia) or disability (e.g., Down's syndrome, spina bifida, and muscular dystrophy). Bowen (1976) notes that "the process is so universal it is present to some degree in all families" (p. 81).

In Bowen's systems theory, the emotional energy arising from the parents' undifferentiation is expressed in one or more of the following ways: (1) marital conflict, (2) dysfunction in one spouse, and (3) projection to the children. The undifferentiation is also absorbed in these three ways. Family members typically shift the weight of the undifferentiation around so that no one member becomes too dysfunctional.

Thus, the children are sometimes projected onto in order to reduce marital conflict or spouse dysfunction. This homeostatic mechanism protects the marriage in the former case, and the adaptive spouse in the latter. According to Bowen (1976), "I have never seen a family in which there was not some projection to a child. Most families use a combination of all three mechanisms" (p. 82).

The projection to the children is not equally distributed. For various unconscious reasons (discussed later), the projection first focuses on one child. If the focus becomes too intense (i.e., if the child becomes too impaired), it is often shifted to another child (a new father–mother–child triangle is created), and so forth. In this fashion, each child may become "triangulated" at some point in the life of the family.

Emotional Cutoff

The final concept in Bowen's theory to be presented here is "emotional cutoff." According to Bowen (1976), individuals with lower levels of differentiation have not separated emotionally from their parents. They have unresolved emotional attachments to their families of origin. "Emotional cutoff" describes the manner in which individuals separate from their parents. Some individuals separate by isolating themselves emotionally, though they continue to live close to their parents. Others may move to a geographically distant area, but remain emotionally dependent on their parents. Still others may sever all communication but remain affected by unresolved attachments. Bowen (1976) notes that many people use a combination of these methods to "cut off."

The more intense the emotional cutoff, the greater the likelihood that an individual will bring the "unfinished business" from the family of origin into his/her present marriage and family. It is also likely that the children of such individuals will cut off in a similar fashion. (Bowen, 1976). Again, parents tend to transmit their level of differentiation to their children.

The preceding discussion has provided a brief overview of the Bowen theory. The concepts provide insight into the ways families function.

CODEPENDENCY

The concept of "codependency" (also called "coalcoholism" when alcoholism is involved) refers to an unhealthy pattern of relating to others that results from being closely involved with an alcoholic or addict (Subby & Friel, 1984). Codependency is a generic term, and it has been defined in various ways, but all definitions describe unhealthy relationship patterns (Beattie, 1987). The chemical abuser in a codependent's life is usually a husband, but it can also be wife, a parent, a close friend, a child, or a coworker.

Koffinke (1991) indicates that the codependent is overly focused on (i.e., overinvolved with) the substance abuser. Their relationship is enmeshed and problem filled. The problems provide endless opportunities for the codependent to be preoccupied with the addict. Hypervigilance is the norm. For women who grew up in chemically dependent families, this behavior seems normal. In fact, some believe that women from such families learn codependent behavior early in life and are thus attracted to chemically dependent mates (Koffinke, 1991). They also find it very difficult, if not impossible, to leave dysfunctional relationships.

As a result of this emotional enmeshment, the codependent tends to lose all sense of "self" or identity, and to become emotionally dependent upon the addict. The addict's mood dictates the codependent's mood. In a sense, the codependent becomes an appendage to the addict and the substance abuse.

The codependent often protects the alcoholic or addict from the natural consequences of substance abuse (Koffinke, 1991). Such behavior is referred to as "enabling." Examples include calling in sick to a dependent spouse's employer when the spouse has been out drinking or using drugs all night, or cleaning up after a spouse who has vomited during the night from too much alcohol. Hence, codependency is considered an unhealthy relationship pattern, whereas enabling is a common behavior arising from it.

In addition, the codependent may purposely isolate himself/herself (and the family) from the extended family and friends, in order to keep the "family secret" and save the family from embarrassment. Unfortunately, this isolation removes opportunities to release feelings of anger, hurt, fear, and frustration (Koffinke, 1991).

Chief Characteristics

Several writers have identified chief characteristics of codependency. Following is a descriptive list of the psychological distress codependents are reported to experience.

1. *Poor self-esteem.* Codependents suffer from low self-esteem; that is, they feel little personal worth and think poorly of themselves. This has many sources. They themselves may have grown up in alcoholic families or in families in which chemical dependency was not an issue but physical or emotional abuse was present nevertheless. It is also possible that they grew up in homes in which the parents were overprotective and domineering.

2. *Need to be needed.* Many codependents believe that their worth depends on how well they take care of loved ones. In our culture, women are especially socialized to be nurturers, so it may come easily for them. As a result, codependence may neglect their own emotional needs for security, love, and attention.

3. *Strong urge to change and control others.* Codependents usually develop the belief that they have the power to control substance dependent spouses. According to Norwood (1985), an overdeveloped sense of responsibility develops in which the codependents come to believe almost grandiosely that they are at the center of the universe and all-powerful in a very unhealthy sense. This may partly explain why some codependent women always seem to end up in dysfunctional relationships with addicted men, and why some women appear to take on unhealthy or impaired men as "rehabilitation projects."

4. *Willingness to suffer*. Norwood (1985) suggests that many codependents ask, "If I suffer for you, will you love me?" (p. 47). They exhibit the tendency to become a martyr. It is as if they gain some satisfaction or reward from suffering. They may not be happy, but they can claim to be superior (i.e., morally, emotionally, or socially) to their impaired spouse (Norwood, 1985). They can also claim to be superior to others who desert the alcoholic/addict. Because many codependents grew up in chemically dependent families, they do not recognize that they are suffering emotionally. They have experienced depression and low self-worth for so long that these conditions seem normal.

5. *Resistance to change*. Codependents typically are immobilized by their own sense of guilt. Leaving the alcoholic/addict is not an option, because they fear being overwhelmed by guilt feelings. These feelings make self-examination very painful; in fact, codependents may develop a great deal of secondary anxiety about feeling guilty. From a systems perspective, these beliefs and feelings preserve the family balance, but they blind the codependents from seeing how they contribute to the drinking and/or drug use.

6. *Fear of change*. Typically, codependents fear and resist change. Again, from a systems perspective, codependents may have an emotional investment in the alcoholic's/addict's continued drinking/drug use. These are almost always unconscious desires. They may fear change (i.e., abstinence/recovery) because they (a) do not want assertive, sober loved ones; (b) may be financially dependent on the substance abuser, and fear that divorce or other disruption would come with sobriety; (c) may want to avoid sexual relations, which could be expected to resume with sobriety; or (d) expect some family conflict or secret to emerge during sobriety.

Rewards Gained by Codependents

The rewards for staying in a codependent relationship are often not apparent to the outside observer. Many inexperienced professionals are amazed at the amount of suffering codependents are willing to endure and have a difficult time understanding why the codependents do not simply leave the alcoholic/addict. Yet a deeper, more thoughtful examination reveals that codependents do attain rewards by staying in dysfunctional relationships. Codependents come to affirm their self-worth by "carrying the cross" of the other person's addiction (or other destructive behavior)—by being a martyr. They may quietly believe that because they suffer, they are special and important. This self-perception represents a misguided grandiosity, which is essentially a shield against feelings, personal inadequacy, and low self-esteem.

CHILDREN IN ALCOHOLIC FAMILIES: CLINICAL ACCOUNTS

Despite recent skepticism about the usefulness of the adult children of alcoholics (ACOA) concept, it is quite true that children growing up in alcoholic families often experience emotional difficulties. Charles Deutsch (1982) describes what growing up in such a household is like from a child's point of view. He relies on extensive interviews with children from alcoholic homes. Deutsch (1982) pays particular attention to three conditions such children experience: (1) inconsistency, insecurity, and fear, (2) anger and hate, and (3) guilt and blame. Each one is described in turn.

Inconsistency, Insecurity, and Fear

According to Deutsch (1982), inconsistency is the hallmark of most actively alcoholic parents. They demonstrate it both when intoxicated and when sober. They can change moods dramatically, swinging from being warm, caring, and jovial to angry and frustrated within minutes. Because the children do not know what to anticipate, they tend to be insecure. The lack of parental predictability breeds distrust and uncertainty. As a result, many children adopt the "don't feel, don't trust, don't talk" rule. As Deutsch (1982) reports one child saying, "We learned to walk on eggshells without cracking a single one" (p. 42).

Domestic violence is reported in many alcoholic homes. A child's insecurity and fear are heightened considerably when an alcoholic parent acts out in a violent way. Deutsch (1982) indicates that the target of the violence does not seem to matter. The alcoholic who only destroys property instills as much fear as the alcoholic who strikes family members. Interestingly, a child often reports that the nonalcoholic spouse is the more violent and feared parent. In such a case, the non-alcoholic spouse may be attempting to force the alcoholic to stop drinking or may be ventilating pent-up anger and frustration about the drinking problem. Deutsch (1982) quotes one child as saying:

> "She tried to kill us, actually kill us. We all had our turns fighting her. Everybody used to say, 'ignore her,' but you can't ignore her when she comes after you with a knife, you know? One time she choked me, I mean, she was on top of me, choking me, and I would have died; I felt like I was dying. My father came in—this was really great—he had a cigarette in his mouth, he came in and my little sister was screaming—it was just me and my little sister at home. My mother had me and she was, I mean, I was blue, I thought I was dying, and my sister was standing there screaming. My father came in and threw the cigarette on the floor. And 'cause we were in my

mother's bedroom, it—started a fire and later our carpet had to be thrown out. My father came in and pulled my mother off me, and I just ran out of the house. When I came back five hours later, she told me, 'Now you're all right, you're all right.' " (p. 44)

Avoiding conflict becomes the primary concern of children in alcoholic homes. Children become preoccupied with not upsetting the alcoholic or violent parent. Conflict is avoided at all costs. One child quoted by Deutsch (1982) described it this way:

"There were things we all did just to placate him, like eating together whether we were hungry or not. We were scared a good deal of the time. One time, he demanded his dinner and my mother threw cereal boxes at him. I sat there thinking, 'now that was stupid, why the hell did you do that?' I wished she hadn't done it because I knew I'd have to keep him off her." (p. 44)

Anger and Hate

Though it may not be difficult to understand why children from such homes hate their parents, the children themselves often find these feelings unacceptable. Just as the alcoholic may deny a drinking problem, the children may deny hateful feelings toward their parents. The denial is unconscious; many of these children are simply unaware of these feelings. The "unacceptableness" stems from cultural norms that prohibit children from hating their parents.

The children's anger and hate may be directed at others or at themselves. It is not usually directed at the alcoholic parent because that would be too dangerous. Deutsch (1982) quotes one 7-year-old boy as saying, "Yeah, sometimes I yell at my teddy bear and sometimes I yell at my teacher when I'm angry at my father. And I know she doesn't like it" (p. 46). Many of these children develop guilt feelings about hating their alcoholic parents. They are unaware that their thoughts and feelings, given the family circumstances, are normal. They feel especially guilty about fantasies they may have in which the alcoholics are killed, die, or just disappear. One adolescent girl confided to Deutsch (1982): "All the time, I used to lay in bed at night and plot how to kill her without getting caught and stuff. I was a mean kid" (p. 47).

Guilt and Blame

Young children are naturally egocentric. They tend to believe that they are the cause of all that goes on around them. Thus, they tend to blame themselves for their parents' problems; this is particularly true of parents' drinking problems. Alcoholic parents often reinforce the children's self-blame with such rationalizations as these:

"I'll stop drinking when you behave the way you're supposed to."
"Why do you think I drink so much in the first place?"
"You kids drive me to drink."
"I can't relax—you kids drive me crazy."

Nonalcoholic parents also teach these children to believe (falsely) that they cause their alcoholic parents to drink. Deutsch (1982) indicates that many children in alcoholic homes hear their nonalcoholic parents instruct them, "Please go with Daddy, it will make him happy," or "You have to be quiet today, Mom seems nervous." Implied in these instructions is the notion that the children have power over their parents' drinking—that they can increase it or decrease it through their actions. Deutsch (1982) believes that these children take this notion of personal power into adulthood. As adults, he believes they continue to feel possessed of power and capable of controlling others. Some clinicians think that these needs to dominate and control others lead to dysfunctional adult relationships at home and work. As noted earlier, many such people refer to themselves today as ACOAs. At ACOA self-help meetings, power and control issues are often the focus of group discussion.

ROLE BEHAVIOR

At several points in this chapter, the chemically dependent family has been described as a closed social system. The family tends to isolate itself, its boundaries are rigid, and outside influences are not allowed to penetrate. This kind of closed, rigid system fosters tension. The tension is managed, in part, by each family member's adopting a specific, predictable role. The roles serve to divert attention from the alcoholic/addict or to reduce the family tension in total.

Family therapists have created a variety of schemes for classifying the types of role behavior in the chemically dependent family. Generally, these schemes have been generated from the clinical experience of therapists, not from empirical studies. Thus, researchers (e.g., Sher, 1997) often question the validity of the classification schemes and the claims made of these typologies. Nevertheless, family role schemes are frequently relied on in clinical settings and the addictions practitioner should have an understanding of these concepts. The following discussion presents one of the common classification schemes. The players in this scheme are (1) the chemically dependent person, (2) the chief enabler, (3) the family hero, (4) the scapegoat, (5) the lost child, and (6) the mascot.

In this model, the family is assumed to be a nuclear one, with two parents and four or more children. Also, because one of the parents is assumed to be chemically dependent, the scheme emphasizes the adaptive roles of the children in the family. Furthermore, it should be noted that although some chemically dependent families have members who clearly fall into a specific role, other families will have members who exhibit characteristics of more than one role; others will have members who shift from role to role as time passes; and in the life of some families certain roles will never appear. Thus, the roles are probably too "neat" for most chemically dependent families. However, for sake of discussion, each one is presented in its stereotypical form.

The Chemically Dependent Person

Within a family systems perspective, the chemically dependent member is not diseased but is playing a role, which is to act irresponsibly. This role has a homeostatic function. Typically, it serves to suppress more basic marital conflict or to divert attention from more threatening family issues.

An important aspect of the chemically dependent role is emotional detachment from the spouse and the children. One consequence of this distancing is the abandonment of parental power. The power is often assumed by the nondependent spouse and an older child (described later). The "first love" of the alcoholic or addict becomes the bottle or the drug. Over time, the self-administration of the substance becomes the central activity in this person's life; family life diminishes in importance.

The Chief Enabler

The second role is often referred to as the "chief enabler," or simply the "enabler." Often, numerous enablers exist in the family; however, the chief enabler is usually the nondependent spouse. Enabling, as discussed earlier, is a behavior that inadvertently supports the addiction process by helping an alcoholic or addict avoid the natural consequences of irresponsible behavior. Most addicts have at least one enabler in their lives, and many have three, four, or more to keep them going.

From a family systems perspective, the chief enabler reduces tension in the family (i.e., maintains family balance) by "smoothing things over" (i.e., making things right). The enabler often faces a dilemma: If he/she (more often she) does not bail the alcoholic/addict out of a bad, sometimes dangerous situation (e.g., a drunk husband alone at a bar), the substance abuser could do serious harm to self or others. A wife of an alcoholic once told me that she knew she was enabling her husband by picking him up from their snow-covered yard but she had no choice, because otherwise he would have frozen to death.

In many cases, the chief enabler is unaware that the enabling behavior is contributing to the progression of the alcoholism or drug addiction. Enablers believe that they are simply being helpful and acting to hold their families together. Though well-intended, their efforts often have destructive long-term consequences for their chemically dependent spouses (Deutsch, 1982).

The Family Hero

The role of the "family hero" is usually adopted by the oldest child. This role is also referred to as the "parental child," the "superstar," and the "goody two shoes" (Deutsch, 1982). This child attempts to do everything right. He/she is the family's high achiever and as such appears quite ambitious and responsible. Given the family circumstances (i.e., a chemically dependent parent), the child is often admired for excelling under difficult conditions.

The family hero often takes on parental responsibilities that the chemically dependent parent gave up. He/she provides care for younger siblings by cooking for them, getting them ready for school, putting them to bed, doing laundry, and so on. The nondependent spouse (i.e., the chief enabler) usually does not have much time for these chores because his/her time is divided between working and caring for the alcoholic or addicted spouse.

Family heroes frequently do well in academic and athletic pursuits (Deutsch, 1982). They may be class presidents, honor students, starters on the basketball team, or the like. They are achievement oriented and frequently develop well-respected professional careers. Deutsch (1982) suggests that many of them later become "workaholics." Some claim that family heroes are prone to "Type A" behavior as adults (Deutsch, 1982). This is a behavior pattern characterized by competitiveness, hostility, time urgency, and an obsession with work, among other features. Such individuals may be susceptible to stress-related disease (e.g., stomach ulcer and coronary heart disease).

The family hero reduces tension in the family simply by doing everything "right." The hero is the source of pride for the family, inspiring desperately needed hope and giving the family something to feel good about. The hero's accomplishments are distinctions around which the family members can rally and say to themselves, "We're not so bad after all."

The Scapegoat

The "scapegoat" role is often adopted by the second oldest child. The scapegoat can be viewed as the alter ego of the family hero (Deutsch, 1982). This child does very little right and is quite rebellious, perhaps even antisocial. Scapegoats may be involved in fights, theft, or other trouble at school or in the community; they are often labeled "juvenile delinquents." Male scapegoats may be violent; female scapegoats may express themselves by running away or engaging in promiscuous sexual activity. Scapegoats of both genders most often abuse alcohol and drugs themselves.

A child in the scapegoat role seem to identify with the chemically dependent parent, not only in terms of substance abuse but in other ways as well (attitude toward authority, attitude toward the opposite sex, vocational interests, etc). The scapegoat typically feels inferior to the family hero; still, the two of them are usually very close emotionally, despite the differences in their behavior. This special bond may continue throughout adulthood.

This child is referred to as the "scapegoat" because he/she is the object of the chemically dependent parent's misdirected frustration and rage. The child may be abused both emotionally and physically by this parent. This is especially true when the chemically dependent parent is the father and the scapegoat his son. In effect, the scapegoat becomes, in common parlance, "his father's son." That is, the son, filled with his father's anger and rage, adopts his father's self-destructive and antisocial tendencies. He models himself after his father despite hating him.

The scapegoat expresses the family's frustration and anger. The child in this role maintains family balance by directing some of the blame from the chemically dependent parent to himself/herself. This allows the chemically dependent parent to blame someone else for his/her own drinking and drug use. It also shields the chemically dependent parent from some of the blame and resentment that would have been directed at him/her; this process of diversion allows the addiction to progress further (Deutsch, 1982).

The Lost Child

Even in functional families, middle children are thought to get less attention than their siblings and seem less certain of their contribution to the family. This tendency is exacerbated in chemically dependent families (Deutsch, 1982). The "lost child" may be a middle child but may also be the youngest. The chief characteristic of the lost child is seeking to avoid conflict at all costs. Such children tend to feel powerless and are described as "very quiet," "emotionally disturbed," "depressed," "isolated," "withdrawn," and so on. These children tend to be forgotten, as they are very shy. They are followers, not leaders. They engage in much fantasy. If they stand out in school in any way, it is by virtue of poor attendance (Deutsch, 1982). If asked to do something they fear doing, they may pretend not to have heard the instructions or claim not to understand them (Deutsch, 1982). These behaviors point to a great deal of insecurity.

According to Deutsch (1982), the lost child is probably the most difficult child in a dysfunctional family to help. He/she may not have close friends or other systems outside the family for emotional support. Also, the child's behavior is usually not disruptive in school; hence, teachers and counselors do not identify this child as needy.

As adults, lost children exhibit a variety of mental health problems. They may complain of anxiety and/or depression. They have difficulty with developmental transitions because they fear taking risks. Thus, they may put off making decisions about careers or where to live. They may also back out of intimate relationships once someone starts to get too close. According to Deutsch (1982), lost children may or may not abuse alcohol and drugs. If they do, their drug of choice is usually different from that used by their chemically dependent parents.

The lost child helps maintain balance in the family by simply disappearing—that is, by not requiring any attention. In essence, the youngster in this role supports the family equilibrium by causing no new problems and requiring minimal attention. In the extreme, the lost child will think, "If I killed myself, Mom and Dad would have one less thing to worry about" (Deutsch, 1982).

The Mascot

The last commonly described role is that of the "mascot,"or "family clown." The youngest child in the family often adopts the role of the mascot. Everyone in the family likes the mascot and is comfortable with having him/her around. The family usually views the mascot as the most fragile and vulnerable; thus, he/she tends to be the object of protection. Deutsch (1982) notes that even the chemically dependent parent treats the mascot with kindness most of the time.

Mascots often act silly and make jokes, even at their own expense. The clownish behavior acts as a defense against feelings of anxiety and inadequacy. Mascots often have a dire need for approval from others. As adults, they are very likable but appear anxious. Deutsch (1982) believes that they may self-medicate with alcohol and/or tranquilizers.

The child in the mascot role helps maintain family homeostasis by bringing laughter and fun into the home. By "clowning around" and making jokes, he/she brightens the family atmosphere, becoming a counterbalance against the tension that is so prevalent and oppressive in dysfunctional families. The mascot may be the one family member about whom no one has a complaint.

THE PROCESS OF FAMILY THERAPY

Rosenberg (1981–1982) has developed a stage model to explain how chemically dependent families tend to respond to therapy as they deal with conflict and struggle to become more functional. This process consists of four phases.

Random Phase

In the initial stage of therapy, the family members typically behave in an unstructured and hostile manner. There often is confusion as to why they, as a unit, are in therapy. The question may emerge, "Why are all of use here? It is our ___ who has the problem." In addition, family members make few, if any, attempts to communicate about problems with each other or with the therapist. Essentially, the family members exhibit denial. They may recognize that there is an alcohol or drug problem within the family, but they are unaware that it has anything to do with family conflict. It is seen only as an alcohol or drug problem of one member. In other words, it is understood in simplistic terms and not linked to more fundamental family conflict.

Recrimination Phase

In the recrimination phase, the family involves itself in accusations and counteraccusations (Rosenberg, 1981–1982). Family members try to engage the counselor in consensus rather than counseling; that is, they make repeated efforts to get the therapist to take sides. Frequently, members resurrect "horror stories" from years past to convince the counselor who is right and who is wrong. In this phase, it is the task of the therapist to remain neutral. Typically, the family divides itself, with the nondependent members pitted against the alcoholic or addicted

member(s). The natural tendency of the therapist is to ally himself/
herself with the nondependent members. This is an impulse that must
be resisted.

Policing Phase

In the next phase, the family begins to test the limits that the therapist
has established for the therapy sessions. For example, certain members may miss sessions; the family may show up late for an appoint-
ment; family members may attempt to talk about the recent use of
alcohol or drugs by another member (when they have been instructed
not to for the time being); or a certain member may appear with alcohol on his/her breath. Rosenberg (1981–1982) indicates that a counselor who is unable to deal assertively with these behaviors usually
loses control of the direction of therapy. Furthermore, the therapist
should understand that the "testing" is an effort by the family to avoid
dealing with more sensitive, emotionally charged issues. By complaining about and challenging the rules, the family members can put off
wrestling with conflict among themselves. Unless the therapist remains
steadfast in enforcing the rules, the family progress will stop or become fixated in this phase.

Realization Phase

In the realization phase, therapeutic work or progress begins
(Rosenberg, 1981–1982). All the prior complaining and "testing" were
simply posturings of sorts to set the stage for actual work. Ideally, the
therapist and the chemically dependent member begin to develop a
therapeutic relationship, and this same member begins to communicate more effectively with the other family members. A transition occurs in which therapy discussion becomes more focused on family problems and concerns, instead of on the rules of therapy. Another
noteworthy shift is the family's efforts to identify solutions that address the needs of all members.

   The task of the realization phase is to help family members develop a positive family image (i.e., "to feel better about us") and an
expanded frame of reference (i.e., to be more adaptive and flexible in
allowing everyone to get his/her needs met) (Rosenberg, 1981–1982).
To accomplish this, the family has to struggle through a hierarchy of
negative feelings. According to Rosenberg (1981–1982), the family's
struggle is analogous to climbing a flight of stairs. The therapist's role is
to provide encouragement and to gently push the members through

the traps of comfort, relief, and satisfaction that they encounter during the struggle. Figure 6.5 illustrates this process.

The family moves through confusion, then anxiety, frustration, fear, anger, hostility, and resentment (Rosenberg, 1981–1982). The effective resolution of these emotions is opposed by such conditions as isolation, denial, resistance, and the desire to maintain the status quo. The combined force of these conditions works against the family's attempts to achieve "elegant change" (see Figure 6.5). These barriers can

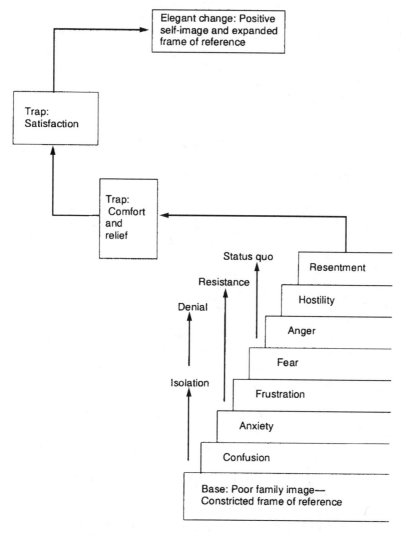

FIGURE 6.5. Family change and growth process.

be overcome with struggle and perseverance. Realistically, though, most families discontinue therapy before they achieve elegant change; many terminate when they find some measure of relief or satisfaction. Though Rosenberg (1981–1982) identifies these as traps, this level of progress is often characterized by a significant decrease in substance abuse. Thus, therapists themselves can find satisfaction in helping chemically dependent families even though the families may not resolve all interpersonal conflicts.

It should also be noted that some families never get to the realization phase. That is, they never begin doing any significant therapeutic work. Generally, these are families that have been dysfunctional and in disarray for many years. The children may be near or into adulthood and perceive their primary need as escaping rather than reuniting with their families of origin. Often the coping strategies and maladaptive roles are so rigidly defined that these seriously impaired families find therapy exceedingly difficult.

FINDINGS FROM THE RESEARCH LITERATURE

Patterson's Parental Family Management Models

For more than a decade, Patterson (1986, 1996) has written extensively about his research on the development of antisocial behavior in children and adolescents. Patterson has relied on rigorous measurement procedures, including the use of structural equation modeling to test hypotheses. His work does not focus specifically on substance abuse, though his models do encompass the problem. Rather, Patterson provides a framework for understanding how adolescent drug and alcohol abuse emerges as one feature of a general pattern of deviant behavior. The assumption here is that early involvement in substance use and delinquency are somewhat different aspects of a unified pattern of antisocial behavior. This assumption can be considered reasonable because antisocial personality disorder (ASPD) and substance use disorders often coexist in adults (Ross, Glaser, & Germanson, 1988).

Importantly, the parental family management models explain how the family mediates between social conditions (e.g., economic cycles, unemployment, and disorganized communities) and the production of delinquency and crime (Patterson, 1996). In Figure 6.6, two paths show how negative or unstable social conditions impact parents and neighborhoods which in turn influences the development of antisocial behavior in adolescents.

The main hypothesis of this research is: "Chronic antisocial behavior is the direct outcome of a breakdown in parental family management" (Patterson, 1996, p. 88). Problem behavior in children and adolescents results from inadequate parenting, particularly a lack of monitoring and poor disciplinary practices. As Figure 6.6 shows, parental antisocial behavior plays an important role here. One of Patterson's empirical models indicates that parental stress, as evidenced by single-parent homes, stepfamily arrangements, and multiple family

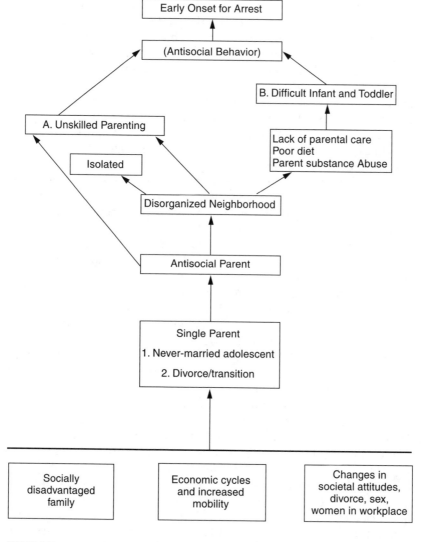

FIGURE 6.6. Two paths to antisocial behavior. From Patterson (1996). Copyright 1996 by Oxford University Press, Inc. Reprinted by permission.

transitions, is not enough to produce boys with an early onset of arrest. The mediating construct is parental antisocial behavior. Under times of stress, parents with antisocial tendencies tend to engage in *irritable discipline*.

Irritable discipline is a feature of a social interaction process that Patterson (1986) describes as *coercion*. The assumption of this model is that the failure of parents to effectively stop a child's relatively innocuous coercive behaviors sets into motion a series of interaction sequences that can be considered aggression training. The provocative idea here is that parent and child train each other to become increasingly aversive (Patterson, 1986). Relatively trivial child behaviors, such as refusing to comply with a simple request, whining, yelling, and so on, provide parents with opportunities to learn "high-amplitude aggressive behaviors" (Patterson, 1986, p. 436). As mentioned previously, parental stress and antisocial tendencies may initiate and exacerbate this coercion process, but other variables are important as well. The confluence of forces includes disorganized or high-risk neighborhoods, poor parenting skills, parental substance abuse, and a difficult temperament of the child (see Figure 6.6).

Transition from simple noncompliance to aggression usually occurs in the older child. The transition appears when the child becomes conditioned by a three-step, escape–avoidant arrangement. This interaction sequence first involves an attack by a parent or other family member, followed by a counterattack from the child, which is followed by the attacker's withdrawal. The attacker may withdraw to reduce the tension of the interaction or to show rejection of the child. In either case, the attacker's withdrawal reinforces or rewards the child's counterattack. Based on observation data collected in homes, Patterson (1982) reports that this sequence may occur hundreds of times a day in some families. About 20% of the coercive behavior of antisocial children falls into the three-step pattern. About one-third of the child's coercive behaviors were provoked by an aversive attack on them, and perhaps most important, about 70% of the time the child's counterattack was successful—meaning the attacker withdrew.

As a result of their work with parents of antisocial children, Patterson and colleagues have identified five critical family management skills: (1) discipline, (2) monitoring, (3) family problem solving, (4) parental involvement, and (5) positive reinforcement.

Parents who have inadequate skills in these areas tend to produce antisocial youth. Adolescent substance abuse is one manifestation of antisocial tendencies. Results from a study I conducted (Thombs, 1997) support this contention. Among a 779 seventh- to twelfth-graders from rural, western New York, I examined correlations among measures of perceived parental involvement and a variety of alcohol use indicators. The teens' perceptions of the parenting they received were factor-analyzed yielding internally consistent measures for parental involvement in their *education*, for establishing *rules* about their drinking and socializing, in developing good *parent/friend relations*,in monitoring school *grades*, in maintaining parent–teen *communication*, and for checking on them by *telephone*.

According to the teens' self-reports, there was considerable variation in parental involvement. For example, about 66% of the sample reported that their parents *never* or *rarely* check with other parents to see if their parties are supervised, 47% of the sample indicated their parents *never* or *rarely* talk to their teachers, and 28% claimed they had *never* had a curfew for being in at night. Canonical analysis of the parental involvement measures and indicators of teenage alcohol abuse showed that there were substantial negative correlations among these measures; teens' who reported low levels of parental involvement were likely to have high levels of alcohol consumption and alcohol problems, including higher rates of driving under the influence of alcohol and riding with alcohol-impaired drivers (Thombs, 1997).

Other Family Influences on Adolescent Alcohol and Drug Use

A large number of studies have examined other family influences on the development of substance abuse. This review highlights some of the important findings from these studies.

It appears that family values are related to teenage substance abuse. Jessor and Jessor (1977) assessed mothers' religiosity, tolerance of deviance, and traditional beliefs. They found that adolescent problem behaviors, including abusive drinking and illegal drug abuse, were less prevalent in families in which the mothers were highly religious, conventional, and traditional. The teens with the greatest prevalence of problem behaviors (e.g., alcohol and drug abuse) had mothers whose ideology deemphasized religion and traditional social values.

Several studies have linked adolescent substance abuse to single-parent families. For example, Burnside, Baer, McLaughlin, and Pokorny (1986) asked a large number of high school students about both their drinking practices and their family structure. The study found that teens in single-parent and stepparent families reported greater alcohol consumption than those in intact families. Furthermore, the parents in the nonintact families used more alcohol than did the parents in the intact families, and the adolescents' alcohol use was positively correlated with that of their parents. The relative influence of nonintact family status versus parental alcohol use in predicting adolescent alcohol consumption was assessed as well; it was determined that nonintact status had an effect on teen drinking that was independent of parental alcohol use.

Family size, sibling spacing, and birth order are family structure variables that have been thought to be linked to the development of alcoholism. However, the findings in this area are equivocal. Barnes (1990), in a review of this literature, concludes that there is little evidence to support the notion that birth order influences alcoholism. The issue of sibling spacing has not been adequately addressed, either. Research findings regarding family size are somewhat clearer; it appears that a disproportionate number of alcoholics come from large families. Zucker (1976) has offered explanations for this relationship: Larger families may exhibit diluted socialization effects, more authoritarian discipline, looser parental controls, or greater sibling rivalries. Any one or a combination of these conditions may explain why a relatively large percentage of alcoholics come from larger families.

Convincing evidence exists that teenage drinking practices are linked with parental drinking behavior (Barnes, 1990). It appears that children and teens learn to drink (or not to drink) through the process of imitation. Young people tend to model their behavior (including drinking) after those whom they observe, especially those with whom they are close. Kandel, Kessler, and Marguiles (1978), for instance, found that parents' use of hard liquor was a moderately good predictor of their adolescents' initiation to the use of hard liquor. In other words, the heavier the parental consumption, the earlier the teens began to use it. Data from a study by Harburg, Davis, and Caplan (1982) indicate that children tend to imitate their perception of their parents' drinking. Moreover, boys particularly imitate their perception of their fathers' drinking, as do girls with their mothers' drinking. However, when parental alcohol consumption was perceived to be extreme (i.e., unusual), imitation decreased; here, "extreme" meant either abstinence or heavy drinking by parents. This effect is consistent with that found by Barnes, Farrell, and Cairns (1986) in which abstaining parents had not only a high proportion of abstaining children but also a high proportion of heavy-drinking children. It appears that children of abstaining parents lack adult role models for sensible drinking. Thus, if they do initiate alcohol use, they have a tendency to drink in a binge-like manner. The reason why this heavy-drinking subgroup initiates use in the first place (when another subgroup of children of abstaining parents abstain) is unclear at this point.

During the teenage years, it can be expected that the peer group will have more influence on adolescent behavior as the family (parental) influence diminishes somewhat. Numerous studies have examined the interaction between peer influences and family influences as they relate to teen drinking. For example, Barnes and Windle (1987) have collected data showing that adolescents who value peer opinions, as opposed to parental opinions, are at heightened risk for alcohol and drug abuse and for other problem behaviors. Kandel and Andrews (1987) found that parental closeness discouraged teen drug use and promoted the choice of non-drug-using friends. This finding is consistent with those of other studies, which have found that adolescents who are close to their parents are less likely to associate with deviant peers (Barnes, 1990). Similarly, Dishion and Loeber (1985) found that lack of parental monitoring had an indirect effect on teen substance abuse by increasing the probability that a teen would "hang out" with deviant peers.

According to Barnes (1990), one of the most neglected areas of research on the development of adolescent substance abuse is that of sibling influence. Though relatively few studies have been done, "siblings may constitute a potentially powerful combination of peer and family socialization agent" (Barnes, 1990, p. 151). In a sample of 9th- and 10th-grade students, Brook, Whiteman, Gordon, and Brenden (1983) investigated older brothers' influence on younger siblings' drug use. It was found that having an older brother who used marijuana had a significant effect on a younger sibling's substance use, even after nonfamily influence was controlled for. Needle et al. (1986) conducted a study in which information was obtained independently from both younger and older siblings. They found that the younger siblings' frequency of drug use was predicted by older siblings' and peers' substance use (each remained significant after the other variable was controlled for). In addition, older siblings, as well as peers, were sources of information about drugs and companions in the use of drugs with their younger siblings. Further research is needed in this area. Though it is not well substantiated at this point, it is not unreasonable to speculate that older siblings in the family may be a potent factor in determining whether younger siblings initiate the use of alcohol and drugs.

Patterns of Interaction in Alcoholic Families: The Life History Model

Some of the pioneering work on how members of alcoholic families interact with one another was done by Peter Steinglass. In one particularly interesting study, 31 alcoholic families were observed in their homes during a 6-month period (Steinglass, 1981). Each family had one alcoholic spouse (husbands = 23, wives = 8) and one nonalcoholic spouse. Trained observers systematically rated the interactional behavior of members in three types of families: *stable wet, stable dry,* and *transition.* Steinglass (1981) refers to these as *family alcohol phases.* They represent long-term phases in the life of alcoholic families. In the study, stable wet families had an actively drinking alcoholic, whereas in the stable dry families, the alcoholic did not drink during the 6-month observation period. Transition families were those in which the alcoholic spouse had cyclic periods of drinking and abstaining.

Multivariate analysis determined that these three family types could be distinguished from one another on two variables: *distance regulation* and *content variability* (Steinglass, 1981). The first variable was concerned with the extent to which family members interacted with one another. Optimal scores were considered to be in the midrange where interaction was not too close or too distant. Content variability was a measure of the extent to which members would raise questions with one another and work to make decisions about them. Here, optimal scores were those in the high range.

Of the three family types, stable dry families were observed to have the best interactional distance; there was balance between intimacy and independence in these families. The stable wet families were characterized by distant relationships and the transition families by relationships that were too close. Commenting on the scores of the transition families, Steinglass (1981) notes they had: "the appearance of huddling together for warmth and protection" (p. 582). In regard to content variability, the stable dry families had the highest scores meaning they were most likely to discuss issues and arrive at decisions about them. The transition families had the poorest functioning in this area. These findings indicate that *family alcohol phase* is a useful construct for understanding how interactional behavior changes during the life phases of alcoholic families.

Day-to-Day Marital Interactions in Alcoholic Families

For 3 months, with eight couples, Dunn, Jacob, Hummon, and Seilhammer (1987) tracked the drinking behavior of alcoholic husbands and both spouse's daily marital satisfaction ratings and psychiatric symptoms. The husbands were of two subtypes: "in-home" drinkers and "out-of-home" drinkers. The findings of the study were distinct for these two groups.

Among the in-home drinkers, the husbands' alcohol consumption was interpreted to prompt positive marital ratings in most couples and decrease negative symptomatology in wives. The researchers concluded that this was particularly likely to occur when: (1) the alcoholic's behavior is predictable and involves steady drinking (not binge drinking), (2) family stress is reduced during drinking times, and (3) the drinking has been accepted and incorporated into family life (Dunn et al., 1987).

In contrast, in the out-of-home drinkers, husbands' alcohol consumption was interpreted to have a negative impact on marital ratings and wives' psychiatric symptomatology. In the out-of-home group, there tended to be more binge drinking. This could not be readily anticipated by wives and thus was probably more disruptive to family life. Also, alcoholic husbands who mostly drink away from home may have more psychopathology (Dunn et al., 1987).

In another study of marital interaction, Haber and Jacob (1997), during three laboratory sessions, observed four groups of couples: (1) alcoholic male ($n = 50$), (2) alcoholic female ($n = 15$), (3) male and female alcoholic ($n = 16$), (4) neither partner alcoholic ($n = 50$). During one of the interview sessions, alcohol was made available to the couples. Thus, there was a "drink"–"no drink" condition. The researchers found that compared to nonalcoholic couples, all alcoholic couple groups demonstrated greater negativity and lower positivity and congeniality toward one another. Furthermore, female alcoholic couples showed high negativity toward one another in the "no-drink" situation, which was erased by the drink session. Couples with two alcoholic partners also demonstrated high negativity in the "no-drink" situation, but this effect was exacerbated by the drink session. These findings suggest that alcohol does have adaptive value for marital interaction, and that there may be unique features to these interactions when the alcoholic is female.

Children of Alcoholics: A Major Research Focus

The research literature on children of alcoholics (COAs) has grown enormously during the last decade. Four major findings can be gleaned from this work. Each is reviewed below.

First, there is a great deal of heterogeneity in families in which alcoholism is present (Chassin, Rogosch, & Barrera, 1991; Jacob & Leonard, 1986; Seilhammer & Jacob, 1990; Zucker, Ellis, Bingham, & Fitzgerald, 1996). Specifically, it appears that not all alcoholic families are equally problematic. Family subtypes exist and some are much more likely to produce adjustment problems and psychopathology in children than others.

Contrary to popular notions, the alcoholic father–child relationship is not always perceived to be unsatisfactory by sons and daughters. Seilhamer, Jacob, and Dunn (1993) found that when children of alcoholic fathers perceive their father as either more pleasant or unchanged when drinking, their daily satisfaction ratings of their relationship with him are positive. However, when children perceive that their father's drinking makes him act strange, become aggressive, spend money that the family needs, or generally causes chaos, then their perceptions of their relationship with him are negative.

Ellis, Zucker, and Fitzgerald (1997) have proposed a probabilistic–developmental model that identifies the biological/genetic, peer, community, and family risk factors that determine COA adjustment (see Table 6.1). The first risk factor is the child's exposure to parental drinking models. Zucker et al. (1995) found that COAs as young as 3 to 5 years of age are more familiar with a wider range of alcoholic beverages and are better able to distinguish among them by smell than are nonCOAs. Furthermore, COAs may be likely to later imitate their parent's drinking if they admire that person. Modeling may not occur when the alcoholic parent is perceived by the child to be severely impaired by drinking or when the parent exhibits severe psychopathology, including aggression.

A second risk factor is the development of alcohol expectancies which may serve as the mediators between observations of parental drinking and decisions about one's own drinking (Reese, Chassin, & Molina, 1994). Alcohol expectancies appear to develop before the child has consumed any alcohol. COAs are inclined to develop positive expectations about drinking; that is, they tend to attribute positive affec-

TABLE 6.1. Family Risk Factors Affecting Alcohol Attitudes and Psychopathology among COAs Compared to Non-COAs

Risk factor	Research finding
Modeling of drinking behavior	COAs are more familiar with a wider range of alcoholic beverages at a younger age and develop alcohol-use schemas earlier than do non-COAs.
Alcohol expectancies	COAs are more likely than non-COAs to expect that alcohol will make them feel good.
Ethnicity and drinking practices	COAs from certain ethnic groups are more likely to hold positive alcohol expectancies.
Parent psychopathology	Subgroups of COAs are raised in families where alcoholic parents have a coexisting psychiatric disorder.
Socioeconomic status	COAs are more likely than non-COAs to come from homes where there is financial stress.
Family dysfunction	Alcoholic families have less closeness or cohesion in relationships, more conflict, and poor problem-solving skills than do nonalcoholic families. COAs are more likely than non-COAs to come from broken homes.
Family aggression/ violence	COAs are more likely than non-COAs to be victims of physical abuse and to witness family violence.
Parental cognitive impairment	COAs are more likely than non-COAs to be raised by parents with poor cognitive abilities in environments which lack stimulation.

Note. Adapted from Ellis, Zucker, and Fitzgerald (1997).

tive changes to drinking. Such expectations may be acquired by observing how drinking transforms their parent(s). The COA's alcohol expectancies may be shaped by the family's cultural heritage as well.

Ellis et al. (1997) also identified a number of family risk factors that influence the COA's overall psychosocial development, rather than just drinking attitudes and behavior. When significant psychopathology coexists with parental alcoholism, particularly ASPD and/or depression, COAs are at much greater risk for adjustment problems. As can be seen in Table 6.1. the other family risk factors associated with poor COA adjustment are low socioeconomic status, low family cohesion/high conflict, aggression and violence, and low intellectual capacity of parents.

In a longitudinal study, Zucker et al. (1996) found that the family risk factors (identified in Table 6.1) tend to aggregate in a nonrandom manner. In other words, they are "nested" within subtypes of alcoholic families. The subtyping is based on the presence or absence of ASPD in the father. Hence, Zucker et al. (1996) classified the families they are tracking as (1) antisocial alcoholic families, (2) nonantisocial alcoholic families, or (3) control families (matched nonalcoholic families recruited from the same communities). To date, their data indicate that antisocial alcoholic families represent a high-risk environment for COAs, ages 3 to 8. On all the assessed child risk indicators, children in the antisocial alcoholic families exhibited more problem behavior than did children in the nonantisocial alcoholic families and the control families. Children in the nonantisocial alcoholic families were similar to those in the nonalcoholic families (Ellis et al., 1997). Table 6.2 summarizes the child risk factors that cluster in antisocial alcoholic families.

A second major finding of COA research is that though COAs, as a group, do experience elevated levels of depression and anxiety and are more likely than non-COAs to have some type of conduct disorder, many of these children do not experience significant mental health or behavioral problems (Sher, 1997). A number of studies have found that the observed differences between COAs and non-COAs on cognitive, emotional, and behavioral measures are not great (e.g., Bennett et al., 1988). Often scores for both groups fall in the normal range. The relatively small group differences may reflect the significant variability in the environments of the alcoholic families in which these children are raised.

The third major finding from COA research is that though ACOAs are at elevated risk for substance use disorders and ASPD, the majority show no evidence of significant mental health problems (Ellis et al., 1997; Searles & Windle, 1990; Sher, 1997). ACOAs are more likely than adult non-COAs to have an alcohol or other drug diagnosis, including tobacco dependence. However, this represents a minority of ACOAs. ASPD is more common in ACOAs than in adult non-COAs, but this may be

TABLE 6.2. Child Risk Factors That Tend to Aggregate in Antisocial Alcoholic Families

One parent has an alcohol or other drug use disorder and ASPD.

Both parents have an alcohol or other drug use disorder and/or other psychopathology (ASPD or depression).

Parental alcohol use is severe and/or problematic.

Dense family history of alcoholism; children are exposed to multiple extended family members with alcohol problems and have higher genetic risk for the disorder.

Parental intellect is relatively low.

There is a relatively high rate of aggression toward the children including aggressive disciplinary practices.

Parents are verbally abusive with one another; there is violence between the parents.

Family socioeconomic status is relatively low.

Note. Adapted from Ellis, Zucker, and Fitzgerald (1997).

attributed to being offspring of antisocial alcoholics rather than a consequence of being raised in alcoholic families (Sher, 1991). There is little evidence that ACOAs are at high risk for other personality disorders other than ASPD. The literature on depression and anxiety disorders in ACOAs is equivocal and no firm conclusions can be drawn at this time (Sher, 1997). One recent study found that ACOAs, as a group, score somewhat higher on measures of state and trait anxiety than do non-COAs, but most often the former group was in or near the normal range on these variables (Maynard, 1997). Hence, it is important that mental health professionals not make assumptions about a client's psychological health solely on the basis of being raised in an alcoholic family.

The final conclusion to be drawn from the COA research is that the portrayals of ACOAs and codependency in many clinical training texts are inconsistent with empirical studies (e.g., Brown, 1995; Doweiko, 1993; Fields, 1995; Stanton & Heath, 1995). Some clinical texts have attempted to balance descriptions of these constructs with cautions about their lack of empirical support (e.g., Doweiko, 1993). However, this is often not the case; one unfortunate outcome could be inaccurate stereotyping of COA clients. Thus, substance abuse counselors must be judicious in their application of the ACOA and codependency concepts.

The research literature indicates that it is difficult to make valid generalizations about COAs (Sher, 1997). A major reason for this is that many alcoholic parents have coexisting psychiatric disorders such as ASPD, major depression, phobia, and so on. Hence, alcoholics and the families they create are not homogeneous. This is highlighted by the work of Zucker and colleagues (described earlier). As Sher (1997) pointed out:

> Thus, some COA's also are children of depressives, children of agoraphobics, children of people with antisocial personality disorder, and so forth. Given the many forms of psychopathology that are possible in parents of COA's, difficulties arise in attributing any apparent COA characteristic specifically to parental alcoholism. (p. 248)

Although the ACOA/codependency movement has maintained that ACOAs suffer from *unique* emotional patterns and problems, research to date has not supported this contention (Gotham & Sher, 1996; Seefeldt & Lyon, 1992). Alterman, Searles, and Hall (1989) found no differences between children of alcoholic fathers and control subjects on a variety of personality variables, mental health problems, and alcohol-related measures. Hence, researchers warned against stereotyping ACOAs as necessarily having a special set of characteristics or problems. Sher (1997) suggests that when COAs do report elevated levels of anxiety and depression, it may be the result of having been raised in a *disruptive home* rather than being exposed to an alcoholic parent.

Seefeldt and Lyon (1992) reached an interesting conclusion about the ACOA/codependency phenomenon. They examined three groups: non-ACOAs (n = 93), ACOAs not in treatment (n = 36), and ACOAs in treatment (n = 18). Subjects were assessed on 11 different personality variables that Woititz (1983) describes as essential features of ACOAs. Seefeldt and Lyon (1992) found no significant differences among the three groups on any of the variables. In fact, the ability of the 11 variables to correctly classify subjects into the three groups (by discriminant analysis) was only slightly better than random assignment.

Some researchers then have attributed the popularity of the ACOA/codependency movement to a tendency known as the "Barnum effect" (Goodman, 1987; Seefeldt & Lyon, 1992). Named after the huckster P. T. Barnum, this is "the tendency to interpret a description that applies to everyone as being particularly valid to one's self" (Seefeldt & Lyon, 1992, p. 588). It is argued that many descriptions of ACOAs and codependents are similar to those used by fortune tellers and astrologers. At first they seem specific, but in reality they are actually quite vague and applicable to almost all persons. If future research does indeed confirm that a Barnum effect is in operation, it is likely that criticism of these constructs will intensify and addiction practitioners eventually will become more cautious about their application in clinical practice.

Child Maltreatment and Violence in the Home

Though popular lore has linked substance abuse, particularly alcohol abuse, with child maltreatment and domestic violence for hundreds of years, it only has been since the mid-1980s that the problem began to receive substantial attention in the research literature (Lee & Weinstein, 1997). Recent studies provide credibility to the anecdotes.

For example, Egami, Ford, Greenfield, and Crum (1996) analyzed self-report data from 9,841 respondents in three communities. About 1.5% of the sample admitted they had *abused* children and an additional 1.4% acknowledged the *neglect* of a child. (We might suspect that these relatively low rates reflect an underreporting bias.) Multivariate analysis showed that lifetime history of an alcohol disorder was significantly associated with both child abuse and neglect (even after controlling for other factors). Thus, people with a past history of alcohol abuse and/or alcoholism appear to be at risk for abusing or neglecting children. Unfortunately, the study design could not directly link intoxication or other alcohol-related behavior to these incidents.

In a review of the impact of alcohol and drug abuse on the child welfare system, Young, Gardner, and Dennis (1998) conclude that 40 to 80% of parents with children in the child welfare system have alcohol or drug problems that interfere with caretaking. One government report has noted that in Los Angeles, New York City, and Philadelphia County, parental substance abuse was a factor for 78% of the children placed in foster care (U.S. General Accounting Office, 1994). A separate investigation found that 55% of families reported to child protective services had one or two caretakers who had a substance abuse problem (Wolock & Magura, 1996). It is important to note that the relationships identified here are correlational and not necessarily causal (National Institute on Alcohol Abuse and Alcoholism, 1993). In some cases, alcohol and drug use may facilitate child maltreatment among caretakers who had a prior proclivity for such behavior; in other cases, there may be mechanisms that mediate between substance use and maltreatment of a child. Regardless, Young et al. (1998) assert that these problems have not been adequately addressed because there are a lack of linkages between the child welfare system (i.e., child protective services, juvenile justice, delinquency and violence prevention, and family counseling) and substance abuse treatment services.

Rivara et al. (1997) conducted a case–control study of the factors associated with 388 homicides and 438 suicides in three large metropolitan areas in the United States. Structured interviews of persons close to the decedents were used to collect information about the alcohol and drug use of the subject. The findings indicated that both homicide and suicide risks were associated with either alcohol or illegal drug abuse. Violent death, in particular, was linked to *chronic* alcohol abuse. Importantly, the researchers also found that nondrinkers and non-drug users living with substance abusers were at increased risk for homicide. This was particularly the case for non–drug-using persons residing in a home with a drug abuser. Rivara et al. (1997) conclude that it is not only the alcohol or drug abuser who is at risk for homicide but others in the home as well.

SUMMARY

It is imperative that substance abuse counselors be familiar with family systems concepts. As the primary social unit, the family exerts a powerful influence over an individual's drinking or drug use. The systems emphasis on reciprocal causality is unique among theories of addictive behavior. It proposes that substance abuse is functional in a certain sense, that it is a manifestation of deeper conflict; and that it helps the individual to minimize, distract from, or cope with interpersonal problems. An understanding of these dynamics is necessary if a counselor is to be an effective helper.

A word of caution about family systems concepts is also in order. Put simply, there is not much empirical support for the efficacy of the systems approach as a treatment for alcoholism and other addictions (Alexander & Barton, 1995; Collins, 1990). Relatively few well-designed studies have tested the effectiveness of family systems therapy. It has been shown to be as effective as individual treatment but less effective than a behavioral treatment (McCrady, Moreau, Paolino, & Longabaugh, 1982; McCrady, Paolino, Longabaugh, & Rossi, 1979). O'Farrell, Cutter, and Floyd (1985) report that a brief family systems intervention is just as effective as more prolonged and intensive treatment. Collins (1990) concludes a review of this literature by stating that "while descriptions of systems approaches to treating alcoholic families abound, the body of methodologically sound empirical research on systems approaches is limited" (p. 296). Considering the reputation of family systems therapy in the substance abuse treatment field, the discrepancy between its prominence and its empirically established validity is conspicuous. Though more research is needed before firm conclusions can be reached, it appears that *behavioral approaches* to marital and family therapy may be effective treatments for substance use disorders (Noel & McGrady, 1993).

REVIEW QUESTIONS

1. What are the sources of literature on addiction and the family?

2. What are "boundaries," "subsystems," "hierarchies," "family rules," and "homeostasis"?

3. What is meant by "reciprocal causality"?

4. How does a person's family of origin affect the person's mate selection and manner of childrearing?

5. How does a teen's fear of separation contribute to his/her abusing drugs?

6. What are "triads"? How do they spur substance abuse?

7. What is the "dance"?

8. What does Bowen mean by "differentiation of self"? What are characteristics of poorly differentiated persons and highly differentiated persons?

9. What does Bowen mean by "triangles"?

10. How does Bowen describe the development of the emotional system in the nuclear family?

11. What does Bowen mean by "family projection process"?

12. What does Bowen mean by "emotional cutoff"?

13. What is "codependency"? What are its chief characteristics?

14. What rewards are gained in a codependent relationship?

15. What three emotional conditions are prevalent in the lives of children living with alcoholic parents?

16. What are the six roles that sometimes develop in chemically dependent families? How does each reduce family tension?

17. According to Rosenberg, what are the four phases of therapy with alcoholic families? Is Rosenberg optimistic about the family's attempts to achieve "elegant change"?

18. What are the components of Patterson's parental family management models?

19. What family factors are linked to adolescent substance abuse?

20. What are the three family alcohol phases identified by Steinglass? What are the characteristics of families in each phase?

21. How does "in-home" versus "out-of-home" drinking affect marital satisfaction? How are the marital interactions of alcoholic couples different from those of nonalcoholic couples?

22. What are the major findings from the COA research?

23. What are the alcohol-specific risk factors and family risk factors that influence COA adjustment?

24. Does research support the link between substance use and child abuse and domestic violence?

REFERENCES

Alexander, J., & Barton, C. (1995). Family therapy research. In R. H. Mikesell, D. D. Lusterman, & S. H. McDaniel (Eds.), *Integrating family therapy: Handbook of family psychology and systems theory.* Washington, DC: American Psychological Association.

Alterman, A. I., Searles, J. S., & Hall, J. G. (1989). Failure to find differences in drinking behavior as a function of familial risk for alcoholism: A replication. *Journal of Abnormal Psychology, 98,* 50–53.

Barnard, C. P. (1981). *Families, alcoholism, and therapy.* Springfield, IL: Charles C. Thomas.

Barnes, G. M. (1990). Impact of the family on adolescent drinking patterns. In R. L. Collins, K. E. Leonard, B. A. Miller, & J. S. Searles (Eds.), *Alcohol and the family: Research and clinical perspectives.* New York: Guilford Press.

Barnes, G. M., Farrell, M. P., & Cairns, A. L. (1986). Parental socialization factors and adolescent drinking behaviors. *Journal of Marriage and the Family, 48,* 27–36.

Barnes, G. M., & Windle, M. (1987). Family factors in adolescent alcohol and drug abuse. *Pediatrician: International Journal of Child and Adolescent Health, 14,* 13–18.

Beattie, M. (1987). *Co-dependent no more.* Center City, MN: Hazelden.

Bennett, L. A., Wolin, S. J., & Reiss, D. (1988). Cognitive, behavioral, and emotional problems among school-age children of alcoholic parents. *American Journal of Psychiatry, 145,* 185–190.

Bowen, M. (1976). Theory in the practice of psychotherapy. In P. J. Guerin (Ed.), *Family therapy: Theory and practice.* New York: Gardner Press.

Brook, J. S., Whiteman, M., Gordon, A. S., & Brenden, C. (1983). Older brother's influence on younger sibling's drug use. *Journal of Psychology, 114,* 83–90.

Brown, S. (1995). *Treating alcoholism.* San Francisco: Jossey-Bass.

Burnside, M. A., Baer, P. E., McLaughlin, R. J., & Pokorny, A. D. (1986). Alcohol use by adolescents in disrupted families. *Alcoholism: Clinical and Experimental Research, 10,* 274–278.

Chassin, L., Rogosch, F., & Barrera, M. (1991). Substance use and symptomatology among adolescent children of alcoholics. *Journal of Abnormal Psychology, 100,* 449–463.

Collins, R. L. (1990). Family treatment of alcohol abuse: Behavioral and systems perspectives. In R. L. Collins, K. E. Leonard, B. A. Miller, & J. S. Searles (Eds.), *Alcohol and the family: Research and clinical perspectives.* New York: Guilford Press.

Deutsch, C. (1982). *Broken bottles, broken dreams: Understanding and helping the children of alcoholics.* New York: Teachers College Press.

Dishion, T. J., & Loeber, R. (1985). Adolescent marijuana and alcohol use: The role of parents and peers revisited. *American Journal of Drug and Alcohol Abuse, 11,* 11–25.

Doweiko, H. F. (1993). *Concepts of chemical dependency* (2nd ed.). Pacific Grove, CA: Brooks/Cole.

Dunn, N. J., Jacob, T., Hummon, N., & Seilhammer, R. A. (1987). Marital stability in alcoholic-spouse relationships as a function of drinking pattern and location. *Journal of Abnormal Psychology, 96,* 99–107.

Egami, Y., Ford, D. E., Greenfield, S. F., & Crum, R. M. (1996). Psychiatric profile and sociodemographic characteristics of adults who report physically abusing or neglecting children. *American Journal of Psychiatry, 153,* 921–928.

Ellis, D. A., Zucker, R. A., & Fitzgerald, H. E. (1997). The role of family influences in development and risk. *Alcohol Health and Research World, 21,* 218–226.

Fields, R. (1995). *Drugs in perspective* (2nd ed.). Madison, WI: WCB/Brown & Benchmark.

Fogarty, T. (1976). Marital crisis. In P. J. Guerin (Ed.), *Family therapy: Theory and practice.* New York: Gardner Press.

Framo, J. L. (1976). Family of origin as a therapeutic resource for adults in marital and family therapy: You can and should go home again. *Family Process, 15,* 193–209.

Goodman, R. W. (1987). Adult children of alcoholics. *Journal of Counseling and Development, 66,* 162–163.

Gotham, H. J., & Sher, K. J. (1996). Do codependent traits involve more than just basic dimensions of personality and psychopathology? *Journal of Studies on Alcohol, 57,* 34–39.

Haber, J. R., & Jacob, T. (1997). Marital interactions of male versus female alcoholics. *Family Process, 36,* 385–402.

Harburg, E., Davis, D. R., & Caplan, R. (1982). Parent and offspring alcohol use. *Journal of Studies on Alcohol, 43,* 497–516.

Jacob, T., & Leonard, K. (1986). Psychological functioning in children and alcoholic fathers, depressed fathers and control fathers. *Journal of Studies on Alcohol, 47,* 373–380.

Jessor, R., & Jessor, S. L. (1977). *Problem behavior and psychosocial development: A longitudinal study of youth.* New York: Academic Press.

Kandel, D. B., & Andrews, K. (1987). Processes of adolescent socialization by parents and peers. *International Journal of the Addictions, 22,* 319–342.

Kandel, D. B., Kessler, R. C., & Marguiles, R. Z. (1978). Antecedents of adolescent initiation into stages of drug use: A developmental analysis. In D. B. Kandel (Ed.), *Longitudinal research on drug use.* Washington, DC: Hemisphere.

Koffinke, C. (1991). Family recovery issues and treatment resources. In D. C. Daley & M. S. Raskin (Eds.), *Treating the chemically dependent and their families.* Newbury Park, CA: Sage.

Laundergan, J. C., & Williams, T. (1993). The Hazelden residential family program: A combined systems and disease model approach. In T. J. O'Farrell (Ed.), *Treating alcohol problems: Marital and family interventions.* New York: Guilford Press.

Lawson, A., & Lawson, G. (1998). *Alcoholism and the family: A guide to treatment and prevention* (2nd ed.). Gaithersburg, MD: Aspen.

Lee, W. V., & Weinstein, S. P. (1997). How far have we come? A critical review of the research on men who batter. *Recent Developments in Alcoholism, 13,* 337–356.

Maynard, S. (1997). Growing up in an alcoholic family: The effect on anxiety and differentiation of self. *Journal of Substance Abuse, 9,* 161–170.

McCrady, B. S., Moreau, J., Paolino, T. J., & Longabaugh, R. (1982). Joint hospitalization and couples therapy for alcoholism: A four year follow-up. *Journal of Studies on Alcohol, 43,* 1244–1250.

McCrady, B. S., Paolino, T. J., Longabaugh, R., & Rossi, J. (1979). Effects of joint hospital admission and couples' treatment for hospitalized alcoholics: A pilot study. *Addictive Behaviors, 4,* 155–165.

National Institute on Alcohol Abuse and Alcoholism. (1993). *Alcohol and health: Eighth special report to the U.S. Congress* (NIH Publication No. 94-3699). Bethesda, MD: National Institutes of Health.

Needle, R., McCubbin, H., Wilson, M., Reineck, R., Lazar, A., & Mederer, H. (1986). Interpersonal influences in adolescent drug use: The role of older siblings, parents, and peers. *International Journal of the Addictions, 21,* 739–766.

Noel, N. E., & McGrady, B. S. (1993). Alcohol-focused spouse involvement with behavioral marital therapy. In T. J. O'Farrell (Ed.), *Treating alcohol problems: Marital and family interventions.* New York: Guilford Press.

Norwood, R. (1985). *Women who love too much.* New York: Simon & Schuster.

O'Farrell, T. J., Cutter, H. S., & Floyd, F. J. (1985). Evaluating behavioral marital therapy for male alcoholics: Effects of marital adjustment and communication from before to after treatment. *Behavior Therapy, 16,* 147–167.

Patterson, G. R. (1982). *Coercive family process.* Eugene, OR: Castalia.

Patterson, G. R. (1986). Performance models for antisocial boys. *American Psychologist, 41,* 432–444.

Patterson, G. R. (1996). Some characteristics of a devlopmental theory for early-onset delinquency. In M. F. Lenzenweger & J. J. Haugaard (Eds.), *Frontiers of developmental psychopathology.* New York: Oxford University Press.

Pearlman, S. (1988). Systems theory and alcoholism. In C. D. Chaudron & D. A. Wilkinson (Eds.), *Theories on alcoholism.* Toronto: Addiction Research Foundation.

Reese, F. L., Chassin, L., & Molina, B. S. (1994). Alcohol expectancies in early adolescence: Predicting drinking behavior from alcohol expectancies and paternal alcoholism. *Journal of Studies on Alcohol, 55,* 276–284.

Rivara, F. P., Mueller, B. A., Somes, G., Mendoza, C. T., Rushforth, N. B., & Kellermann, A. L. (1997). Alcohol and illicit drug abuse and the risk of violent death in the home. *Journal of the American Medical Association, 278,* 569–575.

Rosenberg, D. N. (1981–1982). Holistic therapy with alcoholism families. *Alcohol Health and Research World, 6,* 30–32.

Ross, H. E., Glaser, F. B., & Germanson, T. (1988). The prevalence of psychiatric disorders in patients with alcohol and drug problems. *Archives of General Psychiatry, 45,* 1023–1031.

Searles, J. S., & Windle, M. (1990). Introduction and overview: Salient issues in the children of alcoholics literature. In M. Windle & J. S. Searles (Eds.), *Children of alcoholics: Critical perspectives.* New York: Guilford Press.

Seefeldt, R. W., & Lyon, M. A. (1992). Personality characteristics of adult children of alcoholics. *Journal of Counseling and Development, 70,* 588–593.

Seilhamer, R. A., & Jacob, T. (1990). Family factors and adjustment of children of alcoholics. In M. Windle & J. S. Searles (Eds.), *Children of alcoholics: Critical perspectives.* New York: Guilford Press.

Seilhamer, R. A., Jacob, T., & Dunn, N. J. (1993). The impact of alcohol consumption on parent–child relationships in families of alcoholics. *Journal of Studies on Alcohol, 54,* 1189–198.

Sher, K. (1991). *Children of alcoholics: A critical appraisal of theory and research.* Chicago: University of Chicago Press.

Sher, K. (1997). Psychological characteristics of children of alcoholics. *Alcohol Health and Research World, 21,* 247–254.

Stanton, M. D. (1980). A family theory of drug abuse. In D. J. Lettieri, M. Sayers, & H. W. Pearson (Eds.), *Theories on drug abuse: Selected contemporary perspectives* (DHHS Publication No. ADM 84-967). Washington, DC: U.S. Government Printing Office.

Stanton, M. D., & Heath, A. W. (1995). Family treatment of alcohol and drug abuse. In R. H. Mikesell, D. D. Lusterman, & S. H. McDaniel (Eds.), *Integrating family therapy: Handbook of Family Psychology and Systems Theory.* Washington, DC: American Psychological Association.

Steinglass, P. (1978). The conceptualization of marriage from a systems theory perspective. In T. J. Paolino, Jr., & B. S. McCrady (Eds.), *Marriage and marital therapy.* New York: Brunner/Mazel.

Steinglass, P. (1981). The alcoholic at home: Patterns of interaction in dry, wet, and transitional stages of alcoholism. *Archives of General Psychiatry, 38,* 578–584.

Subby, R., & Friel, J. (1984). Co-dependency: A paradoxical dependency. In *Codependency: An emerging issue.* Hollywood, FL: Health Communications.

Thombs, D. L. (1997). Perceptions of parent behavior as correlates of teenage alcohol problems. *American Journal of Health Behavior, 21,* 279–288.

U.S. General Accounting Office. (1994). *Foster care: Parental drug abuse has alarming impact on young children.* Washington, DC: Author.

Woititz, J. G. (1983). *Adult children of alcoholics.* Hollywood, FL: Heath Communications.

Wolock, I., & Magura, S. (1996). Parental substance abuse as a predictor of child maltreatment re-reports. *Child Abuse and Neglect, 20,* 1183–1193.

Young, N. K., Gardner, S. L., & Dennis, K. (1998). *Responding to alcohol and other drug problems in child welfare: Weaving together practice and policy.* Washington, DC: Child Welfare League of America.

Zucker, R. (1976). Parental influences on the drinking patterns of their children. In M. Greenblatt & M. A. Schuckit (Eds.), *Alcoholism problems in women and children*. New York: Grune & Stratton.

Zucker, R. A., Ellis, D. A., Bingham, C. R., & Fitzgerald, H. E. (1996). The development of alcoholic subtypes: Risk variation among alcoholic families during the early childhood years. *Alcohol Health and Research World, 20*, 46–54.

Zucker, R. A., Kincaid, S. B., Fitzgerald, H. E., & Bingham, C. R. (1995). Alcohol schema acquisition in preschoolers: Differences between children of alcoholics and children of nonalcoholics. *Alcoholism: Clinical and Experimental Research, 19*, 1011–1017.

CHAPTER SEVEN

Social and Cultural Foundations

Previous chapters have explored the factors within the individual and the family that influence substance use. In contrast, this chapter examines the "macroenvironment" (Connors & Tarbox, 1985). Macroenvironmental factors include trends in drug use over time, regional variations in drug use, the role of government regulation, laws, and tax policy (on alcoholic beverages); drug subcultures and crime; and, in general, the social values, beliefs, and norms that influence drug use. These concepts are the social and cultural foundations of substance abuse counseling.

RESISTANCE TO CONSIDERING THE SOCIAL ORIGINS OF ALCOHOLISM

As this volume has described, the etiology of alcoholism, in particular, is multifactorial. Social and cultural factors are part of the mix of variables that spur its development. Vaillant (1995), in a review of his 33-year prospective study of alcoholism in men, notes that ethnicity and number of alcoholic relatives accounted for most of the variance in adult alcoholism. Irish-Americans, "old Americans," and "other Northern Europeans" had the highest rates of alcohol problems, whereas Jews, Italians, and "other southern Europeans" had the lowest rates. In an earlier study, Cahalan (1970) also found heavy drinking was associated with age, sex, ethnicity, and social status. According to the National Institute on Alcohol Abuse and Alcoholism (1997), whites represent the majority of treatment admissions (63%). However, the proportions of African-Americans (22%) and Latino (12%) receiving alcoholism treatment are somewhat higher than their respective proportions in the U.S. population. Asian-Americans (1%) were underrepresented among these admissions, whereas Native Americans

(3%) were overrepresented. These findings suggest that the roots of alcoholism are at least partially sociocultural in nature.

Unfortunately, the importance of social factors has often been discounted by the treatment community in the United States (Peele, 1988). For example, in a book often distributed to patients in alcoholism treatment (*Under the Influence*, by Milam & Ketcham, 1983), it is asserted that the cause of alcoholism is strictly biological. Here is an excerpt from the book:

> In other words, while psychological, cultural, and social factors definitely influence the alcoholic's drinking patterns and behavior, they have no effect on whether or not he becomes alcoholic in the first place. Physiology, not psychology, determines whether one drinker will become addicted to alcohol and another will not. The alcoholic's enzymes, hormones, genes, and brain chemistry work together to create his abnormal and unfortunate reaction to alcohol. (Milam & Ketcham, 1983, pp. 34–35)

This view disregards the possibility that some alcoholics may have no physiological vulnerability at all, and others may only have a mild physiological susceptibility. In such cases, sociocultural (as well as psychological) factors are of great importance in determining alcoholism. The view expressed by Milam and Ketcham implies dangerously that those without this biological vulnerability can use alcohol with impunity.

It is interesting to note that sociocultural theorists do not necessarily rule out the possibility of important pharmacological, metabolic, hormonal, or genetic contributions to alcoholism (Heath, 1988). Yet many proponents of the disease models completely discount social and cultural origins of alcoholism and other addictions, or they consider these influences to be secondary or relatively minor modulators of dependency. This is unfortunate, because any comprehensive theory of alcohol and drug dependence needs to account for social and cultural influences.

TIME AND PLACE AS SOCIAL DETERMINANTS OF ILLICIT DRUG USE

An examination of the etiology of *illicit* drug abuse and dependence requires us to consider the influence of *time* and *place*. Drug availability and drug use norms vary from one region to another and change over time. The data from two federal government surveillance programs track regional variation and changing trends in illicit drug use.

The Substance Abuse and Mental Health Services Administration (SAMSHA) operates one program known as the Drug Abuse Warning

Network (DAWN). Each year DAWN collects data on drug-related emergency room (ER) visits and drug-related deaths (only ER visits are examined here). When an individual is seen in an ER that reports to DAWN, drug-related emergencies are determined and each drug the person used, up to four, is recorded for reporting purposes. Thus, it is important to understand that more than one drug may be mentioned per ER visit. A person could be seen at an ER for a cocaine-induced seizure, but if he also had smoked marijuana both drugs would be "mentioned."

Cocaine-related ER visits were the most frequent incidents reported to DAWN in 1996; it was mentioned in 30% of all ER episodes reported to the system (SAMSHA, 1998). As can be seen in Table 7.1, incidents related to the use of many illicit drugs have increased substantially during the 1990s.

In 1996, 41% of total drug-related ER visits occurred among persons 35 years of age and older. For all drugs identified in Table 7.1, it is the aging user who is increasingly seen in emergency rooms. For instance, between 1994 and 1996, there was a 21% increase in cocaine-related ER visits among persons 35 and older (SAMSHA, 1998). In regard to race, in 1996, 53% of the total drug-related visits occurred among Caucasians, 27% among African-Americans, and 10% among Latinos, and 10% was "other" or unknown. However, a majority of the ER visits for cocaine and heroin were among African-Americans.

A second surveillance system is the Arrestee Drug Abuse Monitoring Program (formerly the Drug Use Forecasting Program). Operated by the National Institute of Justice (NIJ), this program collects urine specimens and self-report information from arrestees in 23 U.S. cities. This system is particularly useful for examining regional differences in substance use. To illustrate the effect of geography, Table 7.2 presents selected data from 5 of the 23 cities.

These statistics show considerable variation in drug use among arrestees across the selected cities. For example, cocaine was detected in the urine of Manhattan and Atlanta arrestees more often than the

TABLE 7.1. DAWN Emergency Room Visits: 1990–1996

Drug	Percent increase in ER visits
Cocaine	78%
Heroin	108%
Marijuana/hashish	219%
Methamphetamine	198%
Any drug	31%

Note. Data from SAMSHA (1998).

TABLE 7.2. Drug Use among Male (and Female) Arrestees in Five U.S. Cities: 1997

City	Any drug	Cocaine	Marijuana	Opiates	Meth- amphetamine
	Percent positive urine test				
Atlanta	72% (74%)	51% (61%)	36% (28%)	1% (3%)	<1% (<1%)
Cleveland	64% (57%)	27% (39%)	46% (22%)	3% (4%)	0% (0%)
Manhattan	79% (81%)	58% (62%)	32% (25%)	19% (20%)	0% (0%)
Phoenix	64% (66%)	32% (33%)	30% (21%)	9% (8%)	16% (26%)
San Diego	73% (73%)	21% (22%)	38% (24%)	7% (12%)	40% (42%)

Note. Data from NIJ (1998).

urine of arrestees in other cities. Marijuana positives were prevalent in Cleveland male arrestees and opiate use occurred at the highest rate in Manhattan female and male arrestees. Methamphetamine presents the greatest variation. There appears to be little use of the drug in eastern cities. However, in western cities methamphetamine appears to be a major drug of abuse, at least among arrestees (NIJ, 1998). The reasons for the variation are not entirely clear, but they may be rooted in the drug trafficking networks in these areas, as well as in the different social beliefs and customs in these particular regions.

THE INFLUENCE OF CULTURE ON DIAGNOSTIC DETERMINATIONS

From a sociological perspective, the problems of alcoholism and other addictions have become "medicalized" (Schwartz & Kart, 1978); that is, because of its vested interests, the medical community has redefined the problem as one of "disease." According to sociologists, this labeling process functions as a means of social control (Schwartz & Kart, 1978). It gives credibility to physicians' efforts to control, manage, and supervise the care given to addicted persons. It makes legitimate such potentially lucrative endeavors as hospital admissions, insurance company billings, expansion of the patient pool, consulting fees, and so forth. It also serves to restrict the number and type of nonmedical treatment providers (e.g., professional counselors, psychologists, social workers, nurses, and marriage and family counselors) who could independently provide care for substance-abusing clients. As a result, much of the treatment of such clients in the United States is carried out under physicians' supervision. In fact, the acceptance of the term "treatment" in the substance abuse field reflects the dominant influence of medicine.

The social process of labeling also functions to restrict alcohol consumption in the community. It defines, for the average citizen, appropriate and inappropriate drinking practices. For example, in our culture, conduct norms typically discourage obvious drunkenness, drinking before noon, drinking at work, impaired driving, and binge drinking. It is interesting to note that many of these popular, "man-on-the-street" notions of alcoholism have found their way into widely used "clinical" assessment instruments, such as the Michigan Alcoholism Screening Test (MAST).

When medicine and the mental health professions formally label problem behaviors, the label is referred to as a "diagnosis." To justify this labeling process, the helping professions have created elaborate sets of criteria based mostly on clinical experience. Of course, the most prominent example in the mental health arena is the fourth edition of the *Diagnostic and Statistical Manual of Mental Disorders* (DSM-IV; American Psychiatric Association, 1994). Labeling theorists have described these professional practices as the *medicalization of deviant behavior* (Conrad, 1992; Conrad & Schneider, 1992). From a sociological perspective, it as an attempt by modern medicine to redefine deviance from "badness" to "sickness." Thus, the control of deviance shifts from the criminal justice system to medicine.

In the sociological perspective, clinical diagnostic criteria for alcoholism (and other addictions) are derived largely from cultural norms. Thus, those drinking practices that are considered "alcoholic" are those that deviate from socially acceptable standards. Alcoholism and other drug addictions are considered social deviance rather than a medical problem. Sociologically, treatment is an effort to force the alcoholic to conform to socially "correct" standards of conduct.

The cultural foundations of alcoholism diagnoses have been recognized by Vaillant (1990, 1995)—a proponent of the disease conception. Vaillant (1990) has stated: "Normal drinking merges imperceptibly with pathological drinking. Culture and idiosyncratic viewpoints will always determine where the line is drawn" (p. 5). The sociocultural origins of diagnoses force us to consider certain possibilities. First, a diagnosis, as applied to a particular client, may not be very different from a personal opinion: It may be based not so much on scientific evidence as on the values and beliefs of the addictions practitioner. The practitioner's own history, relative to his/her use of alcohol and drugs, clearly influences the opinion.

It is also possible that drinking that is considered "alcoholic" in one time or place may not be viewed similarly in another temporal or geographic context. Heath (1988) has noted that 150 years ago, Americans consumed three times more alcohol (per capita) than they consume today. Clearly, the notion of what an alcoholic was then would have differed substantially from our conception today.

These cultural factors also should sensitize counselors as to the consequences, both positive and negative, of applying the diagnosis (i.e., label) of "alcoholism" or "drug addiction" to a particular client. In the best of cases, the diagnosis will motivate the client to adopt abstinence. However, a positive diagnosis also could lead to overly intrusive treatment, social stigma, estrangement from family members, loss of employment, feelings of worthlessness and humiliation, or even exacerbation of existing drinking problems. Obviously, the addiction diagnosis should be made with caution. One can legitimately question the value of making a positive diagnosis (even when one is clearly appropriate) if there is reason to believe that it will adversely affect a client.

SOCIOLOGICAL FUNCTIONS OF SUBSTANCE ABUSE

From a sociocultural vantage point, abuse of alcohol and drugs can be described as having four broad functions. One is the facilitation of social interaction. That is, the use of alcohol (and often illegal drugs as well) enhances social bonds. It makes communication involving self-disclosure easier. Interpersonal trust is strengthened, whereas barriers or guards are diminished. In addition, the intoxicated state and the attending rituals and jargon allow users the opportunity of a shared experience.

A second function is to provide a release from normal social obligations. Alcohol and drug abuse have been characterized as "time-out" periods (Heath, 1988). The purpose of intoxication is to permit people to withdraw from responsibilities that society normally expects teenagers and adults to carry out. In this view, addictive behavior is an effort to escape temporarily from the roles thrust upon individuals (parent, spouse, employee, student, etc.) Intoxication allows for a temporary respite from the stresses and strains inherent in these roles.

A third function of alcohol and drug abuse is to promote cohesion and solidarity among the members of a social or ethnic group. The use or nonuse of a drug can be viewed as a means of group identification. Use or nonuse also establishes group boundaries. That is, substance abuse serves as a social boundary marker, defining who "we" are and who "they" are. For example, Jews generally drink in moderation. It is part of their cultural tradition, one way in which they define themselves. They view drunkenness as a "vice of the Gentiles" (Heath, 1988).

A fourth function of substance abuse, from a sociocultural perspective, is the repudiation of middle-class or "establishment" values. A substance abuse subculture consists of abusers of a particular chemical who all hold similar antiestablishment values. In essence, members of drug subcultures "thumb their nose" at conventional mores and norms, particularly those related to morality and economic productivity. Lifestyles are characterized by hedonistic pursuits, spontaneity, and freedom from family responsibilities. This is a value structure at odds with that of working- or middle-class America.

SOCIAL FACILITATION

Some illicit drug use (e.g., LSD) is associated with motivations unrelated to increased sociability. Alcohol, in contrast to the illegal substances, has a distinctive social function. Because its consumption is legal, alcohol is more closely associated with good times, parties, and fun with others.

The use of alcohol to facilitate social pleasure and interactions with others has been reported for thousands of years among most of the cultures of the world. For example, the Hammurabi Code, the earliest known legal code (promulgated circa 1758 B.C. in Babylon), contains laws governing the operation and management of drinking establishments (McKim, 1986). At another time, the Greek philosopher Plato expressed concern about the drinking of his countrymen, so he established rules for conduct at "symposia," which in reality were drinking parties. He directed that at each symposium a "master of the feast" must be present. This person was to be completely sober. His responsibilities included deciding how much water should be added to the wine and when to bring on the dancing girls (McKim, 1986). Plato observed:

> When a man drinks wine he begins to feel better pleased with himself and the more he drinks the more he is filled full of brave hopes, and conceit of his powers, and at last the string of his tongue is loosened, and fancying himself wise, he is brimming over with lawlessness and has no more fear or respect and is ready to do or say anything. (From Jowett's translation of Plato's Laws; Jowett, 1931, p. 28)

"Drinking" has been thoroughly integrated into mainstream U.S. culture today. Alcoholic drinks have come to be known simply as a "drink." If a person invites a neighbor "to come over for a drink," everyone usually recognizes that alcohol is being offered. Alcohol consumption is expected behavior at various social, family, and business gatherings, both formal and informal. Though individuals are not usually directly pressured to take a drink in such gatherings, a subtle pressure to do so often exists. A blunt refusal often invites puzzlement, covert speculation, or even suspicion as to one's motives.

Frequently, refusing to drink is interpreted as passing on an opportunity to meet and talk in an informal way. This is particularly true in business or other work settings characterized by formal or professional relationships. In such settings, people often desire to escape from the restrictive confines of stiff or rigid professional roles. Drinking together is seen as the way to "loosen up."

The Social Context of Adolescent Drinking

Research by Kenneth Beck and I (DT) confirms that convivial drinking practices are well-established in adolescence. We have developed a social context model to explain adolescent drinking. Derived from factor-analytic studies, this model contends that the adolescent's motivation to drink arises not just from intrapersonal characteristics, such as expectancies or sensation seeking traits, but from situational and temporal aspects of the immediate social environment as well (Thombs & Beck, 1994). Our findings suggest that these three sources of drinking motivation (psychological, situational, and temporal) tend to cluster in unique ways to form distinguishable patterns of social context. Furthermore, this body of research has shown that in young people, social context measures are superior to both alcohol expectancies (Thombs, Beck, & Pleace, 1993) and the sensation-seeking trait (Thombs, Beck, Mahoney, Bromley, & Bezon, 1994) in explaining drinking behaviors.

Results from our factor-analytic studies show that each social context is composed of psychological, situational, and temporal features (Beck, Thombs, & Summons, 1993; Thombs & Beck, 1994). Importantly, the same set of factors emerged from samples of youth residing in different geographic regions. The five contexts of adolescent drinking that we have identified are (1) Social Facilitation, (2) Stress Control, (3) School Defiance, (4) Peer Acceptance, and (5) Parental Control. Among these five factors, Social Facilitation is the contextual pattern that accounts for most of variance in alcohol consumption (Thombs & Beck, 1994; Thombs et al., 1994). This pattern involves drinking in a convivial setting with friends, away from adults, on weekends, at parties, and at friends' homes when the parents are away. Stress Control (done alone for self-medication) and School Defiance (a rebellious pattern) are the contextual patterns of drinking that best discriminate between problem and nonproblem drinkers. Peer Acceptance is a pattern of drinking done to conform with group expectations in reaction to peer pressure. Interestingly, we have found that drinking in this context (as well as that of Parental Control) tend to be linked with the maintenance of lighter and nonproblematic drinking patterns. This finding raises questions about the heavy emphasis placed on peer resistance skill training currently in vogue in prevention programming today (Thombs et al., 1994). It may be an erroneous assumption to conclude that teenagers abuse alcohol because they "cave in" to peer pressure (May, 1993). To the contrary, most adolescents appear to maintain drinking habits because it enhances their social interaction; in problematic patterns, drinking in contexts of self-medication and rebellion tends to be more pronounced.

"TIME OUT" FROM SOCIAL OBLIGATIONS

The Basic Hypothesis

The time-out hypothesis applies to both alcohol and drug abuse. It maintains that the abuse of intoxicants releases individuals temporarily from their ordinary social obligations. By becoming intoxicated, they are excused from their obligations as parents, spouses, students, employees, and so forth. MacAndrew and Edgerton (1969) came upon this notion by observing the fact that many cultures exhibit a certain flexibility in norms that allows for suspension of certain role obligations during times of drunkenness. They were careful to point out that the option of "time out" does not suspend all the rules. In all cultures, certain behavior, even while intoxicated, is considered inexcusable; thus, intoxicated persons are viewed as less responsible rather than as totally unresponsible (Heath, 1988). According to MacAndrew and Edgerton (1969), "the option of drunken time-out affords people the opportunity to 'get it out of their systems' with a minimum of adverse consequences" (p. 169). Heath (1988) notes that the concept is more of a descriptive tool than an analytic one. However, he adds that it may be useful as an early sign of alcoholism. Young people who get intoxicated to avoid, or escape from, social role expectations may be susceptible to developing more serious drinking problems.

Achievement Anxiety Theory

The time-out hypothesis essentially describes "escapist drinking"—that is, drinking to escape role obligations of any sort. Misra (1980) outlined a model that describes substance abuse as an effort to escape a specific class of role obligations. As Misra (1980) sees it, the substance abuser is attempting to evade the pressures placed upon him/her to achieve and produce (e.g., income). Blame is not placed on the individual who abuses drugs but, rather, on U.S. culture and its obsession with materialism, financial success, and personal achievement.

Achievement anxiety theory maintains that drug abuse is a response to a "fear of failure" (Misra, 1980). It allows the abuser to withdraw from the pressures placed on the individual to achieve. At the same time, substance abuse induces and maintains a sense of apathy toward standards of excellence that U.S. culture defines as important. According to Misra (1980), one of the chief characteristics of technologically advanced countries, such as the United States, is anxiety about achievement. Obtaining or reaching socially prescribed goals can become a compulsion in itself (i.e., "workaholism"). Many Americans have a dire need to "be somebody." Such competitive conditions cause people to feel anxious, fearful, inadequate, and self-doubting. As a result of these modern pressures, many Americans, in Misra's view, are likely to rely on chemicals as a way to cope.

According to achievement anxiety theory, drugs are initially used to seek relief from the pressures of achievement and productivity (Misra, 1980). In effect, they provide a quick "chemical vacation" from the stresses of contemporary life. This conceptualization is quite similar to that of "time out." However, Misra (1980) further develops the concept by noting that continued abuse of drugs tends to reduce the difference between "work life" and leisure-time activities. In essence, the chemical vacations gradually change from being infrequent, temporary respites to full-time pursuits (i.e., addiction).

In addiction, the primary goal becomes freedom from productivity. Misra (1980) has labeled this "antiachievement." In this state, relief from achievement anxiety is no longer the goal. Instead, the goal is to maintain a sense of apathy or even hostility toward recognized and socially prescribed standards of excellence. This is the work ethic in reverse. According to Misra (1980):

> Drug abuse is, in a sense, a silent protest against the achieving society. It protects us from a sense of failure: "I may not be achieving what my neighbors and colleagues are, but I do attain a unique feeling of relaxed carelessness." Addictions form the nucleus of a subculture of people who all have the same feeling of nonachievement, and friendships evolve around this theme as efforts are made to create and maintain fellowship among the addicts. (p. 368)

In achievement anxiety theory, leisure, as pursued in technologically advanced countries like the United States, has a special relationship. Misra (1980) notes that Americans have to *plan* to relax. This is typified by those who arrange, well in advance, elaborate, action-packed vacations. Each day is planned out, including hectic travel itineraries. This situation is exacerbated by the fact that holidays for Americans are relatively short in duration and rigidly defined.

Misra (1980) is critical of this approach to leisure. Doing "something" rather than "nothing" has become the hallmark of relaxation in the United States. As Americans creatively jam their leisure time with activity, they become as anxious about their vacations as they are about work. According to Misra (1980), people often come to believe that relaxation must be achieved, here and now. This sense of immediacy for relaxation encourages the adoption of time-saving techniques. Of course, substance abuse fills this perceived need. Alcohol or drug abuse becomes a quick, easy procedure for "getting away from it all" (Misra, 1980).

PROMOTING GROUP SOLIDARITY/ESTABLISHING SOCIAL BOUNDARIES

For hundreds of years, the use of alcohol and drugs has been an important feature of identification with one's ethnic or racial group. With the mainstreaming of various sociodemographic groups into U.S. culture, drinking and drugging practices have served to promote solidarity and cohesion within groups (Heath, 1988). The use of substances also demarcates the boundaries between ethnic and racial groups. It is one source of identity. It solidifies a person's social identity and helps the person define himself/herself in reference to others. The use of alcohol or drugs also shapes the images that individuals want or expect others to have of them (Heath, 1988).

Alcohol as a Boundary Marker

Anthropologists have identified numerous examples of how drinking has functioned to separate social groups and to promote cohesion within themselves. The temperance movement (1827–1919) in the United States is one such example. During the 19th century, temperance groups were widespread in the United States. Initially, temperance groups sought to reduce the consumption of hard liquor and to promote drinking at home, as opposed to saloon drinking. This emphasis on temperance gradually gave way to one demanding abstinence. As could be expected, this led to quarrelsome disputes between "wets" and "drys," and eventually to Prohibition (1919–1933). However, the dispute actually represented deeper ethnic and social class conflict. According to Ray and Ksir (1999):

> Prohibition was not just a matter of "wets" versus "drys," or a matter of political conviction or health concerns. Intricately interwoven with these factors was a middle-class, rural, Protestant, evangelical concern that the good and true life was being undermined by ethnic groups with a different religion and different standard of living and morality. One way to strike back at these groups was through Prohibition. (p. 154)

For those involved in the temperance movement, abstaining (vs. drinking) was a social boundary marker. It served to promote a self-righteous pride within movement workers and was taken as proof that they were morally superior to those who did drink.

For the temperance movement, abstinence was the source of group identification. In other social/ethnic groups, drunkenness was and is the social boundary marker. Heath (1988), in a description of drunkenness among Native Americans, notes that "some Indians embrace the stereotype and use it as a way of asserting their ethnicity, differentiating themselves from others, and offending sensibilities of those whites who decry such behavior" (p. 269). Lurie (1971) has suggested that alcohol abuse by Native Americans is one of the last ways they can strike back or rebel against white America. He refers to their drinking as "the world's oldest on-going protest demonstration" (p. 311).

Situated between the extreme conditions of abstinence and drunkenness are a variety of culturally distinct drinking practices. Again, these serve to facilitate group identification and boundary marking. One widely recognized example, as mentioned earlier, is the Jewish tradition of moderation (Heath, 1988). Alcohol plays a significant role in Jewish family rituals (Lawson & Lawson, 1998); however, excessive consumption, particularly drunkenness, is viewed as inexcusable behavior. Within the Jewish culture, conduct norms allow for frequent but sensible use. According to Glassner and Berg (1980), these beliefs and conduct norms "protect" Jews from developing problems with alcohol. The Yiddish expression *Schikker ist ein Goy* translates to "drunkenness is a vice of Gentiles" (Glassner & Berg, 1980). The Jewish tradition of moderation and sobriety reflects basic values emphasizing rationality and self-control (Keller, 1970). Thus, Jews perceive drunkenness as being irrational and "out of control."

Interestingly, Peele (1985) notes that Jews may express their compulsions by overeating rather than overdrinking. It has been pointed out that Jews refer to overeating as the Jewish version of alcoholism. Peele (1983) suggests: "What this quasi-joking reference meant is that Jews who have emotional and coping problems that lead to substance use that is harmful and degrading would be more likely to eat than to drink excessively" (p. 964). There is some evidence that Jews and members of other ethnic groups who drink less heavily also report greater problems with weight control (Peele, 1985). However, the evidence is probably best considered less than conclusive at this time.

It is generally accepted that Irish Catholics have relatively high rates of alcoholism (Lawson & Lawson, 1998). For example, Vaillant (1983) found that Irish subjects in his sample were more likely to develop alcohol problems than were those of other ethnic backgrounds; in fact, they were seven times more likely to be alcoholic than those of Mediterranean descent. In the same study, Irish subjects were found to be more likely to abstain in an effort to manage a drinking problem. Vaillant (1983) observed: "It is consistent with Irish culture to see the use of alcohol in terms of black and white, good or evil, drunkenness or complete abstinence, while in Italian culture it is the distinction between moderate drinking and drunkenness that is most important" (p. 226). It has been suggested that the Irish have distinctly ambivalent feelings about the use of alcohol (Lawson & Lawson, 1998). Viewing alcohol use dichotomously, as either good or bad, eliminates the middle possibility (i.e., moderate, sensible drinking).

Drinking has never been healthfully integrated into Irish family rituals (e.g., drinking at family wakes) or religious traditions (Lawson & Lawson, 1998). Rather, in Irish tradition, drinking has been viewed as a means of coping with oppression and hard times. In the 19th century, the oppression was largely political in nature and came at the hands of the British. Poverty and famine were widespread, and many an Irishman turned to alcohol in an effort to cope (Bales, 1980). At this time, the terms "Irishman" and "drunkard" became synonymous (Bales, 1980).

What appears to have evolved in Irish culture is the shared norm that "alcohol is an effective way to deal with our hard times that so commonly befall us." Bales (1980) proposed that cultures such as the Irish, which are characterized by suppression of aggression, guilt, and sexual feelings and which condone the use of alcohol to cope with these impulses, will probably have high rates of alcoholism. Alcohol use is seen by the Irish as their way of coping with personal distress. Although on the one hand drinking is viewed as the "curse of the Irish," on the other it is seen as the quintessential Irish act, one embodying all that is "Irish." In a symbolic way, drunkenness connects the Irish to all their similarly anguished ancestors. Though this may be an overly sentimental portrayal of Irish drinking customs, to some degree it captures the socially unifying aspects of drinking within the culture.

Convergence to a False Norm:
Explaining Alcohol Abuse among Young People

Alcohol abuse is a serious problem on college campuses in the United States (Douglas et al., 1998; Wechsler, Dowdall, Maenner, Gledhill-Hoyt, & Lee, 1998). Binge drinking, blackouts, drinking and driving, and an assortment of other alcohol-related problems are more prevalent in this group than in society at large. Though these are not new problems, recent media reporting of unintentional alcohol-related deaths (Associated Press, 1997), fraternity hazing incidents involving alcohol, and so-called riots outside bars in a number of college towns (Associated Press, 1998) have heightened the concern about the problem. Why is it a severe problem?

One explanation that is increasingly relied on is the *convergence to a false norm hypothesis* (Baer, Stacy, & Larimer, 1991; Perkins & Berkowitz, 1986; Thombs, Wolcott, & Farkash, 1997). This model maintains that youthful drinking is maintained by the perceptions of peers' drinking practices. Biased drinking norms tend to develop in relatively insular social environments, such as schools and colleges (Baer et al., 1991). Perceptions of these norms become biased or *exaggerated* because students interact mostly with other students, and less with older adults, and because in these situations, stories about recent drinking episodes tend to be embellished and bragged about in social conversations (see Berkowitz, 1997).

As a result, a large majority of students develop exaggerated perceptions of the extent to which their fellow students are drinking and engaging in related behavior. The belief develops that "everybody is drunk on Thursday, Friday, and Saturday nights," or "if I'm not drinking, I'll miss out on the fun." In other words, students come to perceive that their campus environment is very *permissive*. Students who hold norms that are more conservative tend to increase their drinking over time to conform to the false norm (Prentice & Miller, 1993). These perceptual biases fuel alcohol abuse. Students begin to think "heavy drinking is what we do at ___ University" and "everybody at ___ University knows how to party."

Recent research that I (DT) have conducted with middle school, high school, and college students found that perceived norms are highly correlated not only with alcohol consumption but with drinking and driving and riding with alcohol-impaired drivers (Thombs et al., 1997). Young people who perceived that these behaviors were prevalent among their peers tended to drink heavily as well as engage in drinking and driving and riding with impaired drivers. Interestingly, relatively large majorities of students (66–79%) perceived that other students at their school engaged in these alcohol behaviors more than they did (Thombs et al., 1997). Only a handful of students thought they engaged more frequently in these behaviors than their peers.

Illicit Drugs as Boundary Markers

Illicit drugs have also been used to promote group identity and to establish ethnic boundaries. One frequently described example involves the Chinese laborers who were brought to the western United States in the last half of the 19th century to build the railroad system. Large numbers of Chinese were imported at this time to complete the arduous task of constructing new track; they brought with them their practice of opium smoking. Opium dens were created as places to spend nonworking hours.

The practice of opium smoking never spread to other social groups. Local community leaders in many jurisdictions (who, of course, were Caucasian) passed legislation to forbid the practice. In general, most Americans viewed the use of opium by the Chinese with distaste and repugnance. Thus, for the white majority, opium smoking served as a significant social boundary. It was useful for the white community as a means of identifying who "we" (the good people) were, and who "they" (the Chinese, the bad people) were.

Furthermore, the drug experience (opium smoking) itself made apparent the distinctive value structures of the Chinese versus the white Americans. As noted by Ray and Ksir (1999):

> The opium smoking the Chinese brought to this country never became widely popular, although around the turn of the century about one-fourth of the opium imported was smoking opium. Perhaps it was because the smoking itself occupies only about a minute and is then followed by a dreamlike reverie that may last two or three hours— hardly conducive to a continuation of daily activities or consonant with the outward, active orientation of most Americans in that period. Another reason why opium smoking did not spread was that it originated with Asians, who were scorned by whites. (p. 341)

Opium smoking was consistent with the Chinese emphasis on reflection and introspection. It was at odds with the U.S. orientation toward productivity, action, and settling the West.

The current practice of smoking "Philly Blunts" appears to serve a similar social purpose for some young African-Americans. According to the National Institute on Drug Abuse (NIDA; 1998), "Philly Blunts" are inexpensive cigars in which the tobacco is removed and replaced with marijuana. These are often smoked at "house parties" where the participants are predominately African-American. This practice is largely unknown outside segments of the African-American community.

DRUG SUBCULTURES: REPUDIATION OF MIDDLE-CLASS VALUES

Prior to the 1960s, illicit drug abuse was primarily concentrated among minority ghetto populations. Thus, explaining illicit drug abuse within a subculture framework made a great deal of sense. However, during the 1970s illicit drug abuse became more diffuse among social classes (Oetting & Beauvis, 1988). The availability and use of such substances as marijuana and heroin were not narrowly limited to lower socioeconomic groups, as they were in the 1950s. Thus, sociologists and anthropologists paid somewhat less attention to the subculture concept in the 1970s and 1980s.

There is still value to analyzing drug abuse within a subculture context, however. This is particularly true for examining substance abuse among teens and younger adults. The framework offers insight into how substance abuse is initiated and maintained, and how drug subcultures are related to the youth culture, to the parent culture, and to broad middle-class culture in the United States.

Definitions

Middle-class U.S. culture is characterized by a broad set of rather diverse values and conduct norms for adults. It is essentially a parent culture that includes expectations for what youths can and cannot do. In general, parents expect youths to avoid tobacco, alcohol, and illicit drug use. This expectation is reflected in laws that prohibit youths from purchasing cigarettes and alcohol before the ages of 18 and 21, respectively. To various degrees, the values and conduct norms of the parent culture are internalized by youths. Of course, the extent of this socialization varies from youth to youth and across particular classes of values as well.

The youth culture defines what peers or friends expect each other to do or not to do (Gans, 1962). In its attempt to control and influence young people, the parent culture competes with the youth culture. This competition is an ongoing, dynamic process. The parent culture usually attempts to defend traditional values, whereas the youth culture encourages experimentation with new or novel forms of expression. According to Johnson (1980), the youth culture emphasizes the following conduct norms:

1. The person must be loyal to friends and attempt to maintain group association.
2. Social interaction with the peer group should occur in locations where adult controls are relatively absent.
3. Within such peer groups, a veiled competition exists for status and prestige among group participants and leads to new forms of behavior or operating innovations. (p.111)

"Youth culture" and "peer group" are closely related but distinct concepts. A young person's close circle of friends is his/her peer group. The term "youth culture" refers to a much broader influence—one that touches all peer groups via community, school, church, and media messages. The pervasive influence of the youth culture explains the great similarity among distant peer groups. This is particularly the case today with so many national media targeting youth (e.g., MTV).

A "subculture" consists of a culture within a larger culture (Johnson, 1980). It is characterized by values, conduct norms, social situations, and roles that are distinct from and often at odds with those of the middle class. The term "drug subculture" refers to these same components as they pertain to *nonmedical* drug use (Johnson, 1980).

Excluded from this conceptualization are the values and conduct norms associated with medical and most legal drug use. Thus, psychoactive drugs prescribed by a physician are not included, nor is use of over-the-counter medications or cigarettes. The moderate social use of alcohol is also excluded from a drug subculture analysis because such drinking practices are clearly part of middle-class culture. However, in the subsequent discussion, the values and conduct norms of the alcohol *abuse* subculture are explored.

A relatively unique constellation of values define a subculture. According to Johnson (1980), "the most important elements of a subculture are its values and conduct norms. Values are here understood to be shared ideas about what the subgroup believes to be true or what is wants (desires) or ought to want" (p. 113). The most significant value of a drug subculture is the intention or desire to alter consciousness, or to get "high." This value (i.e., the wish to get high) is the organizing theme of all drug subcultures and their activities. The corresponding conduct norm is an expectation that all subculture participants will partake in the use of a drug, or at least express a desire to do so.

Within subcultures, certain behavior is expected of persons in particular social positions. These performances are referred to as "roles." Three primary roles exist in drug subcultures: seller, buyer, and user (Johnson, 1980). Performance of these roles is almost always illegal, so the execution of them is generally covert, or hidden from the public at large. Thus, the public is generally ignorant of the behavior needed to carry out the role of seller, buyer, or user (Johnson, 1980), which may, in part, explain the great fascination and curiosity nonsubculture members often express about these activities.

Also characteristic of drug subcultures are rituals involving highly valued objects. The objects are usually instruments for self-adminis-tration of drugs. For example, the heroin subculture favors the use of the hypodermic syringe, and incorporates it into rituals in which sev-eral addicts may share the same needle (e.g., in "shooting galleries"). The cocaine subculture has several ritualized practices, depending on the route of administration. Objects include mirrors, spoons, special pipes, vials, and straws or rolled-up dollar bills for snorting. The mari-juana subculture values such objects as "roach clips," water pipes, and rolling papers. These symbolic objects and drug rituals are rarely known outside the subculture but are widely known within it. They bolster group identity and solidarity.

By the time most illicit drug addicts have reached their mid-20s, they have developed a preference for one drug over others. This pref-erence may simply be a function of their participation in a particular drug subculture. The addicts may have an elaborate set of reasons for why their drug is superior to others. Heavily influencing their attach-ment to one drug are their bonds and identification with their peer group. Johnson (1980) noted that subculture participants tend to ig-nore great similarities in the behavior of drug addicts and tend to em-phasize the importance of differences that seem small to outsiders. For example, many cocaine addicts "put down" PCP addicts; they believe that cocaine helps one think more clearly, whereas PCP just makes one "dumb." Alcoholics and heroin addicts take similar views of each other: Alcoholics may perceive heroin addicts as "lowlifes," while many heroin addicts view alcoholics as "wimps" and "crybabies."

Drug Laws as a Means of Striking Back at Low-Status Groups

Drug subcultures are dynamic. Historical, political, economic, and so-ciocultural factors influence their formation and dissolution. However, some of their trends are quite predictable. With much insight, Johnson (1980) noted:

> When patterns of drug use are limited to low-income and low-status groups, societal reaction tends to be punitive, and government pur-sues a prohibitionist policy. When drug use becomes common in many segments of the youth population, public reaction is one of temporary alarm with later adjustment and easing of enforcement effects and legal punishments. (p. 115)

A good example of how public perception shapes U.S. drug laws involves the legal distinction between crack cocaine and powder cocaine (Caulkins, Rydel, Schwabe, & Chiesa, 1997). Under current federal law, a person convicted of possessing just 1.5 grams of crack is subject to a 5-year minimum sentence, whereas 150 grams of powder cocaine is needed for the same sentence (U.S. Sentencing Commission, 1998). Thus, depending on the form of the cocaine, the mandatory minimum sentence for cocaine varies by a factor of 100!

Who tends to be arrested on crack cocaine charges? According to Forst (1995), more than 90% of the defendants are African-Americans. In powder cocaine cases, they comprise only 25% of the defendants. Thus, critics have charged that the differential sentencing guidelines are racist. The situation illustrates how drug laws are sometimes used to strike back at groups that the dominant culture fear.

Changes in drug use, shifts in public opinion and public debate, and new government initiatives are among the dynamic social forces that spur the development of drug subcultures. Therefore, they are not static social groups; subcultures are always changing. Though identification of their chief features can become quickly dated, key aspects of five of today's drug subcultures can be delineated and are described next.

The Alcohol Abuse Subculture

Alcohol is a powerful mood-altering drug. Yet it is legally available and its use is widespread, even expected, in middle-class culture in the United States. Alcohol is viewed as both a beverage and an intoxicant—one that is principally used to facilitate social interaction and relief from stress. There is significant social pressure in this society to drink, at least in moderation. Abstention from alcohol is considered almost as deviant as binge drinking.

In contrast to the sensible, "social" use of alcohol stands the alcohol abuse subculture. The conduct norms of this subculture expect participants to get "wasted," "totaled," "smashed," or "bombed." The emphasis is on excessive consumption. Alcohol is not used as a beverage but as a drug; that is, drunkenness is intentional or purposely sought. Such drinking contrasts sharply with that of the larger middle class, where drunkenness is viewed with embarrassment and met with social disgrace. Many high school and college students become participants of the alcohol abuse subculture, although a sizable proportion seem to "mature out" of it as they assume full-time jobs, get married, and/or have children.

Certain reciprocity conduct norms exist in the alcohol abuse subculture. It is expected that participants will share in the pooling of money to buy relatively large quantities of alcohol (e.g., a case or keg of beer). There is the expectation that one member will buy drinks for other members, and that the favor will later be reciprocated. In some social groups, bottle passing is expected. In others, drinking games (e.g., "quarters," "pass out," and others) and reliance on special paraphernalia (e.g., beer funnels and baseball caps designed to dispense beer) are encouraged. Again, these rituals and objects promote group identity and solidarity.

These social functions become clear when one considers the very high rate of alcohol abuse in college fraternities and sororities (Cashin, Presley, & Meilman, 1998). These Greek-letter organizations are at the center of the alcohol abuse subculture on campus. It is well established by research that members of fraternities and sororities consume substantially more alcohol than do non-Greek students (e.g., Cashin et al., 1998).

Greek student conduct norms for drinking appear to be established to a great extent by the fraternity/sorority *leaders* (Cashin et al., 1998). Thus, on many campuses, some fraternities come to resemble alcohol-dispensing outlets—particularly for underage drinkers. Drinking games are significant features (Engs & Hanson, 1993). They organize binge drinking and ensure participant intoxication. Current campus rituals include the practice of "keg standing" and consuming "jello shots."

Participants of the alcohol abuse subculture are not always young people. Older adults may also be participants of this subculture. The middle class tends to label such adults "alcoholics." Their drinking may also be ritualized (three drinks before dinner, never drinking before noon, stopping at a bar each day after work, etc.). They may set up elaborate liquor cabinets or even full-size bars at home. They may keep large quantities of alcohol in reserve (e.g., a keg of beer on tap in the refrigerator or a dozen or more cases of beer bought at wholesale prices stored in the garage). Decorative mirrors, pictures, posters, clocks, ashtrays, and other "knick knacks" from alcohol retailers may adorn their homes. Heavy drinking is clearly a central activity in their lives (Fingarette, 1988). That is, they organize their lives around the consumption of alcohol.

The Marijuana Abuse Subculture

Among young adults, the marijuana subculture thrived in the 1960s and 1970s. The sharing of marijuana was promoted. Rock music lyrics reinforced this conduct norm (e.g., Bob Dylan emphasized in one song that "everybody must get stoned"). It should be understood, though, that the predominant values were not ones of aggression and pressure; rather, values emphasized peace, love, understanding, and social harmony. Yet a subtle form of peer pressure did exist within the subculture to use the drug.

Usually, no money was exchanged in the sharing of marijuana. Group participants were trusted to reciprocate at some future date. Those who bought relatively large amounts of "pot" were expected to share small amounts with friends, and to sell to friends at cost. There was an expectation that marijuana buyers and sellers were not supposed to turn large profits. Typically, buyers and sellers within this subculture were expected to socialize and smoke together. The business aspects of the transactions were deemphasized.

In this era, there was the naive but persistent belief that marijuana use could correct many of the social ills of the United States. The middle class, particularly the parent culture, was perceived as obsessed with material things, as well as racist, sexist, corrupt, and hypocritical. Marijuana use was naively thought to be the single answer to all social problems. This conviction (among others) helped to forge the youth–parent culture conflict (i.e., the "generation gap") of the 1960s and 1970s.

These social values promoted the acceptance of marijuana and its use was relatively high among youth (Johnson, 1980). However, the 1980s saw a reversal in this trend, with fewer and fewer young people experimenting with it or using it regularly (Johnston, O'Malley, & Bachman, 1989). By 1992, marijuana use among youth had fallen to its lowest level in the 23 years of the national Monitoring the Future Study; about 22% of high school seniors reported using marijuana one or more times in the previous 12 months (Johnston, Bachman, & O'Malley, 1999). Then, in 1993, a second reversal in the trend appeared. Marijuana use among youth increased each year from 1993 to 1997. In 1998, there was a leveling off in use. That year, 38% of high school seniors reported smoking marijuana at least once in the previous 12 months (Johnston et al., 1999).

The reasons for the increase are not entirely clear. Bachman, Johnston, and O'Malley (1998) have determined that perceptions of risk and disapproval related to smoking marijuana have decreased, thereby fueling increased use. Others suggest that prevention programming efforts have become lax since the "Just Say No" days of the Reagan era. Still others have argued that today's youth are likely to have parents who were pot smokers in the late 1960s and 1970s and, as a consequence, have been instilled with values that condone or even support marijuana use.

The provocative findings of a recent study point to yet another possible explanation for the increased use of marijuana by youth in the 1990s. Using a national database, Pacula (1998) tested the hypothesis that among teenagers, marijuana and alcohol were "economic substitutes." This means that the investigator expected to find that marijuana use would increase among youth if the cost of alcohol was increased through taxation. Unexpectedly, Pacula (1998) found no evidence of a substitution effect but, rather, discovered that among teenagers, marijuana and alcohol are *economic complements*. The statistical models she developed suggest that increases in the beer tax would *decrease* marijuana use at least as much as alcohol use, in percentage terms. Thus, it appears that among youth today, marijuana is often used to complement drinking, and both appear to be *price-sensitive consumer products*. This complementary economic linkage suggests that the increased use of marijuana may, in part, be a function of the robust economy of the mid-1990s. Low teenage unemployment, higher wages in jobs held by teenagers, and greater discretionary income as a consequence of increased parental income may contribute to higher levels of marijuana use.

Whatever the reason for the increase, demand for marijuana appears to be high. In response, local, state, and national law enforcement agencies have adopted a tough "zero tolerance" approach to the problem. According to Ray and Ksir (1999), there were more than 600,000 arrests for violation of U.S. marijuana laws in 1996. Despite these law enforcement efforts, there appears to be a substantial underground marijuana market in the United States. In many areas of the country, the local economy is buoyed by the marijuana trade (e.g., Davidson, 1992). All these developments suggest that the marijuana subculture of the 1990s may not resemble that of the 1970s.

The Polydrug Abuse Subculture

Johnson (1980) has identified a drug subculture characterized by polydrug abuse. Substance abuse counselors working in the field today are keenly aware of the use of multiple substances, either simultaneously or on different occasions. Among clients under the age of 40, polysubstance use is prevalent. These patterns are especially common among teens and young adults in their 20s (Chen & Kandel, 1995).

According to Johnson (1980), the polydrug abuse subculture is an outgrowth of the marijuana subculture. One distinguishing conduct norm of this subculture is that participants are expected to use almost any chemical in an effort to alter consciousness. In addition to alcohol and marijuana, the use of cocaine, crack cocaine, tranquilizers, sedatives, narcotics, ketamine ("Special K"), inhalants, methamphetamine, hallucinogenic mushrooms, MDMA ("Ecstasy"), and other designer drugs is encouraged. Conduct norms also require that members be willing to smoke and inhale (snort) a drug, as well as administer it orally. Usually, conduct norms do not expect participants to inject a drug; this is a boundary marker that distinguishes this group from the heroin abuse subculture. Polydrug abuse subculture participants frequently perceive self-administered injection as "going one step too far." They may be heard to say, "That [injection] is the one thing that I would never do."

Sharing drugs (Johnson, 1980) and using combinations of drugs are important in this subculture. A participant who has pills is expected to share with someone who has cocaine, for example. Some drugs are more highly coveted than others; typically, crack cocaine is more highly valued than a drug like PCP (Thombs, 1989). Drug sellers (dealers) are not necessarily expected to socialize with buyers in the polydrug abuse subculture.

One recently reported drug combination involves the use of nitrite inhalants ("poppers"), Viagra (the medication used to treat erectile dysfunction), and possibly methamphetamine (Zamora, 1998). This potentially lethal combination has been reported in some circles in the gay community in California. Apparently, users believe that Viagra can improve sexual performance while under the influence of other substances.

A recent development in the polydrug abuse subculture is the "rave party" (NIDA, 1998). These are all-night dance parties typically attended by older teens and those in their early 20s. Sometimes they are called underground or after-hour parties. Loud "technomusic" is accompanied by laser and light shows. Raves are considered a forum for so-called Generation X. Participants typically wear 1960s- and 1970s-style clothing (bell bottoms, platform shoes) featuring psychedelic colors.

Rave parties are promoted on the Internet, by flyers, private mailing lists, e-mail, and word of mouth. Clubs that hold rave parties usually check identification at the door, but fake IDs are reported to be widely used by underage "ravers." Some rave parties promote themselves as alcohol-free, but others serve alcohol, and some allow participants to bring their own. Nonalcoholic drinks are typically sold, including "smart drinks" consisting of fruit juice, vitamins, amino acids, and caffeine. According to NIDA (1998), the most prevalent drugs at rave parties are LSD, MDMA (Ecstasy), GHB, marijuana, cocaine, methamphetamine, ketamine, and the inhalant nitrous oxide. Participants are reported to freely share drugs with one another, and use of multiple substances is common. Media reports have alleged that at some large parties, organizers distribute substances with the claim that they are legal herbal preparations. One such incident at a New Year's Eve event led to 31 partiers being taken to hospital emergency rooms because they reported difficulty breathing (Canto, 1997).

The Heroin Injection Subculture

Although users may share heroin from time to time, they have strong expectations that peers will reciprocate at a later time (Johnson, 1980). In addition, participants in this subculture are expected to carry out all three drug subculture roles: buyer, user, and seller (Johnson, 1980). Participants provide other participants with information ("connections") regarding where to secure more of the drug. Most participants of the heroin injection subculture were previously involved in the polydrug abuse subculture, and they may continue their contacts with this network on a more limited basis.

The heroin *injection* subculture expects participants to self-administer heroin via hypodermic injection (Johnson, 1980). Heroin can be inhaled or snorted, but in this subculture the conduct norms generally discourage these routes of administration. *Heroin inhalation is more typical of the polydrug abuse subculture.* Snorting (inhalation) is not thought by heroin subculture participants to provide the same "rush" as injection.

Today, conduct norms for injecting heroin vary considerably. Three to four injections a day is typical. However, according to Ray and Ksir (1999), in addition to the 500,000 heroin addicts in the United States, there may be more than 1 million citizens who use the drug on an *occasional* basis. Many of these so-called "chippers" are needle users.

Even occasional needle use increases the individual's risk for contracting HIV, the virus that causes AIDS. Heroin is typically the drug being injected, but other drug use is implicated in HIV transmission as well, including other opiates, cocaine, and methamphetamine. Of course, it should be recognized that HIV infection does not result from the action of illicit drugs. Rather, infection is a consequence of using a contaminated needle (i.e., the sharing of needles). Many injection drug users are known to obtain syringes from the "street" and use them several times. Use of contaminated needles has become the greatest risk factor for contracting HIV in high seroprevalence cities (Friedman, Jose, Deren, Des Jarlais, & Neaigus, 1995).

In many of the world's largest cities, it is estimated that as many as 40 to 50% of the injection drug users had become HIV positive by the early 1990s (Des Jarlais et al., 1995). In the United States today, a substantial number of individuals continue to be exposed to HIV by injection drug use or by having sex with an injection drug user (Centers for Disease Control and Prevention, 1997). The incidence data in

Table 7.3 show the magnitude of this problem in the United States during 1997.

As can be seen in Table 7.3, injection drug use risks for HIV/AIDS vary across groups defined by race and sex. Among Caucasian women, and African-Americans and Hispanics of both sexes, injection drug use is associated with roughly one-third of the AIDS cases. In contrast, Caucasian men tend to be exposed to HIV through homosexual contact (Centers for Disease Control and Prevention, 1997). The data in Table 7.3 also show that across racial groups, women are more likely to be exposed to HIV through sex with an injection drug user than are men.

The Crack Cocaine Subculture

The crack cocaine subculture emerged in the United States during the mid-1980s. According to data collected by the NIJ in 1987, crack use had become prevalent by this time in most major U.S. cities (NIJ, 1988). By 1997, the crack cocaine epidemic appeared to be slowing. According to the NIJ (1998), "1997 data indicate that many communities are dealing with stable or slowly changing cocaine problems. Almost without exception, older age cohorts are testing positive for cocaine at 2 to 10 times the rate of the younger cohorts . . . cocaine use is increasingly a problem of a group of long term users who developed their habits in the early stage of the epidemic" (p. 1). Though the drug is used by a diverse group of people, the typical crack cocaine subculture participant is a 30- to 40-year-old African-American male, often from an impoverished urban neighborhood, who faces significant social and economic barriers to achieving middle-class status.

TABLE 7.3. New U.S. AIDS Cases by Drug Injection Exposure Category, Race, and Sex: 1997

	Caucasian		African-American		Hispanic	
Exposure category	M	F	M	F	M	F
Injection drug use	17%	36%	34%	32%	34%	29%
Sex with an injection drug user	1%	13%	2%	10%	2%	14%
Risk not associated with injection drug use	83%	51%	64%	58%	64%	57%

Note. In 1997, there was a total of 60,634 AIDS cases reported to the Centers for Disease Control. The percentages in Table 7.3 are based only on adolescent and adult cases within each racial group. Pediatric cases ($n = 473$) and cases among Asian/Pacific Islanders ($n = 381$) and American Indian/Alaska Natives ($n = 168$) are not reported. Data from Centers for Disease Control and Prevention (1997).

In the crack cocaine subculture, various conduct norms have developed. It is expected that participants will smoke the drug daily in a binge-like fashion over an 8-, 10-, 12-, or even 24-hour period (NIDA, 1987). The binge or "run" will stop when the addict has run out of money or is too exhausted to continue. The user may "fall out"—that is, have a seizure—and be taken to an emergency room.

Sharing is typically not a conduct norm in this subculture; however, trading a commodity in exchange for crack is common. Participants may swap jewelry, stereos, guns, or even sex for crack. The exchange of sex is particularly true for female addicts, who may engage in prostitution for another "hit."

In many urban settings, crack subculture participants gather in a house, apartment, or other site where the drug can be used in private. In "crack houses," use of the drug may go on 24 hours a day. If the participants come under the scrutiny of police or neighborhood groups, they will probably move to another location. In essence, a crack house is the modern-day version of the "speakeasy" of the Prohibition era.

The distribution conduct norms of the crack subculture are highly secretive. This is hardly surprising, given the harsh legal sanctions that exist for cocaine sale and distribution. However, it appears that the business aspects of the transaction are emphasized. If sellers are cheated in a deal, conduct norms call for retaliation, often involving shootings. Violence and the threat of violence are pervasive in the subculture. In this way, the participants resemble the bootleggers (e.g., Al Capone) of the 1920s. Similar to gangsters of yesteryear, the sellers in this subculture are part of a structured hierarchy in which higher-level distributors attempt to shield themselves from arrest by relying on subordinates. In open-air drug markets, subordinates or "runners" may be young teens who are not subject to the same legal penalties as adults.

IMPLICATIONS FOR COUNSELING

Sociocultural perspectives suggest that addictions treatment must be aware of basic human values in the counseling process. Rokeach and Regan (1980) pointed out that counseling is essentially "values therapy." They assert:

> Every counselor can be conceptualized as being in the business of administering value theory, and if a client's values remain altogether unaffected by counseling it is doubtful that it can be said to have been successful. In short, the successful outcome of counseling can be formulated as always involving either a clarification or a change in specified value priorities and in value-related attitudes and behavior. (p. 576)

Substance Abuse Counseling and Values

Though sociologists and anthropologists are subject to personal biases and value judgments, as Light and Keller (1975) note, "For generations sociologists have labored under the eleventh commandment, 'Thou shalt not commit a value judgment' " (p. 36). Sociocultural analyses do not pass judgment on the "correctness" of addicts' values; instead, they serve as relatively impartial analyses of the social phenomena under scrutiny. If sociologists describe a drug subculture as placing a low priority on economic productivity, they are not insisting that addicts are "lazy." They are simply pointing out that their value structure emphasizes other pursuits, and that this structure deviates from that of the larger middle-class culture.

Many times the "resistance" demonstrated by chemically dependent clients reflects conflicts between their value structure and those of the treatment program/recovery movement (Rappaport, 1997). The noncompliance of the client is usually described as "denial." From a social interaction perspective, noncompliance may not be as much an unconscious defense as a refusal to adopt the values of the treatment provider. A client who indicates that he/she "cannot" attend 90 AA meetings in 90 days is revealing a preference for spontaneity over structure in organizing day-to-day life. A client who will not make a commitment to abstinence may be demonstrating a preference for short-term gratification and excitement over long-term gains (e.g., economic security and family stability) and improved health. Peele (1985), in particular, noted that many addicts place relatively little value on their personal health. The old maxim, "Eat, drink, and be merry, for tomorrow we may die," seems to apply here.

Other addicts may balk at counselors' attempts to encourage introspection and self-analysis. This may reflect a value structure that elevates social relations, fun, and amusement over rational self-control and serious self-understanding. These conflicts are crucial issues to be uncovered, clarified, and discussed in counseling. Many, perhaps most, clients are unaware of their value priorities and of how these relate to their substance abuse. Though it may be painful, counselors should help clients bring these issues to the foreground of consciousness. They reveal sources of resistance and possibly point to suitable treatment goals. In working this way, counselors should maintain an objective attitude toward the clients' value structure.

The consequences of each client's value priorities should be explored. However, it should also be kept in mind that attempts at "bullying" a client into adopting values consistent with popular recovery models will often backfire. Changes in a client's values are likely to evolve slowly. Thus, when a counselor is faced with a client with a dysfunctional value orientation, patience is a much-needed resource.

Multidimensional Treatment

Sociocultural perspectives on addiction do support the view that treatment must be multidimensional in nature. This perspective illustrates that many of the factors that cause addiction and relapse are not "within" the individual (i.e., biological or psychological). As a result, effective treatment will have an impact on other domains of the addict's life. Successful interventions will alter a client's relationships to his/her family, peer group, workplace, and community. According to Galizio and Maisto (1985), these "psychosocial and environmental factors may be most critical in the determination of cessation and relapse" (p. 428).

The social system for many clients in early recovery, is not conducive to abstinence and other recovery-consistent behavior. Various social and environmental factors influence them to drink or use a drug. Mallams, Godley, Hall, and Meyers (1982) cogently describe these pressures in the case of alcohol abuse, and the needed alternative, in the following passage:

> Newly acquired social skills are subject to multiple environmental influences. For example, the physical environment (mass media, advertising, sensory cues for drinking) is structured to increase the likelihood of drinking, and drinking is associated with such social activities as conversation, recreation and dating. Under these environmental influences recovering alcoholics may not only lose existing support, but receive negative sanctions from former drinking associates. Finally, many recovering alcoholics do not have the personal resources (e.g., transportation, family, friends, employment) necessary to engage in new social situations. . . . An alternative approach is to create a new social system in the alcoholics' natural environment that provides wide varieties of social and recreational activities and reinforces the acquisition of appropriate social behaviors. (p. 1116)

Using the community reinforcement training model, Lewis, Dana, and Blevins (1994) identified nine possible treatment plan components that could address the harsh social (and possibly economic) realities of early recovery:

1. Job counseling: helping clients find permanent, full-time, well-paying jobs that would interfere with a return to drinking or drug use

2. Marital counseling: providing counseling for all married couples and arranging "synthetic families" for unmarried clients

3. Resocialization and recreation: arranging alcohol-free social and recreational activities in addition to making referrals to "12-Step" programs

4. Problem-prevention rehearsal: teaching clients how to handle situations that might otherwise lead to drinking and/or drug use

5. Early warning system: providing a mail-in Happiness Scale to be used by clients

6. Disulfiram: developing positive mechanisms to support the use of Antabuse® for alcohol-abusing clients (for impulse control)

7. Group counseling: providing supportive mechanisms that can develop into social or recreational groups after treatment ends

8. Buddy procedure: selecting recovering peer advisors to work closely with each client

9. Contracting: using written contracts to formalize the agreements between counselors and clients regarding the program's procedures and the client's responsibilities (p. 14)

These nine intervention strategies underscore how closely intertwined chemical use (and nonuse) is with the addict's relationships to family, worksite, and peer groups. Drug and alcohol problems cannot be neatly separated from other spheres of the addict's life. They are inseparably entangled with the social experience. The point is that substance abuse counseling should seek to help individuals, not "drug problems."

LIMITATIONS

As a basis for substance abuse counseling, there are two major limitations to sociocultural concepts. First, many of these the concepts lack precision and do not seem applicable to the helping process. In particular, this may be true of such concepts as social boundary markers, subcultures, conduct norms, "time out," and so on. Critics have occasionally charged that sociocultural theorists are the sideline observers of the "war on drugs." Their concepts provide intellectual insight but are not helpful in enhancing the direct delivery of treatment services.

The second limitation pertains to the relative inability of substance abuse counselors (and treatment programs) to significantly alter the social, cultural, and environmental factors that cause addiction and relapse. In this vein, sociocultural perspectives may be viewed as interesting but of little practical value because these variables cannot be manipulated by treatment providers or programs. Substance abuse counselors can do little to alter drinking customs among certain ethnic groups, for example. This lack of practicality is likely to prevent socio-cultural perspectives from gaining more prominent status among theories on addictive behavior.

REVIEW QUESTIONS

1. In Vaillant's prospective study, which ethnic groups had higher rates of alcoholism? Which groups had lower rates?

2. How has the treatment community in the United States often viewed sociocultural perspectives on addiction?

3. Based on DAWN data, what trends in illicit drug use have occurred in the 1990s?

4. What do the data from the Arrestee Drug Abuse Monitoring Program tell us about regional differences in illicit drug use?

5. What is meant by the "medicalization" of addiction? How do cultural factors influence diagnostic determinations?

6. What are the four basic sociological functions of substance abuse? How do they support substance abuse?

7. What are the five social contexts of adolescent drinking? How are these differentially related to alcohol consumption and problems?

8. What is the convergence toward a false norm hypothesis?

9. What is a drug subculture? How is it distinct from middle-class culture?

10. When do government drug policies and laws become especially punitive? What groups tend to be targets?

11. What particular values and conduct norms characterize a drug subculture?

12. What are some of the unique aspects of the alcohol abuse subculture, the marijuana abuse subculture, the polydrug abuse subculture, the heroin injection subculture, and the crack cocaine subculture?

13. What are "raves"?

14. To what extent is drug injection an HIV/AIDS risk in the United States today?

15. How should values be dealt with in substance abuse counseling?

16. What is meant by "multidimensional" treatment?

17. What are the limitations of the sociocultural concepts in substance abuse counseling?

REFERENCES

American Psychiatric Association. (1994). *Diagnostic and statistical manual of mental disorders* (4th ed.). Washington, DC: Author.

Associated Press. (1997, November 18). Colleges need to match words with action on alcohol abuse.

Associated Press. (1998, July 13). Penn State students riot as bars close.

Bachman, J. G., Johnston, L. D., & O'Malley, P. M. (1998). Explaining recent increases in students' marijuana use: Impacts of perceived risks and disapproval, 1976 through 1996. *American Journal of Public Health, 88,* 887–892.

Bales, F. (1980). Cultural differences in roles of alcoholism. In D. Ward (Ed.), *Alcoholism: Introduction to theory and treatment.* Dubuque, IA: Kendall/Hunt.

Baer, J. S., Stacy, A., & Larimer, M. (1991). Biases in the perception of drinking norms among college students. *Journal of Studies on Alcohol, 52,* 580–586.

Beck, K. H., Thombs, D. L., & Summons, T. G. (1993). The social context of drinking scales: Construct validation and relationship to indicants of abuse in an adolescent population. *Addictive Behaviors, 18,* 159–163.

Berkowitz, A. D. (1997). From reactive to proactive prevention: Promoting an ecology of health on campus. In P. C. Rivers & E. R. Shore (Eds.), *Substance abuse on campus: A handbook for college and university personnel.* Westport, CT: Greenwood Press.

Cahalan, D. (1970). *Problem drinkers: A national survey.* San Francisco: Jossey-Bass.

Canto, M. (1997, January 2). Drink sickens concertgoers in L. A.; 31 go to hospitals. *Associated Press.*

Cashin, J. R., Presley, C. A., & Meilman, P. W. (1998). Alcohol use in the greek system: Follow the leader? *Journal of Studies on Alcohol, 59,* 63–70.

Caulkins, J. P., Rydell, C. P., Schwabe, W. L., & Chiesa, J. (1997). *Mandatory minimum sentences: Throwing away the key or the taxpayers' money?* Santa Monica, CA: Rand Drug Policy Research Center.

Centers for Disease Control and Prevention. (1997). *HIV/AIDS Surveillance Report, 9*(2). Atlanta: Division of HIV/AIDS Prevention—Surveillance and Epidemiology, National Center for HIV, STD, and TB Prevention.

Chen, K., & Kandel, D. B. (1995). The natural history of drug use from adolescence to the mid-thirties in a general population sample. *American Journal of Public Health, 85,* 41–47.

Connors, G. R., & Tarbox, A. R. (1985). Macroenvironmental factors as determinants of substance use and abuse. In M. Galizio & S. A. Maisto (Eds.), *Determinants of substance abuse: Biological, psychological, and environmental factors.* New York: Plenum Press.

Conrad, P. (1992). Medicalization and social control. *Annual Review of Sociology, 18,* 209–232.

Conrad, P., & Schneider, J. W. (1992). *Deviance and medicalization: From badness to sickness.* Philadelphia: Temple University Press.

Davidson, J. (1992, December 12). Marijuana farming buoys the economy of rural Kentucky: State's biggest crop supports jobless miners, but police show little tolerance. *Wall Street Journal.*

Des Jarlais, D. C., Hagan, H., Friedman, S. R., Goldberg, D., Frischer, M., Green, S., Tunving, K., Ljungberg, B., Wodak, A., Ross, M., Purchase, D., Millson, M. E., & Myers, T. (1995). Maintaining low HIV seroprevalence in populations of injecting drug users. *Journal of the American Medical Association, 274,* 1226–1231.

Douglas, K. A., Collins, J. L., Warren, C., Kann, L., Gold, R., Clayton, S., Ross, J. G., & Kolbe, L. J. (1997). Results from the 1995 National College Health Risk Behavior Survey. *Journal of American College Health, 46,* 55–66.

Engs, R. C., & Hanson, D. J. (1993). Drinking games and problems related to drinking among moderate and heavy drinkers. *Psychological Reports, 73,* 115–120.

Fingarette, H. (1988). *Heavy drinking: The myth of alcoholism as a disease.* Berkeley: University of California Press.

Forst, B. (1995). Prosecution and sentencing. In J. Q. Wilson & J. Petersilia (Eds.), *Crime.* San Francisco: Institute for Contemporary Studies.

Friedman, S. R., Jose, B., Deren, S., Des Jarlais, D. C., & Neaigus, A. (1995). Risk factors for human immunodeficiency virus seroconversion among out-of-treatment drug injectors in high and low seroprevalence cities. The National AIDS Research Consortium. *American Journal of Epidemiology, 142,* 864–874.

Galizio, M., & Maisto, S. A. (1985). Toward a biopsychosocial theory of substance abuse. In M. Galizio & S. A. Maisto (Eds.), *Determinants of substance abuse: Biological, psychological, and environmental factors.* New York: Plenum Press.

Gans, H. J. (1962). *The urban villagers.* New York: Free Press.

Glassner, B., & Berg, B. (1980). How Jews avoid drinking problems. *American Sociological Review, 45,* 647–664.

Heath, D. B. (1988). Emerging anthropological theory and models of alcohol use and alcoholism. In C. D. Chaudron & D. A. Wilkinson (Eds.), *Theories on alcoholism.* Toronto: Addiction Research Foundation.

Johnson, B. D. (1980). Toward a theory of drug subcultures. In D. J. Lettieri, M. Bayers, & H. W. Pearson (Eds.), *Theories on drug abuse: Selected contemporary perspectives* (DHHS Publication No. ADM 84-967). Washington, DC: U.S. Government Printing Office.

Johnston, L. D., Bachman, J. G., & O'Malley, P. M. (1999, January 5). *Monitoring the future study.* (www.isr.umich.edu/src/mtf)

Johnston, L. D., O'Malley, P. M., & Bachman, J. G. (1989). *Drug use, drinking, and smoking: National survey results from high school, college, and young adult populations* (DHHS Publication No. ADM 89-1638). Washington, DC: U.S. Government Printing Office.

Jowett, B. (Trans.). (1931). *The dialogues of Plato* (3rd ed., Vol. 5). London: Oxford University Press.

Keller, M. (1970). The great Jewish drink mystery. *British Journal of Addictions, 64,* 287–295.

Lawson, A., & Lawson, G. (1998). *Alcoholism and the family: A guide to treatment and prevention* (2nd ed.). Gaithersburg, MD: Aspen.

Lewis, J. A., Dana, R. Q., & Blevins, G. A. (1994). *Substance abuse counseling: An individualized approach* (2nd ed.). Pacific Grove, CA: Brooks/Cole.

Light, D., & Keller, S. (1975). *Sociology.* New York: Knopf.

Lurie, N. (1971). The world's oldest on-going protest demonstration: North American Indian drinking patterns. *Pacific Historical Review, 40,* 311–332.

MacAndrew, C., & Edgerton, R. B. (1969). *Drunken comportment: A social explanation.* Chicago: Aldine.

Mallams, J. H., Godley, M. D., Hall, G. M., & Meyers, R. J. (1982). A social-systems approach to resocializing alcoholics in the community. *Journal of Studies on Alcohol, 43,* 1115–1123.

May, C. (1993). Resistance to peer group pressure: An inadequate basis for alcohol education. *Health Education Research, 8,* 159–165.

McKim, W. A. (1986). *Drugs and behavior: An introduction to behavioral pharmacology.* Englewood Cliffs, NJ: Prentice-Hall.

Milam, J. R., & Ketcham, K. (1983). *Under the influence.* New York: Bantam.

Misra, R. K. (1980). Achievement, anxiety, and addiction. In D. J. Lettieri, M. Sayers, & H. W. Pearson (Eds.), *Theories on drug abuse: Selected contemporary perspectives* (DHHS Publication No. ADM 84-967). Washington, DC: U.S. Government Printing Office.

National Institute on Alcohol Abuse and Alcoholism (NIAAA). (1997). *Alcohol and health: Ninth special report to the U. S. Congress* (NIH Publication No. 97-4017). Bethesda, MD: National Institutes of Health.

National Institute of Justice. (1988, January). *Drug use forecasting (DUF).* Washington, DC: U.S. Department of Justice.

National Institute of Justice. (1998). *Arrestee drug abuse monitoring program: 1997 annual report on adult and juvenile arrestees.* Washington, DC: U.S. Department of Justice.

National Institute on Drug Abuse. (1998). *Assessing drug abuse within and across communities: Community epidemiology surveillance networks on drug abuse* (NIH Publication No. 98-3614). Bethesda, MD: National Institutes of Health.

National Institute on Drug Abuse. (1987). *Drug abuse and drug abuse research.* (DHHS Publication No. ADM 87-1486). Washington, DC: U.S. Government Printing Office.

Oetting, E. R., & Beauvis, F. (1988). Common elements in youth drug abuse: Peer clusters and other psychosocial factors. In S. Peele (Ed.), *Visions of addiction: Major contemporary perspectives on addiction and alcoholism.* Lexington, MA: Lexington Books.

Pacula, R. L. (1998). Does increasing the beer tax reduce marijuana consumption? *Journal of Health Economics, 17,* 557–585.

Peele, S. (1983). Is alcoholism different from other substance abuse? *American Psychologist, 38,* 963–964.

Peele, S. (1985). *The meaning of addiction: Compulsive experience and its interpretation.* Lexington, MA: D.C. Heath.

Peele, S. (Ed.). (1988). *Visions of addiction: Major contemporary perspectives on addiction and alcoholism.* Lexington, MA: Lexington Books.

Perkins, H. W., & Berkowitz, A. D. (1986). Perceiving the community norms of alcohol use among students: Some research implications for campus alcohol education programming. *International Journal of the Addictions, 21,* 961–976.

Prentice, D. A., & Miller, D. T. (1993). Pluralistic ignorance and alcohol use on campus: Some consequences of misperceiving the social norm. *Journal of Personality and Social Psychology, 64,* 243–256.

Rappaport, R. L. (1997). *Motivating clients in therapy: Values, love, and the real relationship.* New York: Routledge.

Ray, O., & Ksir, C. (1999). *Drugs, society, and human behavior* (8th ed.). Boston: WCB/McGraw Hill.

Rokeach, M., & Regan, J. F. (1980). The role of values in the counseling situation. *Personnel and Guidance Journal, 58,* 576–582.

Schwartz, H. D., & Kart, C. S. (1978). *Dominant issues in medical sociology.* Reading, MA: Addison-Wesley.

Substance Abuse and Mental Health Services Administration. (1998). *Preliminary 1996 data from the Drug Abuse Warning Network.* Washington, DC: U.S. Department of Health and Human Services.

Thombs, D. L. (1989). A review of PCP abuse trends and perceptions. *Public Health Reports, 104,* 325–328.

Thombs, D. L., & Beck, K. H. (1994). The social context of four adolescent drinking patterns. *Health Education Research, 9,* 13–22.

Thombs, D. L., Beck, K. H., Mahoney, C. A., Bromley, M. D., & Bezon, K. M. (1994). Social context, sensation seeking, and teen-age alcohol abuse. *Journal of School Health, 64,* 73–79.

Thombs, D. L., Beck, K. H., & Pleace, D. J. (1993). The relationship of social context and expectancy factors to alcohol use intensity among 18- to 22-year-olds. *Addiction Research, 1,* 59–68.

Thombs, D. L., Wolcott, B. J., & Farkash, L. G. E. (1997). Social context, perceived norms, and drinking behavior in young people. *Journal of Substance Abuse, 9,* 257–267.

U.S. Sentencing Commission. (1998). *Federal sentencing guidelines (1998).* Washington, DC: Author.

Vaillant, G. E. (1983). *The natural history of alcoholism.* Cambridge, MA: Harvard University Press.

Vaillant, G. E. (1990). We should retain the disease concept of alcoholism. *Harvard Medical School Mental Health Letter, 6,* 4–6.

Vaillant, G. E. (1995). *The natural history of alcoholism revisited.* Cambridge, MA: Harvard University Press.

Wechsler, H., Dowdall, G. W., Maenner, G., Gledhill-Hoyt, & Lee, H. (1998). Changes in binge drinking and related problems among American college students between 1993 and 1997: Results of the Harvard School of Public Health College Alcohol Study. *Journal of American College Health, 47,* 57–68.

Zamora, J. H. (1998, July 29). Viagra a killer when combined with "poppers." *San Francisco Examiner.*

CHAPTER EIGHT

Conditions That Facilitate and Inhibit Change in Addictive Behavior

This volume has provided an in-depth review and critique of contemporary theories of addictive behavior and supporting research in each area. Each perspective has offered concepts that can be used in clinical practice to guide the design of individual treatment plans.

In recent years, there has been greater focus on treatment planning that addresses the issue of client *motivation* (Miller & Rollnick, 1991). Often, alcohol and drug abusers are ambivalent about change. Their ambivalence may delay or even block them from seeking treatment. Other clients may reach a decision to enter treatment, only to quickly change their mind and drop out. Many also work hard to change themselves, but after a while lose their commitment and return to substance use. These are problems of establishing and maintaining motivation to change.

Traditionally, clinicians have found fault with clients for being "unmotivated" to change. When a client prematurely terminated treatment, there was the tendency to blame the client—not the treatment model. Recently, however, there has been growing recognition that inflexible treatment models contribute to this problem, and that an explicit goal of psychosocial treatment should be motivation enhancement (Miller, Zweben, DiClemente, & Rychtarik, 1992; Rappaport, 1997). Stated another way, *client motivation is influenced not only by the client's personal characteristics and dispositions but by conditions external to them as well.* This position requires respect for the client's perspective, empathy, and an openness to a variety of treatment options.

This chapter briefly reviews the models identified in this volume to point out their utility for enhancing client motivation. In light of these models, I then review Prochaska, DiClemente, and Norcross's

(1992) stages-of-change model. Finally, there is a discussion of important treatment practices and related issues (i.e., coercion and managed care pressures) that facilitate and inhibit client motivation and change.

ADDICTIVE BEHAVIOR MODELS AND CLIENT MOTIVATION

The Disease Models

The disease models are important for historical reasons. Without the shift from sin to malady, there would be no basis for offering treatment. Punishment, including incarceration, would be perceived by most of society as the only means of addressing the problem. Thus, there would be little hope for persons with substance abuse problems. Aside from its historical importance, clients who readily accept the disease conception often seem to become motivated to participate in their treatment. For some clients, the disease conception appears to reduce shame and guilt and thereby removes a psychological barrier to change. The model also may be a good fit for those who perceive themselves to be genetically vulnerable and for those who have significant biomedical complications.

For some time, the disease concept of treatment has been associated with the use of confrontational group therapy (Yalisove, 1998). There was a tendency among many disease model practitioners to challenge or even punish clients who were ambivalent about change. Today, competent addictions practitioners consider this type of confrontation to be counterproductive because it usually does little to motivate ambivalent clients, and because it increases their probability of dropping out of treatment (Lewis, Dana, & Blevins, 1994). This issue is discussed in more detail later in this chapter.

Psychoanalytic Formulations

Psychoanalytic formulations provide keen insights into the dynamics of compulsive drug use. First and foremost, this perspective emphasizes the role of unconscious forces in the maintenance of addictive behavior. Defense mechanisms, such as denial and rationalization, certainly have to be considered in motivation enhancement strategies. These defense mechanisms may indicate weak "ego strength." That is, many clients in early recovery lack strong internal controls and will benefit from strong external support and encouragement. This is particularly true of the early recovery period.

Conditioning and Contingency Management Models

Incentive is the core concept in the conditioning approach. By the time many chemically dependent clients reach treatment, the self-administration of drugs is often the only source of pleasure in their lives. Family, social, and recreational activities have been given up, or drug use has been incorporated into them. In either case, clients usually find the period of early recovery to be one of *deprivation*. The old rewards (i.e., reinforcers) have been removed, but the alcoholic or addict knows they are still readily available. Thus, "slips" or full-blown relapses always remain a possibility; this is especially true during the first 3 months following treatment (Miller & Hester, 1986).

Motivation enhancement strategies should include activities that help clients identify nonchemical rewards and then make use of them to maintain gains achieved in recovery. This is not an easy task for the counselor. Sometimes clients have limited experience with recreational activities, hobbies, or other enjoyable pursuits. However, if enjoyable alternatives to the chemical experience can be found and used, clients may be able to build a stable recovery relatively quickly and without enormous struggle.

Cognitive Models

Social cognitive theory provides us with a framework for understanding the cognitive dynamics of addictive behavior. It should be understood that social cognitive explanations are entirely consistent with the conditioning model of drug self-administration. However, social cognitive theory goes further by elaborating on the unobservable cognitive processes that accompany reinforcement from drug use. For example, "outcome expectancies" mediate between drug availability and drug use. The latter is likely to occur when the drug's anticipated effects on mood are positive.

Self-efficacy theory points to strategies for relapse prevention. As applied to recovery, this is (roughly) the client's confidence in his/her ability to perform those tasks deemed necessary in treatment (refrain from substance use, attend counseling sessions and Twelve-Step programs, take Antabuse as prescribed, etc.). A feature of low self-efficacy is having little optimism about one's ability to avoid alcohol and drug use. Clients with low self-efficacy will be likely to relapse (Burling, Reilly, Moltzen, & Ziff, 1989). Those with strong self-efficacy, on the other hand, are likely to be successful at recovery efforts.

Strategies have been identified to bolster clients' self-efficacy; they involve the teaching of skills to enhance coping. An important concept in this skill-building approach to relapse prevention is the "abstinence violation effect," or the tendency of clients committed to recovery to exaggerate the significance of a "slip." Clients often engage in intense self-downing after an initial drink or use of a drug; as a result of the self-condemnation, they continue to abuse substances, rather than just limiting their use to a "slip."

The Family System

These models view addiction as having an adaptive value for the family (Steinglass, 1981). That is, during intoxication many families show behaviors that are adaptive as characterized by increased positive interaction. These functional aspects of substance use suggest that whenever possible, the client's family members should be included in the treatment process. The poorly motivated client may be "stuck" because of systemic forces, such as a dysfunctional marital relationship. Failure to include the family system in treatment planning may explain the chronic relapsing in some clients.

Social and Cultural Foundations

Sociocultural concepts point out that values and life goals play a pivotal role in clinical strategies to facilitate client change. Values based on immediate gratification, intense stimulation, rebellion, and so on, block or undermine the change process. Thus, efforts to enhance client motivation can be seen as "values therapy." This is particularly the case when clients experience a discrepancy between their current behavior and broader life goals (Miller & Rollnick, 1991).

STAGES OF CHANGE IN ADDICTIVE BEHAVIOR

Motivation is a particularly critical issue in helping clients to change. Prochaska et al. (1992) have developed a *transtheoretical, stage model* to explain how people change unwanted behavior as well as maintain new habits. The "stages of change" model is not another theory but a framework that can organize existing theories to help explain the process people use to change themselves—with or without professional assistance. Within each stage, constructs from various theories can be used to explain movement. It is important to note that the model does not explain why people change but rather *how* they do so.

Practitioners and researchers have shown much interest in the model because it provides a structure for understanding client motivation. The model has been applied to a variety of health behavior problems characterized by relapse. These problems have included medication adherence in AIDS treatment (Bradley-Springer, 1996), smoking cessation (DiClemente et al., 1991), recovery from alcohol/drug addiction (DiClemente, 1991), weight control (Prochaska & DiClemente, 1985), and psychological distress (Prochaska & Norcross, 1983).

Research has shown that the stages-of-change model is particularly useful for matching patients with treatments based on their readiness for change. Prochaska and DiClemente (1992) noted that many psychosocial and medical treatment programs have poor outcomes because they assume that new clients (or patients) are highly motivated to participate in their own treatment; the issue of motivation is ignored in treatment planning. In reality, across a broad range of behavioral and medical disorders, clients often do not possess a high level of readiness for change at the onset of treatment. Prochaska and DiClemente (1992) have estimated that across populations with active health problems, roughly 10 to 15% are prepared to take action to improve their condition upon entering treatment.

The stages-of-change model consists of five stages (Prochaska & DiClemente, 1992). Each stage and its treatment implications for substance abusing clients is described here. It is important to point out that patient progression through these stages does not usually occur in a linear fashion. Patients who reach the latter three stages often recycle to the first two. However, research does indicate that for most patients, relapsing is not an endless process (Prochaska & DiClemente, 1992). Most of the time patients do not regress all the way back to where they began. It appears that many individuals do learn from their mistakes and relapses become less frequent over time.

Precontemplation

Precontemplation describes a stage in which there is no intention to change behavior in the foreseeable future. Often, precontemplators do not define the behavior as a problem (DiClemente, 1991). Bell and Rollnick (1996) have described the precontemplator as the "happy user." However, external observers such as their friends, families, employers, and so forth identify their behavior as problematic.

DiClemente (1991) argues that there is more to precontemplation than just "denial" and "resistance." Some precontemplators simply lack knowledge about the risks associated with their behavior. Others are rebellious because they have a heavy investment in maintaining the problem behavior. On the other hand, some precontemplators are characterized by resignation. They are overwhelmed by the problem and see themselves as incapable of change; they have no hope and believe it is too late to modify their behavior. Finally, some precontemplators involve themselves in rationalizing away the problem (e.g., "What's the use of going through all the hassle of treatment, you only live once.").

DiClemente (1991) argues that there is a pervasive myth in the helping professions pertaining to precontemplators. The myth maintains that the more serious the health or behavior problem, the more intense the education, treatment, or confrontation must be to "help" the person. With precontemplators, "more" help may actually be harmful or, more commonly, just ignored. Reviews of the research on brief interventions indicate that they are as effective as more intensive treatment and more effective than no treatment (Miller & Rollnick, 1991; National Institute on Alcohol Abuse and Alcoholism, 1997). This may be particularly the case when the focus of the brief intervention is to motivate the client to make a commitment to change.

Contemplation

Contemplation is a stage at which many patients stay for an extended period. Typically, this stage involves an extended "risk–reward analysis" (DiClemente, 1991). Patients are involved in the frequent weighing of the costs and benefits of change. They mull over costs and benefits again and again. In contrast to the precontemplator, the contemplator is willing to consider change, but his/her ambivalence often makes this state chronic. For instance, DiClemente and Prochaska (1985) followed a group of 200 cigarette smokers in the contemplation stage for 2 years and found that the group's modal or most common response was unchanged during this period.

Contemplators have an interest in change but little *commitment*. They demonstrate this lack of commitment by asking about treatment options but not following through, or by scheduling appointments only to not show up for them. DiClemente (1991) indicates that contemplators often offer reasons for why "now is not the right time" to begin a program (p. 195).

In working with contemplators, the challenge for addiction practitioners is to facilitate movement toward the next stage: preparation. The content of the information given to contemplators is important. First, it should be *personally relevant* to the individual; a cocaine-dependent person considering treatment may not be swayed by information about Alcoholics Anonymous or long-term sobriety. Second, there is a need to emphasize the *benefits of change* (e.g., "Stop wasting money on crack") rather than attempting to arouse fear (e.g., "You're damaging your heart and lungs," or "You are going to end up in prison"). A focus on the benefits of change can create incentives for the contemplator. Fear arousal messages (scare tactics) generally should be avoided because they serve to undermine self-efficacy; that is, they destroy optimism about the prospects for change by implying that "it may already be too late for you."

Preparation (or Determination)

In the preparation stage, persons form an intention to change a behavior in the near future (Prochaska & DiClemente, 1992). Their determination is often demonstrated by small behavior changes. People are typically in this stage for only brief periods. Their experimenting does not necessarily propel them into the next stage: action (DiClemente, 1991). Experiencing barriers to change may result in a return to contemplation.

DiClemente (1991) notes that an important task in helping the patient in preparation is to encourage the development of a *realistic* plan of action. Many determined patients fail to recognize or dismiss the difficulties they will encounter when they take action (e.g., enter treatment). A realistic plan anticipates these barriers and identifies solutions or responses for them.

Action

The next stage, action, involves implementing a plan. Here, people modify their behavior and/or their environment to overcome a problem. However, as Prochaska and DiClemente (1992) note:

> Modifications of the addictive behavior made in the action stage tend to be most visible and receive the greatest external recognition. People, including professionals, often erroneously equate action with change. As a consequence, they overlook the requisite work that prepares changers for action and the important efforts necessary to maintain the changes following action. (p. 1104)

Individuals who seek out professional help sometimes have already initiated behavioral changes in their lives; obtaining substance abuse treatment may be just one part of their change efforts. Studies have found that it is not unusual for clients to initiate abstinence days or even weeks before entering treatment (Maisto, Sobell, Sobell, Lei,

& Sykora, 1988; Tucker, Vuchinich, & Pukish, 1995). According to DiClemente (1991), these are the clients who make therapists feel good about themselves; these are the "easy clients," and the "miracle cures" (p. 199). Clients already in action sometimes enter counseling to (1) make a public commitment to action, (2) obtain external confirmation of the plan, (3) seek support and confidence, and (4) create external monitors of their activity (DiClemente, 1991).

DiClemente (1991) maintains that the primary tasks of treatment personnel for helping patients in action is to identify ways to enhance client self-efficacy (e.g., introducing clients to peer support networks) and, if possible, to remove any bureaucratic barriers that may impede their progress. Individuals are classified as in "action" if they successfully alter their behavior for a period of 1 day to 6 months. After 6 months of success, they are considered to have moved to the next stage (Prochaska & DiClemente, 1992).

Maintenance

In maintenance, people continue their efforts to prevent relapse and to consolidate gains made in treatment. Prochaska and DiClemente (1992) do not view maintenance as a static state but, rather, as a continuation of change. The threat of relapse becomes less and less intense with the passage of time. However, relapse to another stage remains a possibility.

Here, an important task for addictions practitioners is to develop, with the patient, a relapse prevention plan that anticipates, and protects against, "abstinence violation effects." As discussed in Chapter Five, these are the intense, negative emotional reactions, often involving self-downing, that many patients experience when they have a small setback or "lapse." The significance of a lapse is exaggerated and leads to feelings of doom. In turn, these emotional reactions undermine self-efficacy and typically result in a more severe relapse than otherwise would be the case. One particularly deleterious consequence of abstinence violation effects is that out of embarrassment or shame, many clients conceal their return to drinking and/or drug use or, even worse, drop out of treatment. Relapse prevention plans must be realistic in educating clients about setbacks or "backsliding" and prescribe health-enhancing response options.

Figure 8.1 is the "wheel of change," which shows how people cycle through the stages. Notice that precontemplation is not part of the motion of the wheel, which represents the static state of precontemplation. Most people who attempt change move around the wheel

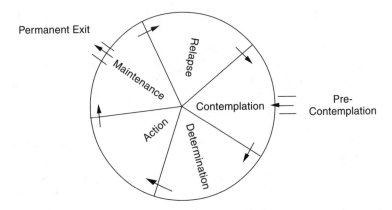

FIGURE 8.1.   Prochaska and DiClemente's six stages of change.

several times before achieving permanent change (Miller & Rollnick, 1991).

If we conceptualize treatment as an effort to facilitate movement through the stages of change, it becomes necessary to examine both our helping strategies and the social ecology in which these services are delivered to the client; treatment services are not provided in a social vacuum. Issues such as legal coercion affect client motivation as well. Further complicating this mix are dramatic shifts in thinking about how to help difficult-to-reach clients (e.g., harm reduction approaches) and new ways to finance treatment services (managed care). Next we look at some of the most pressing issues in treatment today and examine their impact on client motivation.

COERCION

There is disagreement about how to define "coercion" (Marlowe et al., 1996). For the purpose of this discussion, coercion is defined as the "imposition of an aversive stimulus to deter further substance use." In substance abuse treatment, many clients are subject to multiple coercive pressures. Legal coercion is not the only source. Other domains of coercion are social, familial, and medical (Marlowe et al., 1996). Often, coercion is used as a "lever" to push clients into treatment. Sometimes these pressures are applied by treatment personnel or programs. However, a mix of pressures can be exerted on an individual client when applied by some combination of the family, employer, criminal justice system, and so on. There is limited research on the use of coercion (Marlowe et al., 1996), and when it does exist it usually focuses on the most extreme methods, such as compulsory residential treatment (Leukefeld & Tims, 1988).

Coercion is thought to operate on an escape or avoidance reinforcement schedule in which an aversive stimulus precedes the desired event or behavior (entering treatment, providing a "clean" urine, etc.). The client can avoid the aversive stimulus by engaging in the target conduct (Crowley, 1984). A rationale for using coercion in mental health care has been put forth by the Group for the Advancement of Psychiatry (1994). This group postulates that under optimal conditions, clients appropriately forced into treatment eventually make the following transitions: initial defiance to reluctant compliance to a therapeutic alliance to a successful outcome.

Only a few coercive practices are briefly mentioned here. A historical example is the civil commitment of narcotic addicts in the United States. From 1965 to 1975, some states, most notably California and New York, operated compulsory treatment programs—primarily for intravenous heroin users involved in criminal activity. In the California Civil Addict Program (CAP), addicts were forced into inpatient treatment, for an average of 18 months, and subsequently released to supervised community follow-up programs that relied on urine drug testing (Anglin, 1988). The full civil commitment procedure was 7 years in duration. At the end of this period, the CAP program appeared to reduce nondrug arrests by 40% and daily drug use by 7%. A number of other positive outcomes were observed, but these were of modest magnitude (Anglin, 1988). According to Inciardi (1988) and Inciardi, McBride, and Rivers (1996), other states and the federal government also operated civil commitment programs for narcotic addicts from 1965 to 1975, but these were often poorly managed and when they were evaluated, the outcomes were quite poor.

The civil commitment programs of the 1960s and 1970s were the forerunners of today's "drug courts." The more official name for these units is "court-enforced drug treatment program." Though the structure and operation of these programs vary, there are some common features (Inciardi et al., 1996):

1. Nonviolent drug offenders are either diverted to treatment or sentenced to treatment as a part of probation.
2. Treatment is court-supervised—drug court judges essentially act as case managers.
3. Urine testing is relied upon to monitor compliance.
4. There is an emphasis on processing a large number of cases as efficiently as possible.

In a review of drug court evaluation studies, Inciardi et al. (1996) found that these programs substantially reduce *justice system costs* (decreased time from arraignment to disposition and sentencing, fewer jury trials, reduced days spent in jail, etc.). However, at this time, there appears to be little evidence that any particular drug court model significantly reduces *drug use* among offenders.

Another example of a coercive strategy involves requiring convicted drinking drivers to install ignition-interlock devices in their cars as a condition of probation (Elliott, Morse, & Mihalic, 1993). These devices require the operator of a motor vehicle to provide an alcohol-free breath sample in order to start a car, as well as to continue to operate. Preliminary studies suggest that ignition-interlock technology has some deterrence effect (Baker & Beck, 1991; Elliott et al., 1993). However, some offenders do attempt to thwart the system.

Other coercive methods exist (drug testing, referrals by employee assistance programs). These are not reviewed here. In general, it appears that coercive methods, when properly applied, do motivate some individuals to change their behavior. *However, the magnitude of the impact does not seem great over an extended period*; when the aversive stimulus is removed it might be expected that substance use and related risk behavior will return to previous levels.

When are coercive methods likely to produce *internal motivation* to reduce or eliminate substance use? The stages-of-change model suggests that coercion may best influence the contemplator (i.e., the substancer user who has been wrestling with whether to change but is waiting for a compelling reason to do so). External pressure in the form of a mandate from the court or an employer may provide the needed rationale to change oneself. The external control may bolster what the psychoanalyst refers to as "weak ego strength" or the social cognitive therapist may identify as "low self-efficacy." Cognitively, exposure to coercive requirements may be accompanied by heightened negative expectancies. Thus, in the risk–reward analysis of the contemplator, the balance between positive drug expectancies and negative social consequences could shift toward the latter.

In contrast, the response of the precontemplator to legal or worksite directives to change will likely be met with rebellious acting out, attempts at evasion, or even absconding in some cases. When coercive methods are poorly managed as a result of inadequate monitoring and inconsistent enforcement, precontemplators are likely to attempt to evade the external control. Theory then suggests that coercive methods are best used selectively in the addictive behaviors. How this would be accomplished within the boundaries of civil rights and the bureaucracy of the criminal justice system is an open question.

CONFRONTATIVE TREATMENT

The use of confrontation has long been associated with substance abuse counseling (Fisher & Harrison, 1997; Lightfoot, 1993; Lewis et al., 1994). The conventional view has been that substance abusers are "manipulative" and in "denial." Therefore, confrontation is necessary to break down this pattern of conduct and accompanying psychological defenses. This view is still prevalent today, especially in criminal justice settings. Torres (1997), a professor of criminal justice, writes:

> For the probation officer, the most effective approach in supervising the substance-abusing offender is to set explicit limits, to inform the probationer/parolee of the consequences for noncompliance, and to be prepared to enforce the limits in case of violations. The preferred course of action for many, if not most, users is placement in a therapeutic community, with credible threats and coercion if necessary (p. 38).

Such views are common in settings in which there is an emphasis on external controls and a concern about appearing strong or "credible." In the past, some addiction treatment programs, such as therapeutic communities, shared this philosophy (Fisher & Harrison, 1997); many addictions practitioners believed that confrontation was the only counseling skill needed to work with people who have alcohol and other drug problems (Doweiko, 1993; Lewis et al., 1994).

Views about confrontative counseling have changed during the past decade or so. Concerns have been raised that there was an overreliance on confrontative methods. The two negative outcomes that have been identified are counselor disillusionment or "burnout," and clients avoiding or dropping out of treatment (Brown, 1995). *Increasingly, it is recognized that much of what has been described as denial, resistance, and so on, is actually a consequence of the therapist's style* (Bell & Rollnick, 1996; Lightfoot, 1993; Miller et al., 1992; Taleff, 1997). For example, one study randomly assigned problem drinkers to two different therapist styles: confrontational/directive versus motivational/reflective (Miller, Benefield, & Tonigan, 1993). Clients who received the confrontational/directive therapy showed more resistance, were less likely to acknowledge their problems, and less often voiced the need to change. Furthermore, these patterns were predictive of less long-term change (Miller et al., 1993).

Why does client motivation appear to be dampened by confrontation? Several of the theories reviewed in this volume offer explanations. From a psychoanalytic perspective, being confronted evokes anxiety, particularly among clients with weak ego strength, and this triggers psychological defenses necessary for coping. Thus, resistance actually may be an attempt to protect the self from threat; leaving treatment prematurely should be expected in such situations. In behavior-analytic terms, confrontation creates an aversive condition which the person will usually attempt to escape. Self-efficacy theory would predict that confrontation does little to increase client optimism about treatment success or to enhance coping with stress. If the client was raised in an addictive family, confrontation and conflict may well be threatening experiences that they associate with substance use rather than abstinence. In short, there does not appear to be much theoretical basis for using confrontational therapy to help persons with substance abuse problems.

MOTIVATION ENHANCEMENT

William Miller, Stephen Rollnick, and colleagues developed motivation enhancement therapy (MET) to deal with the critical issue in helping a person with an addiction problem: *ambivalence about change.* MET (also known as "motivational interviewing") is a departure from traditional methods in that the purpose of counseling is to enhance the client's readiness for change. According to Miller et al. (1992):

> In sum, people with alcohol problems do not, in general, walk through the therapist's door already possessing high levels of denial and resistance. These important client behaviors are more a function of the interpersonal interactions that occur during treatment. An important goal in MET, then, is to avoid evoking client resistance (antimotivational statements). Said more bluntly, *client resistance is a therapist problem.* How you *respond* to resistant behaviors is one of the defining characteristics of MET. (p. 22)

The theoretical basis for MET is the stages-of-change model (Miller et al., 1992; Rollnick & Morgan, 1995). To a great extent, MET focuses on helping clients move from contemplation to preparation. In contemplation, the client is *unsure* about change. The preparation stage involves getting *ready* for change. Rollnick and Morgan (1995) describe this movement as passing through a "decision gate." There are five important clinical implications of this model (Rollnick & Morgan, 1995):

1. Clients approach and move away from the decision gate;
2. Confrontation by the counselor about moving away from the gate can prompt greater backward movement;
3. Ambivalence about change increases as the client moves toward the decision gate;

4. When the counselor jumps ahead of the client, the client is perceived as resistant;
5. Resistance results when the counselor indicates the client *should* change.

An important strategy of MET is eliciting self-motivational statements from the client (Miller et al., 1992). In other words, MET is working when the client, rather than the counselor, provides reasons for change. The basic principles that guide this effort are as follows (Miller & Rollnick, 1991; Miller et al., 1992):

1. Express empathy for the client.
2. Develop and amplify a discrepancy, in the client's mind, between his/her substance use and broader life goals.
3. Avoid argumentation about these issues.
4. "Roll with" the client's resistance.
5. Support the client's self-efficacy.

An interesting question is whether MET constitutes "treatment" in the traditional sense, or is more appropriately considered an attempt to facilitate *self-change* among clients who are ambivalent? In the medical model, treatment involves procedures that are designed to somehow alter the patient. With its grounding in the stages-of-change model, MET seems to follow the client's movement, hoping to facilitate change among contemplators, at the same time respecting the reluctance of precontemplators. This is not a criticism of MET but, rather, to point out that it may be capitalizing on self-change (or natural recovery) processes in the addictions that only recently have been subject to investigation (Sobell, Sobell, & Toneatto, 1992; Sobell, Cunningham, Sobell, & Toneatto, 1993). The preliminary work suggests that self-change might be much more common in the general population than was previously thought.

HARM REDUCTION APPROACHES

The previous discussion might suggest there is little that can be done to help the precontemplator. Coercion may have only a modest impact on this group, that is, if it can be applied at all. Furthermore, there is not much reason to expect that precontemplators will benefit from confrontational therapy, and MET may be best suited for those who have moved beyond precontemplation.

A controversial intervention strategy known as "harm reduction" offers help to those who are resistant to conventional treatment options (Erickson, Riley, Cheung, & O'Hare, 1997). The goal of harm reduction strategies is to minimize personal risks among chronic or recalcitrant users based on the recognition that abstinence is not always realistic for all segments of the addicted population (Rotgers, 1996). Harm reduction programs do not view substance use as intrinsically immoral and the user is not viewed to be abnormal. The focus is mostly on the *problems* caused by the substance use rather than on the substance use itself. Furthermore, these programs are "user centered," meaning they encourage users to make their own choices about how to protect themselves, and they avoid marginalizing or stigmatizing participants (Erickson et al., 1997).

Harm reduction programs tolerate some level of substance use and are primarily concerned with extending help to high-risk groups. As a public policy, the harm reduction concept represents a middle ground between the harsh "zero tolerance" stance and the extremely permissive drug legalization position. According to Erickson et al. (1997), the harm reduction movement avoids *unnecessary* constraints imposed by moral, legal, and standard medical interpretations of substance use. The public health community usually advocates for harm reduction programs, whereas the criminal justice system often opposes such efforts when they extend help to illicit drug users (Marlatt & Tapert, 1993).

This approach is quite congruent with Prochaska and DiClemente's stages-of-change model. In stages-of-change jargon, harm reduction aims to provide some level of protection to those who are in precontemplation and contemplation about their risk behavior, as well as to offer an alternative form of "action" and "maintenance" to those who reject abstinence. Some of these strategies are more controversial than others. Those that seek to reduce harm associated with illicit drug use usually draw the most vocal opposition. Some examples of harm reduction strategies for substance abuse include (1) syringe-exchange programs for injection drug users, (2) methadone and heroin maintenance, (3) addict registration programs, (4) nicotine replacement therapies, (5) controlled drinking training, and (6) designated driver and safe-ride programs. These strategies provide a way to reach treatment-resistant individuals. Participation in these types of programs can prompt contemplation about the risk behavior, particularly when the service has an educational or coping skills component. Thus, harm reduction strategies show much promise for reducing risk and increasing readiness to change in a broader spectrum of people than that traditionally served by abstinence-oriented treatment and prevention.

THE IMPACT OF MANAGED CARE

The rapid development of managed care organizations (MCOs) in the United States has produced dramatic changes in virtually all aspects of health care delivery, including public and private addiction treatment services (Miller, 1999; Morey, 1996; National Institute on Alcohol Abuse and Alcoholism, 1997). Managed care can be defined as a program designed to control access to care, including types of care, and to constrain the overall costs of care (Wells, Astrachan, Tischler, & Unutzer, 1995). Cost containment is accomplished through utilization reviews that rely on preadmission approval for care as well as in-treatment review to determine the necessity of continuing care. The review process typically relies on placement criteria that specify the type of care a person can receive from his/her MCO. According to Morey (1996), MCO use of placement criteria has "significantly challenged the alcohol field" (p. 38). Many addiction practitioners may consider this to be an understatement.

The primary impact of managed care pressures on addiction treatment has been to severely restrict access to inpatient care, shift clients to outpatient settings, and increase use of nonmedical approaches, such as halfway houses and nonmedical residential programs (National Institute on Alcohol Abuse and Alcoholism, 1997). It might be expected that the decreased utilization of inpatient services would be accompanied by an increase in use of outpatient services. Unfortunately, this has not been the case. *The use of outpatient services decreased during the period that access to inpatient services was restricted as well* (Mechanic, Schlesinger, & McAlpine, 1995).

As a result of these changes, addictions practitioners have turned to brief therapy models and placed greater emphasis on helping clients use Twelve-Step Programs such as Alcoholics Anonymous (Miller, 1999). Skill building to prevent relapse must start at the beginning of treatment. Under these conditions, assessment of client readiness for change becomes critical. The time constraints compel practitioners to focus on client motivation at the onset of treatment and to make decisions based on these initial judgments.

Unfortunately, at this time, there is little empirical basis for making decisions about client placement and level of care. The American Society of Addiction Medicine (ASAM) has developed a set of criteria for this purpose, but it has been not validated to determine whether it improves treatment outcomes (Morey, 1996). Nevertheless, the criteria are an important starting point and they do attempt to account for the role of client motivation in making these critical decisions about care.

Under the ASAM guidelines, there are four levels of care ranging from outpatient to partial inpatient to nonmedical inpatient to medical inpatient. The client's level of care should be determined by six dimensions that reflect the severity of the client's problems. The ASAM dimensions include (1) acute intoxication at admission and/or potential for withdrawal, (2) the possible presence of biomedical conditions and complications, (3) emotional and behavioral conditions and complications, (4) treatment acceptance/resistance (i.e., readiness for change), (5) relapse potential, and (6) recovery environment. Morey (1996) notes that criticisms of the ASAM guidelines abound. They have not been uniformly accepted in the private or public sectors; in fact, MCO placement criteria tend to be more restrictive. Thus, more research is needed to develop tools that will improve treatment outcomes and thereby justify the provision of services in the managed care environment.

There is little doubt that managed care has had a dramatic impact on the delivery of addictions treatment in the United States. Services of all types have decreased significantly with the advent of MCOs. The irony of the situation is that the health care industry has justified its cost-containment practices on the grounds that findings from outcome research do not support a higher level of service delivery. In essence, past efforts to improve clinical practice through research have been used against the treatment community. Out of necessity, the treatment community will now have to collaborate more closely with the research community to develop more effective treatment tools.

REVIEW QUESTIONS

1. What was the traditional view of the unmotivated client?

2. What aspect of client motivation does each model of addictive behavior focus on?

3. What are the stages of change that clients cycle through in an effort to change addictive behavior?

4. What is the role of the counselor at each change stage?

5. Under what conditions might coercion be effective?

6. Based on theory and research, is confrontational treatment effective?

7. What are the features of motivation enhancement therapy?

8. What is the "harm reduction" concept? What are examples of harm reduction strategies?

9. In what ways has managed care affected addictions treatment in recent years?

REFERENCES

Anglin, M. D. (1988). The efficacy of civil commitment in treating narcotic addiction. In C. G. Leukefeld & F. M. Tims (Eds.), *Compulsory treatment of drug abuse: Research and clinical practice* (NIDA Research Monograph 86;

DHHS Publication No. ADM 88-1578). Washington, DC: U.S. Government Printing Office.

Baker, E. A., & Beck, K. (1991). Ignition interlocks for DWI offenders: A useful tool. *Alcohol, Drugs and Driving, 7,* 107–115.

Bell, A., & Rollnick, S. (1996). Motivational interviewing in practice: A structured approach. In F. Rotgers, D. S. Keller, & J. Morgenstern (Eds.), *Treating substance abuse: Theory and technique.* New York: Guilford Press.

Bradley-Springer, L. (1996). Patient education for behavior change: Help from the transtheoretical and harm reduction models. *Journal of the Association of Nurses in AIDS Care, 7,* 23–33.

Brown, S. (1995). *Treating alcoholism.* San Francisco: Jossey-Bass.

Burling, T. A., Reilly, P. M., Moltzen, J. O., & Ziff, D. C. (1989). Self-efficacy and relapse among inpatient drug and alcohol abusers: A predictor of outcome. *Journal of Studies on Alcohol, 50,* 354–360.

Crowley, T. J. (1984). Contingency contracting treatment of drug-abusing physicians, nurses, and dentists. In J. Grabowski, M. L. Stitzer, & J. E. Henningfield (Eds.), *Behavioral intervention techniques in drug abuse* (NIDA Research Monograph 46; DHHS Publication No. ADM 86-1282). Washington, DC: U.S. Government Printing Office.

DiClemente, C. C. (1991). Motivational interviewing and the stages of change. In W. R. Miller & S. Rollnick, *Motivational interviewing: Preparing people to change addictive behavior.* New York: Guilford Press.

DiClemente, C. C., & Prochaska J. O. (1985). Processes and stages of change: Coping and competence in smoking behavior change. In S. Shiffman & T. A. Wills (Eds.), *Coping and substance abuse.* New York: Academic Press.

DiClemente, C. C., Prochaska, J. O., Fairhurst, S. K., Velicer, W. F., Velasquez, M. M., & Rossi, J. S. (1991). The process of smoking cessation: An analysis of precontemplation, contemplation, and preparation stages of change. *Journal of Consulting and Clinical Psychology, 59,* 295–304.

Doweiko, H. E. (1993). *Concepts of chemical dependency* (2nd ed.). Pacific Grove, CA: Brooks/Cole.

Elliott, D. S., Morse, B. J., & Mihalic, S. W. (1993). *In-vehicle BAC test devices as a deterrent to DUI, final report.* Rockville, MD: National Institute on Alcohol Abuse and Alcoholism.

Erickson, P. A., Riley, D. M., Cheung, Y. W., & O'Hare, P. A. (1997). *Harm reduction: A new direction for drug policies and programs.* Toronto: University of Toronto Press.

Fisher, G. L., & Harrison, T. C. (1997). *Substance abuse: Information for school counselors, social workers, therapists, and counselors.* Boston: Allyn & Bacon.

Group for the Advancement of Psychiatry. (1994). *Forced into treatment: The role of coercion in clinical practice.* Washington, DC: American Psychiatric Press.

Inciardi, J. A. (1988). Some considerations on the efficacy of compulsory treatment: Reviewing the New York experience. In C. G. Leukefeld & F. M. Tims (Eds.), *Compulsory treatment of drug abuse: Research and clinical practice* (NIDA Research Monograph 86; DHHS Publication No. ADM 88-1578). Washington, DC: U.S. Government Printing Office.

Inciardi, J. A., McBride, D. C., & Rivers, J. E. (1996). *Drug control and the courts.* Thousand Oaks, CA: Sage.

Leukefeld, C. G., & Tims, F. M. (Eds.). (1988). *Compulsory treatment of drug abuse: Research and clinical practice* (NIDA Research Monograph 86; DHHS Publication No. ADM 88-1578). Washington, DC: U.S. Government Printing Office.

Lewis, J. A., Dana, R. Q., & Blevins, G. A. (1994). *Substance abuse counseling: An individualized approach* (2nd ed.). Pacific Grove, CA: Brooks/Cole.

Lightfoot, L. O. (1993). The offender substance abuse pre-release program: An empirically based model of treatment for offenders. In J. S. Baer, G. A. Marlatt, & R. J. McMahon (Eds.), *Addictive behaviors across the life span: Prevention, treatment, and policy issues.* Newbury Park, CA: Sage.

Maisto, S. A., Sobell, L. C., Sobell, M. B., Lei, H., & Sykora, K. (1988). Profiles of drinking patterns before and after outpatient treatment for alcohol abuse. In T. Baker & D. Cannon (Eds.), *Assessment and treatment of addictive behaviors.* New York: Praeger.

Marlatt, G. A., & Tapert, S. F. (1993). Harm reduction: Reducing the risks of addictive behaviors. In J. S. Baer, G. A. Marlatt, & R. J. McMahon (Eds.), *Addictive behaviors across the life span: Prevention, treatment, and policy issues.* Newbury Park, CA: Sage.

Marlowe, D. B., Kirby, K. C., Bonieskie, L. M., Glass, D. J., Dodds, L. D., Husband, S. D., Platt, J. J., & Festinger, D. S. (1996). Assessment of coercive and noncoercive pressures to enter drug abuse treatment. *Drug and Alcohol Dependence, 42,* 77–84.

Mechanic, D., Schlesinger, M., & McAlpine, D. D. (1995). Management of mental health and substance abuse services: State of the art and early results. *Milbank Quarterly, 73,* 19–55.

Miller, G. A. (1999). *Learning the language of addiction counseling.* Boston: Allyn & Bacon.

Miller, W. R., Benefield, R., & Tonigan, S. (1993). Enhancing motivation for change in problem drinking: A controlled comparison of two therapist styles. *Journal of Consulting and Clinical Psychology, 61,* 455–461.

Miller, W. R., & Hester, R. K. (1986). The effectiveness of alcoholism treatment: What research reveals. In W. R. Miller & N. Heather (Eds.), *Treating addictive disorders: Processes of change.* New York: Plenum Press.

Miller, W. R., & Rollnick, S. (1991). *Motivational interviewing: Preparing people to change addictive behavior.* New York: Guilford Press.

Miller, W. R., Zweben, A., DiClemente, C. C., & Rychtarik, R. G. (1992). *Motivational enhancement therapy manual: A clinical research guide for therapists treating individuals with alcohol abuse and dependence* (DHHS Publication No. ADM 92-1894). Washington, DC: U.S. Government Printing Office.

Morey, L. C. (1996). Patient placement criteria: Linking typologies to managed care. *Alcohol Health and Research World, 20,* 36–44.

National Institute on Alcohol Abuse and Alcoholism. (1997). *Alcohol and health: Ninth special report to the U. S. Congress* (NIH Publication No. 97-4017). Bethesda, MD: National Institutes of Health.

Prochaska, J. O., & DiClemente, C. C. (1985). Common processes of change in smoking, weight control, and psychological distress. In S. Shiffman & T. Wills (Eds.), *Coping and substance abuse.* New York: Academic Press.

Prochaska, J. O., & DiClemente, C. C. (1992). Stages of change in the modification of problem behaviors. In M. Herson, R. M. Eisler, & P. M. Miller (Eds.), *Progress in behavior modification* (Vol. 28). Sycamore, IL: Sycamore.

Prochaska, J. O., DiClemente, C. C., & Norcross, J. C. (1992). In search of how people changes: Application to addictive behavior. *American Psychologist, 47,* 1102–1114.

Prochaska, J. O., & Norcross, J. C. (1983). Psychotherapists' perspectives on treating themselves and their clients for psychic distress. *Professional Psychology: Research and Practice, 14,* 642–655.

Rappaport, R. L. (1997). *Motivating clients in therapy: Values, love, and the real relationship.* New York: Routledge.

Rollnick, S., & Morgan, M. (1995). Motivational interviewing: Increasing readiness to change. In A. M. Washton (Ed.), *Psychotherapy and substance abuse: A practitioner's handbook.* New York: Guilford Press.

Rotgers, F. (1996). Behavioral theory of substance abuse treatment: Bringing science to bear on practice. In F. Rotgers, D. S. Keller, & J. Morgenstern (Eds.), *Treating substance abuse: Theory and technique.* New York: Guilford Press.

Sobell, L. C., Cunningham, J. A., Sobell, M. B., & Toneatto, T. (1993). A lifespan perspective on natural recovery (self-change) from alcohol problems. In J. S. Baer, G. A. Marlatt, & R. J. McMahon (Eds.), *Addictive behaviors across the life span: Prevention, treatment, and policy issues.* Newbury Park, CA: Sage.

Sobell, L. C., Sobell, M. B., & Toneatto, T. (1992). Recovery from alcohol problems without treatment. In N. Heather, W. R. Miller, & J. Greeley (Eds.), *Self-control and the addictive behaviors.* Botany Bay, NSW, Australia: Maxwell Macmillan.

Steinglass, P. (1981). The alcoholic at home: Patterns of interaction in dry, wet, and transitional stages of alcoholism. *Archives of General Psychiatry, 38,* 578–584.

Taleff, M. J. (1997). *A handbook to assess and treat resistance in chemical dependency.* Dubuque, IA: Kendall/Hunt.

Torres, S. (1997). An effective supervision strategy for substance-abusing offenders. *Federal Probation, 61,* 38–44.

Tucker, J. A., Vuchinich, R. E., & Pukish, M. M. (1995). Molar environmental contexts surrounding recovery from alcohol problems by treated and untreated problem drinkers. *Experimental and Clinical Psychopharmacology, 3,* 195–204.

Wells, K. B., Astrachan, B. M., Tischler, G. L., & Unutzer, J. (1995). Issues and approaches in evaluating managed mental health care. *Milbank Quarterly, 73,* 57–75.

Yalisove, D. (1998). The origins and evolution of the disease concept of treatment. *Journal of Studies on Alcohol, 59,* 469–476.

Author Index

Subject Index